UNDERSTANDING, EVALUATING, AND CONDUCTING SECOND LANGUAGE WRITING RESEARCH

Understanding, Evaluating, and Conducting Second Language Writing Research speaks to the rapidly growing area of second language writing by providing a uniquely balanced approach to L2 writing research. While other books favor either a qualitative or quantitative approach to second language acquisition (SLA) research, this text is comprehensive in scope and does not privilege one approach over the other, illuminating the strengths of each and the ways in which they might complement each other. Part I will help novice researchers consider the best approach to use for answering their research questions. It will also help more experienced researchers expand their repertoire in terms of approaches and help them consider both cognitive and social aspects of L2 writing. Part II will prove useful for both novice and experienced researchers when they are faced with choices regarding data collection and analysis. Containing an array of focal studies and suggestions for further reading, this text is the ideal resource for students beginning to conduct L2 writing research as well as for more experienced researchers who wish to expand their approach to conducting research.

Charlene Polio is Professor in the Department of Linguistics & Germanic, Slavic, Asian, and African Languages at Michigan State University, USA. She is currently co-editor of the *Modern Language Journal*.

Debra A. Friedman is Assistant Professor in the Department of Second Language Studies at Indiana University, USA.

Second Language Acquisition Research Series

Susan M. Gass and Alison Mackey, Series Editors

De Costa Ethics in Applied Linguistics Research: Language Researcher Narratives (2015)

Mackey and Marsden Advancing Methodology and Practice: The IRIS Repository of Instruments for Research into Second Languages (2015)

Tomlinson SLA Research and Materials Development for Language Learning (2016)

Gass/Mackey Stimulated Recall Methodology in Applied Linguistics and L2 Research, Second Edition (2017)

Polio/Friedman Understanding, Evaluating, and Conducting Second Language Writing Research (2017)

Of Related Interest:

Gass Input, Interaction, and the Second Language Learner (1997)

Gass/Sorace/Selinker Second Language Learning Data Analysis, Second Edition (1998)

Mackey/Gass Second Language Research: Methodology and Design (2005)

Gass/Selinker Second Language Acquisition: An Introductory Course, Third Edition (2008)

UNDERSTANDING, EVALUATING, AND CONDUCTING SECOND LANGUAGE WRITING RESEARCH

Charlene Polio
MICHIGAN STATE UNIVERSITY

Debra A. Friedman
INDIANA UNIVERSITY

Routledge
Taylor & Francis Group
NEW YORK AND LONDON

First published 2017
by Routledge
711 Third Avenue, New York, NY 10017

and by Routledge
2 Park Square, Milton Park, Abingdon, Oxon, OX14 4RN

Routledge is an imprint of the Taylor & Francis Group, an informa business

Library of Congress Cataloging in Publication Data
A catalog record for this book has been requested

ISBN: 978-1-138-81467-7 (hbk)
ISBN: 978-1-138-81468-4 (pbk)
ISBN: 978-1-315-74729-3 (ebk)

Typeset in Bembo
by Apex CoVantage, LLC

Printed and bound in the United States of America by
Edwards Brothers Malloy on sustainably sourced paper

CONTENTS

Conclusion   253

ACKNOWLEDGMENTS

Many people have contributed their help and feedback to the preparation of this book. Jessica Williams helped us shape the volume with her detailed feedback on the first half of the book. Jung Min Lim and Magda Tigchelaar provided feedback on many of the chapters as did Meg Malone, and Stacy Sabraw assisted with detailed editing. Much thanks goes to our research assistants Ji-Hyun Park and Yunona Shcherbina, and especially Jongbong Lee, who promptly found relevant studies and tirelessly compiled the reference list.

1

INTRODUCTION

Second language (L2) writing is both a *cognitive process*, in which a writer draws upon a set of internalized skills and knowledge to produce a text, and a *situated activity* that takes place in a specific context with a specific goal and for a specific audience. As a result, L2 writing research encompasses a wide range of topics while drawing on a wide variety of research traditions. This diversity also reflects the field's roots in the areas of both second language acquisition (SLA) and first language (L1) composition. The former has tended to be more cognitively oriented and use quantitative and experimental research methods, whereas the latter has tended to be more socially oriented and to use qualitative and naturalistic methods. L2 writing research has consistently drawn on both quantitative and qualitative paradigms, probably more so than any other area of applied linguistics. We see this as a positive phenomenon because it gives researchers a variety of tools to use, allows them to answer many different types of research questions, and helps them to tap into both the cognitive and social aspects of writing. In this book, we discuss the different epistemological traditions behind the various approaches to L2 research in more detail, but we maintain that no one research approach should be privileged; rather, the approach should emerge from the research questions that one wishes to answer. Furthermore, qualitative and quantitative approaches can inform and complement each other in mixed methods research (see Chapter 5). We begin this chapter by explaining what we see as the scope of L2 writing research. We then provide a description of two studies, one quantitative and one qualitative, to illustrate how two very different approaches to research can inform the field of L2 writing. We then end with a description of the organization of this book.

The Scope of Second Language Writing Research

The types of research that fall under the scope of L2 writing research are varied and broad, and different volumes divide up the field in different ways. Probably the most basic distinction between types of research is related to a pedagogical distinction, namely the difference between writing as way to learn language and writing for real-life purposes. These have been described as *writing-to-learn* and *learning-to-write approaches* (e.g., Manchón, 2011). A writing-to-learn-language focus would be on activities or tasks not done outside of the classroom. One example of such an activity is a dictocomp, an activity in which students reconstruct a text after listening to it. Although the associated text could be related to real-life purposes, the activity is often used to get students to learn to use the language from the text. We also might include here studies that focus on corrective feedback. Although grammar feedback might be given on any type of assignment, research in this area focuses on language learning, not on the task as it is used outside the classroom. On the other hand, a learning-to-write activity might teach students how to write a literature review for an academic paper. There would be a focus on the language used, for example through explicit instruction or feedback, but also a focus on the content, organization, and audience. The goal is for students to be able to write a literature review in their respective academic fields. In the classroom, these approaches are not mutually exclusive. In research, they may not be either, but there is often a focus on one or the other. For example, consider a study that manipulates task complexity and then examines the effect on writers' language (e.g., Kuiken & Vedder, 2008). The goal of the study is to understand what teachers can do to help students produce more complex language without necessarily considering students' real-life goals. Conversely, consider Lillis and Curry's (2010) volume on the politics of publishing in English. They studied scholars with real-life writing goals and how those scholars went about producing English texts within their research networks. There was little emphasis on how such scholars' language learning was affected. Both of these studies fall within the area of L2 writing. Although we are considering only writing research in which learners produce texts beyond the sentence level, we include both research in which the writing is used for real-life purposes and writing that is done only for the purposes of language learning.

Another way to distinguish approaches to L2 writing research is based on the phenomenon being studied. Articles and books about L2 writing research have divided up the field in different ways. For example, Polio (2001) classified writing research according to the following foci: writers' texts, writers' processes, participants in the learning and teaching process, and the context within and outside of the classroom. Hyland (2009), in his volume on teaching and researching writing, included four foci: practitioners, L2 writers' texts and target text, writers and their processes and attitudes, and readers and their expectations and evaluations. In a comprehensive review of L2 writing research, Leki, Cumming, and Silva (2008) divided their book into three sections: contexts for L2 writing, instruction and assessment, and basic research, which included writer characteristics, composing processes, textual issues, and grammatical issues. Finally, the new *Handbook of Second and Foreign Language Writing* (Manchón & Matsuda, 2016) covers a variety of topics that can be subsumed under the categories of writers' texts, processes, identity, backgrounds and goals; the context for L2 writing; and teacher research. The point is that L2 writing research may concern something as language focused as how L2 writers use lexical phrases (Li & Schmitt, 2009) or something as contextually focused as how L2 writers learn to write in a writing center (Severino & Cogie, 2016).

One can also consider the range of L2 writing research against a background of the studies' theoretical perspective. We do not have the space to go into detail on the different theories of L2 writing, but we refer readers to Cumming (2016), who details four theories: contrastive rhetoric, cognitive models of composing, genre theories, and sociocultural theory. In addition, he mentions other theories such as critical theory, goal theory, and dynamic systems theory. The point that should be kept in mind is that despite the tendency of certain theories to be linked to certain approaches, no one theory goes with one method. One example comes from contrastive rhetoric, which, simply put, is the idea that writers from different cultures organize their writing differently. The theory has changed and developed since first proposed by Kaplan (1966), and the ways that researchers working within the theory have conducted research have also varied. Many researchers have taken a text-based approach, examining differences in the organization of writers writing in their first and second languages (e.g., Hirose, 2003). Others, such as Shi (2003), used interviews to understand what Western-trained Chinese scholars perceived to be differences between Chinese and English writing and why those differences existed.

Different Questions, Different Approaches

As noted previously, both quantitative and qualitative approaches have been used to investigate issues of interest in L2 writing, with the choice between them depending on the questions to be answered or the phenomenon to be explored. For example, establishing causal relationships between a practice and an outcome (e.g., a particular instructional technique and writing improvement) requires an experimental quantitative study in which the researcher controls and manipulates variables by assigning participants to random groups and designing tasks for them to perform. However, if one wants to examine how a teacher implements the instructional technique and how students feel about it, one would employ qualitative methods such as observing participants in the course of their everyday classroom activities and eliciting their perspectives through interviews.

Although we emphasize that these different approaches to research are equally valid and suitable for understanding different aspects of the complex processes involved in L2 writing, others would argue that they are inherently irreconcilable, as they represent distinct sets of beliefs, or *paradigms*, regarding the nature of reality (*ontology*) and ways of knowing (*epistemology*). Research paradigms have been classified and labeled in various ways, but the most essential distinction is between *postpositivist* and *postmodern* (or *poststructuralist*) paradigms (Lincoln & Guba, 2000). Postpositivism is embodied in the scientific method and rests on an assumption that objective truth exists. For researchers working from this perspective, the aim of research is to discover this truth to the extent possible and to generate findings that can be generalized to other contexts. Those adopting a postmodern paradigm, on the other hand, assume that there are multiple perspectives on reality and that what we call *truth* is a social construction. Such researchers do not aim to discover universal and generalizable facts but to provide a detailed picture of particular settings or participants in order to explore and document the diversity of individual experience.

For some postmodern researchers, the postpositivist assumptions and emphasis on *generalizability* (or *external validity*; see Chapter 2) and *replicability* (see Chapter 12) that underlie quantitative and experimental studies are ill-suited to the study of human activities such as writing that are shaped by multiple social practices, beliefs, and values, thus making each instance unique. For others, there are concerns that holding qualitative research to such standards risks marginalizing it as unscientific, descriptive, and ungeneralizable. Our position is that while these paradigms clearly represent different worldviews, they need not be in contention. In a discussion of this issue in the social sciences, Lincoln and Guba (2000) noted the increased acceptance of nonpostpositivist research (a trend that can also be found in the field of SLA in general and in L2 writing research in particular) and argued for the value of "dialogue, consensus, and confluence" where possible (p. 167). Moreover, we also note that quantitative and qualitative approaches do not map neatly onto postpositivist (quantitative) and postmodern (qualitative) paradigms. Much L2 writing research, both quantitative and qualitative, has reflected and continues to reflect a postpositivist orientation, and a postmodernist need not take what Lincoln and Guba (2000) called an "antiquantitative stance" (p. 174). As we hope to show in the remainder of this volume, it is precisely the openness of the field of L2 writing to a range of research paradigms, approaches, and methods that has allowed for the emergence of a body of work that has enriched understandings of the complex social and cognitive processes that constitute L2 writing.

Two Example Studies

To illustrate how different approaches can be used to answer different but related questions, we present in Box 1.1 two studies on peer review (also called peer editing, peer response, or peer feedback). The first study (Lundstrom & Baker, 2009) is a well-constructed experimental study that manipulated a treatment condition in an attempt to disentangle variables related to peer review that can affect learners' revisions. The second study (Zhu & Mitchell, 2012) is a qualitative case study that attempted to understand why learners take different stances toward peer review. It did not attempt to manipulate any variables but rather sought to document and understand students' behavior in a particular context.

Both studies begin by reviewing work on peer review but immediately diverge. Lundstrom and Baker (2009) discuss the purported benefits of peer review to the reviewer and cite studies from L1 research that suggest the benefits to writers of reviewing their peers' work. They note the lack of similar research on L2 writers and the fact that L1 studies do not address the added complications of having to do peer review in one's L2. They also note the lack of experimental research on this issue:

> [M]ost of the studies do not use experimental research methods (i.e., they do not quantitatively compare two groups), nor do these studies examine the types of improvements students made, whether in global (i.e., organization, development, and cohesion) or local (i.e., grammar, vocabulary, and mechanics) aspects of writing.
>
> *(p. 32)*

What makes this study a typical quantitative experimental study is that it is concerned with the outcomes of peer review and the relationship between those outcomes and specific roles (i.e., as giver or receiver of peer comments). This focus is reflected in the research questions presented in Box 1.1.

BOX 1.1   COMPARISON OF A QUANTITATIVE AND A QUALITATIVE STUDY ON PEER REVIEW

Lundstrom, K. & Baker, W. (2009). To give is better than to receive: The benefits of peer review to the reviewer's own writing. *Journal* of *Second Language Writing, 18*, 30–43.

Zhu, W. & Mitchell, D. (2012). Participation in peer response as an activity: An examination of peer response stances from an activity theory perspective. *TESOL Quarterly, 46*, 362–386.

Background information

- Teaching students to review their peers' work might positively affect the reviewers' writing.
- Sociocultural theory and past research suggests that writers can scaffold for reviewers, not just reviewers for writers.

- Previous studies have shown that student background influences interaction in peer review.
- Other studies have shown that students take different stances (e.g., authoritative, interpretive, collaborative).

- Early work on L1 writers suggested that teaching peer review helps students revise their own writing, but this has not been studied experimentally.

- According to activity theory, people complete different tasks for different reasons, and motives are essential to understanding behavior.
- Learners' motives will affect interaction and possibly outcomes.

Research questions

- Do students who review peer papers improve their writing ability more than those who revise peer papers (for both beginning and intermediate students)?
- If students who review peer papers do improve their writing ability more than those who revise them, on which writing aspects (both global and local) do they improve? (p. 32)

- Why do students adopt different peer response stances? (p. 364)

Participants and context

- US university ESL program
- 45 students in level 2 of the program (beginners)
- 46 students in level 4 of the program (low-advanced)

- US university academic ESL writing class
- Two students were chosen as focal participants from a larger study because their cases were "illuminating" (p. 367).
- Rosa: 30s, from Colombia, finance major in home country
- Ingrid: 40s, from Spain, physics major in home country

Design and data sources

- Experimental and control groups from two intact classes at each level were used.
- Experimental (Givers) provided peer feedback but did not receive it.
- Control (Receivers) received feedback but did not give it.

- Students met in peer groups of three, read essays at home following a checklist with questions about features of the essays.
- Peer response sessions were audio-recorded.

- Pretest-posttest included timed essay rated on an analytic rubric for organization, development, cohesion/coherence, structure, vocabulary, mechanics.
- Treatment was provided four times during the semester; students were instructed on giving or using feedback.
- Students gave feedback on or revised sample essays each time.

- Semi-structured interviews were conducted with Rosa and Ingrid after the last peer response session of the semester.

Data analysis

- ANOVA for group differences and repeated measures ANOVA for time were conducted.
- Overall score and six subscores were examined.

- Two researchers independently read transcripts of peer response sessions to identify participants' stances and orientations to the task as both readers and writers.
- Interview transcripts were coded for features regarding purpose of peer response, beliefs about peer response.
- Stances were compared in relation to stated motives within each case and across the two cases.

Results

- A significant effect for time was found as well as a treatment by time interaction for beginners on some aspects of writing.
- A significant effect for time was found but not treatment by time for intermediate learners.
- When new and returning students were separated in the intermediate group, a treatment effect was found for the new students.
- More of the time and group differences were related to global aspects of writing than to local ones.

- Students' stances are guided by their motives for participating in peer review.
- From an activity theory perspective, different motives guided Rosa's and Ingrid's behavior.
- Peer review is often seen as a way to enhance audience awareness, but Rosa did not see peer review as such.
- Students performed the task in accordance with their own learning purposes.

The Zhu and Mitchell (2012) study also discusses previous research on peer review but then details research related to what happens in peer-review groups. In other words, they focus on the process of peer review as opposed to the outcome. They summarize research by Lockhart and Ng (1995) that found that students in peer response groups take different stances while reading their peers' work and note the gap in the literature in this way:

> Although existing studies have provided classifications for and descriptions of peer response stances, little has been done to explain the reasons for the observed stances. Why do students adopt different peer response stances? Answering this question is critical for peer response research because examining the why of students' peer response stances affords a deepened understanding of students' participation in peer response. In the study we report on in this article, we address this gap in peer response research by not only presenting students' peer response stances but also identifying what underlays the observed stances.
>
> *(p. 364)*

In addition to these different foci, these two studies vary in terms of the perspectives they represent. Lundstrom and Baker (2009) privilege an *etic* (outsider) perspective; that is, it is the researchers who evaluate the effects of different types of peer-review training by assessing the quality of the essays produced before and after this training. Zhu and Mitchell (2012), on the other hand, incorporate both an etic perspective (i.e., it is the researchers who analyze the data) as well as the *emic* (insider) perspective of participants as elicited through interviews.

These different perspectives are reflected in the designs and data sources used in the two studies. The experimental study, which should actually be classified as quasi-experimental because of a lack of random group assignment (see Chapter 2), has 91 participants with few specific details about their backgrounds, while the qualitative study provides more details on the two focal participants (Ingrid and Rosa) and the class in which the research was conducted. The former study did not make an attempt to select specific participants and instead chose intact classes. The latter study chose the two participants from a larger study because they were "illuminating" (p. 367), but it is not clear how representative they were of the students in the larger study, and the researchers explicitly do not attempt to generalize their participants' stances and motives to other learners with similar linguistic/cultural backgrounds. In other words, their point is that each learner has to be viewed as an individual, not as a representative of some larger type.

With regard to study design, the Lundstrom and Baker (2009) study manipulated the treatment (i.e., type of instruction or activity) that the students participated in. One group gave feedback and one received it, but neither group did both, as is normally done in a writing class. In fact, prior studies such as Berg

(1999), which found that peer feedback training had a positive effect on students' writing, could not determine if the training improved how students gave feedback to each other or if it improved the actual writing and revision skills of the writers. In other words, it could have been the feedback from the trained readers or the training itself that improved the students' writing. Lundstrom and Baker attempted to disentangle these two independent variables. To measure progress, they used a pretest-posttest design in which students wrote before and after the treatment. The essays were then rated on a variety of factors. The scores were compared across time and between groups using an analysis of variance (ANOVA).

The Zhu and Mitchell (2012) study did not, as far as we know, manipulate the instructional context; all the students participated in the same instructional activities, which are typical of an ESL writing class, meaning that the study can be said to be more naturalistic. The peer response sessions were recorded and analyzed in an attempt to understand the process of peer review, but the outcome, the final essays, were not examined, presumably because they were not seen as relevant to answer a research question that focused on process. In addition, and perhaps more importantly, the participants were interviewed to get their perspectives on peer review. By observing the peer-review sessions and interviewing the students, the authors were able to obtain more than one perspective on peer review. The transcripts of the peer-review sessions were coded by the researchers to identify the participants' stances and task orientations (an etic perspective), and the interviews with the participants were coded to examine the views of the participants (an etic and emic perspective).

The results of the two studies also illustrate differences between the approaches. Lundstrom and Baker (2009) found that both groups improved over time on their overall essay scores and that for the beginners, the type of treatment (giving or receiving feedback) made a difference, with the givers getting better scores at the end of the treatment sessions. They did not find such a treatment effect in the intermediate group and reasoned that some of the returning students may have already participated in peer review. When they separated out the students who were new to peer review, they found the same treatment effect that they did with the beginners. Furthermore, they looked at different subscales to determine where the improvement occurred, and it was generally in the global skills (e.g., content, organization) as opposed to local ones (e.g., grammar, vocabulary). What is notable here is the attempt to isolate the cause and effect; at first it seemed that proficiency may have had a mediating effect on the treatment, but instead, it was actually writing instruction experience. Moreover, even though the researchers found an effect on the overall scores, they attempted to isolate exactly which aspects of writing were affected.

The results of the Zhu and Mitchell (2012) study are presented by describing the two participants' stances, attitudes, and motives in detail supported by examples taken from the peer-review sessions and interviews. For example, they found that Ingrid as a writer was reader-centered: She explained her purpose as a writer, checked readers' comprehension, and asked for clarifications on feedback. As a giver of feedback, she focused on the clarity of her peer's text from her personal perspective as a reader. The researchers link this behavior to her motive (as stated in the interview) to make her paper clear and easy for others to read. As a writer, Rosa was cooperative during peer review, but took a less active role than Ingrid. She was more active as a feedback giver and saw her role as an instructor whose feedback recycled concepts learned in class. Unlike Ingrid, Rosa specifically mentioned during the interview that she found providing feedback to be valuable to her own writing, which would provide a possible motivation for her primary role in peer review as a feedback provider.

From these two studies we learn about different aspects of peer review. In the experimental study, we learn that giving feedback may have a stronger effect on students' writing than receiving feedback and that the positive effect may be limited to certain global aspects of writing. Furthermore, these effects seem to occur only with students who have not participated in peer review before. The qualitative study shows that different students may have different motives for participating in peer review, and these motives affect how they interact in the peer-review sessions.

Although these studies were both well designed, they have limitations and shortcomings; it is often logistically difficult to design the perfect study. In the Lundstrom and Baker (2009) study, there was a lack of random assignment to experimental and control groups; no reliability was reported for the subscores on the rubric; and some of the different subscores seemed to measure the same constructs. These issues are discussed in more detail in Chapter 2. In addition, there was no description of what kind of feedback the giver group received. This last point illustrates a general weakness of quantitative research: It sometimes does not describe what happened during the treatment. On the other hand, Zhu and Mitchell's (2012) conclusions are limited because we do not know how representative the students were; only two cases were presented, the number of examples from the data is small; and the researchers do not provide their coding scheme to allow readers to evaluate the robustness of their coding categories (see Chapter 10). Furthermore, collection of other types of data, such as student papers, would have added another layer of description; that is, we might see students' stances via their behavior in the peer review, their comments in the interviews, *and* their response to the peer review in their texts. Such additional data would have enhanced the credibility of the researchers' claims.

Most of the features used to contrast these two studies are discussed in more detail throughout the book. We hope these examples, however, serve to introduce readers to the basic differences between quantitative and qualitative research on a topic in the realm of L2 writing research.

Organization of the Book

The focus of this book is on *what* is researched and especially *how* it is researched but less on the findings of research. This book is divided into two main sections. Part I covers four different broad approaches to L2 writing research. Chapters 2 and 3 address experimental and correlational/causal-comparative research, which are quantitative, whereas Chapter 4 addresses ethnographic and case study research, which are qualitative approaches. Chapter 5 covers mixed methods research, an approach that is becoming more popular in applied linguistics. In these chapters, we talk about the major tenets of the approach and the types of research questions that each can address. Each of these four chapters includes a table of representative studies with the research questions, the research context, and notes about the study design.

Part II presents six different methods (or what some might call *techniques* or *tools*) used for data collection and analysis in L2 writing research. These are chosen after the researcher has decided on an approach to answer the research questions. Some of these methods tend to be associated with certain approaches; for example, interviews are likely to be part of an ethnography or case study, while learner text analysis is likely to be part of an experimental study. These associations are only tendencies, and with the trend toward mixed method approaches (see Chapter 5), we should not assume that a specific method is always tied to a specific approach or vice versa. Each chapter in Part II describes a method, how it has been used in L2 writing research, and what we can find out by using it. This is followed by variations on the method and a discussion of issues that need to be considered when using the method, including choices the researcher has to make, potential problems with the method, and related practical issues. Chapters in this section also include a table of representative studies that focus on the research questions and contexts, as well as a second table that lists variations of the methods, and a representative study. Throughout the book, studies included in the tables of sample studies and in the boxes are bolded in the text when they are mentioned. In addition, each chapter includes suggestions for further reading.

The book ends with a chapter on future directions in L2 writing research. Here we include a discussion of methods that are not yet widely used in L2 writing research but more so in other areas of applied linguistics, in education, or in L1 composition. We also discuss general issues related to L2 writing research methods and give suggestions for future research.

This book is organized so that it can be used by both novice scholars as an introduction to L2 writing research as well as by experienced researchers who wish to know more about certain approaches and methods. The representative studies included in the tables in each chapter serve as examples, and the suggested readings will allow readers to examine specific issues in more depth. The book can be used as a reference book, as a course book for a class on L2 writing, or as a supplemental text in a research methods class. We have italicized what we consider to be key terms in the field so as to alert novice researchers of their importance.

PART I

Approaches

2

EXPERIMENTAL RESEARCH

Descriptions of how to design an experimental study in the social sciences are numerous, but here we address the basic concepts as they apply to L2 writing research. Simply put, experimental research attempts to control and manipulate variables to determine cause-effect relationships. The variables that are manipulated are the *independent variables* (also called the treatment or intervention), while the outcome variables are the *dependent variables*. As an example from L2 writing research, consider a study by van Beuningen, De Jong, and Kuiken (2012). The authors wanted to determine the effect of comprehensive written corrective feedback, a type of treatment, on accuracy in writing. The independent variable in this case is the feedback, and accuracy is the dependent variable. In addition to research on corrective feedback, other purposes for conducting experimental research are first addressed in this chapter. This is followed by a discussion of the central issues related to experimental research and the discussion of a sample study.

Overview of Experimental Research

Although studies of feedback often come to mind first when thinking about experimental L2 writing research, a variety of other independent variables have been investigated. Examples of these studies are included in Table 2.1. For examples, studies have been conducted on the effect of the writing task itself, often in terms of topic, genre, or complexity. Kuiken and Vedder (2008) manipulated the complexity of the writing task itself to understand how the task affected the language used in the students' essays. Other studies have examined other aspects of the context in which texts are produced. For example, several studies have examined different aspects of planning by manipulating the conditions before

TABLE 2.1 Representative Experimental Studies

Study	Context, participants, and task	Research questions	Comments
van Beuningen, De Jong, & Kuiken (2012)	• Students learning Dutch in Dutch secondary schools • The population had a range of L1s, with 20% coming from Dutch L1 backgrounds. • Both the pre- and two posttest tasks included a 10-minute presentation on a science-related topic. • Students had 20 minutes to write a 15-line email to a classmate who missed the presentation.	1. Is comprehensive written CF useful as an editing tool—that is, does it enable learners to improve the accuracy of an initial text during revision? 2. Does comprehensive written CF yield a learning effect—that is, does it lead to improved accuracy in new texts written one week and four weeks after CF has been provided? (p. 10) 3. Five additional related questions were asked.	• This was a well-designed study that included an appropriate task for the control group. • The study did not consider long-term effects of the treatment.
Kuiken & Vedder (2008)	• 91 Dutch learners of Italian and 76 Dutch learners of French at a Dutch university at three levels of proficiency • Students wrote letters for 40 minutes with the use of a dictionary allowed. Their letters had to be at least 150 words.	1. What is the effect of manipulating cognitive task complexity on syntactic complexity, lexical variation, and accuracy of learner output? 2. Is the output of low- and high-proficient learners affected by the manipulation of task complexity? (p. 51)	• Task complexity was operationalized as the number of factors the students had to consider when making a choice. • It is not clear if the participants were randomly assigned to groups.
East (2007)	• 47 secondary school students of German as a foreign language in New Zealand • Students wrote two timed 50-minute argumentative essays.	1. Does use of a dictionary make a difference to the quality of L2 test takers' writing, as measured by the test scores? (p. 332)	• This was a repeated measures study with task and condition counterbalanced. • Interrater reliability is reported but only on scores after a discussion of discrepancies. • A lack of difference on an ANOVA does not prove that no difference exists.

Wigglesworth & Storch (2009)	• 144 ESL students from an Australian university • Students writing alone wrote a 40-minute argumentative essay, and students writing collaboratively wrote for 60 minutes.	1. What are the differences in the essays of students who compose alone versus in pairs?	• This study also collected data from the pairwork condition to understand what the students were focusing on. • Time-on-task could not be strictly controlled because the collaborative condition takes more time.
Yang, Hu, & Zhang (2014)	• 95 Chinese university EFL students • Students wrote an argumentative essay with no time constraints, but there was a word-limit of 400 words for both the baseline and experimental condition task.	1. Does concurrent verbal reporting, be it metacognitive or nonmetacognitive, have any effects on the writing fluency, linguistic complexity, formal accuracy, and overall writing quality of texts produced by L2 learners? 2. Do MTA and NMTA differ in their effects, if there are any, on the aforementioned measures of texts written by L2 learners? (p. 56)	• The training for the think-aloud task included an extensive five-step procedure in which students watched examples. • The researchers do not present data showing that the students in the two experimental conditions were actually following the instructions given. • Participants were allowed to speak in English, Chinese, or a mix while performing the think alouds.
Zhang (2013)	• 29 students in a US university intensive English program • Students were given two hours to read two related readings and write an essay using the information from the readings.	1. Does the quality of intermediate ESL students' synthesis essays improve after one semester's instruction? 2. What is the effect of instruction on intermediate ESL students' overall synthesis essay quality compared to the students who did not receive instruction? (p. 54)	• Intact classes were used, but students were randomly assigned to those classes. • A detailed description of what both groups did is provided. • The appendix includes one full set of readings and the associated prompt as well as the scoring rubric. • The prompts were counterbalanced.

(Continued)

TABLE 2.1 (Continued)

Study	Context, participants, and task	Research questions	Comments
Ong (2014)	• 106 pre-university Chinese students studying in Singapore • Students wrote a 30-minute argumentative essay.	1. What are the effects of planning time conditions and task on the frequencies of five metacognitive processes during planning and writing?	• The study used retrospective questionnaires to measure the dependent variables, namely, different aspects of the writing process. The variables were assessed in terms of frequency of different behaviors.
Short, Fidelman, & Louguit (2012)	• Over 400 US ESL middle and secondary school students • Students took a writing test that included writing a story based on a prompt and one based on a picture. An indirect multiple-choice test of writing was also included.	1. Will ELLs in one district with teachers who received professional development in the SIOP model show significantly higher achievement in reading, writing, and oral proficiency in English on a standardized measure than ELLs in a comparable district with teachers who had no SIOP professional development? (p. 339)	• The study measured changes in oral language as well. • This was a quasi-experimental study matching two school districts on a variety of features.
Hartshorn et al. (2010)	• 47 ESL students studying at a US university • Students wrote 30-minute argumentative essays for the pre- and posttests.	1. Will students who received dynamic corrective feedback for a semester do better on a writing posttest than students in a contrast group?	• This was a well-designed study because it was longitudinal and because it examined a variety of writing features, not only accuracy. • It appears that the students in the treatment group wrote more than the students in the contrast group. • Intact classes were used for the different groups, so this is a quasi-experimental study.

students write, while others have manipulated the condition during which students write or revise, including Ong and Zhang (2013), discussed in Box 2.1. Other conditions that can be manipulated include a condition for writing such as dictionary use (East, 2007) or collaborative versus individual writing (Wigglesworth & Storch, 2009).

Some studies have manipulated data collection conditions, such as having students think aloud while writing, to examine the effect on the quality or various features of the text. (See Chapter 8 for a further discussion of thinking aloud.) These studies were conducted not necessarily to investigate a pedagogical benefit but rather to understand how the act of collecting data may affect students' writing. Yang, Hu, and Zhang (2014) studied the effects of different types of thinking aloud on a variety of text features as well as on overall quality.

Another type of independent variable is some type of instruction, broadly defined. For example, a study might focus on one aspect of writing such as fluency training or explicit versus implicit instruction of a certain grammatical point. Zhang (2013) examined, specifically, the effect of synthesis instruction in a writing class. Other studies have examined the effect of program-level instruction, meaning that students are in different types of classes for an extended period of time, such as in Short, Fidelman, and Louguit (2012). They studied the effect of a teacher professional development program in a large-scale study spanning two school districts and found positive effects on students' written skills.

The majority of experimental studies use either text quality or some text feature such as accuracy or complexity as their dependent variable. However, a few studies have examined the effect of an intervention on some part of the writing process, as opposed to the texts. These studies are challenging because the dependent variables (i.e., various aspects of the writing process) in such studies may be difficult to operationalize. Most studies of the writing process use introspective methods, such as thinking aloud while writing, or retrospective methods, such as stimulated recall, both described in Chapter 8. Ong (2014), on the other hand, studied the effects of task conditions and planning time on the frequencies of different metacognitive processes by using a retrospective questionnaire.

Issues Involved in Conducting Experimental Research

It is obvious from the earlier discussion that experimental studies seek to determine cause and effect, which many researchers see as their strength. The studies are controlled so as to isolate the independent variables. These studies are not always easy to design, however, often because of difficulties in operationalizing and isolating the independent variable to ensure *internal validity* (are the effects really due to the causes studied) and in choosing a reliable and valid way to measure the dependent variable. Furthermore, experimental studies may be criticized for being too *reductionist*; in other words, the focus is so narrow that other factors related to teaching and learning are ignored. In addition, the study may lack *external* and *ecological validity*, which are related to how generalizable the study's results are. Each of these points is addressed here.

Operationalizing the Independent Variable and Ensuring Internal Validity

As mentioned, operationalizing an independent variable such as written corrective feedback necessitates that the researcher make several choices. Consider Kuiken and Vedder (2008), who had to operationalize task complexity. There have been volumes written on what makes a task, both written and oral, more complex. Kuiken and Vedder may or may not have chosen the most agreed-upon definition, but they reviewed the literature, made a decision, and described the tasks in their article. Yang, Hu, and Zhang (2014) had to operationalize a procedure, think-aloud protocols, and they too included a discussion of the different types of think alouds and the instructions given to the participants. In both of the cases, there were a variety of ways to operationalize the independent variable. No one way can be considered the best way, but it is essential that the researchers describe and explain their decisions, not only so that the study can be evaluated but so that it can be appropriately compared to other similar studies. For example, in Truscott's (2007) meta-analysis (see Chapter 12) of corrective feedback, he explained that not all studies operationalized grammar feedback in the same way. Specifically, some studies included feedback on spelling and punctuation while others did not. Such differences can affect the conclusions the study makes about feedback.

After the variables are properly operationalized, internal validity has to be considered as the study is designed. A study is said to be internally valid if the outcome can be clearly attributed to the independent variable, but some independent variables create comparability issues that may result in internal validity problems. For example, Wigglesworth and Storch (2009) used as their independent variable individual versus collaborative writing. In some ways, this appears easy to operationalize, but there are still decisions that the researcher has to make. As Wigglesworth and Storch pointed out, writing collaboratively takes longer. They chose to give the participants writing in pairs 60 minutes while giving those writing alone only 40 minutes. The dilemma here is clear: This design may privilege the collaborative group, whereas giving all participants the same amount of time would give the individual group an advantage. Thus, the difficulty is not in how the researcher defines the variable but how he or she operationalizes it so that it is the only variable being manipulated. Although certain choices are not always obvious, the researcher has to make a decision, be clear about how the study was done, and justify that decision.

When the independent variable is a type of instruction, such as in Short, Fidelman, and Louguit (2012) or Zhang (2013), the researcher has other challenges that may affect a study's internal validity; in other words, the researcher has to ensure that the group differences are related only to the instruction. Zhang wanted to investigate a very specific type of instruction, discourse synthesis instruction, on students' ability to write an essay using source texts. Some studies that examine a specific type of instruction include a treatment that may last only a short time, possibly one class session or one session done outside of class (e.g., Shintani & Ellis, 2013), but Zhang's instructional treatment lasted over the course of a semester, with the experimental group receiving five cycles of synthesis writing instruction. Such an extended treatment with two different classes increases the possibility of some external factor, such as classroom dynamics, having an effect on the students' learning. Thus, it is important to describe exactly what the two groups were doing and how the control group, who did not receive the synthesis instruction, differed from the treatment group. Zhang included a table showing what the control group was doing and even the materials that were used in the experimental group. He stated, "The only difference in instruction between the two classes was whether there was instruction on (and therefore practice in) synthesis writing" (p. 57) indicating that he was aware of external factors and attempted to minimize them.

Longitudinal experimental studies like Zhang's (2013) sometimes use intact classes, meaning that the participants were not randomly assigned to groups. In such cases, student selection into class could be a factor in their learning. For example, students who choose a morning class may be more motivated. Zhang used intact classes but was fortunately able to randomly assign students to classes and teach both the classes himself. Such a design is still not ideal, because other factors can affect the students' learning, such as classroom dynamics or the time of day that the class is conducted. Although Zhang taught both classes himself, which may appear to eliminate any teacher-associated factors (e.g., knowledge, enthusiasm), the author knew which class was the experimental group and therefore he could have subconsciously treated the experimental group differently. Also, if the students knew that they were part of an experimental treatment, it could have caused a change in their performance. This phenomenon is a well-documented effect in social science research called *the Hawthorne effect*, which says that any noticeable change in routine can cause a temporary improvement in behavior (see Chapter 4). An alternative design could have had the synthesis instruction online as homework so that students in both the control and experimental groups would have had the same classroom experience but different discourse synthesis instruction. With such a design (i.e., the treatment as homework), it is important to give the control group some type of writing experience so that they spend an equal amount of time writing. Again, this would help ensure internal validity because the only difference between the two groups would be the synthesis instruction.

In some cases, where random assignment is not possible, researchers have to use intact classes, and the study is then classified as a *quasi-experimental* study. If the groups are not equivalent on certain measures, there are certain statistics that can be used to account for the lack of equivalence. These statistics are beyond the scope of this book, but see Thyer (2012) for more details. Another type of quasi-experimental design would be a study that has a pretest-posttest design with no control group. We have not included any such studies in Table 2.1 because they are problematic in that the researcher has no way of determining cause and effect. In other words, if a group produces fewer errors after a year of receiving feedback, we cannot attribute that improvement to the feedback; instead, the improvement may have occurred because the students were writing more during the year. Such studies generally lack internal validity.

Hartshorn et al. (2010), a longitudinal feedback study, and Short, Fidelman, and Louguit (2012) were not able to assign students to groups randomly, so they can be considered quasi-experimental. Hartshorn et al.'s treatment-group students and control-group students were in different classes with different teachers, with a few students from each group sharing a teacher. Hartshorn et al. discussed the lack of random assignment at length in their article. They explained how students were assigned to the classes and provided a table comparing the students' native languages and genders. Furthermore, they provided pretest scores for both groups suggesting that they were similar before the treatment. Nevertheless, we cannot ignore the fact that the students did not have exactly the same instruction over the course of a semester. Furthermore, most statistical tests such as an ANOVA, which the authors used to show that there were no initial group differences, are designed to show that groups differ, not that they do not differ. (For a more detailed discussion of this issue see Godfroid & Spino, 2015, also discussed in Chapter 8.)

Short, Fidelman, and Louguit (2012) wanted to investigate the effects of a professional development program on student learning including on a writing test that involved two story-writing tasks. Their study spanned two school districts in northern New Jersey. In one district, the teachers participated in a series of workshops, summer institutes, and classroom observations related to a model of instruction called *sheltered instruction observation protocol* (better known as SIOP). The control group from another district did not participate. Given the existing differences in both teachers and students, conducting an internally valid study was extremely challenging, but Short et al. stated:

> The districts were matched as closely as possible on five contextual and participant factors: student diversity in linguistic and cultural backgrounds, size of student population, socioeconomic status, student achievement scores on state exams, and language program design at the middle and high school levels.
>
> *(p. 339)*

They provided detailed information on both the treatment and control groups to show how the participants, that is, students and teachers, were similar.

Another possible research design that can help ensure internal validity is a repeated measures design. This is when the participants are in both the experimental and the control or comparison groups. East (2007) had students write under two conditions: with and without a dictionary. In a repeated measures study, the researcher has to counterbalance the order of the conditions as well as any other factors that could influence the dependent variable. In East's study, half of the students wrote without a dictionary first and the other half wrote with a dictionary first. This was to account for the possibility that students' writing improved on the second essay because of practice or that their writing got worse because of boredom, for example. Because different topics were used, the order of the topic matched with the condition also had to be counterbalanced in case one topic was inherently more difficult than the other.

Finally, studies that include any type of instructional treatment should include a description of what actually happened during the treatment, not only a description of what was supposed to happen. This is another way to ensure that the outcomes are related to the independent variable. Long (1980) discussed this issue with regard to L2 instructional research and referred to studies of language classes that looked only at outcomes as *black box* studies. He argued that observations had to accompany such studies. The Short, Fidelman, and Louguit (2012) study did include observations to ensure that teachers were implementing the SIOP model. Wigglesworth and Storch (2009), in their study of collaborative versus individual writing, included a description of what students were actually doing when working in pairs. Had they not done so, we would not have known if the students collaborating really were talking to one another and sharing in the writing task. Again, these additional data sources help ensure internal validity.

Measuring the Dependent Variables: Practicality, Reliability, and Validity

Researchers have to choose not only how to elicit the data used to assess the outcomes of the treatment but also which measures to use to assess the outcomes. In experimental L2 writing research, the investigation usually focuses on some aspect of text quality, and so these issues are also discussed in more detail in Chapter 6. Occasionally, however, experimental researchers may focus on the composing or revision process. In any case, researchers need to choose measures that are *practical* and *reliable* as well as *valid*.

When collecting data from which to assess outcomes, generally, the more the better, both in terms of number of participants but also in terms of examples of the behavior that the research wants to assess. Nevertheless, practicality has to come into play. Consider again the Short, Fidelman, and Louguit (2012) study in which they wanted to determine the effects of a model of teaching and teacher development on students' writing. They had to first decide what writing they would consider. In assessment, usually the more data one has from a student, the more accurately one can assess that student. In an ideal world, the researchers would likely have obtained writing samples on a wide variety of genres on which to assess writing. But instructional context, student fatigue, and cost, among other factors, have to be considered, which is likely why only two different writing tasks were used.

Conditions under which the data are collected can affect the *reliability* of the data. Reliability refers to the idea that if the study were repeated, the researcher would get the same results each time. Sometimes the conditions under which data are collected can affect reliability. For example, in any of the experimental studies in Table 2.1, if students had produced writing in some type of harsh condition (e.g., poor lighting, uncomfortable temperatures), their writing quality may have suffered. Another consideration when collecting data might be the researcher's behavior. If some researchers cause anxiety among participants but other researchers don't, different data will be obtained in each data collection session or in different studies.

Perhaps the most difficult issue to deal with in experimental research is the reliability and validity of the measure used for the dependent variable. In order for a measure to be reliable, the researcher has to ensure that the results of the measure are consistent and would be obtained by other researchers. For example, one might want to determine the accuracy of a student's vocabulary by counting the number of lexical errors. It's difficult, however, to get coders to agree on what is to be counted as a lexical error, and thus the results of the measure might differ across coders, thus making the measure unreliable. Researchers need to take steps to make sure that the measures they use are consistent and that others using the same measure will get the same results on the same or similar data. As the majority of dependent variable measures in experimental L2 writing research are related to text features, the issue of reliability is dealt with more in Chapter 6, but simply put, guidelines for coding need to be established. In the case of measures of text quality, detailed rubrics and norming of raters are needed. All of these steps will help coders or raters achieve agreement or *interrater reliability.* Some studies also report *intrarater reliability,* in which one rater or coder uses a measure at different points in time to determine if he or she is consistent. Such a step is helpful but does not ensure that other researchers will get the same results.

Reliability is important because if a measure is not reliable, more error is introduced into the measure, causing a researcher to possibly miss group differences. For example, a study might teach students to use different graphic organizers to help them write more coherent essays. If those essays are assessed using an unreliable measure of text organization and no effect of the treatment is found, there is no way of knowing whether the lack of findings is due to error in the measure or no effect from the treatment.

Although reliability is important, it is only one part of choosing a measure. It is possible to have a reliable measure that is not *valid,* meaning that it does not measure what it says it measures. A study may wish to get students to use more sophisticated vocabulary in their writing through an intervention that involves explicit vocabulary teaching. If that study assessed vocabulary by having coders count the number of nouns, the measure would likely be very reliable, but it would not tap into the level of lexical sophistication of the essay; thus it would not be valid. And while determining reliability is relatively straightforward, determining validity is not. Determining the validity of specific text measures is addressed in Chapter 6, but many experimental studies use rubrics. There is a huge body of work in the language-testing literature related to different types of test validity, including construct validity (i.e., the idea that a test measures a broad concept such as writing proficiency or discourse competence). (For an overview on related assessment issues, including validity, see Kunnan, 2013). Many studies on L2 writing that assess quality rely on previously used rubrics, which are assumed to be valid, but other studies use rubrics that may not have been validated. East (2007), for example, like most studies, did not empirically validate the rubric used, but he described its theoretical basis and justified his decision to use the rubric.

Again, most of the L2 experimental writing research focuses on constructs related to writers' texts, and the validity of these measures is addressed in Chapter 6. Consider, though, a study such as Ong (2014). In this study, the frequency of metacognitive processes was the dependent variable, and determining a valid measure of such a variable is not easy. Ong used a questionnaire and stated:

> To reduce distortion of self-reports due to memory failure or reconstruction of memory, we administered the questionnaire immediately after the writing task experiment and we designed the questionnaire to be task-specific (see Schellings & Van Hout-Wolters, 2011) and focused only on five metacognitive processes.
>
> *(p. 23)*

In this case, the procedure, or timing of the questionnaire, was related to the questionnaire's validity or ability to measure what it was supposed to measure. Ong also addressed the practicality issue, saying:

> Despite the methodological drawbacks of retrospective questionnaires, they were used in this present study for several reasons. First, it was the least intrusive method for examining the writers' metacognitive processes as this method minimized disruption of their cognitive processes while they composed. Second, it allowed the collection of data from a larger sample of writers. Third, the complexity of the experimental design and the sample size made it impractical to incorporate on-line methods such as think-aloud and introspection.
>
> *(p. 23)*

Whether a questionnaire is the best way to measure cognitive processes or not, Ong justified her decision with a discussion of practicality but also validity.

Finally, experimental research aims to determine group differences based on the dependent variables. Determining if the differences are meaningful is a complex matter that has been long debated. One way to determine if group differences are meaningful is to conduct *a test of statistical significance*, such as an analysis of variance (ANOVA), to determine whether or not they are due to chance. Tests of significance alone, however, do not provide a full picture of the differences, and the use of such tests continues to be debated (e.g., Norris, 2015). For example, a test may conclude that there is a 99.99 percent chance of a group difference, but the difference might very small. Most studies now include *effect sizes* as way to assess the magnitude of the difference. We refer readers to applied linguistics statistics literature in the suggestions for further reading section at the end of the chapter for more information. These references discuss choosing an appropriate test of statistical significance, the debate on statistical significance testing, and issues related to effect size.

External Validity, Ecological Validity, and Reductionism

We are often concerned with the extent to which the results of an experimental study can be extended to other instructional contexts and other populations. This concern is called *external validity* (also known as *generalizability*) and is related to any experimental study. In Yang, Hu, and Zhang's (2014) study of the reactivity of thinking aloud, participants were Chinese EFL students at a Chinese university. These students likely had a high degree of metalinguistic knowledge because of Chinese language teaching practices. These participant characteristics could have influenced the results of the study because the students were used to talking about language. In contrast, for students not used to talking about grammar, thinking aloud could have helped them focus on their grammatical errors in a way that they normally did not. Thus, for this and most studies, readers need to consider how the results of any study can or cannot be extended to other populations. Researchers should provide detailed descriptions of their study populations so that readers can consider studies' possible implications for other groups.

Ecological validity refers to the extent to which the study is related to real-life situations. In SLA research, this has been addressed by postulating whether or not laboratory studies are related to real classrooms (e.g., Gass, Mackey, & Ross-Feldman, 2005; Hulstijn, 1997). Consider again Hartshorn et al. (2010). They employed an intensive and sustained system of corrective feedback in their study. On the one hand, it was conducted in a classroom, so they can argue that their study has ecological validity, but their treatment may be difficult to realize in most classroom contexts. Another example is Sachs and Polio (2007), who studied the effects of error correction versus reformulation on students' accuracy in a revision task. In their study, the researchers rewrote the students' essays with the correct grammar. It is clear that this type of intervention cannot be done in most L2 classrooms because it is too time-consuming. However, the fact that an intervention cannot be replicated in a classroom or that real-life pedagogical contexts may require modification of a treatment does not negate a study's importance. Although ecological validity is important to consider, any study that gives researchers and teachers insight into how students write can be potentially helpful, as it may guide future research or help us build models of the L2 writing process.

A related but more philosophical issue about experimental research concerns what has been called a *reductionist* approach to research. The criticism is that the focus of experimental research may be so narrow that it ignores important contextual factors. Recall that a study is internally valid if the results can be attributed to the independent variable, meaning that the researcher has to design a study that controls for extraneous variables, that is, those not related to the independent variable in question. Block (1996), who is critical of experimental research, stated that "the extraneous variables are possibly the most interesting part of a study because they are specific context defining" (p. 74). A similar point of view is taken by Atkinson (2014), who argued that SLA is complex and we cannot isolate cognitive factors (or variables) from social ones.

Atkinson (2014) and Block (1996) represent one ontological view of SLA that probably cannot be reconciled with experimental research, but we can still consider problems related to the isolation of variables in experimental research. In studies that examine the effect of a treatment on students' writing, researchers may focus on just one or a few variables. Research on written corrective feedback, for example, uses measures of accuracy. It is highly likely, however, that students' attention to accuracy may cause other features of their writing to suffer, which was the crux of Truscott's (1996) argument that written corrective feedback was harmful. However, corrective feedback studies such as Hartshorn et al. (2010) and van Beuningen, De Jong, and Kuiken (2012) addressed this concern by considering other aspects of writing, such as the complexity of the language, so as to provide a bigger picture of the students' writing. In sum, it is important to consider how the dependent variable that is the focus may interact with other variables.

BOX 2.1 FOCAL STUDY

Ong, J. & Zhang, L. J. (2013). Effects of the manipulation of cognitive processes on EFL writers' text quality. *TESOL Quarterly, 47*, 375–398.

Background

Writing is a cognitively complex and demanding task, but there are ways to reduce the cognitive demands through prewriting activities. In addition, different tasks will have different cognitive demands. Controversy exists with regard to both theory and empirical research as to whether freewriting or planning will have a more positive effect on text quality. Research has also been conducted on the conditions under which revision of an essay takes place and how those conditions affect text quality.

Research Question

1. What is the effect of planning condition, subplanning condition (i.e., the amount of information given in the prompt), and revising condition on essay quality?

Method

Chinese EFL students were given a writing pretest in which they wrote in three different genres. Based on the results of the test, the students were divided into three proficiency levels and randomly assigned one of each of the following: a planning condition (planning, prolonged planning, freewriting, control); a subplanning condition (task given, task content given, task content and organization given); and a revising condition (with or without their original draft present). The 107 participants wrote an opinion essay and then revised it. The drafts and revisions were scored using an analytic rating scale.

Results

There was minimal effect from the planning condition, but those in the subplanning conditions, in which content or both content and organization were given, wrote higher quality essays. There was an interaction effect for planning and revising; the participants in the freewriting condition who had their essays removed wrote essays of higher quality.

Discussion of an Experimental Study: Ong and Zhang (2013)

Ong and Zhang (2013) took a very cognitively oriented approach to the study of L2 composing by discussing all the various cognitive demands on writers as they write. Many have argued, from different theoretical perspectives, that if students have time to plan before they write, their essay quality should improve. In relation to our earlier discussion about operationalizing variables, it is clear that the researchers needed to operationalize planning as well as essay quality. They did so by first reviewing research in which planning was operationalized as freewriting, thinking silently, outlining, thinking aloud, and even online planning, which means that students were given unlimited writing time. Most of the studies they reviewed were conducted with L1 writers, and several found some effects of planning on some text features. In Ong and Zhang's study, students were assigned to one of four planning conditions: planning, in which students had 10 minutes to plan and 20 minutes to write; prolonged planning, in which they had 20 minutes to plan and 10 minutes to write; freewriting, in which students were told to start writing immediately; and a control group that was not given specific instructions.

As discussed earlier, one of the challenges in experimental research is to make sure that the groups differ only according to the independent variable. Ong and Zhang did this in two ways. First, they gave participants a writing test that consisted of three essays. Based on the scores of this test, students were assigned to one of three proficiency levels. The researchers used *stratified random sampling*, meaning that the participants were randomly divided within their proficiency level (i.e., low, average, or high). This technique better ensures that the four groups are equivalent, something that is particularly important with smaller sample sizes. Although the study had a relatively large sample size of 107 participants, there were four groups in the different planning conditions, with each having 26 to 28 participants. Because of the relatively small number of students in each group, stratified random sampling was an excellent choice for this study. The second design feature that allowed Ong and Zhang to isolate the effects of the planning variable was to control for time-on-task. As mentioned earlier, controlling for time can be challenging in many social science and applied linguistics studies. Ong and Zhang designed their study so that all groups were engaged in some aspect of the writing process for 60 minutes. Had they designed the study so that the students in the planning condition were simply given additional time to plan, with all groups writing for the same amount of time, we can see the unfair advantage the planning group would have had. While some studies are often not clear about time-on-task, Ong and Zhang provide a detailed and clear table regarding the allocation of time across all phases of writing for all four groups.

Ong and Zhang also were interested in two other aspects of the writing condition, namely, what kind of information was given in the prompt and whether or not the students' first draft was accessible as they revised. A previous study by Kellogg (1988) failed to show that students' writing improved when they were provided with additional information about the topic or organization in the prompt, which countered the idea that students' writing would improve if their cognitive load was reduced. Galbraith and Torrance (2004) examined L1 writers in a variety of revision conditions and found that the best quality essays were those in which students were told to first write a draft without worrying about the organization and then had that draft removed while rewriting, that is, removing the draft allowed the students to make more global revisions that improved the quality of their essays. Given these two lines of research, Ong and Zhang added two other variables: task condition (task only, content given, content and organization given) and revising condition (draft-accessible, draft removed). (Note that the authors call task condition *subplanning* in their study because the prompt will affect how students plan. We have chosen to call it *task condition* here.) These two variables are more straightforward, so the authors did not go into as much detail describing them. In the article, they provided the writing prompt that was common across all conditions, which is an important detail, but they did not provide the specific instructions that each group had. This would have been useful to include in the appendix for other researchers who might want to replicate the study.

The next point to consider is how the authors measured the dependent variable, text quality. Recall that the purpose of the research was to determine the effect of various independent variables on text quality. Ong and Zhang used an analytic writing rubric in which scores are given for various essay components. They used the Jacobs, Zinkgraf, Wormuth, Hartfiel, and Hughey (1981) scale, which has been used in many L2 writing studies. It is composed of five categories: content, organization, vocabulary, language, and mechanics. Some studies choose to report scores on these five individual components, but Ong and Zhang reported only the total score and not the individual components. Such practice is completely acceptable; there are several advantages to using analytic, as opposed to holistic, scales, even if the individual components are not dependent variables.

As discussed earlier, reliability and validity of the measures is a major concern in experimental research. Whether measuring overall quality or a specific construct such as complexity or accuracy it is important to report reliability. Ong and Zhang had two raters rate 40 percent of the essays and had one of the researchers rate all of the essays twice, three months apart. Thus, this study reported both inter- and intrarater reliability, which for the essays written before revision were .62 and .93, respectively. A few points are worth mentioning. Most studies using rating scales report interrater reliability on 100 percent of the data (but studies using other coding schemes tend to report it on only a portion of the data). Given that the components of the analytic scale are high-inference, meaning that the rater has to make many judgments, it seems that the authors should have had two raters rate all the essays, not just a portion. On the other hand, most studies do not report intrarater reliability on even a portion of the data, and this calculation adds another check on the measure. Another concern is the low interrater reliability in this study. It does not discredit the significant findings, but it may have masked other significant relationships. Furthermore, the low interrater reliability suggests that others using the scale may not obtain the same ratings, thus making replication of the findings difficult.

To calculate the results and determine the relationship between the first two independent variables, planning and task condition, Ong and Zhang calculated a two-way ANOVA. This allowed them to look at not only each variable separately but also how those two variables interacted. They found that the effect of planning approached statistical significance but did not reach it; a post-hoc test showed that the contrast between the freewriting condition and the prolonged planning condition was nearly significant, with the students in the freewriting condition doing the best and the students in the prolonged planning condition doing the worst. With regard to the task condition, the students in the conditions where they were provided with the content or both the content and organization did better than the control, or prompt-only, groups. There was no interaction effect between the two independent variables. As with most recent experimental studies, Ong and Zhang reported effect sizes, another way to consider group differences. (See suggested readings.)

The participants also had a chance to revise in one of the two revision conditions. The interrater reliability on the scores of the revised essays was also low, at .56, so the authors took the unusual step of having the raters discuss the essays on which they disagreed widely to resolve discrepancies. They found that there was an interaction effect between the planning and revision conditions. Specifically, students in the freewriting condition did better when their essays had been removed before revising, but the students in the control group did better when they had their essays as they revised. They report other contrasts, but what stands out is that the revising condition alone did not affect group differences, and that there were large differences for students in the planning and freewriting groups.

Suggestions for Further Reading

General Research Design and Statistics

- Fields, A. (2013). *Discovering statistics using IBM SPSS statistics.* Los Angeles: Sage.
- Fraenkel, J., Wallen, N. E., & Hyun, H. H. (2014). *How to design and evaluate research in education.* Boston: McGraw Hill.
- Thyer, B. (2012). *Quasi-experimental research design.* Oxford: Oxford University Press.

Research and Design Issues Related to Experimental Applied Linguistics research

- Hudson, T. & Llosa, L. (2015). Design issues and inference in experimental L2 research. *Language Learning, 65*(Suppl.), 76–96.
- Larsen-Hall, J. (2016). *A guide to doing statistics in second language research using SPSS and R* (2nd ed.). London: Routledge.
- Lowie, W. & Seton, B. (2012). *Essential statistics for applied linguistics.* New York: Palgrave Macmillan.
- Norris, J. (2015). Statistical significance testing in second language research: Basic problems and suggestions for reform. *Language Learning, 65*(Suppl.), 97–126.

- Plonsky, L. (2013). Study quality in SLA: An assessment of designs, analyses, and reporting practices in quantitative L2 research. *Studies in Second Language Acquisition, 35*, 655–687.
- Plonsky, L. (2014). Study quality in quantitative L2 research (1990–2010): A methodological synthesis and call for reform. *Modern Language Journal, 98*, 450–470.
- Plonsky, L. (2015). Statistical power, *p* values, descriptive statistics, and effect sizes: A "back-to-basics" approach to advancing quantitative methods in L2 research. In L. Plonsky (Ed.), *Advancing quantitative results in second language research* (pp. 23–45). New York and London: Routledge/Taylor Francis.
- Plonsky, L. & Oswald, F. L. (2014). How big is "big"? Interpreting effect sizes in L2 research. *Language Learning, 64*, 878–912.
- Porte, G. (2010). *Appraising research in second language learning: A practical approach to critical analysis of quantitative research.* Amsterdam and Philadelphia: John Benjamins.
- Porte, G. (Ed). (2012). *Replication research in applied linguistics.* Cambridge: Cambridge University Press.
- Turner, J. L. (2014). *Using statistics in small-scale language education research: Focus on non-parametric data.* New York and London: Routledge.

3

CAUSAL-COMPARATIVE AND CORRELATIONAL RESEARCH

Causal-comparative and correlational research are similar to experimental research in that they attempt to quantitatively measure a variety of variables. For this reason, these types of research need to consider the measurement issues addressed in Chapters 2 and 6. Although many of the issues related to conducting causal-comparative and correlational research are covered in other chapters, we felt it was important to separate them from experimental research because they differ in one crucial way: In these types of research, researchers do not manipulate an independent variable as they do in experimental approaches, but instead describe relationships among existing variables (see Table 3.1). Despite the ultimate goal of determining cause-effect relationships in much of the research, causal-comparative and correlational research are similar in that they generally cannot show clear cause-effect relationships, but they differ in the types of variables investigated. Both may consider the same outcome variable, such as writing proficiency, but causal-comparative research examines existing differences between groups, and these groups are labeled by *nominal* variables that cannot be quantified, such as L1 or gender. Correlational research, on the other hand, uses *ordinal* or *continuous* variables that can be measured. For example, a correlational study might examine the relationship between writing proficiency and writing anxiety. In this chapter, we first discuss the kinds of questions that researchers using these two approaches wish to answer about L2 writing and then discuss the issues related to conducting descriptive research. We end with a discussion of a sample study. This chapter is shorter because many of the important issues are covered in Chapters 2 and 6, but the discussion of the focal study is more detailed because of the study's complexity.

TABLE 3.1 Representative Causal–Comparative and Correlational Studies

Study	Context, participants, and instruments	Research questions	Comments on study design
Cheng (2002)	• 165 university-level English majors from Taiwan • Four different anxiety questionnaires	1. What is the relationship between L1 writing anxiety and L2 writing anxiety? 2. What is the relationship between L2 writing anxiety and gender, and L2 writing anxiety and class level?	• This study was both correlational and causal comparative. • Reliability was reported for each of the questionnaires. • Factor analysis was used to reduce the number of variables. A regression was then done to see which factors predicted L2 writing anxiety. An ANOVA was used to examine group differences.
Doolan & Miller (2012)	• 67 students in a developmental writing class at a US community college	1. Does Generation 1.5 students' writing exhibit more total identified errors than does their developmental L1 classmates' writing? 2. Are there any differences with regard to specific types of identified errors produced by Generation 1.5 students and their L1 classmates? 3. Are there any qualitative differences with regard to verb errors produced by Generation 1.5, L1, and more traditional L2 classmates? (p. 4)	• The two groups had comparable holistic essay scores. • A *t*-test and a series of nonparametric tests were used to examine group differences.
Friginal, Li, & Weigle (2014)	• Highly rated essays from 24 NNSs and 51 NSs enrolled in US universities	1. How do profiles from highly rated native speaker and nonnative speaker essays differ?	• The study used the Biber tagger (2006) for the initial coding of the essays. • Cluster analysis was used.

Study	Research questions	Notes
Yang & Plakans (2012)	1. What is the relationship between strategy use and test performance on an integrated reading-listening-writing test? (p. 84)	• Factor analysis was used on the questionnaire to determine the related variables. • Reliability scores were given for the questionnaire and integrated test. • Structural equation modeling was used to test a model of strategy use and test performance.
Kim (2012)	1. What patterns of performance are observable among KFL learners and KHL learners completing the same writing tasks? (p. 344)	• Five heritage and four L2 Australian high school learners of Korean • Very small sample size did not allow for inferential statistics. • Students wrote two different types of essays, both scored on an analytic scale.
Lu (2011)	1. Which measures of linguistic complexity distinguish among different proficiency levels?	• 442 timed argumentative essays from Chinese university EFL students • An automated complexity analyzer was used for 14 measures of linguistic complexity.
Bulté & Housen (2014)	1. Which measures of linguistic complexity best show change over time? 2. Which measures of linguistic complexity correlate with overall measures of quality?	• 45 university ESL students at the beginning and end of a semester of ESL study • 30-minute descriptive essays counterbalanced for topic • This study used a corpus analyzed by others for different features as described in Connor-Linton and Polio (2014).
Yu (2010)	1. What is the relationship between L2 learners' lexical diversity in spoken and written discourse?	• 25 students from a range of backgrounds • MELAB • A simple correlation was used to check the relationship between lexical diversity on oral and written production. • Vocd was used to measure lexical diversity.
Kokhan (2012)	1. Does the correlation between TOEFL iBT and a university placement test depend on the time between taking these two tests?	• Over 2,500 ESL students at a US university • TOEFL iBT and university placement test • Pearson correlations were calculated for students who took the TOEFL and university writing placement tests with different intervening intervals.

An Overview of Causal-Comparative Research

Causal-comparative research, like experimental research, studies group differences, but these differences already exist when the study is conducted. Such group differences may include gender, L1, field of study, school district, or other demographic variables that cannot be manipulated and that require labeling participants according to nominal variables. Cheng (2002), for example, examined gender differences in L2 writing anxiety, which was measured through the use of a questionnaire, and found that females had higher L2 writing anxiety. In addition, he looked at the relationship between language anxiety and language class level. In this case, class level was treated as a nominal variable (i.e., placement into one of three groups based on year in school), and an ANOVA was used to test for group differences. In contrast, if placement test scores (a continuous variable) had been used instead of class placement, this part of the study would have been *correlational* (discussed later). In neither case, however, can a cause-effect relationship between class level and anxiety be assumed; language anxiety can negatively affect learning and poor progress can affect anxiety. Doolan and Miller (2012), another causal–comparative study, examined differences in the errors of L1 and Generation 1.5 writers, that is, writers distinctly different from international students in that they have lived in the US for an extended period of time and usually have strong oral skills. The authors found that Generation 1.5 writers made more errors overall and more of certain error types. In this case, we do not know what factors (e.g., language input at home, educational background, motivation) related to being a Generation 1.5 writer caused the difference in errors.

In addition to Doolan and Miller (2012), other studies have tried to characterize differences in the writing of different groups of students. Friginal, Li, and Weigle (2014) looked at differences between native speaker (NS) and nonnative speaker (NNS) essays. They focused on only essays that received the highest score using the TOEFL iBT rubric. Instead of simply comparing the sets of essays on a range of features, they investigated how the various features grouped together in all of the highly rated essays. To do this, they used a technique called *cluster analysis* to identify six clusters that shared common features (also used by Jarvis, Grant, Bikowski, & Ferris, 2003). For example, cluster 4 included features of texts with an informational, as opposed to narrative, focus, while cluster 1 essays were longer and more lexically diverse. Friginal et al. (2014) were able to show that NS essays and NNS essays receiving the same holistic scores had different groups of features from each other. Again, while we cannot identify causes in this study, the characteristics that the researchers identified may inform writing curricula. Furthermore, any of these causal-comparative studies can lead to experimental studies that involve interventions with the groups studied.

An Overview of Correlational Research

Correlational research is similar to causal-comparative research in that it addresses the relationship among variables. At its simplest, it will take two continuous variables and show the relationship between them using a Pearson correlation (a number from −1, a negative relationship, to 1, a positive relationship, with 0 indicating no relationship). For example, in L2 writing research, studies may investigate the relationship between quantifiable learner behaviors (e.g., strategy use) or characteristics (e.g., motivation) and L2 writing proficiency, or, alternatively, studies may examine the relationship among behaviors, attitudes, or learner characteristics without actually examining learners' writing. Cheng (2002), described earlier, also included a correlational aspect to his study. He studied the correlations among four variables: L2 writing anxiety, L2 class anxiety, L1 speaking anxiety, and L1 writing anxiety and found that correlations were higher between language-specific measures (.66 for the relationship between L2 speaking and L2 writing; .56 between L1 speaking and L1 writing) than between skills (.19 between L1 speaking and L2 speaking; .07 between L1 writing and L2 writing). In statistical terms, the correlation squared indicates the amount of shared variance. For example, because there is a correlation of .66 between L2 speaking and L2 writing anxiety, we can say the two constructs share 43 percent of the variance between them. While they are clearly two different constructs, there could be a common element, such as language proficiency, affecting them both in some way.

Cheng (2002) did not include students' writing in his study, but researchers might also be interested in the relationship between students' writing test scores and other skills' tests (e.g., reading or listening) or a general proficiency test. They also might want to correlate a specific feature of the students' writing with an overall writing score to help validate the measure (see Chapter 6). Yu (2010) conducted research on lexical diversity in both oral and written language examining the relationship between lexical diversity measures and holistic scores of oral and written discourse. He also examined the correlation between measures of oral and written lexical diversity. He found that the written lexical diversity score and holistic score had a correlation of .33 (for speaking it was higher, at .48). As for the relationship between oral and written lexical diversity, the correlation was .45, suggesting that the construct in the two modalities are related but not the same.

Much of the correlational research on L2 writing is found in the area of language testing. This is likely because language testing researchers often have access to large amounts of test data, which allows them to use sophisticated statistical techniques such as *structural equation modeling* (see the discussion of Schoonen, van Gelderen, Stoel, Hulstijn, & de Glopper, 2011, in Box 3.1). The use of existing test data, however, does not allow researchers to manipulate the variables, thus making experimental research impossible. Often, questionnaire data can be collected along with the assessment instruments to study issues such as strategy use, motivation, or other individual differences. Yang and Plakans (2012) studied the relationship between strategy use and test performance on an integrated reading-listening-writing test. With the results from a strategy questionnaire, *a factor analysis* was conducted. This technique determines how the questionnaire items grouped together to form different factors. Yang and Plakans found six distinct factors, including discourse synthesis strategy use, monitoring, and test wiseness. Using the results of the factor analysis and the test data, the authors were able to test a model of the relationship between strategy use and test performance with structural equation modeling.

Issues Involved in Causal-Comparative and Correlational Research

Many of the issues related to descriptive quantitative research are the same as in experimental research, namely, reliably and validly measuring variables and operationalizing complex constructs such as writing proficiency (see Chapter 2). In other words, the need to find reliable, valid, and practical measures of the dependent variables discussed in the last chapter also apply to correlational research. We note, however, that most correlational research does include reliable measures of language ability with tests that have often been independently validated. This is likely because much of this research is associated with the field of language testing, where reliability and validity are central concerns. There are, however, other issues related specifically to correlational and causal-comparative research that arise.

Creating Groups in Causal-Comparative Research

Comparing groups of students can be difficult. In some cases, such as when examining gender differences, assigning students to groups can be straightforward, but this does not mean that the groups are similar on other factors. For example, consider a context in which male and female students are taught separately. This would result in a wide variety of variables that could affect learning. In other words, it may not be gender itself but the type of instruction or social expectations for the two different genders that account for any difference in the dependent variables. Furthermore, it is difficult to collect data on all variables that could affect learning; for example, most applied linguistics studies do not collect data on socioeconomic status. There is no easy solution to this problem in causal-comparative research, so it is important to carefully describe the groups in any study so that the study can be evaluated.

As an example, Kim (2012) compared the writing of heritage and L2 learners of Korean on two writing tasks. These are especially difficult groups to compare because, as is the case when comparing L2 and Generation 1.5 students, it is difficult to match the groups on the basis of proficiency and socioeconomic status. Complicating the matter, the term *heritage learner* has been defined differently across studies (see the discussion in Carreira, 2004), so it is possible that some of the heritage learners had more in common with the L2 learners than with each other. Some studies report group differences in test data to show equivalence. For example, in a study comparing heritage and L2 learners, a researcher might report writing proficiency test scores for the two groups to show that they are similar in terms of writing proficiency. Such information is helpful, but it is difficult to statistically demonstrate that there are no group differences, since most statistics used in applied linguistics are not appropriate for determining *a lack of difference*. (See Godfroid & Spino, 2015, for discussion of this issue, as well as Chapter 8). Cross-sectional studies of writing development (i.e., studies that are interested in change over time) are, in effect, studies of group differences. Students can be placed into groups by an institutional policy including a placement test or prior language learning experience. If students are placed in levels (i.e., groups) by different means, they may not vary only, or at all, on the variable of language proficiency. When class level is used, as in Lu (2011), who examined differences in written linguistic complexity across of range of levels in a corpus of Chinese EFL learners, the study becomes causal-comparative because it compares pre-existing groups. An alternative to causal-comparative studies of writing development is to conduct longitudinal research and compare the same group of students at different points of time using a repeated measures test. This was done in Bulté and Housen (2014), who studied linguistic complexity. What was particularly interesting about their study was that it also included a correlational component in which holistic scores were correlated with complexity scores, similar to Yu (2010). Bulté and Housen found that developmental changes (i.e., over time) in complexity and changes related to quality (i.e., essay scores) were not the same. Thus, studies that group students by a score from an essay or writing proficiency test may not find the same results as studies that group students by time or level.

Using Questionnaire Data

Because much correlational research uses large data sets, questionnaire data is often used in addition to test data. Questionnaires, as opposed to interviews, allow researchers to collect data from a large number of participants. However, anyone using questionnaires needs to be familiar with the range of issues related to creating and administering good and reliable questionnaires. Issues related to constructing and piloting surveys and reporting reliability are addressed in Dörnyei and Csizér (2012) as well as in other sources in the suggestions for further reading at the end of this chapter. Yang and Plakans (2012), who used a questionnaire to identify students' strategy use during an integrated writing test, provided a detailed discussion of the creation of their instrument. They had experts assess the instrument, and they piloted it with a small number of students to check for wording problems. They also eliminated items with poor reliability. Because some items may have tapped into similar strategies, they conducted a factor analysis to reduce the number of variables to six factors. Good questionnaires require extensive piloting and the use of advanced statistics to interpret them.

Using and Interpreting Statistics

Over the last several years, researchers have begun to use advanced statistical techniques that go beyond correlations and ANOVA. Although a detailed discussion of these sophisticated statistical techniques are beyond the scope of this chapter (but see the suggested readings at the end of this chapter), we will briefly outline some issues involved in using them. One particular issue for correlation research is that multiple measures correlate with each other, so it is not clear which to use. Bulté and Housen (2014) used 10 different measures of linguistic complexity, which had significant correlations with each other. In their study, they wanted to look at each measure separately, but sometimes researchers simply want to measure a specific construct and do not know whether to use one measure or several. This is an issue in experimental research as well, but large sample sizes in correlational research allow for advanced techniques including different types of factor analysis (i.e., principal component analysis, exploratory factor analysis, or confirmatory factor analysis). These types of analyses allow researchers to take a range of measures and choose from the best combinations among them. Which type of analysis to use in applied linguistic research has been debated (e.g., Ellis & Loewen, 2007; Isemonger, 2007) and is not a straightforward issue. If one then wishes to use structural equation modeling (SEM), training in advanced statistical packages is needed; packages like SPSS cannot perform confirmatory factor analysis or structural equation modeling. Winke (2014) discusses other issues that need to be resolved in SEM studies.

Generally, correlational research cannot determine cause-effect relationships, with the exception of some structural equation modeling research (see Pearl, 2012 for a discussion of cause-effect relationships in structural equation modeling research). How then should we interpret or use the results of correlational research? Some research on group differences can lead to a close examination of curriculum and changes in how writing is taught, as with heritage versus non-heritage learners. Ideally, the research will lead to experimental studies that test any instructional changes.

Another issue related to correlational research is how researchers should interpret a correlation coefficient. Just because a correlation is statistically significant does not mean that it is meaningful. For example, assume that one wants to determine the relationship between two tests in order to decide if they are similar enough to say that they are measuring the same construct. Written texts are time consuming to grade, and interrater reliability needs to be established. If a published test, such as the TOEFL, has a high correlation with an expensive and time-consuming institutional test, then replacing one test with another may be appropriate for placing students into classes in a program. Only if there is a very high correlation between the two tests would we argue that they are measuring the same thing. This was the issue addressed by Kokhan (2012), who investigated the correlation between the TOEFL iBT and a university placement test and was able to show that the correlation was strong when the two tests were taken close together in time. We might compare this to Yu (2010), discussed earlier, who included a correlation between lexical diversity and holistic scores and found a correlation of .33 (or that lexical diversity accounted for 11 percent of the variance in the test scores). A correlation of .33 might be considered high when determining the contribution of lexical diversity to a holistic score and therefore would be an important component in an automated scoring program, but it is too low to claim the lexical diversity is sufficient for measuring writing quality.

BOX 3.1 FOCAL STUDY

Schoonen, R., van Gelderen, A., Stoel, R., Hulstijn, J., & de Glopper, K. (2011). Modeling the development of L1 and EFL writing proficiency of secondary school students. *Language Learning, 61*, 31–79.

Background

A variety of factors in different studies have been shown to have a relationship to the ability to write well, including linguistic knowledge and the ability to access that knowledge quickly, as well as rhetorical knowledge, awareness of appropriate writing strategies, and L1 writing ability, among others. Little is known about how these various factors change over time and how they may interact differently at different times in a student's development of both L1 and L2 skills.

Research Questions

1. Does the L1 Dutch and EFL writing proficiency of secondary school students improve (from grade 8 to 10), and how predictive are initial levels of writing proficiency for later levels of proficiency?
2. Are linguistic knowledge, processing efficiency (i.e., speed of processing linguistic knowledge), and metacognitive knowledge related to (development in) writing proficiency in L1 Dutch and EFL? That is, what are the relative contributions of knowledge and speed of processing predictors to writing development?

3. What are the developmental differences between Dutch and EFL writing with respect to the roles of the three proficiency components mentioned in research question 2. (linguistic knowledge, processing efficiency, and metacognitive knowledge)?
4. How does L1 writing proficiency relate to EFL writing proficiency in the course of the writing development? (p. 39–40)

Design

389 Dutch students learning English completed a series of writing tasks in both their L1 and L2s over a period of three years from grade 8 to 10. The variables used to predict L1 and L2 writing scores included metacognitive knowledge, vocabulary knowledge, grammatical knowledge, spelling knowledge, speed of lexical retrieval, and speed of sentence construction.

Results

EFL writing proficiency improved more over time than L1 writing and had a higher correlation with linguistic knowledge and fluency than L1 writing. Although there was a strong relationship between L1 and L2 writing, the models for development across time were not the same.

Discussion of a Correlational Study: Schoonen, van Gelderen, Stoel, Hulstijn, and de Glopper (2011)

This complex study of writing proficiency development is notable for the precision with which the design is reported and the careful choices made in good correlational research. It also serves to illustrate a complex statistical technique, structural equation modeling, that is best described through an example. For these reasons, we have included a lengthy discussion of the study as an example of how to design and carry out correlational research.

Schoonen et al. (2011) were interested in writing proficiency development over time in both learners' L1s and L2s. The study is based on the idea that writing proficiency is "multicomponential" (p. 32), with various cognitive and linguistic factors affecting both L1 and L2 writing. Therefore, in addition to tracking writing proficiency, the researchers examined a number of variables thought to have an effect on or to predict writing proficiency. Furthermore, the researchers addressed the issue of the relationship between L1 and L2 writing, namely, whether or not L1 writing skills can transfer to the L2; one of the central issues in the literature, and well summarized in the study, is whether or not a threshold level of L2 proficiency is needed for writers to draw on their L1 writing skills. The study is complex because the relationship of the 11 predictor variables among each other and writing proficiency can change over time, as can the relationships between L1 and L2 writing.

The study followed 389 students in Dutch schools starting at grade 8 (about 13–14 years old) over three years. As stated earlier, large sample sizes are needed for advanced statistical techniques such as structural equation modeling (see Winke, 2014), and this study is a good example of a rare L2 writing study that qualifies. Problems, of course, arise with large sample sizes, particularly when studies are longitudinal. The obvious problem is the loss of participants over time. Schoonen et al. began with 397 participants from eight secondary schools, and they used data from 389 students, which is a very low drop-out rate for a three-year study. Nevertheless, they had to address missing data from missed test sessions, and the authors explain the statistical procedure used in structural equation modeling for dealing with missing data. One very important point they make is that some methods assume that the data is missing randomly, which is unlikely in most L2 longitudinal studies; lower proficiency students are more likely to miss test sessions. However, the method that they use simply assumes that the missing data can be predicted from the available data.

Another issue related to large sample sizes can be finding comparable participants. In multilingual societies such as the Netherlands, it is difficult to find participants who have similar language backgrounds, among other factors. While different backgrounds of the participants will not negate any results, such differences are an additional source of variation. Schoonen et al. carefully describe their participants and note that 29 percent of what they call *Dutch L1 learners* actually had other L1s. However, all the students began their schooling in Dutch at an early age, had Dutch as their dominant language, and were literate in Dutch. We do not see this as a flaw in the study and, in fact, appreciate the level of detail with which the participants were described.

The variables in this study are clearly described and carefully measured. The first variables, writing proficiency in the L1 and L2, are called the dependent variables with the assumption that some of the 11 predictor variables have an effect on them. The 11 predictor, or independent, variables included metacognitive knowledge, L1 vocabulary knowledge, L2 vocabulary knowledge, L1 grammatical knowledge, L2 grammatical knowledge, L1 spelling knowledge, L2 spelling knowledge, L1 lexical retrieval speed, L2 lexical retrieval speed, L1 sentence construction speed, and L2 sentence construction speed.

Writing proficiency, as stated by the authors, "is notoriously difficult to measure and more than one writing assignment is required to obtain satisfactory generalizabilities" (p. 41). Thus, this study uses three different writing assignments at each of the three data collection points. The writing prompts in their study provide information about various aspects of a context and tried to connect the situations "to young people's life as much as possible to aim for acceptable levels of ecological validity" (p. 42). Nevertheless, students were allowed only

20 minutes to plan and write, so while the prompt may have had ecological validity, the writing conditions may not have. Because the study was longitudinal, the authors raised concerns about the comparability of the prompts. It is not clear why the prompts were not counterbalanced, which would have eliminated the comparability issue. Instead, one prompt from the previous year was included in time 2 and time 3 to look at prompt equivalence.

When measuring writing proficiency, researchers also have to consider how to evaluate the writing. There is no one correct way to do this, but whatever method is chosen needs to be carefully described, and the reliability of the rating needs to be discussed. Schoonen et al. explained that they used a primary-trait analysis in which raters gave one score related to whether or not the writing fulfilled the purpose. In norming sessions, raters were provided with benchmark texts, and each essay was scored by two raters with high levels of interrater reliability for both the English and Dutch essays. An issue in their study related to longitudinal research, but not specific to correlational, is that the ratings were done after each data collection and not by the exact same raters. Thus, the essays were not rated blindly, meaning that the raters knew which data collection point was being rated.

As noted, 11 predictor variables were included. Five of the constructs were measured in both the L1 and the L2, while metacognitive knowledge was not because it was considered to be language independent. To measure metacognitive knowledge, students were given a questionnaire, presumably in Dutch, that asked general questions about reading, writing, and text organization, with some referring specifically to L2 use, and the questionnaire was found to be reliable. Vocabulary, spelling, and grammar knowledge tests were measured with a variety of discrete point tests, each with acceptable reliabilities reported. The last two constructs, speed of lexical retrieval and speed of sentence construction, were measured with reaction time data in which students performed tasks in their L1 and L2 at the computer. For example, students had to read the beginning of a sentence and then decide on one of two ways to finish the sentence as quickly as possible. Reaction time data raise an entire other set of issues that we do not address here because they are not used often in L2 writing research. (The authors do address these issues, such as eliminating outliers, in their study, but we recommend seeing N. Jiang, 2012, for a further discussion of reaction time data.)

In structural equation modeling, the procedure is to propose a model based on theory (Winke, 2014) and then test the fit of the data to the model. Schoonen et al. first tested two models, one for Dutch writing proficiency and one for English, and found that they were different. Specifically, writing proficiency and individual differences related to writing proficiency did not change over time in Dutch, whereas they did in English. The researchers next looked at which variables predicted English and Dutch writing proficiency separately by using backward deletion in which variables are entered into a regression model and then successively eliminated to come up with a parsimonious model, meaning a model that had as few variables as possible. The English model was more complex because of the change in the relationship of variables over time. Finally, the researchers combined the models of Dutch and English writing development, which were also different, to examine how writing in Dutch contributed to English writing proficiency, and they found that including it improved the fit of the model.

One goal of factor analysis, backward deletion regression, and structural equation modeling is to reduce the number of variables, as many may correlate with each other, or to create latent variables that are not measured directly but are composed of different items or factors. In Schoonen et al., this point is often mentioned as they work toward coming up with a parsimonious model. For example, although many variables were measured, metacognitive knowledge, grammatical knowledge, and typing speed accounted for 61 percent of the variance in Dutch writing proficiency. As mentioned earlier, the Dutch data did not change over time, so time did not need to be taken into consideration. (However, as discussed by Winke, 2013, many factors related to individual differences are not static, so a model might need to take into account time.) Factors related to English writing proficiency included more factors (including lexical retrieval speed), and these factors changed over time.

Schoonen et al. include a lengthy and excellent discussion of their findings in relation to their design, noting, for example, the use of multiple assessments reduces the amount of error in measuring writing proficiency. They do note, ultimately, that their study was only correlational, but it does lay the groundwork for future experimental research related to the development of writing proficiency. They propose, for example, an experimental study of metacognitive knowledge instruction to test its effects on writing. Overall, this study stands out as a detailed and sophisticated correlational study that can serve as a model.

Suggestions for Further Reading

Statistical References for Social Sciences

- Costello A. & Osborne J. (2005). Best practices in exploratory factor analysis: Four recommendations for getting the most from your analysis. *Practical Assessment, Research & Evaluation, 10,* 1–9.
- Henson, K. R. & Roberts, J. K. (2006). Use of exploratory factor analysis in published research: Common errors and some comment on improved practice. *Educational and Psychological Measurement, 66,* 393–416.
- Hoyle, R. (Ed.). (2012). *Handbook of structural equation modeling.* New York: Guilford.
- Pett, M. A., Lackey, N. R., & Sullivan, J. J. (2003). *Making sense of factor analysis: The use of factor analysis for instrument development in health care research.* Thousand Oaks, CA: Sage Publications Inc.

- Tabachnick, B. G. & Fidell, L. S. (2001). *Using multivariate statistics* (4th ed.). Boston: Allyn and Bacon.
- Thompson, B. (2004). *Exploratory and confirmatory factor analysis: Understanding concepts and applications.* Washington, DC: American Psychological Association.
- Widaman, K. F. (1993). Common factor analysis versus principal component analysis: Differential bias in representing model parameters. *Multivariate Behavioral Research, 28,* 263–311.

Readings Related to Correlational Research in Applied Linguistics

- Hancock, G. R. & Schoonen, R. (2015). Structural equation modeling: Possibilities for language learning researchers. *Language Learning, 65*(Suppl.), 160–184.
- Jeon, E. H. (2015). Multiple regression. In L. Plonsky (Ed.), *Advancing quantitative methods in second language research* (pp. 131–158). New York: Routledge/ Taylor Francis.
- Kunnan, A. J. (1998). An introduction to structural equation modelling for language assessment research. *Language Testing, 15,* 295–332.
- Loewen, S. & Gonulal, T. (2015). Exploratory factor analysis and principal components analysis. In L. Plonsky (Ed.), *Advancing quantitative methods in second language research* (pp. 182–212). New York: Routledge.
- Norris, J. (2015). Discriminant analysis. In L. Plonsky (Ed.), *Advancing quantitative methods in second language research* (pp. 305–328). New York: Routledge.
- Schoonen, R. (2015). Structural equation modeling in L2 research. In L. Plonsky (Ed.), *Advancing quantitative methods in second language research* (pp. 213–242). New York: Routledge.
- Winke, P. (2014). Testing hypotheses about language learning using structural equation modeling. *Annual Review of Applied Linguistics, 34,* 102–122.

Designing Questionnaires

- Dörnyei, Z. & Csizér, K. (2012). How to design and analyze surveys in second language acquisition research. In A. Mackey & S. Gass (Eds.), *Research methods in second language acquisition: A practical guide* (pp. 74–94). Malden, MA: Wiley-Blackwell.
- Dörnyei, Z. & Taguchi, T. (2010). *Questionnaires in second language research: Construction, administration, and processing* (2nd ed.). New York: Routledge/ Taylor Francis.

4

ETHNOGRAPHY AND CASE STUDY

The emergence of the so-called *social turn* (Block, 2003) in second language research over the past 20 years has been accompanied by an increased focus on language learning as a social process and an emphasis on the contexts of learning (e.g., Ortega, 2012; K. Richards, 2009; Swain & Deters, 2007; TESOL, 2014). The field of L2 writing has seen a corresponding rise in the number of studies using theoretical frameworks such as second language socialization (Duff, 2010), sociocultural theory (Lantolf & Thorne, 2006), activity theory (Engeström, 2015; Leontiev, 1981), community of practice (Lave & Wenger, 1991), biliteracy (Hornberger, 1989), new literacy studies (Gee, 2012; Street, 1995), and identity theories (Ivanič, 1998; Norton & McKinney, 2011) that view writing as situated within multiple overlapping social and political contexts and emphasize co-construction of knowledge. As the field has shifted from a purely cognitive focus to encompass more socially oriented frameworks and from a concentration on *texts* to the *con-texts* in which writing is taught, learned, and produced, ethnographic and case study research on L2 writing has expanded from a handful of exemplars in the 1990s (e.g., Atkinson & Ramanathan, 1995; Carson & Nelson, 1996; Cumming, 1992; Prior, 1995; Spack, 1997) to become increasingly evident in applied linguistics and L2 writing journals (see Table 4.1).

This chapter introduces ethnographic and case study approaches to the study of L2 writing as a situated social practice. The chapter begins by outlining the basic principles and methodologies of these two related yet distinct traditions and what each can contribute to the study of L2 writing. We will then review some key issues relevant to ethnographic and case study research such as sampling, data triangulation, generalizability, and ethical issues particular to small-scale situated research and how these have (or have not) been dealt with in existing qualitative research on L2 writing.

TABLE 4.1 Representative Ethnographies and Case Studies

Study	Participants, context, and data	Research questions/focus	Comments on study design
Lillis & Curry (2010)	• Book-length "text-oriented ethnography" (p. 2) of multilingual scholars publishing in English conducted over 8+ years • 50 scholars located at 12 institutions in Slovakia, Hungary, Spain and Portugal • Participants' texts; text-based and language history interviews; correspondence related to texts; observational field notes; documents related to departmental, institutional, and national policy	1. How is the dominance of English affecting scholars who use languages other than English and live/work in non-English dominant countries? 2. In what ways is the position of English as an "academic lingua franca" influencing academic knowledge production and exchange in the twenty-first century? 3. Which texts are successful or unsuccessful in being accepted for publication, and why? 4. What are scholars' experiences in writing and publishing their research in English? 5. What meanings does publishing in English have for scholars? 6. What pressures do scholars face in this enterprise? 7. What barriers to publishing in English do scholars encounter? 8. What does and doesn't get published, and why? (p. 2)	• The study provides a detailed and informative account of research methods. • Experiences of individual scholars are situated within their local settings, disciplinary communities, and the larger context of international academic publishing.
Harman (2013)	• Critical ethnography of a fifth-grade classroom conducted over one academic year • Teacher (Julia) and 14 students; focal participants were two Puerto Rican students from bilingual or monolingual Spanish homes • Audio and video recordings and field notes of classroom interaction; interviews with instructor; students' texts; instructional materials; school, university, and state policy documents	1. How and to what extent did Julia's instructional focus on intertextuality support focal language minority students in learning how to appropriate particular lexicogrammatical resources from children's literature to build cohesion in their writing? In other words, how did the instructional approach support them in expanding their meaning-making processes? 2. How can the tools of functional linguistics be used to document how students' intertextual borrowings help them develop lexical cohesion to build meaning in their literary and academic writing? (p. 126)	• An extensive data set allows for method triangulation. • The paper focuses primarily on analysis of source and students' texts, with select examples from classroom interaction and interviews used to contextualize.

Molle & Prior (2008)	• Ethnography of written genres at a US university • International graduate students from four disciplines enrolled in an EAP writing course; disciplinary faculty • Interviews with students and faculty, student assignments in the disciplines (most with instructor comments), course materials, observation of selected classes	1. What are the characteristics of the genres that EAP graduate students read and produce in their disciplines?	• Ethnographic data (e.g., preparatory classroom activities, interviews with instructors regarding assessment criteria) provide a context for analysis of individual assignments.
Seloni (2014)	• Textography of a multilingual writer (Jacob) from Columbia writing his MA thesis in visual culture at a US university • Multiple text-based interviews with Jacob over one year; written materials such as assignments, multiple drafts of his thesis, other documents	1. What are some of the rhetorical enactments and literacy practices Jacob developed around his thesis writing? 2. What writerly identities are constructed in art-oriented, new humanities thesis/dissertation writing? (p. 84)	• The study is well contextualized with multiple examples of Jacob's writing, materials used to produce this writing, and his own comments on the writing process.
Lee & Schallert (2008b)	• Case study of the effect of teacher–student relationships on students' response to feedback • Female Korean teacher of English and two male students in an English composition course at a Korean university • Students' writing with teacher's written comments; interviews with teacher and each student (in Korean); observation and audio-recordings of class sessions and individual teacher-student conferences • Data collected over one semester	1. Looking at the relationship between a teacher and two of her students in an EFL college composition classroom, what impacted the development of a trusting relationship in the one case and a more troubled relationship in the other case? 2. How did the relationships, in the one case trusting and in the other more troubled, influence the ways the teacher provided written comments on the students' drafts and the processes by which the students used these comments as they revised their drafts? (p. 167)	• Focal participants were chosen from a larger study (14 students) because they illustrated contrasting relationships with the teacher. • A detailed description of the course, participants, and teacher's feedback practices contextualize the study. • Multiple examples from written texts, interviews, and conferences enhance credibility of findings.

(Continued)

TABLE 4.1 (Continued)

Study	Participants, context, and data	Research questions/focus	Comments on study design
Fránquiz & Salinas (2011)	• Case study of a sheltered world history class at a US high school comprising 11 newcomer Spanish-heritage students and their teacher • Observation and audio-recording of lessons over three months; collection of students' written work	1. How does the writing of newcomer students reflect growing mastery of English literacy and historical thinking? (p. 198)	• Researchers worked with the teacher to design lessons. • Three lessons are analyzed in detail; students' writing around these lessons is examined for evidence of development in English language and historical thinking skills.
Leki (2007)	• Book-length multiple case study of acquisition of English academic literacy • Four L2 English students at a US university followed over five years • Biweekly interviews with participants; observation of classes and interviews with instructors; recordings of writing center sessions; collection of syllabi; class texts, exams, and drafts of writing assignments; weekly journals kept by participants	1. How do NNES students experience and respond to the literacy demands of an undergraduate course of study in an English-medium university? 2. How and how well did their experience in their English-language and writing classes help them in meeting literacy demand across the disciplines? 3. How do these students become initiated into the specific discourses of their disciplines?	• The rich database is used to provide in-depth descriptions of individual participants and to document their literacy development over time. • Use of multiple participants from diverse backgrounds and academic disciplines allows for generalization beyond the study.

| Yi (2013) | • Case study of multiple literacy practices and identities of a Korean male *Jogi Yuhak* ("early study abroad") student (Hoon) sent by his family to study in a US high school
• Observations in ESL classes, interviews, weekly literacy activity checklist kept by participant, examples of written coursework, informal face-to-face and online chats collected during Hoon's junior and senior years | 1. What are the characteristics of an adolescent multilingual writer and what is the context in which Hoon engages in writing practice?
2. What are Hoon's academic writing experiences, opportunities, and resources?
3. How does he access them?
4. What is a possible relationship, if any, between his stigmatized ESL-student identity and academic literacy learning? (p. 209) | • The report is part of a larger study on five Korean students' literacy practices in the US.
• The study includes a high level of transparency regarding researcher's relationship with Hoon and a detailed description of analysis methods.
• Interpretations were member-checked with Hoon; however, alternative perspectives (e.g., Hoon's teachers) are not provided. |

(*Continued*)

TABLE 4.1 (Continued)

Study	Participants, context, and data	Research questions/focus	Comments on study design
Gentil (2005)	• Case study of the biliteracy practices of three French-speaking students at an English-medium university in Québec over 2½ years • Audio-taped interviews (45 hours total, in French); collection of participants' academic writing (in English and French); participant observations and field notes in an EAP writing course and a written technical communication course from which focal students were recruited; collection of relevant documents (e.g., graduate program guidelines)	1. How do the participants define their level of commitment to developing and maintaining academic literacies in English and French in response to the perceived stakes and contexts of learning to write academically in these languages? Are they committed to developing academic literacies in both their first and second language? Why or why not? 2. How do the participants develop biliteracy as they negotiate academic discourses with professors, peers, and other mediating agents in and across English and French? What challenges do they face when writing bilingually and shuttling across language and discourse communities? What strategies and resources do they use? 3. How do the micro and macro learning contexts facilitate or impede the participants' sustained development of academic biliteracy? (pp. 427–428)	• There is a detailed description of data collection, but little about analysis procedures. • Preliminary results were shared with participants; their responses contributed to subsequent analysis.
Li (2006)	• Case study of a Chinese doctoral student in physics writing a research article in English, from first draft to publication • Major drafts of the article; correspondence between student and target journals; interviews with student and his advisors	1. What is the process through which a Chinese doctoral student of physics writes a paper for international publication?	• The report is part of a larger study on apprentice Chinese scholars in the sciences. • Data from multiple sources are triangulated to construct an account of the student's publication experience.

An Overview of Ethnographic Research

The aim of ethnography is to describe and interpret the behaviors, beliefs, and practices of human social groups and communities. Ethnographic research is typically qualitative and situated within a postmodern paradigm (see Chapter 1) with a strong emphasis on *emic* (insider) perspectives. Although the term *ethnographic* is sometimes used over-broadly to describe any qualitative study, ethnography has a clearly delineated set of criteria and methods for data collection and analysis (see Hammersley, 2007; Watson-Gegeo, 1988). First, as its objective is to understand what a group's practice means to its members, ethnography requires a *longitudinal* research design in which the researcher is immersed in the research setting for an extended period of time; studies lasting a year or more are the norm. In some studies researchers are outside observers; in others, they act as *participant observers* who participate in the community in some capacity. There are also studies in which the researcher is already an insider (e.g., the instructor of the class that is the focus of the study) and becomes what Erickson (1986, p. 157) calls an *observant participant* whose role shifts between practitioner and observer of his or her own practice. Although the latter is controversial among ethnographers (on the grounds that being too much of an insider can cause the researcher to miss important details), neither role is seen as a source of interference in the research but as a means of gaining deeper understanding of community practices.

Ethnographers do not design tasks for participants to perform or otherwise organize activities for purposes of the research but engage in *open* and *naturalistic inquiry* in which they observe participants engaging in routine community activities. They typically begin a project with an open mind, allowing the focus of the research to emerge and evolve during data collection and analysis. Ethnography also has a *holistic* orientation that considers all aspects of the context, both at the macro-level (e.g., curriculum, school or state educational policies, participants' race and social class) and the micro-level (e.g., physical layout of the classroom, lesson organization and activities) as potentially relevant to an analysis. It therefore draws from multiple sources of data, such as extensive observation at the research site documented through detailed field notes, collection of materials such as textbooks and assignments, and interviews with participants. Many ethnographies include audio or video recordings of routine community activities (e.g., lessons, writing conferences), which allow for more detailed analysis than what can be achieved with field notes alone.

Ethnography in L2 Writing Research

In L2 writing, ethnographic research has been advocated as a way to "close the gap between text analysis and context analysis" (Lillis, 2008, p. 382). By situating individual writers within the contexts in which they work, ethnography allows for an exploration of not only the *whats* of L2 writing (the texts) but also the *whys* and *hows* (the process of writing and the various social factors that shape it). An excellent example of this approach is Lillis and Curry's (2010) book-length "text-oriented ethnographic" study (p. 2) of 50 multilingual scholars' experiences writing and publishing in English. The primary data source for this extensive study was the "text histories" (p. 3) of participants' professional writing documented through analysis of multiple drafts and text-based interviews (see Chapter 9) with the authors. However, the study also includes many features of ethnography, such as a longitudinal research design (eight years and counting), multiple interviews with participants, detailed field notes from visits to the sites where the scholars work, and collection of emails and other documents related to their writing.

Ethnography can also be a way to extend L2 writing research beyond the study of texts to the contexts in which these texts are produced. For example, Harman's (2013) ethnography of a fifth-grade classroom combined a systemic functional linguistics analysis (see Chapter 11) of students' texts with observations of the lessons of a teacher trained in genre-based pedagogy over the course of an academic year. The study documented how strategies for lexical cohesion that were taught in class later emerged in L2 students' writing by linking students' texts to the classroom practices or other discourses that contributed to their production. Similarly, Molle and Prior's (2008) use of ethnographic methods (e.g., observation of content classes) to investigate the genre needs of international graduate students enrolled in an English for academic purposes (EAP) class revealed the complexities and "discursive hybridity" (p. 558) of the texts these students were required to produce in their disciplines and the mismatch between these genres and those being taught in the EAP course.

L2 writing research also includes a form of ethnography called *textography*, a term coined by Swales (1998a, 1998b) to describe a study that is "something more than a disembodied textual or discoursal analysis, but something less than a full ethnographic account" (1998a, p. 1). As its name implies, textography focuses on the texts produced in a particular discourse community but also considers the contexts in which those texts are produced and may include data from sources such as on-site observations and writer perspectives elicited through text-based interviews (see Chapter 9). Textography has been promoted as a way to extend genre research beyond a structural or linguistic analysis (e.g., Paltridge, 2008) but has also been used in other L2 writing research, such as Seloni's (2014) textography of a Colombian art historian writing his MA thesis in English. Encompassing emails, an array of materials related to the participant's thesis writing (e.g., assignments, drafts, source materials), and interviews, including a text-based interview in which the participant narrated his writing process, the study examined how this writer drew upon multiple languages as he planned, drafted, and revised his thesis.

An Overview of Case Study Research

Case study "is not a methodological choice but a choice of what is to be studied" (Stake, 2000, p. 435). In a case study, the focus of analysis is the *case*, defined as a "bounded system" (Merriam, 1998, p. 27) that most often comprises an individual person but can also be several individuals (in a multiple case study) or entities such as classrooms, institutions, or even countries. The case is typically studied in depth as an instance of a more general phenomenon, that is, as a case *of* something, such as multiliteracy or writing a dissertation.

Although usually classified as qualitative, case study research covers a range of paradigmatic orientations and can involve both quantitative and qualitative methods or an experimental research design (Duff, 2008); the focus in this chapter will be on qualitative case studies (for mixed methods case study research, see Chapter 5). Case study research has a focus on the particular and aims to provide a detailed picture of the case(s) in question by bringing out individual characteristics and exploring these in depth. Similar to ethnography, qualitative case studies tend to study a phenomenon in natural settings (e.g., classrooms) and employ an *inductive* form of analysis with the aim of building theory (i.e., an explanation of the focal phenomenon) from detailed study of particular instances. Achieving in-depth analysis of the case(s) typically involves collecting data from multiple sources, such as interviews with participants, observations of participants in one or more settings (sometimes audio- or video-recorded), and documents or other artifacts. Additional sources of data may include participants' journals or process logs, surveys and questionnaires, stimulated recall protocols, and elicitation tasks. Although many case studies track participants over long periods of time, a longitudinal research design is not an inherent feature of this approach, and case studies may be of relatively short duration.

The fact that a case may be a group (e.g., a classroom) as well as an individual somewhat blurs the line between case study and ethnography, as does the focus on individual focal participants (i.e., cases) in many ethnographies and the emergence of *sociopolitically oriented* (Casanave, 2003) or *interpretive* (Duff, 2014) case study research in which the study of individual cases is situated within a social context. But although it is possible to understand ethnography as a kind of case study, most case studies would not qualify as ethnographies, as they lack the emphasis on sociocultural explanations for the behaviors and values exhibited by study participants that are hallmarks of ethnographic research (see Table 4.2).

Case Study in L2 Writing Research

In a reflection on future directions for L2 writing research, Casanave (2003) argues for the use of qualitative case study "to explore social and political aspects of *local* knowledge and *local* interactions of *particular* L2 writers in *particular* settings" (p. 86, our italics). This focus on the local and particular points to a strength of case study research in which a small sample size enables a close

TABLE 4.2 Characteristics of Ethnography and Case Study

	Ethnography	*Case study*
Focus	Human social or cultural groups (e.g., classrooms, workplaces, discourse communities) as contexts for writing and/or learning how to write	Single or multiple cases (e.g., individuals, institutions) as representative of some larger phenomenon (e.g., writing a dissertation in an L2)
Methodological approach	Typically qualitative	Qualitative or quantitative
Basic principles	• Longitudinal • Open inquiry (i.e., focus emerges from data collection) • Naturalistic • Holistic; emphasis on context • Inductive • Emic perspective	• In-depth analysis of individual cases • May be longitudinal • Usually naturalistic, but may involve experimental design or elicited data • Usually inductive
Data collection	• (Participant) observation • Interviews, questionnaires • Collection of artifacts (e.g., texts, assignments) • May involve audio or video-recording	• Observation • Interviews, surveys • Collection of artifacts (e.g., texts, assignments) • May involve stimulated recall, journals, process logs, elicited data

investigation of individual differences that may be lost in large-scale analyses. For example, Lee and Schallert's (2008b) case study of how two English composition students in Korea differentially responded to feedback illustrates how these responses were shaped by the varying degrees of trust that existed between the students and their Korean instructor. Case studies also allow for an in-depth study of processes that unfold over time, such as the experiences of individuals as they acquire L2 academic literacy. Although covering a relatively brief period (three months), Fránquiz and Salinas's (2011) case study of a newcomer classroom in a US high school provides a rich account of L1 Spanish students' increasing facility in "historical thinking" (i.e., the ability to critically evaluate historical narratives, p. 197) and English language literacy as documented through multiple examples of students' texts. Leki's (2007) multiple case study of four international and immigrant undergraduates at a university in the southeastern United States followed participants for five years as they negotiated the complex literacy demands of college.

Longitudinal case studies have also examined individuals engaging in writing in multiple settings (e.g., different classrooms or in school vs. out of school) or in multiple languages and the variety of identities that may be performed by or ascribed to them in each. In a case study of a Korean adolescent (Hoon) at a US high school, Yi (2013) described the contrasting identities (i.e., a stigmatized nonproficient English speaker vs. a high-achieving student) that Hoon constructed in his ESL and mainstream classes and how these affected his (non)acquisition of academic literacy in English. Gentil's (2005) 2½–year case study of three French-speaking students at an English-medium university in Québec documented participants' varying levels of success in developing academic literacy in both French and English. Drawing from multiple interviews, written assignments in both English and French, and observations of participants' EAP and technical writing classes, Gentil created narratives of each individual's academic literacy experiences over time and across languages and the contextual factors that shaped these experiences.

In addition, case study has been a productive approach for researchers interested in taking a social, rather than cognitive, view of the writing process. Using a community of practice framework (Lave & Wenger, 1991), Li (2006) followed her case study participant, a Chinese doctoral student in physics, as he drafted and revised a research article for publication (see also Li, 2007). By supplementing her analyses of drafts with data collected from correspondence with the target journals and interviews with faculty who reviewed (and occasionally rewrote) the student's text, Li documented the many voices (the student, his advisors, reviewers, editors) involved in its construction, thus demonstrating the final article to be a community, not just individual, product.

Several of the studies cited here also point to an emerging trend in L2 writing case study research toward increased emphasis on the political aspects of learning, teaching, and practicing writing (see Casanave, 2003; Duff, 2008). For example, in Fránquiz and Salinas (2011), students' responses to lessons that focused on race, immigration, and civil rights were linked to their identities as members of a linguistic minority group to make a larger point about how "identity texts" (i.e., writing that reflects a personal critical stance toward the topic, p. 200) evince appropriation (and not simply replication) of knowledge. Leki's (2007) study is richly contextualized with a description and critique of the institutional practices and biases that often worked against her participants' full participation in the academic community and how participants accommodated to, negotiated, or resisted these forces. Li's (2006) analysis of a doctoral student's (ultimately successful) struggle to be published in a prestigious Western journal illustrates the complex power relationships involved in producing a published article that Li refers to as a "sociopolitical artifact" (p. 373).

Issues Involved in Ethnographic and Case Study Research

Problematizing Culture and Community

The 2003 *TESOL Quarterly* research guidelines (Chapelle & Duff, 2003, pp. 172–178) define ethnography as "a firsthand, contextualized, naturalistic, hypotheses-generating, emic orientation to the study of TESOL through the study of *culture*" (p. 172, our italics). In research on L2 writing the term *culture* usually refers to what Holliday (1999) calls *small cultures*: that is, sets of beliefs, values, and behaviors that are supposedly shared by some collectivity, such as a classroom, a program, or an institution. For example, in an early example of ethnographic L2 writing research, Atkinson and Ramanathan (1995) contrasted the "cultures of writing" of ESL and mainstream writing programs at the same university; similarly, Hyland (2004) uses genre analysis of academic texts to explore the "disciplinary cultures" of the university.

However, *culture* is an elusive concept that has come in for a great deal of criticism in many academic disciplines, including applied linguistics and L2 writing (e.g., Atkinson, 2003, 2004; Kubota, 1999; Matsuda, 2001; Ramanathan & Atkinson, 1999). The primary issue is that the term seems to presume an essentialized and bounded set of practices that are equally shared by members of a group and thus fails to capture the diversity and inequality that may exist within the group as well as the individual agency of group members. Postmodern critiques of culture have further observed that group homogeneity and supposedly shared values may be imposed from above and represent a manifestation of the power of a dominant group to assign meanings and define valued knowledge (e.g., Kubota, 1999). In addition, many have questioned the relevance of the concept in an increasingly open world in which individuals typically participate in multiple cultures, whose fluid boundaries challenge the very idea of an easily defined and delimited cultural group (Eisenhart, 2001). Related concepts that are commonly found in L2 writing research, such as *discourse community* (Swales, 1990) and *community of practice* (e.g., Casanave & Li, 2008), have been similarly criticized. Although the former continues to be widely used in research on genre, Swales himself has expressed some ambivalence regarding the extent to which many so-called discourse communities actually constitute functioning communities with a shared set of goals and practices (e.g., 1998b, pp. 196–208). Similarly, the application of the *community of practice* model to educational settings has been questioned on the grounds that it ignores the inequality and marginalization that is often experienced by nonmainstream participants, such as L2 speakers (e.g., Haneda, 2006).

The response to these critiques may lie not in abandoning these concepts but in reconceptualizing the assumptions that underlie them. The 2003 *TESOL Quarterly* guidelines specify that "culture [in ethnographic TESOL research] . . . is treated as heterogeneous, conflictual, negotiated and evolving, as distinct from unified, cohesive, fixed and static" (Chapelle & Duff, 2003, p. 173), and this view has been reflected in L2 writing research in a number of ways. First, there has been a trend away from focusing on a single site to consideration of the multiple communities with which L2 writers engage (Lillis & Curry, 2010; Yi, 2013) or the multiple languages and writing practices that they draw upon in constructing texts and textual identities (e.g., Gentil, 2005; Seloni, 2014). Research on communities of practice and discourse communities has also begun to shift from studying how novices acquire established community norms to considering how they may resist these norms and establish their own voices (e.g., Li, 2006), thus highlighting the dynamic, contested, and co-constructed nature of such communities. Nevertheless, an understanding of culture (or discourse community or community of practice) as "conflictual, negotiated, and evolving" (Chapelle & Duff, 2003, p. 173) also carries a reminder that researchers cannot take the existence of such communities for granted. Rather, it is their responsibility to establish that participants understand themselves to be part of a community and to document the processes through which a shared body of practices comes into being.

Ethics

Although ethics are rarely discussed in published reports beyond a statement that the researchers followed standard protocols for protection of research subjects, there are a number of ethical issues particular to small-scale situated research such as ethnography and case study that need to be considered. For example, although it is possible to disidentify participants in a large-scale experimental study, protecting privacy and confidentiality in a study that focuses on a single site or a small number of individuals can be challenging (e.g., see Lillis & Curry, 2010, pp. 28–29). In addition, the level of commitment required of participants in a longitudinal study that can extend over several years and involve multiple interviews and extensive observation means that the question of potential benefits of the research to participants may take on more urgency than it might in a study in which participants spend 30 minutes performing an experimental task. Researchers may also need to make decisions on delicate matters such as whether they will report on (and possibly criticize) participants' questionable behaviors recorded during observations and how they will represent participants or their work in published reports, both directly (e.g., as "unsuccessful" students or "insensitive" instructors) or indirectly (e.g., as nonproficient users of English, as evidenced in passages quoting from written texts or interviews).

These issues are complex, as they involve striking a balance between procedures needed to produce good research and sensitivity to participants' concerns (Kubanyiova, 2008). For example, although a basic tenet of ethnography and case study is to provide detailed information about the setting and participants in order to contextualize the study, there may be times when this information could risk revealing a participant's identity. A full discussion of these ethical issues is beyond the scope of this chapter; however, we will here note a few basic practices that ethnographers and case study researchers commonly employ to mitigate such concerns (see also De Costa, 2015; Duff, 2008, pp. 144–151; Guillemin & Gillam, 2004; Kubanyiova, 2008). One recommendation is to cede control over the research to participants to the extent possible, that is, to allow participants to decide their level of participation (e.g., to be observed but not interviewed), withdraw from all or part of the research, refuse to answer any interview question, or ask that audio or video recorders be turned off at any point. In addition, some researchers provide participants with copies of transcripts or the final research report in order to give them some control over how they are represented, although in such cases one will have to decide how to respond if a participant's perspective conflicts with that of the researcher (see Kubanyiova, 2008). Concerns over possible exploitation of participants can be at least partially addressed by offering something in exchange for their participation. Some L2 writing researchers have acted as tutors or otherwise provided assistance to those that they research (e.g., Yi, 2013), and classroom researchers often work closely with teachers to design projects to improve pedagogy (e.g., Fránquiz & Salinas, 2011; Harman, 2013). However, general principles such as these cannot cover all of the issues that may arise in the course of situated research, and researchers may be faced with "ethically significant moments" (Kubanyiova, 2008, p. 506) for which such principles offer insufficient guidance. It is therefore necessary to be attentive to situation-specific *microethics* operating at the level of day-to-day research practice as well as the more general *macroethics* that are grounded in internal review board (IRB) standards (Guillemin & Gillam, 2004; Kubanyiova, 2008).

Observer's Paradox

Another issue involves the effects of the researcher and the research on participants' behavior and how these might affect findings. Although this issue is not limited to ethnographic and case study research (e.g., see Chapter 8), it may be particularly acute in studies that aim to examine participants' "natural" behavior while documenting that behavior through intrusive techniques such as making recordings. Two terms that often arise during discussions of this question are the *Hawthorne effect* and *observer's paradox*. The former, named for a study on worker productivity at the Hawthorne Works factory near Chicago in the 1920s, proposes that individuals will change their behavior when they know they are being observed, supposedly because the increased attention makes them more aware of their actions. Observer's paradox, a term coined by sociolinguist William Labov (1972), refers to a similar phenomenon in which individuals being interviewed change their speech style to bring it closer to the standard (an issue for a sociolinguist endeavoring to obtain nonstandard speech samples). At the core of both concepts lies a concern that research participants may put on a performance to impress the researcher; for example, during an observation a teacher may use techniques that she knows to be best practices even though she may not use these techniques in her regular teaching.

How one addresses this issue will depend in large part upon the paradigm in which one is working (see Chapter 1). Both the Hawthorne effect and observer's paradox reflect a postpositivist assumption that a singular reality or truth exists (i.e., how people really talk, think, or act) but that it surfaces only when we are not there to observe it (hence the paradox). Those concerned about this possibility can mitigate its effects in a number of ways. For example, by comparing observational data with data from other sources (e.g., interviews, comments on assignments), researchers can check whether observed behavior is consistent with stated beliefs or behaviors that occur outside the observation. In addition, regular observations over a period of time, as is the norm in ethnographic and longitudinal case study research, allow participants to become used to the presence of the researcher and decrease the chance that they will perform in ways that are at variance with their regular practice.

On the other hand, those operating from a postmodern perspective begin with an assumption that all forms of truth, including research findings, are co-constructed; thus, the researcher is simply one more aspect of the research context to be incorporated into an analysis. This stance requires engaging in the process of *reflexivity*; that is, reflecting on "aspects of your own background, identities or subjectivities, and assumptions that influence data collection and interpretation" (Chapelle & Duff, 2003, p. 175; see also Duff, 2008; Lee & Simon-Maeda, 2006; Norton & Early, 2011; Starfield, 2013, 2016; Talmy, 2010). Although L2 writing researchers may practice reflexivity, it rarely surfaces explicitly in published accounts beyond a brief acknowledgement that the researcher's identity (e.g., as an authority figure or an outsider to the community being researched) may have affected participants' behavior; how (or whether) this effect was considered during analysis of the data is often unclear. More transparency on this point is needed.

Evaluative Criteria

Determining evaluative criteria for qualitative research has generated much discussion within many academic disciplines, including applied linguistics (e.g., Duff, 2006; Edge & Richards, 1998; Lazaraton, 2003). On the one hand, it is clear that standard criteria for quantitative and experimental research cannot be directly applied to qualitative research; for example, small sample sizes and emphasis on local contexts mean that findings of qualitative research cannot be generalized as they might be in a randomized large-scale experimental study, and lack of control of variables and the interpretive (i.e., subjective) analytical methods of qualitative research do not lend themselves to the usual techniques for establishing internal validity (see Chapter 2). Moreover, the postpositivist assumptions upon which these standards rest (e.g., that there are universal truths that can be verified statistically and generalized to other contexts) are incompatible with postmodern research paradigms under which much ethnography and case study research is conducted. On the other hand, it is equally clear that qualitative studies should not be exempt from any and all standards; as the qualitative researchers Lincoln and Guba (2000) have noted, any researcher who wishes to make recommendations for change based on research results (as most L2 writing researchers do) needs a basis for feeling confident that these results are "faithful enough to some human construction" (p. 180) to be acted upon.

Debates over evaluative criteria for research essentially revolve around a single question: "What warrant do you have for the statements that you make?" (Edge & Richards, 1998, p. 342). Some answer this question by adapting conventional notions of reliability and validity to qualitative studies, for example, having two researchers code interview data and comparing the results to establish intercoder reliability (see Chapter 10). More commonly, however, the nature of qualitative research requires that researchers take a different route toward the goal of establishing that research findings are *credible* (plausible interpretations of the data), *dependable* (consistent), and potentially *transferable* (applicable to other contexts). Here we focus on three key concepts—*triangulation, contextualization*, and *transparency*—as well as how qualitative L2 writing researchers have addressed issues regarding generalizability (see also Chapelle & Duff, 2003; Duff, 2006, 2008; K. Richards, 2003, 2009).

Triangulation

Triangulation is the primary method for enhancing dependability and credibility in ethnographic and case study research. The term, borrowed from navigation and land surveying, simply means that any data point (the apex of the triangle) should be supported by two or more sources (the two corners at the base of the triangle). For postpositivists, triangulation provides a means of validating interpretations; if two or more sources lead the researcher to the same conclusion, that conclusion is more likely to be valid. Postmodern researchers take a somewhat different perspective on triangulation, seeing it as a means of incorporating multiple perspectives into an analysis, thus enabling researchers to "explain more fully the richness and complexity of human behavior by studying it from more than one standpoint" (Cohen, Manion, & Morrison, 2000, p. 254).

Denzin (1978) has proposed four types of triangulation. The first, *data triangulation*, requires that data be gathered from different individuals, different points in time, or different places. The second, *investigator triangulation*, results when multiple researchers are involved in collecting or analyzing the data. *Member checking*, in which participants are asked to verify or contribute to the researcher's interpretations, is a variant of investigator triangulation that also contributes to the emic perspective favored in ethnographic research. *Theoretical triangulation* involves interpreting the data through more than one theoretical lens. The final type, *methodological triangulation*, is achieved through use of multiple data collection methods.

Methodological triangulation is the most common form in L2 writing research; however, many studies involve multiple types. For example, Lillis and

Curry's (2010) ethnographic study of European scholars publishing in English involved methodological triangulation (observations, interviews, collection of texts and other relevant documents), data triangulation (multiple participants who were interviewed multiple times, multiple drafts of each text), and investigator triangulation. On the other hand, Seloni's (2014) textography of a student writing his MA thesis involved only one researcher and one participant; however, methodological triangulation (analysis of multiple texts and interviews), theoretical triangulation (application of cultural-historic activity theory and theories of translingualism), and data triangulation achieved through collecting data at multiple points over the course of the participant's second year of graduate studies contribute to strengthening claims.

Researchers may occasionally confront a situation in which different data sources disagree; for example, different participants may provide contradictory accounts of the same event, or participants' accounts may not coincide with the researcher's observations. Rather than discarding the data as unreliable, one may attempt to reconcile these disparities. A classic example comes from Leki (2007), who noted that observations of one of her case study participants (Jan) in class presented an image of "the very model of the diligent, industrious international student" that contradicted his representation of himself in interviews as a "shrewd manipulator" who cut corners and gamed the system whenever possible (p. 127). She presented both sides of Jan in her report, eventually concluding that they represented two facets of a complex young man who "lived his contradictions" (p. 122) and who wanted to succeed academically even as he struggled to find a way to do so (see also Leki, 1999). Ultimately, researchers who aim to incorporate multiple viewpoints into their work may sometimes have to accept that these viewpoints will diverge and to see this as evidence of the diversity of human experience rather than as threats to validity.

Contextualization

Another method for enhancing dependability and credibility is contextualization. Similar to *thick description* (Geertz, 1973), contextualization aims to build a detailed picture of a setting, event, or practice that is sufficient to enable outsiders (e.g., readers of the study) to understand and hopefully confirm the researcher's interpretations. Contextualization does not simply mean collecting data from multiple sources; the researcher also needs to make clear how these multiple sources inform the analysis and support the findings. A good example can be found in Fránquiz and Salinas's (2011) study of a sheltered world history class of 11 newcomer high school students from Spanish-speaking countries in which findings were contextualized with detailed descriptions of three focal lessons, including information about topics, procedures, materials, activities, writing prompts, and samples of students' work, and further situated within the state-mandated history curriculum. However, because of space limitations, ethnographic and case study researchers cannot include all of their data in a single report, and much relevant context can be lost when insufficient care is taken during the process of data selection. For example, a case study may have involved interviews, observations, written documents, and other sources of data, and the researcher may have drawn upon all of these when making interpretations and drawing conclusions. However, if the report only presents data from interviews with no discussion of how other sources support the analysis, dependability and credibility of the findings can be called into question.

Transparency

Transparency refers to careful documentation of the research process, such as how participants or sites were selected, how participants were recruited, and how the data were analyzed; it can also involve the researcher's reflections on his or her identity or role(s) in the research process (e.g., as a participant observer, tutor, outsider, or insider). For example, in her longitudinal case study of a Korean student at a US high school, Yi (2013) explained how and where she met the focal participant, her relationship with him as a tutor and bilingual aide in his ESL class, and their continued contact via a social networking site after the study had ended, and also includes detailed information regarding the process of data collection and analysis as it evolved over the course of the two-year study. By opening up the research process for scrutiny, such transparency allows others to evaluate the quality of Yi's research design and identify potential factors that may have affected her interpretations, thus contributing to dependability. In addition, documenting the extent of her engagement with her participant also enhances the credibility of her analysis as an informed interpreter of his experiences.

Although not an isolated instance, this level of transparency appears to be the exception rather than the rule in the studies reviewed for this chapter, especially in article-length reports in which space limitations preclude lengthy discussions of methodology. Particularly problematic is the sparseness of information on analytical procedures; in some cases this consists of little more than a general statement that analysis was "inductive," which is akin to saying that the analysis in a quantitative study was "statistical." At a minimum one should specify the chosen analytical methods and describe how they were applied to the data, as well as how emerging themes and patterns were linked across multiple sources of data for each site or individual (*within case analysis*) or across multiple sites or individuals (*cross-case analysis*).

Generalizability

Generalizability (also external validity as discussed in Chapter 2) concerns how study findings relate to the world beyond the study itself. As standard criteria for establishing generalizability are grounded in postpositivist assumptions of experimental and quantitative research approaches, they are highly controversial among ethnographic and case study researchers. For many, generalizability is irrelevant to research in which "a single case or small nonrandom sample is selected precisely *because* the researcher wishes to understand the particular in depth, not to find out what is generally true of the many" (Merriman, 1998, p. 208) and which may seek to identify differences as well as (or instead of) similarities across individuals or sites. This concept is also seen as antithetical to postmodern paradigms that see truth as multiple and grounded in individual perspectives and local contexts and thus not generalizable elsewhere.

Nevertheless, ethnographic and case study researchers who want their findings to be seen as relevant beyond the immediate research context must establish a basis upon which such claims can be made. One approach is to choose individual cases or sites based on reasoned criteria in what is called *purposive* (or *purposeful*) *sampling* (Duff, 2008; Merriam, 1998; Yin, 2014). Alternatively, having multiple cases in a case study or multiple sites in an ethnography allows for a cross-case analysis that can demonstrate how typical or general a phenomenon is, especially if the chosen cases or sites differ in important ways. Lillis and Curry's long-term ethnographic work on international scholars publishing in English (Curry & Lillis, 2004; Lillis & Curry, 2006, 2010) has drawn from data collected from 50 individuals in two disciplines (psychology and education) and four countries (Hungary, Slovakia, Spain, and Portugal), which has enabled them to identify broad patterns and general trends that operate across these diverse individuals and thus to contribute to larger issues related to this area of inquiry. Leki (2007) included four students from different backgrounds (an immigrant student from China, an immigrant student from Poland, an international student from China, and an international student from Japan) majoring in different disciplines (engineering, business, nursing, and social work). This diverse data set enabled her to provide in-depth accounts of each participant's literacy experiences and development over time as well as draw larger conclusions regarding literacy instruction for L2 students in US undergraduate education.

Finally, researchers can extend findings of small-scale studies beyond the immediate research context by situating them within theories and previous literature on a similar topic, thus contributing one more piece to a larger puzzle. One area of L2 writing research that has benefitted from this approach is case study research on L2 students' strategies for writing from sources (e.g., Abasi, Akbari, & Graves, 2006; Li & Casanave, 2012; Thompson, Morton, & Storch, 2013). The small number of participants (ranging from one to 13) in each of these studies makes them nongeneralizable in the usual sense; however, when taken together the findings have been building an increasingly complex picture of what is commonly dismissed as plagiarism and has contributed to deeper understandings of this widespread and controversial issue. Nevertheless, as Duff (2008, pp. 44–45) notes, the onus is on the researcher to make these connections to theory or other published research visible.

BOX 4.1 FOCAL STUDY

Kibler, A. K. (2014). From high school to the *noviciado*: An adolescent linguistic minority student's multilingual journey in writing. *The Modern Language Journal, 98*, 629–651.

Background

Part of a larger ethnographic study, this longitudinal case study follows Maria, a Spanish-English bilingual adolescent, over the course of five years, from high school to postsecondary training at a bilingual Catholic *noviciado* (novitiate) program. The stated purpose of the study is to fill what Kibler identifies as a gap in the literature on adolescent and college-age L2 writers that has thus far focused primarily on monolingual institutional settings (e.g., English-medium classrooms), which she argues may lead researchers to overlook the full range of languages and practices that shape the literacy development of bilingual youth.

Research Question

1. How do features of an English-medium high school experience either support or hinder Maria's writing development and transition to a bilingual postsecondary setting?

Method

Data collection took place over four years (grades 9–12) in high school and one year in the novitiate program. It included selected writing samples (both academic and nonacademic) in both English and Spanish, discourse-based interviews (see Chapter 9), and observations of lessons connected to writing assignments in high school; however, Kibler was not allowed to observe in the novitiate program. Data for Maria comprised a total of 57 written texts, 15 interviews, and over 20 observations. Interviews and field notes were coded inductively (see Chapter 10) and crosschecked against written texts. Kibler also shared her analytic memos with Maria to confirm interpretations. The analysis draws primarily on Ivanič's (2004) model of language and literacy (texts, cognitive processes, events, sociocultural and political processes), although Kibler makes two important changes. First, given that her research design did not permit access to Maria's cognitive processes, Kibler instead focuses on what she calls "orientations to writing" (p. 633), that is, Maria's perspectives on her writing as reflected in interview data. Second, she supplements this model with Hornberger's (2003) continua of biliteracy to examine the effects of Maria's bilingualism on her writing development.

Results

Although Maria's high school was officially monolingual, Maria's Spanish literacy received some limited support through courses such as "Spanish for Native Speakers" as well as outside literacy activities. In addition, her L2 (English) writing development was supported through bilingual "events" (e.g., discussing and receiving feedback on papers from Spanish-speaking peers and faculty). However, there appeared to be no direct transfer of literacy skills learned in high school to the novitiate, given the very different literacy demands in the latter setting (i.e., primarily note taking and short answer questions on exams). Nevertheless, Maria's increasingly sophisticated writing ability (as seen through analysis of her texts over time) and growing confidence in her English language proficiency (documented through interviews) that was developed in high school subsequently gave Maria a solid foundation for successfully coping with the literacy demands of the novitiate program, which she completed successfully.

Discussion of an Ethnographic Case Study: Kibler (2014)

This longitudinal case study of a Spanish–English bilingual adolescent called Maria (see Box 4.1) illustrates the sometimes fuzzy boundaries between ethnography and case study. Drawn from an ethnographic study of five Latino students in a California high school, it is primarily a case study of the writing development of a single individual, yet it also situates this development within two distinct writing communities (high school and the Catholic novitiate that Maria attended after graduation) and includes extensive descriptions of the literacy practices that were valued and promoted in each community. It might therefore be classified as an ethnographic case study. The study also exemplifies a number of emerging trends in L2 writing research, such as biliteracy, an approach to investigating literacy that emphasizes how individuals learn to write in multiple languages or how they use their full linguistic repertoire when composing (Gentil, 2011); multisited ethnographic research; and socially oriented case study (Casanave, 2003), in which a case study approach is used to explore the sociopolitical contexts of writing.

The phenomenon being investigated is the multilingual writer transitioning between secondary and postsecondary settings. Kibler's stated interest in providing an in-depth account of socially situated writing development over time makes this study well suited for an ethnographic, longitudinal case study design. Although the focal participant might be seen as atypical due to her choice of postsecondary education (a novitiate program to prepare young women to become nuns), Kibler justifies her selection as motivated by her interest in a multilingual approach to the study of L2 writing development, noting that Maria's case provides an opportunity to study the same individual in both a monolingual (US high school) and bilingual (novitiate program) setting. In addition, the contrast between the latter and the community college or university setting in which L2 writing is commonly researched allows Kibler to test the applicability of the findings of prior research to a new context and thus to support or challenge its broader implications and claims.

The credibility and dependability of the study is enhanced through multiple forms of triangulation and a high degree of contextualization. Triangulation includes data triangulation (collection of data across a five-year period in two different settings), theoretical triangulation (use of Ivanič's (2004) model, Hornberger's (2003) continua of biliteracy, and sociocultural theory), and methodological triangulation (texts, interviews, and observations), all of which are brought together to support claims. In addition, Kibler's use of member checking (consulting with Maria to clarify questions) adds some degree of investigator triangulation and contributes to an emic perspective. The findings are also well contextualized, with data drawn from multiple sources at both the micro (Maria's texts) and macro (school policies) level taken from different points in time and framed around Kibler's adapted version of Ivanič's (2004) model of language and literacy. For example, her analysis of Maria's school-based writing compares multiple drafts of the same text as well as texts written at various points during her high school years to document Maria's development as an L2 writer. Observations and interviews with Maria provide information about events (i.e., interactions with peers or teachers in both Spanish and English), which are analyzed as *mediational tools* (Lantolf, 2000, as cited in Kibler, 2014) that contributed to this development. Interview data also reveal shifts in Maria's orientations to writing that parallel her increasing facility in both English and valued school genres, evident in the texts. Maria's experience is also set within a sociocultural and political context in which the official monolingualism evident in school policies was to some degree contested by the presence of bilingual teachers, courses such as "Spanish for Native Speakers," and use of Spanish in unofficial contexts (e.g., among students during breaks), all of which influenced Maria's literacy experiences. Data from the school setting is also compared with information about Maria's out-of-school literacy activities (e.g., online, in enrichment programs, at her church) and the novitiate, thus cumulatively building up a thick description of Maria's literacy development across time and space.

The study also benefits from transparency and reflexivity. Considering space limitations and the large volume of data to be reported, there is a reasonable amount of detail regarding data collection and analysis procedures as well as background information about the focal participant and the ethnographic study from which this paper was drawn. Multiple examples of texts are provided to support analyses, along with some direct quotations from interviews to provide an emic perspective, and sources of information (e.g., from observation or through an interview) are well documented. In addition, in line with standards for ethnographic research (e.g., Chapelle & Duff, 2003), Kibler provides an account of her own positioning as a researcher and how this may have affected the research, including how her race (white), age (in her 30s), and status as an instructional coach at the high school during the early phase of the study may have marked her as a teacher-like authority figure in the eyes of her participants. She also admits that, as a non-Catholic, she had difficulty understanding Maria's religious beliefs and decision to become a nun, which may have affected her interpretations of Maria's literacy experiences in the novitiate. On the other hand, Kibler also claims that her long relationship with Maria and her use of Spanish when speaking with her made Maria more willing to open up in interviews and somewhat compensated for the issues listed earlier. However, as is often the case in ethnographic studies, it is not clear how Kibler's awareness of her own positioning was taken into account in the analysis, as it is not mentioned further in the presentation of findings.

Although the study focuses on a single, somewhat atypical, participant, Kibler connects her findings to previous research on multilingual adolescents, noting, for example, how Maria's experiences were similar to those of participants in those studies in terms of types of writing required, out-of-school literacy activities, privileging of English, and the different literacy demands of secondary and postsecondary settings. However, she also points to a number of important differences, such as the availability of bilingual support in high school and the bilingual environment of the novitiate. Kibler highlights the insights that Maria's unique experience has revealed, such as the occasional incongruity between macrolevel policy (e.g., the school's English-only policy) and microlevel practices (the availability of bilingual support from teachers) and the importance of *literacy sponsors* (Brandt, 1998, cited in Kibler, 2014), who seemed to have a greater effect on Maria's writing development than her classroom experiences. She expounds on the larger implications of these findings, in particular on the need for future research on L2 writers to consider the potential effects of multilingual resources beyond the classroom.

Although this is in many respects an exemplary study, there are also a few shortcomings. In light of Kibler's research question, the most problematic aspect is the difficulty in drawing any firm conclusions regarding the transferability of literacy skills due to the very different literacy demands of the novitiate as well as the fact that Kibler was not allowed to observe there and had to rely on Maria's accounts. Kibler is frank about how these circumstances limit her ability to make claims regarding this question. In addition, although some descriptions of events that supported Maria's writing draw upon direct observations as well as Maria's accounts of these events as recalled in interviews, others rely entirely on the latter; given the controversies regarding the reliability of interview data (see Chapter 9), some consideration might have been given to how factors such as Kibler's researcher identity might have influenced such accounts.

Suggestions for Further Reading

General Guides to Ethnographic Research

- Goetz, J. P. & LeCompte, M. D. (1993). *Ethnography and qualitative design in educational research* (2nd ed.). San Diego: Academic Press.
- Hammersley, M. (2007). *Ethnography: Principles in practice* (3rd ed.). New York: Routledge.
- Hornberger, N. H. (1994). Ethnography. *TESOL Quarterly, 28,* 688–690.
- Richards, K. (2003). Observation. In K. Richards (Ed.), *Qualitative inquiry in TESOL* (pp. 104–171). London: Palgrave Macmillan.
- Spradley, J. P. (1980). *Participant observation.* New York: Holt, Rhinehart, & Winston.
- Toohey, K. (2008). Ethnography and language education. In K. A. King & N. H. Hornberger (Eds.), *Encyclopedia of language and education: Vol 10: Research methods in language and education* (2nd edn., pp. 177–187). New York: Springer.
- Watson-Gegeo, K. A. (1988). Ethnography in ESL: Defining the essentials. *TESOL Quarterly, 22,* 575–592.

Ethnography in L2 Writing Research

- Lillis, T. (2008). Closing the gap between text and context in academic writing: Ethnography as method, methodology, and "deep theorizing." *Written Communication, 25,* 353–388.
- Paltridge, B. (2008). Textographies and the researching and teaching of writing. *Ibérica, 15,* 9–24.
- Ramanathan, V. & Atkinson, D. (1999). Ethnographic approaches and methods in L2 writing research: A critical guide and review. *Applied Linguistics, 20,* 44–70.
- Swales, J. M. (1998). Textography: Toward a contextualization of written academic discourse. *Research on Language and Social Interaction, 31,* 109–121.

General Guides to Case Study Research

- Duff, P. A. (2008). *Case study research in applied linguistics.* New York: Routledge.
- Duff, P. A. (2011). How to carry out case study research. In A. Mackey & S. Gass (Eds.), *Research methods in second language acquisition: A practical guide* (pp. 95–116). Malden, MA: Wiley-Blackwell.
- Duff, P. A. (2014). Case study research on language learning and use. *Annual Review of Applied Linguistics, 34,* 233–255.
- Merriam, S. B. (1998). *Qualitative research and case study applications in education.* San Francisco: Jossey-Bass.

- Stake, R. (2005). Qualitative case studies. In N. K. Denzin & Y. S. Lincoln (Eds.), *Handbook of qualitative research* (2nd edn., pp. 435–454). Thousand Oaks, CA: Sage.
- Yin, R. (2003). *Case study research: Design and methods* (3rd edn.). Thousand Oaks, CA: Sage.

Case Study in L2 Writing Research

- Casanave, C. P. (2002). *Writing games: Multicultural case studies of academic literacy practices in higher education.* Mahwah, NJ: Lawrence Erlbaum.
- Casanave, C. P. (2003). Looking ahead to more sociopolitically-oriented case study research in L2 writing scholarship (But should it be called "post-process"?). *Journal of Second Language Writing, 12,* 85–102.
- Dyson, A. H. & Genishi, C. (2005). *On the case: Approaches to language and literacy research.* New York, NY: Teachers College Press.

Defining Culture and Community

- Atkinson, D. (2004). Contrasting rhetorics/contrasting cultures: Why contrastive rhetoric needs a better conceptualization of culture. *Journal of English for Academic Purposes, 3,* 277–289.
- Eisenhart, M. (2001). Educational ethnography past, present, and future: Ideas to think with. *Educational Researcher, 30,* 16–27.
- Haneda, M. (2006). Classrooms as communities of practice: A re-evaluation. *TESOL Quarterly, 40,* 807–817.
- Holliday, A. (1999). Small cultures. *Applied Linguistics, 20,* 237–264.

Ethical Issues

- De Costa, P. (Ed.). (2015). *Ethics in applied linguistics research: Language researcher narratives.* New York, NY: Routledge.
- Guillemin, M. & Gillam, L. (2004). Ethics, reflexivity, and "ethically important moments" in research. *Qualitative Inquiry, 10,* 261–280.
- Kubanyiova, M. (2008). Rethinking research ethics in contemporary applied linguistics: The tension between macroethical and microethical perspectives in situated research. *The Modern Language Journal, 92,* 503–518.

Evaluative Criteria

- Chapelle, C. A. & Duff, P. A. (Eds.). (2003). Qualitative research guidelines. *TESOL Quarterly, 37,* 163–178.
- Duff, P. A. (2006). Beyond generalizability: Contextualization, complexity, and credibility in applied linguistics research. In M. Chalhoub-Deville, C. A.

Chapelle, & P. Duff (Eds.), *Inference and generalizability in applied linguistics* (pp. 65–95). Amsterdam: John Benjamins.

- Edge, J. & Richards, K. (1998). May I see your warrant, please? Justifying outcomes in qualitative research. *Applied Linguistics, 19*, 334–356.
- Lazaraton, A. (2003). Evaluative criteria for qualitative research in applied linguistics: Whose criteria and whose research? *The Modern Language Journal, 87*, 1–12.
- Starfield, S. (2013). Researcher reflexivity. In C. A. Chapelle (Ed.), *Encyclopedia of applied linguistics* (pp. 1–7). Malden, MA: Wiley-Blackwell.
- Starfield, S. (2016). Ethnographic research. *TESOL Quarterly, 50*, 51–54.

5

MIXED METHODS RESEARCH

Mixed methods research (MMR), a design in which quantitative and qualitative methods are combined within a single project, has been receiving increasing attention in the social sciences in recent years, with the publication of several handbooks (e.g., Bergman, 2008; Creswell & Plano Clark, 2011; Greene, 2007; Tashakkori & Teddlie, 2010) as well as the debut of a dedicated journal, *Journal of Mixed Methods Research*, in 2007. Researchers in applied linguistics and TESOL have also begun to consider the potential of MMR to expand and deepen understandings of the multilayered processes involved in L2 acquisition and teaching (e.g., Brown, 2014; Dörnyei, 2007; Hashemi, 2012; Hashemi & Babaii, 2013; Jang, Wagner, & Park, 2014; Riazi & Candlin, 2014). In a recent review of major applied linguistics journals, Hashemi and Babaii (2013) identified 205 articles published between 1995 and 2008 that employed some form of MMR design, while Riazi and Candlin's (2014) more narrowly focused overview of language teaching research found 40 studies published between 2002 and 2011 that combined quantitative and qualitative methods to some degree.

Originally, MMR was proposed as a form of triangulation (see Chapter 4) under the assumption that bringing in multiple methods (both quantitative and qualitative) and multiple perspectives to investigate an issue would strengthen validity of findings and enhance understandings of complex social phenomena (see Creswell & Plano Clark, 2011; Dörnyei, 2007). Other purposes that have been advanced for engaging in MMR include counterbalancing strengths and weaknesses of each methodology, expanding a researcher's toolkit when neither quantitative nor qualitative methods alone are sufficient to address a research problem, using one method to develop a study based on the other (e.g., to enhance sampling or design of instruments), and dealing with divergent or puzzling findings derived from one method by investigating them with the other method (Creswell & Plano Clark, 2011; Greene, 2007; Greene, Caracelli, & Graham, 1989; Jang et al., 2014; Riazi & Candlin, 2014).

MMR would seem to hold great potential for an interdisciplinary field such as L2 writing in which both cognitive and social factors interact in intricate ways. It has also been recommended as an approach to L2 writing research that can investigate both quantitative (e.g., increased grammatical accuracy) and qualitative (e.g., increased understanding of academic writing conventions) changes in L2 learners' knowledge (Tardy, 2006). Nevertheless, the blending of quantitative and qualitative approaches raises several theoretical, methodological, and practical questions. This chapter will begin with an overview of how MMR has been defined and a description of the different types of MMR studies. This is followed by the kinds of issues that L2 writing researchers have explored using this methodology. It will continue with a discussion of some ongoing issues related to MMR, such as whether, how, and when quantitative and qualitative methods should be combined and how such studies should be evaluated.

An Overview of Mixed Methods Research

At the most basic level, MMR involves use of at least one quantitative and one qualitative element. However, a mixed methods design requires not only the presence of both quantitative and qualitative data and/or methods, but their *integration* at some stage of the research. That is, MMR is more than quantitative research that involves some qualitative data (e.g., a few open-ended questions on a Likert-scale survey) or qualitative research that includes a few numbers (e.g., frequency counts of how often a topic arose during interviews). Although how and when such integration should be achieved is a matter of some debate, there is general agreement that in order for an MMR design to reach its full potential, both quantitative and qualitative approaches should contribute to the study in a substantive way.

Definitions of MMR have proliferated in the literature (for an overview, see Johnson, Onwuegbuzie, & Turner, 2007). For the purposes of this chapter we have chosen to adopt the following from Dörnyei (2007):

> A mixed methods study involves the collection and analysis of both quantitative and qualitative data in a single study with some attempts to integrate the two approaches at one or more stages of the research process. In other words, mixed methods research involves the mixing of quantitative and qualitative research methods or paradigm characteristics.
>
> *(p. 161)*

This definition, which incorporates the key criteria for MMR while also allowing for some degree of flexibility in terms of when and how integration of multiple methods is achieved, allows for a fuller exploration of how this methodology has been adopted and adapted to investigate issues relevant to the field of L2 writing.

Types of MMR Designs

Mixed methods studies can be classified along several dimensions. The first concerns timing (Greene, 2008), that is, the order in which data are collected and analyzed. In a *simultaneous* (or *concurrent*) design, quantitative and qualitative data are collected at approximately the same point in the study, are analyzed separately, and are integrated only at final stages of the research, during which findings from both sets of data are used to make inferences and draw conclusions. In a *sequential* design, on the other hand, the data are collected and analyzed in phases, with findings from the first phase used to develop the second. This latter point is especially important; that is, *sequential* does not simply refer to the order in which quantitative and qualitative methods were employed, but implies a relationship between the two phases of the research.

The second dimension involves what Greene (2008, p. 14) calls *status*, that is, whether one methodology is dominant or both are given equal weight. This relationship is usually expressed by using all capital letters to designate the dominant methodology, for example QUAL-quan for a design that is primarily qualitative (QUAL) with some quantitative (quan) elements, QUAN-qual for a study in which the quantitative element is dominant, or QUAN-QUAL for a design in which each methodology contributes equally. Finally, MMR designs can vary in terms of when and how much the mixing of methodologies occurs.

These options can be implemented in a variety of combinations, resulting in a wide array of possible design types, labels, and classification schemes. One frequently referenced typology comes from Creswell and Plano Clark (2011) and comprises six design types (Table 5.1; see also Creswell & Plano Clark, 2011, pp. 73–76), although each of these also has a number of possible variants. However, other typologies as well as other ways of conceptualizing MMR designs exist (e.g., see Guest, 2013), and not all MMR studies fit neatly into this typology. What follows should therefore not be taken as a definitive list but as a starting point for thinking about potential options for MMR. More information on each of these designs and how to implement them can be found in the suggested readings listed at the end of this chapter.

In the first design type, convergent parallel (formerly called *triangulation*; see Creswell & Plano Clark, 2007), quantitative and qualitative data are collected and analyzed separately at approximately the same point in the research process and brought together only at the end for the purpose of interpretation and triangulation. An example would be a study in which both quantitative and qualitative data were combined at the analysis stage to answer a single research question (e.g., see Neumann, 2014 in Box 5.1). In an embedded design, one type of data is embedded within a study that employs the other type of data.

TABLE 5.1 A Typology of Mixed Methods Designs

Type	Category	Characteristics	Why Use It
Convergent parallel QUAN + QUAL	Concurrent	• QUAN and QUAL collected at same point • Methods have equal weight • Analyzed separately, brought together at end	• Inform or validate interpretations through triangulation
Explanatory QUAN → qual	Sequential	• QUAN data collected first • Qual phase designed to follow up on results	• Explain results or clarify issues from QUAN phase
Exploratory QUAL → quan	Sequential	• QUAL collected first • QUAL results used to design Quan phase	• Explore a phenomenon in depth then measure it on a wider scale • Identify key variables or develop instruments
Embedded QUAN (qual) QUAL (quan)	Concurrent/ Sequential	• Either QUAN or QUAL data is primary • Secondary type embedded within design built around primary type • Secondary data type collected before, during, or after primary data type	• Different research questions require different types of data • Examine process (QUAL) as well as outcomes (QUAN) • Use secondary data type to supplement results from primary data type
Transformative (Varies)	Concurrent/ Sequential	• Research is framed within a transformative theoretical framework (e.g., feminist theory) • Theory guides decisions regarding issues such as timing and status	• To conduct MMR that identifies and responds to social problems
Multiphase QUAN + QUAL	Concurrent/ Sequential	• Combines concurrent and sequential strands within a larger plan of research conducted in phases over time	• The research objective requires multiple phases (e.g, program evaluation)

Adapted from Creswell, J. & Plano Clark, V. L. (2011). *Designing and conducting mixed methods research* (2nd ed.). Thousand Oaks, CA: Sage.

For example, a researcher doing a qualitative observational study of an L2 writing classroom might note that students were struggling with paraphrasing and embed an instructional intervention (using a pre- and posttest design) to see if instruction made a difference (concurrent). In a sequential embedded design, a researcher conducting an experimental study on the efficacy of various types of written corrective feedback might interview participants following the posttest regarding whether they noticed the feedback and how they interpreted it; these findings would then be incorporated into the interpretation of the experimental results.

In an explanatory design, one method (usually qualitative) is used to further explore or explain the results generated by the other method (usually quantitative). For example, one might begin by conducting a quantitative survey of a large sample of L2 students to determine the kinds of writing assignments they are required to do in their content classes and whether their L2 composition classes adequately prepared them to do these assignments. The key findings from the survey (e.g., that these students struggle with paraphrasing and summary writing) would then be used to develop questions for interviews with a subset of survey participants in order to determine the reasons behind these findings (e.g., asking participants about the kind of instruction in these skills they received in their L2 composition classes). In an exploratory design, on the other hand, results from (usually) qualitative data are used to develop a (usually) quantitative study; for example, the study outlined here could instead begin with interviews with a small group of L2 composition students who were taking content classes in order to determine what aspects of writing they found to be most problematic, with the results used to develop items for a survey that could explore these same issues among a larger pool of participants.

In a transformative design, an MMR study is situated within a theoretical framework such as critical theory, feminist theory, or emancipatory pedagogy with the overall aim of critiquing social inequality and advocating for change (e.g., see Mertens, 2007). Creswell and Plano Clark (2011) stress that in a transformative design, the theory is primary and guides all other methodological decisions, including timing and status of each method. In L2 writing, this design might be applied by a researcher taking a critical approach in a study that examines differential access to test preparation for high-stakes L2 writing exams using a combination of quantitative (questionnaires, test scores) and qualitative (e.g., interviews, observations in test preparation classes) data. The final design type, multiphase design, is most commonly found in large-scale research, such as program evaluation, that is implemented in stages over time. For example, evaluation of a new writing curriculum in an ESP program might comprise multiple studies conducted at different points in time over the course of the first year, each of which may use qualitative (interviews, observations of writing classes), quantitative (surveys, analyses of student texts, exam scores), or mixed methods to determine how the new curriculum is being implemented and its impact on student achievement.

In L2 writing research, concurrent designs appear to be the most common, a finding that is consistent with patterns found in reviews of MMR in the applied linguistics literature more generally (e.g., Hashemi & Babaii, 2013; Jang et al., 2014; Riazi & Candlin, 2014). Concurrent designs are an optimal choice for many research purposes, such as studies that employ different methods to investigate different facets (e.g., social and cognitive) involved in L2 writing or those in which MMR is used for triangulation. However, this pattern suggests that the potential of sequential designs, especially those that serve the purposes of explanation or development, may not be fully exploited in the field. For example, although the combination of quantitative surveys and qualitative interviews is not uncommon in L2 writing research (e.g., Evans & Green, 2007; Ferris, 2014; Yasuda, 2011), these methods are typically implemented in a concurrent design in which interview questions are written (and interviews may be conducted) before the surveys are analyzed rather than in a sequential design in which interview questions are formulated for the express purpose of delving more deeply into survey findings (e.g., why a majority of students in a survey indicated a negative attitude toward writing). Similarly, selection of interview participants, even when purposive, is usually not based on their responses on the survey but on independent factors such as language proficiency (but see Busse, 2013). Expanding L2 writing research to encompass a broader range of MMR designs and purposes is an area for future work.

MMR on L2 Writing

Although it is not uncommon to find L2 writing research that employs both quantitative and qualitative methods, it is still relatively rare for researchers to describe their study as mixed methods and even more unusual to find studies in which the researcher designates the type of MMR research design employed or the purpose for using it. In selecting studies for this review, we have therefore chosen to take a fairly expansive view of MMR and to include any study that integrates quantitative and qualitative methods in a way that enriches the overall findings, whether or not it is expressly labeled as mixed methods (see Table 5.2).

A frequent purpose for mixing methods in L2 writing research is to complement the researcher's (usually quantitative) analysis with the perspectives of study participants (usually elicited through interviews), with the aim of generating a deeper or alternative understanding of the phenomenon under investigation. One example is Sasaki's (2007) longitudinal study that compared the English writing development of two groups of Japanese students: those who participated in study-abroad programs in Canada and the US and those who stayed in Japan (see also the discussion of Sasaki, 2004 in Chapter 8). While primarily quantitative (English proficiency tests, analyses of elicited essays, stimulated recall based on recordings of writing sessions), the study also included data from interviews in which participants were shown the results of the quantitative measures of

TABLE 5.2 Representative Mixed Methods Studies

Citation	Participants, context, and data	Research questions/focus	Comments on study design
Sasaki (2007)	• Two groups of Japanese EFL learners: seven study-abroad (SA) students and six at-home students, studied for one year • Proficiency tests, elicited essays, video recordings of composing sessions used for stimulated recall (SR), interviews, written reports from SA students • QUAN analysis of proficiency and writing test scores; SR data coded and quantified • QUAL analysis of interviews and written reports	1. How did study abroad affect students' overall writing ability and composing processes?	• Most data collected at three points during the study; interviews at the end • Interview participants were shown QUAN results and asked to comment. • Results reported based on QUAN results with quotations from interviews to provide participants' perspectives
Kobayashi & Rinnert (2013)	• Longitudinal case study (2½ years) of a multilingual (Japanese, English, Chinese) Japanese university student • Elicited essays in each language collected at two points during the study; video recordings of three composing sessions (one per language), used for stimulated recall (SR); six interviews • QUAN analysis of essays for fluency and complexity • QUAL analysis of SR sessions and interviews	1. How does L1 and L2 writing by a multicompetent writer change over two and a half years in terms of linguistic development (fluency, sentence length, and lexical diversity) and text construction (choices of text features)? 2. What similarities and differences are there in the multicompetent writer's text construction and composing processes across L1, L2, and L3? 3. How are individual and social factors, particularly attitude and identity, related to the development of L1/L2/L3 writing? (p. 8)	• Multiple data sources are integrated throughout. • Fluency/complexity measures are not compared statistically between two time periods.

(Continued)

TABLE 5.2 (Continued)

Citation	Participants, context, and data	Research questions/focus	Comments on study design
Lee & Coniam (2013)	• 167 students and two teachers in a Hong Kong secondary school • Six-item Likert-scale questionnaire on students' attitudes toward writing (pre- and poststudy) pre- and posttests of students' writing; observational field notes from two classrooms (four lessons each over one year); interviews with teachers and 12 students from these classrooms • QUAN analysis of questionnaire (paired t-tests) and writing tests (rated for accuracy, vocabulary, sentence structure, complexity) • QUAL analysis of interviews	1. To what extent and how did teachers bring AFL [Assessment for Learning] to the EFL writing classroom? 2. To what extent did teachers' attempts to implement AFL affect students' motivation and writing performance? 3. What were the factors that facilitated or inhibited the implementation of AFL in the EFL writing classroom? (p. 37)	• Results reported based on research questions; RQ2 draws from both QUAL and QUAN analyses, but others rely primarily on QUAL • Observations used as validity checks for teacher interviews but not otherwise analyzed
Williams (2004)	• Four writing center [WC] tutors and five L2 writers • Student drafts (pre- and post-WC session); video recordings of WC sessions; interviews and stimulated recall (SR) sessions with WC tutors and students • QUAN analysis of drafts to measure revisions; all drafts also rated holistically • QUAL analysis of videotaped WC sessions	1. Do L2 writers revise their drafts following sessions at the WC? 2. What kinds of revisions are they most likely to make? 3. Do the revisions lead to improvement in the quality of the drafts? 4. Is there a relationship between *what* is addressed in the session and what writers choose to revise? 5. Are there significant revisions *not* linked to issues raised in the session? 6. Is there a relationship between *how* issues are addressed in the session and what is revised? (p. 177)	• Procedures for analyzing revisions outlined in detail • Report of findings integrates QUAN analysis of revisions with examples from WC sessions. • There is no discussion of interview or SR data, so it is not clear how they informed the findings.

Study	Data and methods	Research questions	Notes
Busse (2013)	• Students studying German at two British universities • Questionnaires about motivation (94 students), semi-structured interviews (12 students), student papers with feedback used in interviews (but not analyzed) • QUAN analysis of questionnaires • QUAL analysis of interviews	1. What are the characteristics of first-year students' motivational profiles and how do they relate to the contextual characteristics of the learning environment? 2. How do first-year students' perceptions of feedback practices in the particular instructional contexts influence their motivational thought processes? (p. 411)	• Detailed information is provided about sampling and procedures for data collection/analysis. • QUAL sample chosen based on QUAN results • Results focus on QUAL data, with references to relevant questionnaire results.
Ferris (2014)	• Writing instructors at eight colleges in California • 26-item online survey (129 instructors), interviews with 23 survey respondents, sample student texts with instructor comments (supplied by interview participants) • QUAN analysis of surveys and feedback on sample student texts • QUAL analysis of interviews	1. What are the response practices (including providing written and oral feedback and facilitating peer response) of college writing instructors, and how do they compare with "best practices" recommendations by L2 experts? 2. How do college writing instructors describe their own philosophies toward response, and how/where did they acquire those views? 3. Are college writing instructors' statements about their practices and philosophies consistent with their observed written response behaviors? (p. 9)	• Interview data were summarized but not coded. • Analysis of student texts used for triangulation with participants' accounts of feedback practices • Data were combined into case study narratives for each interview participant. • Findings from QUAL analysis were not applied to the survey sample.

(Continued)

TABLE 5.2 (Continued)

Citation	Participants, context, and data	Research questions/focus	Comments on study design
Plakans & Gebril (2012)	• L1 Arabic EFL students at a university in the Middle East • 145 students did a reading–writing task and questionnaire on source use in the task using think-aloud (TA) protocols and were interviewed • QUAL analysis of TA and interview data • QUAN analysis of questionnaire based on patterns from QUAL analysis	1. How well do L2 writers comprehend the source texts in an integrated task? 2. How do writers use source texts in their process of composing an integrated reading-writing task? 3. Are writers' scores related to reported comprehension and source use in the integrated task? (p. 21)	• Categories from QUAL analysis are reported and matched to survey items. • QUAN and QUAL analyses are integrated in discussion of results. • QUAL sample was sample of convenience (volunteers), so may not be representative of larger sample.
Barkaoui (2010)	• Novice (31) and experienced (29) ESL essay raters • QUAN analysis of raters' holistic and analytic scores on 180 essays • QUAL analysis of raters' written explanations for holistic scores	1. What aspects of writing explain the holistic scores that raters assign to ESL essays? 2. To what extent and how do the aspects of writing that explain ESL essay holistic scores vary in relation to rater experience? (p. 34)	• Codes from QUAL analysis were quantified for each rater and compared. • Results of QUAN and QUAL data are reported separately and integrated in discussion section.

Study			
Hu & Lei (2012)	• 270 undergraduates from two universities and four disciplines in China • Questionnaire on competence in source use; tasks in which participants evaluated texts that were copied (blatant plagiarism) or paraphrased (subtle plagiarism); participants' written comments on their evaluation • QUAN analysis of questionnaire, scores from tasks • QUAL analysis of evaluative comments	1. How well can Chinese university students detect blatant plagiarism (i.e., unacknowledged copying) and subtle plagiarism (i.e., unacknowledged paraphrasing) in actual English writing samples? 2. What stances do they take toward these two forms of intertextual practices if they identify them as plagiarism? 3. Do such factors as discipline, gender, length of academic training, knowledge of plagiarism, and competence in source use and referencing in English writing relate to their ability to recognize blatant and subtle plagiarism? (p. 823)	• Detailed discussion of QUAN analysis; QUAL analysis is briefly described, but resulting categories are not reported. • Results of QUAN and QUAL analyses are reported separately and integrated in discussion section.
Kang (2009)	• 42 Korean (intermediate-level EFL) and 28 American (L1 English) college students • Narrative essays in English (all participants); narrative essays in Korean (Korean participants) • QUAN analysis of frequency of use of referential forms • QUAL analysis of discourse functions of nonobligatory NPs	1. Are there any crosslinguistic differences in the referential choices in English and Korean extended written narrative discourse? 2. In what ways are Korean English learners' reference management and anaphoric strategies in English similar to or different from NES'? Are there any possible L1 transfer effects of L1-determined referential strategies in marking reference continuity–discontinuity in L2 at the discourse level? (p. 443)	• Detailed discussion of both QUAN and QUAL analysis • Extensive examples are given to illustrate discourse functions of noun phrases in Korean and English essays.

writing development and asked for their comments. Inclusion of the qualitative data allowed Sasaki to consider how students' varied experiences in each setting (Japan and North America) contributed to the changes in proficiency or use of writing strategies observable in the quantitative results. Using a similar research design, Kobayashi and Rinnert (2013) documented the writing development of a multilingual (Japanese, English, Chinese) student (Natsu) over two and a half years. In the quantitative phase, the researchers analyzed the fluency and complexity of Natsu's writing in each language at different periods of time and compared the results with the mean scores for the same measures (in English and Japanese) for other Japanese EFL writers in order to determine how Natsu's exposure to multiple languages might be affecting her overall writing development in each language. In addition, stimulated recall protocols were used to examine the functions of pausing during composing processes (with results reported as frequency counts), while interviews provided Natsu's perspective. Throughout the paper, data from the interviews are interwoven with the results of the quantitative analyses, providing a multifaceted picture of Natsu's emergence as a multicompetent writer.

Quantitative and qualitative methods may also complement each other in studies that investigate process, outcomes, and the links between the two. Lee and Coniam's (2013) study of the implementation of assessment-for-learning practices in secondary school EFL writing classes in Hong Kong explored process through observations of two classrooms and interviews with teachers (analyzed qualitatively), while the outcomes—changes in student attitudes toward writing and overall writing ability—were measured both quantitatively (pre- and post-study Likert-scale questionnaires and writing tests) and qualitatively (interviews with six students from each class). Williams's (2004) research on the effect of writing center (WC) conferences on revisions focused on a qualitative analysis of video recordings of writing center interactions between four tutors and five Generation 1.5 students to identify incidents in which the tutor or tutee pointed to a problem in the writing. These incidents were compared against quantitative analyses of the revisions made by each tutee following the WC session. While direct linkages between process (discussion of a specific problem) and outcomes (a revision that addressed that problem) proved to be elusive, the integrated analysis allowed Williams to document more global patterns (e.g., the types of interactional patterns that tend to lead to revisions) and to identify issues related to how writing center tutors interact with L2 students. Another example is Busse's (2013) study on the effect of written feedback on L2 German learners' motivation, which combined data elicited through motivation questionnaires administered at the beginning and end of the academic year with multiple interviews with a subset of participants about their feelings on the feedback that they received on written assignments. Broad categories developed through qualitative coding of the interview data (e.g., *satisfaction with feedback, dissatisfaction with feedback*) were compared with participants' quantitatively analyzed responses on the motivation questionnaire in order to determine how the feedback may have engendered changes related to various facets of motivation (e.g., self-efficacy).

Other L2 writing studies have sought to combine the strengths of quantitative methods (such as larger sample sizes, comparability across participants, and establishing statistically significant correlations among variables) with those of qualitative methods (e.g., deeper exploration of topics and individual variation) to investigate a range of issues. Ferris (2014) used an online survey (analyzed quantitatively) of 129 English composition instructors (both ESL and mainstream) to construct a broad picture of the instructors' experience in working with both ESL and non-ESL students and their feedback practices (e.g., written comments, use of peer response activities, and teacher–student conferences), which were then compared with best practices as outlined in the pedagogical literature. Interviews with 23 of the survey participants and analysis of feedback on student essays (provided by interview participants and used for triangulation) allowed her to probe more deeply into the issues addressed by the survey (see also Ferris, Brown, Liu, & Stine, 2011). In a study of L2 writers' use of sources in integrated writing tasks, Plakans and Gebril (2012) began with a qualitative analysis of think-aloud protocols (see Chapter 8) and interviews with nine participants to identify participants' purposes for using the source during the task, which they then matched with items on questionnaires about in-task source use completed by 136 participants who had completed the same writing task. The qualitative data allowed for a more detailed accounting of students' source use than what would have been feasible with a larger sample and also provided more direct evidence (through the think alouds) of students' composing processes versus the self-reports generated by the questionnaire. On the other hand, the integration of the qualitative results with those from the quantitative data enabled the researchers to extend their findings to a larger population.

Researchers have also used qualitative methods to provide additional information about behaviors (e.g., assigning scores to writing samples) measured through quantitative methods. Barkaoui (2010) used statistical analyses to compare the scores given by expert and novice essay raters on sample TOEFL essays using both holistic and analytic rating scales in order to determine what aspects of writing (e.g., organization, linguistic accuracy) raters focused on when giving the scores. He then compared these results with those from a qualitative analysis of the written comments raters had made explaining the reasons for their holistic scores, with the qualitative results used to supplement and (in some cases) support the results of the quantitative analysis. Hu and Lei (2012) used multiple methods to explore Chinese undergraduate students' recognition of and attitudes toward plagiarism. Participants rated two short essays, one of which had been copied almost verbatim from a source text (supplied by the researchers) and one of which was a paraphrase of the source text; participants' written comments were used to ascertain whether they recognized that the essays had been plagiarized. Comparative quantitative analyses (two-way ANOVAS) of scores were used to determine whether identification of plagiarism resulted in lower scores, while a qualitative analysis of the comments provided further information about participants' stances toward copying.

Finally, a combination of quantitative and qualitative methods can be applied to a single set of data in order to address different aspects of the same phenomenon. Kang (2009) began with a quantitative analysis to compare use of referential forms (e.g., third-person singular pronouns, zero anaphora) in personal narratives written by Korean L2 English learners (in Korean and English) and L1 English speakers (in English). However, arguing that this approach "cannot provide information about the narrators' discourse competence as opposed to linguistic competence" (p. 443), Kang extended the inquiry to incorporate a qualitative analysis of the functions of nonobligatory noun phrases (e.g., repeating a noun phrase such as *my friend* to refer to a recurring character in the story rather than using a pronoun) in each essay. Although the quantitative results showed no significant differences between the Korean and English L1 writers in terms of frequency of nonobligatory noun phrases in the English essays, the qualitative analysis revealed considerable disparities in terms of the discourse functions of these noun phrases, suggesting that although these learners had good control over form, they had not yet mastered the usage of noun phrases as a cohesive device. Overall, the results point to the additional insights that can be gained through using different methods in analysis of learner texts.

Issues Involved in Mixed Methods Research

Theoretical Issues

The main theoretical issue facing mixed methods researchers is whether quantitative and qualitative approaches are, in fact, commensurable. This question has arisen because quantitative and qualitative research are often seen as situated within seemingly incompatible sets of epistemological and ontological assumptions that underlie postpositivist (quantitative) and postmodern (qualitative) paradigms (see Chapter 1). As Greene (2008) has put it:

> Can one simultaneously hold contrasting, even competing, assumptions about what matters in human action? Is it possible for one inquirer to dialectically tack (Geertz, 1983) or make mind shifts (Patton, 2002) between up-close and distant perspectives or between thinking about generalities and honoring contextual particularities?
>
> *(p. 10)*

MMR researchers have responded to such questions in a variety of ways. One approach has been to differentiate *methods* (e.g., survey and interview) from *methodology* or *approach* (e.g., experimental or ethnographic) and *paradigms* (e.g., postpositivist or postmodern). For example, Lincoln and Guba (2000) have argued that although it is possible to combine quantitative and qualitative approaches at the level of method, it is not possible to do so at the levels of methodology or paradigm, as this would require violating key principles of one or the other methodology or paradigm and thus be unacceptable. Bergman (2008) also makes a distinction between methods and paradigms, questioning whether quantitative and qualitative methods are as distinct as is often claimed and noting that it is quite possible to interpret interview data from a (post)positivist perspective or to interpret numerical survey data as socially constructed (see also Bryman, 2008, for a similar argument).

Others have proposed taking a *dialectic stance* that views MMR as a way of generating insights through "a respectful conversation between different ways of seeing and knowing" (Greene, 2007, p. 79). This position acknowledges both the diversity and usefulness of paradigms but sees them as mutable perspectives open to negotiation rather than fixed dogmas that rigidly govern a researcher's behavior. A third possibility that has gained favor with many MMR researchers is to represent MMR as a new alternative paradigm, referred to as *pragmatism*, that embraces methodological diversity as a strength and emphasizes the practical need of researchers to utilize whatever methods (quantitative, qualitative, or both) enable them to answer research problems and generate useful findings rather than the purity of research designs (e.g., Morgan, 2007; Tashakkori & Teddlie, 2010).

Because of this range of possible paradigmatic orientations, MMR researchers are encouraged to reflect upon their own position and to be transparent about it in MMR reports (Creswell & Plano Clark, 2011). However, the absence of such reflection in the studies reviewed for this chapter makes it difficult to make a clear determination of how (or even whether) L2 writing researchers are considering and resolving potential methodological incompatibility. The prevailing stance appears to be one of pragmatism; that is, L2 writing researchers who have adopted an MMR design appear to do so because it provides the best approach for addressing the specific research problems that have motivated the study. For example, Kang (2009) justified her choice to add a qualitative analysis to her quantitative study of Korean EFL learners' use of referential forms on practical grounds, noting that this choice allowed her "to have a closer look at the Korean EFL learners' reference management at the discourse level because the number of certain referential forms included in the narratives reveals a limited picture of the learners' discourse skills and motivation behind their referential choices" (p. 462). The question may appear to be abstract and thus of secondary concern, but how one answers it can have implications for choice and implementation of MMR designs and thus should not be lightly dismissed.

Methodological Issues

Integration

Integration is a definitional concept in MMR and a requirement if the methodology is to serve the purposes for which it is intended. Indeed, the concept is of such importance that some MMR methods texts propose that at least one research question directly address the issue of integration, for example, the extent to which the findings from each method confirm, explain, support, or expand upon those derived from the other (e.g., Brown, 2014; Creswell & Plano Clark, 2011). However, a frequent finding in reviews of MMR across disciplinary fields, including applied linguistics, has been that integration is often absent or only minimally implemented (e.g., Greene et al., 1989; Hashemi & Babaii, 2013; Jang et al., 2014; Riazi & Candlin, 2014). For example, in their overview of MMR in the field of language testing (including writing assessment), Jang et al. (2014) found that a majority of the studies analyzed and discussed the results of the quantitative and qualitative strands separately or used them to answer different research questions, resulting in studies that might better be classified as what Yin (2006) calls *parallel* (i.e., a synthesis of separate studies) rather than *mixed* (a single study). Similarly, Riazi and Candlin (2014) conclude their review of MMR in language teaching and learning research by noting that many researchers take what they term an *eclectic* position that "adding another component (either qualitative or quantitative) to their study could work to strengthen it, but without effecting any systematic integration" (p. 167). A similar statement could be made about the majority of L2 writing studies reviewed for this chapter.

Achieving meaningful integration in an MMR study can be a challenging task, and a number of suggestions have been offered for accomplishing it. Yin (2006) argues for integration at every stage of the research, from research questions and sampling to data collection and analysis. None of the studies that we reviewed for this chapter met this ambitious aim, but many did achieve some degree of integration on at least one or two of these levels. A number of studies were integrated at the level of research questions by including questions that were addressed by combining both quantitative and qualitative results; for example, "To what extent did teachers' attempts to implement AFL [assessment for learning] affect students' motivation and writing performance?" (Lee & Coniam, 2013, p. 37) or "Is there a relationship between *what* is addressed in the [writing center] session and what writers choose to revise?" (Williams, 2004, p. 177). Integration at the level of sampling was sometimes addressed by employing *nested sampling* in which the qualitative sample was drawn from the larger quantitative sample (e.g., Busse, 2013; Lee & Coniam, 2013). Integration at the level of data collection or analysis was less common, although this was partially achieved in some studies with techniques such as formulating (quantitative) survey questions and (qualitative) interview questions that examined the same issues (e.g., Ferris, 2014) or using each method to examine different aspects of the same data set (e.g., Kang, 2009).

Caracelli and Greene (1993) emphasize integration at the analysis stage and offer four strategies. The first, *data transformation*, involves converting one type of data into the other, for example, by quantifying qualitative data that has been thematically coded (e.g., Barkaoui, 2010). In the second strategy, *typology development*, one type of data is used to develop categories that are then applied to analyze the other type (e.g., Busse, 2013; Plakans & Gebril, 2012). The third strategy proposed by Caracelli and Greene, *extreme case analysis* (identifying unusual cases from one type of analysis and using the other type of data analysis to confirm or disconfirm them), was not found in the studies reviewed for this chapter, perhaps because it requires a sequential MMR design that, as noted earlier, is rarely used in the field. The final strategy, *data consolidation/merging*, involves bringing both data types together into a single data set, expressed either quantitatively or qualitatively. For example, Ferris (2014) combined data from quantitative analyses of survey and teacher feedback with those from qualitative analyses of interviews to construct narratives for each focal participant, which then became the basis for answering her research questions.

Sampling

As noted previously, sampling can be an issue in MMR studies that aim to integrate and compare data from quantitative and qualitative methods. In some MMR studies, the participants in the quantitative and qualitative phases are identical (e.g., Sasaki, 2007; Williams, 2004). However, it is not uncommon for quantitative and qualitative samples to be of unequal size and thus comprise different individuals. While there are valid reasons for using a smaller sample for the qualitative portion of a study (e.g., to enable a more in-depth investigation of the issue under consideration), it also raises issues of comparability of the two data sets and thus the ability to make meaningful inferences based on their integration. Onwuegbuzie and Collins (2007) discuss several options for MMR sampling designs, including *parallel sampling* (the samples are drawn from two different but comparable groups), *nested sampling* (the qualitative sample comprises a subgroup of the qualitative sample), and *multilevel sampling* (the two samples are drawn from different levels of the study; for example, a survey of students in a writing program combined with interviews with their teachers). This third approach is most commonly found in exploratory MMR designs in which the results of the first (qualitative) stage are used to develop instruments to be administered to a different population in the second (quantitative) stage (Creswell, Plano Clark, & Garrett, 2008). Of these options, the one most commonly found in L2 writing studies is nested sampling (e.g., Busse, 2013; Ferris, 2014; Lee & Coniam, 2013; Plakans & Gebril, 2012). When using nested sampling, however, care must be taken to ensure that the subset of participants is representative of the larger sample, a particular problem when, as is often the case, this subset is self-selected (i.e., individuals who volunteer to participate). Although self-selection often cannot be avoided, it is possible to take a more purposeful approach to selecting participants in such studies; for example, Busse (2013) selected 12 interview participants (out of 28 volunteers) in order to obtain a sample that represented the various motivational profiles and gender distribution identified in the questionnaire stage of the study. Regardless of which sampling method is used, providing a clear explanation of how sampling was done at each stage of the research is essential in establishing a basis for valid (or credible) inferences.

Practical Issues

On a practical level, there have been questions regarding the readiness of researchers to take on the challenge of conducting studies that require expertise in both quantitative and qualitative methods (e.g., Bryman, 2008; Creswell & Plano Clark, 2011; Dörnyei, 2007; Johnson & Onwuegbuzie, 2004). As Creswell and Plano Clark (2011) note, "at a minimum, researchers should be acquainted with both quantitative and qualitative data collection and analysis techniques" and also have "a solid grounding in mixed methods research" (pp. 13–14). However, it is not clear whether L2 writing researchers conducting MMR studies have such skills; many of the studies reviewed for this chapter evinced weaknesses in one or the other methodology as well as lack of familiarity with the literature on MMR. A recent survey on statistical literacy in the field of applied linguistics (Loewen et al., 2014) paints a relatively reassuring picture regarding the ability of applied linguists to handle the statistical analyses that are central to quantitative research, although the authors note that their self-selected sample may have been biased in favor of quantitative researchers. Unfortunately, we know of no comparable study regarding knowledge of qualitative methodologies. Although it is likely that the situation has improved since Lazaraton (1995) expressed concern regarding the lack of training in qualitative research offered by TESOL and applied linguistics programs, the often cursory (and sometimes nonexistent) discussions of qualitative analytical procedures in many of the studies reviewed for this chapter makes it difficult to ascertain researchers' familiarity with the basic principles and practices of qualitative research. Ensuring that L2 writing researchers have been trained in the array of skills necessary to produce quality MMR studies is an issue that will need to be resolved if this approach is to progress in the field.

Evaluative Criteria

Judging the quality of research that combines quantitative and qualitative approaches, each of which comes with its own distinct (if not necessarily mutually exclusive) epistemologies and sets of evaluative criteria, presents a challenge that has not been fully resolved within the MMR community. The relative newness of MMR as a distinct research approach and the diversity of research designs and philosophical orientations that characterize it have made it difficult to develop a single set of evaluative criteria on which MMR researchers can agree. On the one hand, there seems to be a general consensus that what is called *quality of data* (related to methodology) can be evaluated according to established criteria for quantitative and qualitative methods; that is, one can use criteria such as validity and reliability (see Chapter 2) to evaluate the quantitative portions of an MMR study and criteria such as credibility and dependability (see Chapter 4) to evaluate the qualitative portions (e.g., Creswell & Plano Clark, 2011; Greene, 2008; Tashakkori & Teddlie, 2010). However, MMR researchers have also noted that evaluating the *quality of inferences* made from MMR research requires a more integrated approach that draws from both traditions (e.g., Greene, 2008; Onwuegbuzie & Johnson, 2006; Tashakkori & Teddlie, 2010). In addition, many have argued that if MMR is to be considered a distinct methodology that generates results beyond what could be accomplished with either method alone, it needs its own set of standards that addresses issues that are specific to integrated research designs (e.g., Bryman, 2008; Creswell & Plano Clark, 2011). Among the frameworks for judging research quality in MMR, the two most prominent have been proposed by Onwuegbuzie and Johnson (2006) and Tashakkori and Teddlie (2003, 2008). In an effort to avoid terms such as *validity* or *credibility* that are seen as too closely associated with either quantitative or qualitative research, these researchers have named their frameworks *inference quality* (Tashakkori & Teddlie) and *legitimation* (Onwuegbuzie and Johnson). Each of these will be discussed briefly; for a fuller discussion, see the references at the end of this chapter.

Tashakkori and Teddlie's (2003, 2008) framework for judging inference quality in MMR focuses on *meta-inferences,* a term that they use to refer to the broad conclusions that are drawn by combining the inferences that have resulted from each phase (quantitative and qualitative) in a MMR study. Meta-inferences can be evaluated along two dimensions, *design quality* (which directly affects the quality of resulting inferences) and *interpretive rigor.* Design quality may be measured in terms of general criteria such as appropriacy of the design for answering the research questions (*design suitability*), how well it has been implemented (*design adequacy/fidelity*), the extent to which various elements of the design work together (*within-design consistency*), and the suitability of the chosen analysis techniques (*analytic adequacy*). For example, L2 writing studies utilizing surveys and interviews (e.g., Ferris, 2014; Lee & Coniam, 2013; Plakans & Gebril, 2012) have achieved within-design consistency by ensuring that the interview questions focused on the same topics as those explored on the survey; that respondents in both phases were similar in terms of age, level of education, and L1 background; and that the same language was used to collect data in each part of the study.

Tashakkori and Teddlie's (2003, 2008) criteria for measuring interpretive rigor include *interpretive consistency* (the extent to which inferences from the quantitative and qualitative strands of the study are supported by results and are consistent with each other), *theoretical consistency* (the extent to which inferences are consistent with relevant theories), *interpretive agreement* (whether other researchers or study participants would agree with the conclusions), *interpretive distinctiveness* (whether the final conclusion is more plausible and defensible than other possible conclusions based on the data), and *integrative efficacy* (the extent to which inferences made based on the quantitative and qualitative data have been integrated into a meta-inference). For example, a problem with interpretive consistency would arise if the conclusions drawn from the quantitative and qualitative portions of the study lead in different directions; this lack of convergence should cause the researcher either to review and revise the inferences or to conduct further research to investigate the discrepancies (e.g., see the discussion of Neumann, 2014, Box 5.1).

Onwuegbuzie and Johnson (2006) begin from the premise that the primary purpose of MMR is to build on the "complementary strengths and non-overlapping weaknesses" (p. 51) of quantitative and qualitative methods and that MMR must therefore be judged on how well it has achieved this aim. Their legitimation framework draws from both quantitative and qualitative traditions to create multiple *legitimation types* that evaluate the quality of integration along various parameters, such as sampling, incorporating both insider and outsider perspectives, conversion (quantifying qualitative data or vice versa), compensating for the weaknesses of each approach, and whether the design has yielded high-quality inferences. For example, Barkaoui (2010) legitimated his use of conversion (i.e., quantification of data from the written comments made by each evaluator) by providing a clear and detailed description of procedures for coding the comments and an explicit rationale for converting these data into numbers (p. 37). In this case, answering the research questions required comparing the frequency of certain criteria across raters; thus, converting the qualitative data into a form that could be subject to a correlational analysis led to better-quality inferences than what would have been the case had the conversion not taken place.

BOX 5.1 FOCAL STUDY

Neumann, H. (2014). Teacher assessment of grammatical ability in second language academic writing: A case study. *Journal of Second Language Writing, 24*, 83–107.

Background

Noting that the assessment literature on L2 writing has largely focused on high-stakes testing situations, Neumann argues for the importance of examining how writing teachers assess grammar at the classroom level. She proposes to investigate this issue through a mixed methods design that incorporates the perspectives of teachers and students.

Research Questions

1. What indicators of grammatical ability do teachers attend to in their students' L2 academic writing when assigning grades for grammar on an analytical rating scale?

2. What knowledge do students have about the indicators their teachers look for when assigning a grade for grammar in writing?
3. What do students perceive to be the impact of their teachers' assessment criteria on their way of writing and learning in the L2 writing classroom? (p. 86)

Method

Participants were 33 students and their teachers in two ESL writing classes at an English-medium university in Canada. The quantitative portion comprised an analysis of student essay exams for accuracy and complexity, which were then compared with teacher grades using Pearson product-moment correlation coefficients. Stakeholder perspectives were elicited through an open-ended questionnaire (33 students) and interviews with eight students and two teachers, all of which were subjected to a qualitative thematic analysis. Data from all sources were brought together at the end of the study to inform and triangulate findings.

Results

Quantitative results showed a statistically significant correlation between grammar grades and accuracy but none between grammar grades and complexity, indicating that the primary factor in determining grades was number of errors. This focus on error reduction also emerged as highly salient in both student and teacher interviews. Taken together, the data suggest that an emphasis on accuracy may have discouraged students from taking risks by attempting more complex sentence structures, thus negatively impacting their further grammatical development.

Discussion of a Mixed Methods Study: Neumann (2014)

Neumann's stated aim in this study is to "examine the construct of grammatical ability that is assessed in L2 academic writing courses" (p. 84), in particular, how teachers balance the competing criteria of grammatical accuracy and grammatical complexity when assessing students' in-class writing exams. She further proposes to bring in the voices of students on this issue on the grounds that their perceptions of the criteria being used to assess them have an impact on how they approach a writing task. The study addresses this dual focus through a mixed methods design that uses quantitative methods (correlations between grammar grades and analyses of accuracy and complexity in students' texts) to investigate what teachers do and qualitative methods (an open-ended questionnaire and interviews) to investigate what teachers and students say about the role of grammar in assessing writing.

The study was conducted in two intact L2 writing classes (high-intermediate and advanced) at an English-medium university in Canada. It follows what Creswell and Plano Clark (2011) call a convergent parallel design (formerly called a triangulation design; Creswell & Plano Clark, 2007) in which data were collected in three phases and analyzed independently, with findings from each phase brought together at the end to answer the research questions and draw conclusions. In the first phase Neumann analyzed students' essay exams for accuracy and complexity (see Chapter 6) and computed Pearson product-moment correlation coefficients to explore relationships between these measures and grammar grades assigned by each teacher. The second phase focused on the students and comprised open-ended questionnaires completed by all 33 student participants and follow-up interviews with eight of these in order to probe more deeply into the questionnaire results. Both the questionnaires and the interviews examined students' perceptions of their instructors' criteria for assessing grammar and what the students themselves focused on when writing an essay exam. In the final phase, Neumann interviewed both teachers about how they assessed grammar. Data from the questionnaires and interviews were thematically coded (see Chapter 10) for qualitative analysis.

Of the three research questions, only the first, which addressed the aspects of grammatical ability that teachers attend to when assigning grammar grades, drew upon results from both the quantitative and qualitative phases of the study. The quantitative results were mixed; the only statistically significant correlation was a negative one between grammar grades and independent measures of accuracy (errors per 100 words) for one of the two teachers. However, the negative (albeit weak) correlation between the number of errors and grammar grades for the second teacher along with the lack of statistically significant correlations between grades and measures of complexity (clauses per t-unit and words per clause) pointed to the relative importance of accuracy versus complexity in assessing writing for both teachers. Neumann supports this interpretation of the quantitative results with data from the teacher interviews, in which attention to grammatical accuracy emerged as an important theme. Overall, the use of multiple methods allows Neumann to better address this research question than would have been possible had she used only a text analysis or only interviews, with each method compensating for the weakness of the other in what Onwueg-buzie and Johnson (2006) call *weakness minimization*.

Discussion of the remaining two research questions, both of which focused on students' perceptions, is based entirely on qualitative analyses of questionnaire and student interview data. These indicated that students also saw accuracy as the primary factor determining their grammar grade, and a number of students commented that this perception made them less likely to take risks by writing more complex sentences. In the discussion section, Neumann links these results to those derived from the text analyses and teacher interview data and draws meta-inferences (Tashakkori & Teddlie, 2008) regarding possible negative washback effects on students' overall writing development engendered by this emphasis on accuracy. She further argues that the parallels between results from the student interviews and those of the other phases of the study add further support to her overall claim that accuracy was privileged over complexity in these classrooms. By integrating the researcher's perspective (through text analyses) with those of teachers and students (through questionnaires and interviews) to generate these meta-inferences, the study meets one of Onwuegbuzie and Johnson's (2006) criteria for legitimation that calls for utilizing both insider and outsider views.

However, student interview data are less well integrated into the overall study than they might have been. Including a research question that directly compared student perceptions and teachers' actual practices or making a stronger connection between the student data and the quantitative analyses of their essays (e.g., a comparison between what an individual student said about the focus on accuracy vs. complexity and what he or she actually did in the essays) would have enhanced this aspect of the study. In addition, there could have been more clarity regarding the extent to which the smaller interview sample was representative of the larger pool of student participants. Although this sample included an equal number of students from each class, it was apparently a sample of convenience (i.e., volunteers), meaning that the data generated from the interviews might not represent the views of the students as a whole.

The focus of all of the research strands on a single construct (grammatical ability) means that the study is strong in terms of within-design consistency (Tashakkori & Teddlie, 2008), and this aspect of the study is further enhanced by using the major themes that resulted from analysis of the questionnaire data as the basis for the interview questions. Although the design appears to have been well implemented overall, evaluating the qualitative portion is complicated by the fairly generic (and thus less informative) description of qualitative analytical procedures. In addition, although Neumann reports the percentage of students in each class who mentioned grammatical accuracy as important (85 percent in one class and 75 percent in the other), the overall themes and number of mentions of each theme that resulted from the analyses of the interview data are not reported, which somewhat weakens the credibility of these results and thus the quality of the meta-inferences that are in large part derived from them.

In terms of interpretive rigor (Tashakkori & Teddlie, 2008), the integration of the results from each strand of the study into a single meta-inference regarding washback effects means that the study succeeds at the level of integrative efficacy. However, the failure to fully achieve interpretive consistency (i.e., the discrepancy between the weak correlations found in the quantitative analysis vs. the frequent mentions of accuracy in the interviews) somewhat weakens the study in this respect. The quantitative results do at least suggest a correlation between accuracy and grades (and lack of correlation between complexity and grades), and Neumann discusses some possible reasons for the failure of the quantitative analysis to generate statistically significant findings. Nevertheless, this issue might have been engaged with more fully. In addition, the lack of clear results from the quantitative analysis leads Neumann to rely more heavily on the qualitative results as evidence for her interpretations, which, given issues related to the reliability of interview data (see Chapter 9), could be problematic. A more extensive discussion that relates these meta-inferences to the literature on possible trade-offs between accuracy and complexity would have strengthened claims and also contributed to the evaluative criterion of theoretical consistency.

Overall, Neumann does a credible job situating her study within the field of MMR, including the provision of a clear description of her MMR design, illustrated by a figure that outlines the relationship among the three phases of her research (p. 87). It is true that, in common with much of the L2 writing literature that utilizes quantitative and qualitative methods, she does not engage with the broader theoretical issues regarding compatibility of quantitative and qualitative methods that are seen by some MMR researchers (e.g., Onwuegbuzie & Johnson, 2006) as central to establishing the legitimacy of MMR inferences. Doing so would require a discussion of how the different paradigms, worldviews, or standards for validity that characterize quantitative and qualitative methodologies were reconciled or combined in a way that allowed for greater insights into a research problem. However, this does not constitute a failure on the part of this particular study but rather reflects the new and still emergent nature of MMR in the field. Despite the shortcomings outlined here, this study provides a good example of how an MMR design might be approached to study an issue of relevance to L2 writing research and the potential benefits that can accrue from expanding one's methodological framework beyond the quantitative/qualitative dichotomy.

Suggestions for Further Reading

General Guides to Mixed Methods Research

- Bergman, M. M. (Ed.). (2008). *Advances in mixed methods research*. Thousand Oaks, CA: Sage.
- Bryman, A. (2008). Mixed methods research: Combining quantitative and qualitative research. In A. Bryman (Ed.), *Social research methods* (3rd ed., pp. 602–626). Oxford: Oxford University Press.
- Creswell, J. W. & Plano Clark, V. L. (2011). *Designing and conducting mixed methods research* (2nd edn.). Thousand Oaks, CA: Sage.
- Greene, J. C. (2007). *Mixed methods in social inquiry*. San Francisco, CA: Jossey-Bass.
- Greene, J., Caracelli, V. J., & Graham, W. F. (1989). Toward a conceptual framework for mixed-method evaluation designs. *Educational Evaluation and Policy Analysis, 11*, 255–274.

- Johnson, R. B., Onwuegbuzie, A. J., & Turner, L. A. (2007). Toward a definition of mixed methods research. *Journal of Mixed Methods Research, 1,* 112–133.
- Tashakkori, A. & Teddlie, C. (2010). *Sage handbook of mixed methods research in social and behavioral research* (2nd edn.). Thousand Oaks, CA: Sage.

Mixed Methods Research in Applied Linguistics

- Brown, J. D. (2014). *Mixed methods research for TESOL.* Edinburgh, UK: Edinburgh University Press.
- Dörnyei, Z. (2007). *Research methods in applied linguistics: Quantitative, qualitative, and mixed methodologies.* Oxford: Oxford University Press.
- Hashemi, M. R. (2012). Reflections on mixing methods in applied linguistics research. *Applied Linguistics, 33,* 206–212.
- Hashemi, M. R. & Babaii, E. (2013). Mixed methods research: Toward new research designs in applied linguistics. *The Modern Language Journal, 97,* 828–852.
- Jang, E. E., Wagner, M., & Park, G. (2014). Mixed methods research in language testing and assessment. *Annual Review of Applied Linguistics, 34,* 123–153.
- Riazi, A. M. & Candlin, C. N. (2014). Mixed-methods research in language teaching and learning: Opportunities, issues and challenges. *Language Teaching, 47,* 135–173.

Issues in Mixed Methods Research

- Caracelli, V. J. & Greene, J. C. (1993). Data analysis strategies for mixed-method evaluation designs. *Educational Evaluation and Policy Analysis, 15,* 195–207.
- Creswell, J. W., Plano Clark, V. L., & Garrett, A. L. (2008). Methodological issues in conducting mixed methods research designs. In M. M. Bergman (Ed.), *Advances in mixed methods research* (pp. 66–83). Thousand Oaks, CA: Sage.
- Greene, J. C. (2008). Is mixed methods social inquiry a distinctive methodology? *Journal of Mixed Methods Research, 2,* 7–22.
- Mertens, D. M. (2007). Transformative paradigm: Mixed methods and social justice. *Journal of Mixed Methods Research, 1,* 212–225.
- Morgan, D. L. (2007). Paradigms lost and pragmatism regained: Methodological implications of combining qualitative and quantitative methods. *Journal of Mixed Methods Research, 1,* 48–76.
- Onwuegbuzie, A. J. & Collins, K. M. T. (2007). A typology of mixed methods sampling designs in social science research. *The Qualitative Report, 12,* 281–316.

- Onwuegbuzie, A. J. & Johnson, R. B. (2006). The validity issue in mixed research. *Research in the Schools, 13*, 48–63.
- Tashakkori, A. & Teddlie, C. (2008). Quality of inferences in mixed methods research: Calling for an integrative framework. In M. M. Bergman (Ed.), *Advances in mixed methods research* (pp. 101–119). Thousand Oaks, CA: Sage.
- Yin, R. K. (2006). Mixed methods research: Are the methods genuinely integrated or merely parallel? *Research in the Schools, 3*, 41–47.

PART II
Methods

6

LEARNER TEXT ANALYSIS

As explained in Chapter 2, most experimental research focuses on some aspect of writers' texts. Features of the text are usually the dependent variables that must be measured to assess the outcomes of some treatment. The reverse, however, is not true: Many studies analyzing learners' texts are not experimental studies and instead have goals other than to assess the outcomes of a treatment. In addition, analyses of learners' texts may be combined with other methods, particularly in case study research that seeks to describe students' development over time with regard to text features. The various goals for analyzing learners' texts are addressed in the first section of this chapter. In the second section, we provide a taxonomy of ways to analyze learners' texts with a discussion of the issues related to choosing and using the techniques. We have included here mostly studies of L2 writers' texts but include a few that also examine native speakers' texts as a point of comparison to validate a measure or to show how learners' texts differ from those of native speakers. The third part of this chapter focuses on issues related to using the various measures and text analysis techniques. We end with a description of how to design a study using text data, followed by a discussion of a focal study. We note that many experimental and correlational studies use holistic or analytic rubrics to assess features of students' writing with regard to the quality of their writing. There is a large volume of research on assessing writing and validating holistic and analytic rubrics, but the development of such rubrics is beyond the scope of this book. We focus here, instead, on the more narrow and arguably objective measures to distance ourselves from the notion of quality per se.

Purposes for Analyzing Learners' Texts

L2 writing studies vary in their purposes for analyzing learners' texts (see Table 6.1). Some are descriptive while others are experimental (see Chapter 2)

TABLE 6.1 Sample Studies That Use Text Analysis

Citation	Participants, context, and writing task	Research questions	Comments
Chan (2010)	• 387 Cantonese speakers from Hong Kong universities and secondary schools • Two timed "freewriting" (p. 299) tasks	1. What types of lexicogrammatical errors do Hong Kong Cantonese learners make in their English writing?	• The text analysis was supplemented with focus group interviews about the sources of the errors. • The sources of the errors are speculated on, but there is no comparison group with a different L1.
Bardovi-Harlig (2002)	• 16 low-level ESL students in an intensive English program • A variety of text types over the course of seven to 17.5 months	1. Do ESL learners begin by using formulaic chunks to express the future, and what is the sequence of acquisition?	• Oral texts were also collected so that the use and emergence of the future tense could be compared. • Written data included journals, exams, compositions, and elicited narratives.
Benevento & Storch (2011)	• 15 secondary school students in Australia who had been studying French for five years • Three different topics and genres over the course of the year	1. Does writing among secondary school French learners develop or improve over a period of six months? 2. What aspects of writing, if any, develop or improve? (p. 99)	• The topics and genres were not counterbalanced. • The essays were coded for complexity and accuracy. • Detailed coding descriptions are provided, with good reliability reported for accuracy. • Few details on the coding of chunks are provided.
Crossley & McNamara (2009)	• About 200 native English speakers from a US university and 200 Spanish EFL students • Persuasive essays	1. Can lexical differences in essays distinguish between L1 and L2 writers?	• The essays were taken from two corpora that included persuasive essays written on comparable topics across the two corpora. • Many of the measures calculated were related to cohesion among the lexical items, but word frequency, usually a measure of lexical complexity, was also calculated.

Study		Research Questions	
Lu (2011)	• Chinese English majors from nine Chinese universities • Three different genres with a total of 16 different prompts	1. What is the impact of sampling condition, including institution, genre, and timing condition, on the mean values of any given syntactic complexity measure? (p. 46)	• Many different measures of syntactic complexity from Lu's syntactic complexity analyzer were used. No handcoding was done. • The data were taken from a large corpus of learner texts.
Shintani & Ellis (2013)	• 49 ESL students at a US university • A picture-story task	1. What is the effect of direct corrective feedback and the provision of metalinguistic explanation without feedback on learners' use of the indefinite article?	• Accuracy of indefinite article use was scored by calculating the number of correct uses divided by total of obligatory context plus overused forms. Reliability is reported. • In addition to examining students' writing, this study investigated students' explicit knowledge based on the results of an error correction test.
McCarthy & Jarvis (2010)	• Two corpora covering a wide range of English written texts including nonlearner texts	1. What is the most valid measure of lexical diversity?	• This study is not a study of L2 writing per se but rather one that attempted to validate a measure used in L2 writing.
Verspoor, Schmid, & Xu (2012)	• 489 Dutch EFL learners at five levels of proficiency • Short narratives on different topics, depending on age of the learners	1. How do various text features change over time and which discriminate best among different proficiency levels?	• 64 different measures were used. • Writing tasks differed among the levels. • Reliability of the measures is not reported.

or causal-comparative (see Chapter 3). Some combine text analysis with other methods, and most calculate some type of measure, but a few do not.

Chan (2010) is an example of a descriptive study that does not try to measure a construct (e.g., complexity or accuracy) but instead provides a taxonomy of lexicogrammatical errors made by Cantonese writers of English. In addition, Chan included interviews in order to triangulate the data. Bardovi-Harlig (2002) is a descriptive study that did not focus on writing per se but that used written data to examine a linguistic function, namely, the expression of future time. By following 16 ESL learners for a period of seven to 17.5 months, she was able to track forms used to express the future including how the future was expressed in formulaic chunks. Although these two studies both tallied features of learners' texts, they are quite different in terms of their orientation to language learning. Chan focused on errors and the purported source of those errors, whereas Bardovi-Harlig focused on the emergence and use of a particular temporal function.

Unlike descriptive studies, other studies seek to describe learners' texts in a particular context by measuring a construct. These studies tend to be quasi-experimental with no control group. Benevento and Storch (2011) wanted to determine what aspects of learners' text developed among secondary L2 learners of French and did so by measuring *accuracy* and *complexity* and by examining the use of *chunks*, all of which are discussed in more detail later in this chapter. Other studies seek to describe the texts written by different populations of students. These studies are examples of causal-comparative research (see Chapter 3). Crossley and McNamara (2009), for example, compared native English speakers' texts with those written by Spanish EFL students. They used Coh-Metrix, an automated computational tool designed to measure a variety of text features including different types of cohesion and lexical proficiency.

Experimental studies vary the condition under which learners produce texts or provide some intervention that is expected to affect text features (see Chapter 2). Lu (2011) compared Chinese students' English language texts in three different genres and found differences among some of the measures of linguistic complexity. Shintani and Ellis (2013) examined the effect of feedback and the provision of metalinguistic information without feedback on students' accuracy of the use of indefinite articles. In other words, their measure of accuracy was narrow and focused only on indefinite articles in contrast to some of the other studies measuring accuracy discussed here.

Finally, there are studies of writers' texts that focus on the measures themselves. The goal of these studies is to determine the best measure for a particular construct or to *validate* the measure (see the discussion of measure validation in the section on Issues Involved in Learner-Based Text Studies later in the chapter). There are a variety of ways to validate measures, and Table 6.1 includes two such studies, each very different from each other in their design. McCarthy and Jarvis (2010) examined measures of lexical diversity using a variety of validation methods including how similar or different the measures were from other related measures. This is called convergent and divergent validity, respectively. Their study was done using a wide variety of texts including nonlearner texts from published sources. Verspoor, Schmid, and Xu (2012), taking a different approach, examined 64 different text measures focusing on accuracy, complexity, lexical sophistication, and formulaic chunks. Using a cross-sectional design, they were able to determine which measures showed development among the different proficiency levels. In other words, some measures distinguished groups at the lower levels and some at the higher.

Types of Text-Based Analyses

Polio (2001) outlined different approaches to analyzing learners' texts, categorizing the focus of the studies into the following categories: overall quality, linguistic accuracy, linguistic complexity, lexical features, content, mechanics, coherence and discourse features, fluency, and revision. Most of these categories are still relevant in current research, but what has changed since then are the number of different specific measures in each category. For example, Polio identified only a few different measures of syntactic complexity, but recent measures are much more varied and capture different aspects of syntactic complexity. Furthermore, automated analyses have also allowed researchers to examine collocations and formulaic chunks more easily, and this has coincided with trends in usage-based approaches to language learning (e.g., N. Ellis, 2012). Table 6.2 shows 11 broad categories or constructs that have been used in the last 15 years in L2 writing research. Here, we discuss the CALF measures (i.e., complexity, accuracy, lexical complexity, and fluency) followed by less commonly used text-based analyses.

CALF Measures

Wolfe-Quintero, Inagaki, and Kim (1998) drew attention to CALF measures in their monograph that reviewed measures used in L2 writing development studies. Around the same time, there was an increased focus on these constructs in SLA research. Specifically, Peter Skehan (1996, 1998) proposed the limited attention capacity hypothesis, which suggests that in a given task, if learners focused on accuracy, for example, their fluency or complexity might suffer. Similarly, if a task called for more complex language, their accuracy or fluency would decrease. With Peter Robinson's (2001, 2011) counterproposal, the cognition hypothesis, which suggested that attention was not a limited capacity construct and that learners could improve on both complexity and accuracy if the task conditions were correct, even more studies using the constructs were conducted. Some of the studies testing these theories are discussed in Chapter 2 and in Box 6.1 in this chapter. Although at least two studies have expressed some doubts about applying these theories to L2 writing (Jackson & Suethanapornkul, 2013;

TABLE 6.2 Categories of Text-Based Measures and Analyses

Construct or focus	Specific measure or analysis	Example
Accuracy	Percentage of error-free clauses	Ellis & Yuan (2004)
	Percentage of correct verb forms (tense, aspect, modality, and subject–verb agreement)	Ellis & Yuan (2004)
	Number of errors per words	Truscott & Hsu (2008)
Syntactic complexity	Sentence length (words per sentence)	Vyatkina (2012)
	Clausal complexity (finite verbs per sentence)	
	Coordination (coordinating conjunctions per 100 words)	
	Subordination (subordinating conjunctions per 100 words)	
	A variety of measures using the syntactic complexity analyzer	Lu (2011)
Lexical measures	Density	Li (2000)
	Diversity (Guiraud index)	Verspoor, Schmid, & Xu (2012)
	Diversity (*D*-value)	Kormos (2011)
	Sophistication (average word length)	Gebril & Plakans (2013)
	Sophistication (frequency of word use)	Kormos (2011)
Fluency	Words per text	Storch (2005)
	T-units per text	
	Clauses per text	
	Syllables per minute	Ellis & Yuan (2004)
	Dysfluencies (number of words crossed out)	
Formulaic sequences	Lexical phrases	Li & Schmitt (2009)
	Lexical bundles	Cortes (2004)
	Modifier–noun collocations	Durrant & Schmitt (2009)
Cohesion	Variety of cohesive devices	Liu and Braine (2005)
	Measures using Coh-Metrix	Crossley, Weston, Sullivan, & McNamara (2011)
Paraphrasing and text copying	Number and types of quotations	Petrić (2012)
	A four-way taxonomy of paraphrase types	Keck (2006, 2014)
	Indirect source use, direct source use, verbatim source use, number of source use T-units	Gebril & Plakans (2013)
Revision process	Change in response to grammar feedback code	Lavolette, Polio, & Kahng (2015)
	Word-level changes	M. Suzuki (2008)
	Sentence-level changes	
	Discourse-level changes	
	Successful vs. unsuccessful revision	W. Suzuki (2012)

Yoon & Polio, 2016), L2 writing research on these hypotheses continues (e.g., Frear & Bitchener, 2015; Ruiz-Funes, 2015).

Another possible reason for an increase in the use of measures related to complexity, fluency, and accuracy is likely Norris and Ortega's (2009) call for a multidimensional approach to examining complexity. Norris and Ortega explained that the various measures of complexity were not necessarily measuring the same constructs and argued that focusing on only one measure of complexity, such as the amount of subordination, might cause researchers to miss other types of complexity. Finally, there was likely a realization that examining only one aspect of writers' texts is too reductionist (see the discussion in Chapter 2) and that we need to assess a range of constructs to better describe writers' texts. For example, studies of written corrective feedback now tend to consider a variety of CALF measures instead of measuring only accuracy (e.g., Hartshorn et al., 2010; van Beuningen et al., 2012). In addition, there is a realization that, with CALF measures, we need also to consider how they interact (see also Larsen-Freeman, 2006; Verspoor et al., 2012). Because of the pervasiveness of CALF measures in the L2 writing research, we begin with a discussion of these four categories (see Table 6.2).

Accuracy

Accuracy is on one hand easy to define but, on the other hand, somewhat challenging to measure. Researchers agree that accuracy means absence of error, but what constitutes an error is not always agreed on by coders or native speakers; thus, coding reliability can be particularly problematic to achieve. Furthermore, although counting the number of errors may seem like the best way to measure accuracy, it can be quite challenging because sentences can often be revised in a number of different ways that will lead to different error counts (e.g., there may be a simple fix or a more complicated one depending on how the coder interprets the writer's meaning). Although some researchers do use error counts, many opt for counting error-free units, either clauses or *T-units* (an independent clause and all of its dependent clauses) because it is easier. For example, Ellis and Yuan (2004) used error-free clauses per number of clauses, while Truscott and Hsu (2008) used number of errors per words. Unlike complexity measures, all accuracy measures measure similar constructs related to the number of errors (e.g., error-free clauses and error-free T-units) and so will necessarily correlate highly with each other. Polio and Shea (2014) detailed the full range of measures use to assess accuracy in recent L2 writing research, but unfortunately were unable to conclude that any one measure is the most reliable or valid.

Complexity

Syntactic and lexical complexity have been discussed at great length in the L2 writing (and oral) research. The most comprehensive review of syntactic and lexical complexity is Bulté and Housen (2012), who reviewed task-based studies, including oral studies, and found 44 different measures of complexity. It is important to understand that all measures of syntactic complexity cannot be measuring the same construct when they target different parts of the sentence. For example, a study that focuses on the number of clauses per sentence or T-unit misses features of noun phrase complexity as well as complexity achieved through coordination. Table 6.2 includes two studies that used a variety of complexity measures. Vyatkina (2012) examined students' writing development in German using four measures that targeted different complexity features. Lu (2011) used an automated analyzer that he developed. His syntactic complexity analyzer calculated 14 different measures related to length of a unit (i.e., clause, T-unit, and sentence), subordination, coordination, and specific grammatical structures. In both studies, the measures are not completely independent; for example, sentence length will be affected by the number of clauses.

Lexical complexity measures have also received a great deal of attention. While lexical diversity and lexical sophistication are probably the constructs most often discussed, lexical density, the proportion of content words, has also been used (e.g., Li, 2000). Lexical diversity, which refers to the range of different words used in a piece of writing, has been studied extensively, although the construct has recently been problematized by Jarvis (2013). One way to assess lexical diversity is by using a type-token ratio (i.e., the number of different words divided by the total number of words), but such a measure can be affected by the length of a text, so many researchers have chosen to use the Guiraud index (Verspoor et al., 2012) or D (Kormos, 2011; see Box 6.1), which take length into account. Other measures are discussed in detail by McCarthy and Jarvis (2007, 2010). Measures of lexical sophistication attempt to assess the level of individual words used. Gebril and Plakans (2013) defined this construct as average word length, while others consider the frequency of each word (Crossley, Weston, Sullivan, & McNamara, 2011); that is, a less common word is considered more sophisticated. One point of note is that all of the analyses using these measures are done by a computer and generally do not consider whether or not a word was used correctly.

Fluency

Fluency is a construct often measured by examining writers' texts for the number of words written in a given period of time. Some studies have also included the number of T-units or clauses written (e.g., Wigglesworth & Storch, 2009). Fluency is fairly straightforward, but some discussion of the construct as manifested in writing exists. Wolfe-Quintero, Inagaki, and Kim (1998) argued that length-of-structure measures (e.g., words per T-unit) were related to fluency, but this has been refuted (e.g., Bulté & Housen, 2012; Norris & Ortega, 2009) on the basis that such measures are capturing an aspect of complexity. The issue of exactly what fluency is in writing, as opposed to speaking (e.g., Segalowitz, 2010), has been addressed by Abdel Latif (2013), who argued that text-based production measures may be problematic because the amount of text one writes can be influenced by a range of variables, include topic familiarity. In their study of writing fluency, Baba and Nitta (2014) argued that text length does not adequately assess fluency. Indeed, a few studies have assessed fluency through nontext-based methods such as think alouds (Chapter 8) or keystroke logging (Chapter 12), but such methods involve another step in data collection. We note that a few studies such as Ellis and Yuan (2004) included both syllables per minute as well as the number of dysfluencies, that is, the number of words crossed out and changed. While such measures provide some type of information about what the writer is doing, it is also true that we cannot fully capture the writing process by looking only at texts; the writers could be composing and reformulating in their heads without anything being put on paper.

Other Types of Measures and Analyses

There are a wide variety of analyses; Table 6.2 lists some of the more commonly used measures. *Formulaic sequences*, also called *chunks, lexical bundles*, or *routines*, have received much attention in L2 writing research (e.g., Hyland, 2012). Throughout the applied linguistics and psycholinguistics literature, there have been different types of chunks identified (see the discussion in Wray, 2002). In a review of recent longitudinal writing research, Polio and Park (2016) found a few studies that focused primarily on chunks, such as Li and Schmitt (2009), but many others included chunk identification as one type of feature examined among a variety of measures (e.g., Benevento & Storch, 2011; see also Yasuda, 2011, discussed in Chapter 2). How such chunks are identified is not a simple matter. They can be identified by hand, as in Li and Schmitt, who had a panel of judges identify what they called *lexical phrases* so that they could trace the learners' use of the phrases over time. Another approach is to look at *lexical bundles*, the co-occurrence of words as identified by a computer; these bundles may intuitively be a unit (e.g., *statistically significant*) or they may not be (e.g., *look in the*). This approach, discussed more in Chapter 7, was taken by Cortes (2004), who compared the writing of published works in history and biology to student writing in those disciplines. One type of chunk is *collocations*, which can take a variety of forms (e.g., adjective plus noun, noun plus verb). Durrant and Schmitt (2009) compared native and nonnative speakers' texts by focusing on modifier-noun collocations and found that nonnative speakers were more likely to use high-frequency combinations than combinations of words that were strongly associated with one another.

Researchers are sometimes interested in measures of cohesion to capture the relationship among sentences. Liu and Braine (2005) addressed problems that Chinese students had with cohesion and the relationship between cohesion and text quality. They handcoded a variety of cohesive devices in three categories: reference, conjunction, and lexical. Each of these categories included specific text features; for example, reference devices included pronouns, demonstratives, definite articles, and comparatives. However, more studies are now analyzing cohesion through automated programs, particularly Coh-Metrix (McNamara, Graesser, McCarthy, & Cai, 2014). We do not have space to discuss the full extent of features analyzed by Coh-Metrix, which can analyze complexity and lexical sophistication as well, but to give one example, Coh-Metrix can measure content word overlap, that is, how often a content word is used across sentences. Various Coh-Metrix measures have been used to analyze L2 texts (e.g., Crossley & McNamara, 2014). Crossley et al. (2011), which analyzes L1 writing as a function of grade level, best illustrates the range of cohesive measures that Coh-Metrix can provide.

Other discourse features often studied are related to how students use outside sources. A growing number of studies have examined the way in which students do or not use verbatim language from other texts, sometimes in the context of integrated writing tests in which source texts are provided. For example, Gebril and Plakans (2013) looked at source use in an integrated writing task and identified paraphrases and summaries, direct quotations, and verbatim strings of three or more words. In other types of writing, Petrić (2012) investigated how students who had written high- and low-rated master's theses used direct quotations. Keck (2006) had coders identify attempted paraphrases in ESL students' summaries, and each attempted paraphrase was subsequently classified as one of four types.

Finally, texts have been examined to understand students' revision processes. While it is much more common in this area of research to use think alouds (see Chapter 8), stimulated recall (see Chapter 8), or keystroke logging (see Chapter 12), some researchers have examined changes from one text to another. Coding for revision is extremely difficult because there is often no clear *unit of analysis*. (A definable unit of analysis might be a sentence or a T-unit.) For example, if a student changes two related parts of a sentence, it can be counted as either one or two changes. Faigley and Witte (1981) developed a comprehensive hierarchical revision coding taxonomy, but no studies have reported reliability beyond the highest level (e.g., Berg, 1999), in part because the unit of analysis is not obvious. M. Suzuki (2008) coded revisions based on the level of change (i.e., word, sentence, or discourse), while other studies have simply reported changes in response to a certain type of feedback (e.g., Ferris & Roberts, 2001). Ferris and Roberts's type of coding is much easier because the unit of analysis is *any* type of change related to an instance of feedback. This was also done in both Lavolette, Polio, and Kahng (2015) and W. Suzuki (2012), who noted changes in response to an error code and reformulation, respectively.

In sum, there are a number of ways to analyze learners' texts. Most methods result in some type of quantification, but others result in qualitative descriptions and are sometimes combined with other data sources. Some measures are related to constructs from SLA that are often investigated in oral language as well, but many others are unique to the written modality (e.g., cohesion and writers' interaction with sources).

Issues Involved in Learner Text-Based Studies

The major issues regarding the analysis of learners' texts are the *reliability* and *validity* of the measures (see Chapter 2). These are discussed here, followed by issues related to automated and crosslinguistic coding. Other procedural matters, such as eliciting data and combining text data with other types of data, are addressed in the next section of this chapter.

Reliability

In quantitative research, if any kind of text data is coded and presented, the researcher needs to make sure that the coding is *reliable*. (Compare this to *emergent coding* for some qualitative research discussed in Chapter 11.) What this means is that if someone else were to code the data, he or she would get the same results. Similarly, if the researcher were to go back to the data at another time and code, he or she would get the same results the second time the data were coded. If another researcher wants to replicate a study and fails to get the same results, we cannot draw any conclusions unless we are sure that the measures are reliable. A test, such as a multiple-choice, can be assessed for its reliability using a variety of statistical methods, but here we focus on interrater or intercoder reliability in L2 writing research.

Some types of coding are easy to do and will always result in high interrater reliability. For example, a T-unit is defined the same way in the literature, and unless a writer makes severe syntactic errors, T-units are easy to identify (see more on this later). Polio (1997) found that two raters achieved .98 interrater reliability when counting T-units, so it is probably not necessary to have two coders. (Note anything over .80 is generally considered acceptable, so .98 is very high.) But consider a measure such as clauses per T-unit. The coder has to determine not only the T-unit but also the number of clauses in the T-unit. Once one segments the T-unit into smaller units, coding becomes more difficult. Furthermore, definitions of clauses differ across studies. Generally only finite clauses are considered, but those can be difficult to identify. Consider the following sentences:

> Example 6.1: The wedding guests ate, drank, and danced all night.
> Example 6.2: Even though the guests enjoyed themselves, a lot of preparations.

In example 6.1, depending on how a clause is defined, there could be one or three clauses because the subject is deleted before two of the verbs. In the second example, the writer likely meant there were a lot of preparations but deleted the subject and copula. Certainly clear guidelines for coding are needed, but even with guidelines, some types of coding are more difficult to do.

Accuracy is notoriously difficult to code because it can be challenging for coders to agree on what an error is. For example, in academic writing one needs to consider whether a register variation, such as *who* for *whom* or *gonna* for *going to*, is an error. Grammatical errors also can be difficult to identify because of differing coder dialects (e.g., *by accident* vs. *on accident*) as well as difficulty in understanding a writer's intended meaning. For example, consider example 6.3:

Example 6.3: The student are always must leave early from the class.

If we are coding error types, we need to know if the writer is talking about one or more students to determine if the subject should be singular (i.e., verb error) or plural (i.e., plural inflection on noun error). Also, even with more context, it might be difficult to decide if the writer should have included the definite article before *class* or not. In addition, coders need to decide whether or not spelling and punctuation errors are to be coded. Again, all these decisions need to go into coding guidelines to help ensure reliability. If we instead decide to count the number of error-free T-units, our task becomes easier: The T-unit is or is not error-free. Polio and Shea (2014), however, did not find error-free T-units or clauses to be more reliable measures, perhaps because they gave a separate code to T-units that were not comprehensible or contained more than five errors (see the guidelines in the appendix of their article). Of the specific error types they coded, only the number of lexical errors had low reliability.

We have chosen to focus on accuracy here as an example of issues related to coding, but coding for any type of text feature needs to be reliable. Yet even with accuracy, which is probably the most difficult construct to code for, not all studies report reliability (see discussions in Polio, 2012; Polio & Shea, 2014), and some studies report reliability on only a portion of the data. If two coders achieve a reliability of .95, then it is probably not necessary to have both coders code all the data. Finally, with more text analyses being done by computer programs, reliability becomes a nonissue: A computer will give the same results each time. Instead, validity becomes the concern: Can a computer program make valid judgments about certain constructs? This issue is addressed later in the chapter.

Finally, one point that is not often addressed in the L2 writing literature is which measure of interrater reliability to use. Many studies use a simple Pearson correlation. If the data are categorical, percentage agreement or Cohen's Kappa are generally used. There are, however, other methods available, particularly from biostatistics (e.g., Shoukri, 2010), and exploring other methods with L2 writing data might be worthwhile.

Validity

In the assessment literature, validity refers to the idea that a test measures the broad construct that it says it measures (e.g., listening proficiency, pragmatic competence). In this chapter, we discuss the validity of text-based measures, which refers to how well they measure more narrow constructs. There are a variety of ways to determine validity; we here focus on those approaches used in the L2 writing literature. Wolfe-Quintero, Inagaki, and Kim (1998) tried to find measures of L2 writing that best captured development and to validate the measures by reviewing previous empirical research. By examining longitudinal and cross-sectional studies, the researchers examined which measures changed over time or correlated with proficiency level. In other words, if a measure shows change over time or distinguishes among students across proficiency levels, one could argue that it is valid. However, there are a few problems with this conclusion. First, the converse is not necessarily true. If a measure does not show change, it may still be valid; it could be that no change in the construct occurred. Second, because the development of different constructs may not be linear (e.g., Verspoor et al., 2012), the conclusions of any research are limited by the range of proficiency levels of the students. For example, students might improve on one complexity measure at a lower proficiency level and on a different one at a higher level. Verspoor et al. found that between the two lowest levels of proficiency in their study, mostly lexical changes occurred, but between the second and third level, mostly syntactic changes occurred. As mentioned earlier, although Polio and Shea (2014) found no change over time in any of the accuracy measures except preposition use and their attempt to validate a measure of accuracy was not successful, the measures of accuracy themselves could still be valid.

Some of the studies in Wolfe-Quintero, Inagaki, and Kim (1998) correlated specific CALF measures with measures of holistic quality (i.e., as measured by a rubric), which is another way to assess validity. Again, if a relationship exists, it is possible that the measure is validated. For example, we would expect a measure of lexical sophistication or grammatical accuracy to correlate with essay quality. If there is no correlation, however, our conclusions are limited. Bulté and Housen (2014) found a relationship between essay quality and measures that considered the amount of subordination in a text. Even though the subordination measures were not related to change over time, the fact that they were related to quality indicates that they may be measuring some aspect of complexity.

More sophisticated statistical techniques are available for investigating validity but are not used often in L2 writing research (but see McCarthy & Jarvis, 2010, who investigated four types of validity to determine the best measure for lexical diversity). Factor analyses can also be used. Norris and Ortega (2009) reported on two unpublished studies that used factor analysis to determine how specific measures cluster together, including Oh (2006 cited in Norris and Ortega), who found that the number of words per T-unit and per clause were not associated with measures of fluency but with complexity.

Automated Coding

Related to reliability and validity, as well as practicality, is the issue of hand versus machine coding. Lexical measures are always done by a computer because it is much easier and because they generally do not involve human judgment, as with type-token ratios. Lexical measures can be done using a variety of free software such as the Natural Language Toolkit. Unlike with handcoded measures, reliability is not an issue with automated measures because all researchers will get the same results each time. Instead, the validity of the measures needs to be discussed. For example, one could problematize the fact that lexical errors are ignored. On the one hand, accuracy of the lexical items may be considered a separate construct. On the other hand, a student misusing a wide range of less frequent vocabulary will receive high scores for lexical diversity and lexical sophistication.

Coh-Metrix (McNamara et al., 2014) and the Syntactic Complexity Analyzer (Lu, 2010) are both available for calculating a variety of complexity measures. The former was originally developed to measure the readability of texts but has been applied to L2 writing, as discussed earlier. The latter was developed specifically for L2 writing. The developers of both pieces of software discuss the rationale behind their systems, but the programs are difficult to evaluate without a background in natural language processing. Again, both programs are clearly reliable, but how they deal with the complexities of interpreting L2 writing is an empirical question. We know of no studies that have compared handcoding of complexity measures using Coh-Metrix. Lu (2010) and Yoon and Polio (2016), however, have reported adequate correlations of the analyzer with handcoding. In contrast, accuracy is still a measure that requires handcoding. Some software, such as the Educational Testing Service's Criterion, can provide feedback to students on their grammatical errors, but such software was not intended to code all errors for research purposes (see Lavolette et al., 2015 for a discussion of errors Criterion can identify).

Crosslinguistic Measures

Finally, little has been written about whether the various text analyses and measures work across a variety of languages. Most of the research discussed in this chapter has been conducted on English texts, with some research on German as well. Some L2 writing research has been conducted on other languages, but little attention has been given to whether or not constructs can be measured in the same way across languages. Considering the range of text features examined, we would need to look at each construct separately to determine if measures could be imported from English. If we take accuracy as an example, counting the number of errors in a language other than English might be valid, particularly if one is not comparing English texts to texts in another language. In other words, the numbers of errors as a measure of accuracy for texts in any language written under different conditions might be appropriate, but comparing the number of errors across texts in two different languages might be inappropriate without normalizing the scores in some way. Using a measure such as error-free clauses or T-units could work in other languages as well. W. Jiang (2013) discussed this issue for Chinese and was able to use T-units as a unit of analysis for accuracy and complexity measures. Validating measures across languages is clearly an area that needs to be investigated, and programs for automated analyses of languages other than English need to be developed.

How to Design a Study Using Text Data

Eliciting Data

Once a researcher has determined that text data can be used to answer a research question, he or she needs to decide how to elicit that data. For example, the Kuiken and Vedder (2008) study (see Chapter 2) had to both operationalize task complexity and decide on the conditions under which the students would write. These conditions involve decisions related to the use of sources, modality, and time. They also had to determine the details of the prompt. In addition, they had to choose which constructs to measure and then decide how to measure those constructs. Each of these points is discussed here.

Experimental studies of L2 writing tend to have students write for short periods, usually under an hour, on topics that do not require outside reading. In other words, the type of writing often resembles a timed testing situation such as in the TOEFL independent writing task. Students generally do not have access to outside sources, and the writing is done by hand or using a text editor, as opposed to a word processor, which has spelling and grammar-check functions. These timed short writings are used to control for extraneous variables. For example, some students might spend a lot of time with the grammar checker and as a result write shorter but more accurate essays, while others might not use it at all. By controlling the writing conditions, more of the variation should be attributable to the independent variable. Modality has to be decided on as well: Should the students type or handwrite the essay? For beginners not used to a target-language keyboard, an essay produced by typing may not represent their true writing ability. For advanced students, however, handwriting might slow them down. Typing has practical advantages that the data is easier to prepare for analysis (see later in the chapter), but sometimes getting access to a computer for all participants at the same time can be logistically difficult.

The length of time that students should have to write may be difficult to determine as well. In any type of research or assessment context, the general rule is *the more data the better*, and students can write more, up to a point, if they have more time. But of course practicality, logistics, and student fatigue intervene. Piloting prompts with a population of students similar to those to be used for the study can be helpful to determine how much the students can write in a given time period. If the essays are too short, they will not be appropriate for any type of quantitative analysis.

In addition to considering issues of sources, time, and modality, one has to choose a prompt. If the prompt itself is an independent variable, then it is determined, in part, by the research question. However, in a study such as East (2007), which investigated the effects of dictionary use on writing, no specific prompt was suggested by the research question. East chose two prompts that required students to choose a point of view and argue that point of view. One possible reason for this choice is that students had been exposed to argumentative essays in their instructional contexts. Regarding the topics, East said that they were chosen because they did not require specialized knowledge. Topic familiarity is an important issue to consider. If some students are not familiar enough with the topic, they will not be able to write much, thereby introducing more unwanted variance. Some studies use prompts that require students to describe a picture or tell a story about a series of pictures. These types of prompts might avoid the topic familiarity problem; however, how students choose to write about picture prompts, particularly picture stories, can vary widely. For example, some students may write in the past tense and some in the present, or some students may write separate descriptions of each picture while others will tell a coherent story without reference to individual pictures. Again, making choices about all these factors can be helped by piloting the prompts.

Writing conditions and prompts choices are also related to ecological validity (see Chapter 2) in that the short timed writings used in experimental research may not be indicative of actual writing that L2 learners have to do in other contexts. Take for example the series of studies in Connor-Linton and Polio (2014). The corpus used in those studies was created from writings that elicited descriptive essays with topics such as *Describe your hometown* that would likely not be used outside of a low-level writing class. The topics were used to ensure genre comparability at each point in time; keeping the genre consistent reduces variability. However, the prompts tended to elicit five-paragraph essays, a questionable genre that might not exist outside of writing classes.

Making Coding Decisions

Another decision in conducting a study using text data is which constructs to measure or which text features to focus on. In some cases, the construct is fairly obvious, such as in the studies of planning or task complexity, which usually focus on the CALF measures. In other studies, such as those that ask general questions about writing development in a specific context, the text features to analyze are not obvious. Take for example the Benevento and Storch (2011) study in which they wanted to determine what changed in secondary school students' L2 French writing over six months of instruction. In addition to using a rubric to assess overall quality, they chose to examine accuracy, complexity, and the use of chunks; however, they could have also looked at cohesion or various discourse markers.

If texts are to be analyzed automatically, one will need to consult the instructions for the given software about how to prepare the data. If the data will be handcoded, it will have to be prepared for the coders. Generally, all hand-written essays should be typed, with identifying information such as proper names redacted. Otherwise, the essays should be typed exactly as written with anything illegible noted in some way, such as *xxx* for each illegible word. The data then needs to be formatted for the coders. When coding for accuracy or complexity, probably the most common practice is to divide up the essays into T-units using a table or spreadsheet. The coders can then tally what they are counting in each row. This could include the number of clauses, the number of errors, the number of certain error types, or the number of specific discourse markers. Spreadsheets can be merged to calculate reliability or average counts of the various features.

Once this is done, clear and detailed guidelines about how to code the data need to be developed. This is important so that the guidelines can be included in the appendix of the studies for others to see and use if they wish to replicate the study (see Chapter 12). Many times decisions regarding coding are not obvious, and, as noted earlier, there are a variety of ways to code. When there is no best way to code, one must simply make a decision and be clear about that decision in the guidelines. Having clear guidelines also helps coders achieve reliability. Guidelines are generally developed when two coders, using a set of data not used in the study, sit down together and discuss the result of their coding. This process is similar to norming test graders using a rubric. As mentioned earlier, having two coders for all or only some of the data depends on how much judgment needs to be exercised by the coders.

Supplementing with Other Data

The last point that needs to be considered is whether or not other methods besides text analysis should be used. If the study is a case study (or multiple case study), it is essential to use other techniques to triangulate the data. But even a large-scale study might benefit from supplementing text data with other types of data or methods (see the discussion of mixed methods research, Chapter 5).

BOX 6.1 FOCAL STUDY

Kormos, J. (2011). Task complexity and linguistic and discourse features of narrative writing performance. *Journal of Second Language Writing, 20*, 148–161.

Background

Although much research has been conducted on the effects of task complexity, most of it has focused on oral language. Skehan and Foster's (2001) limited attention capacity model suggests that as complexity increases, learners may pay more attention to certain aspects of performance while others suffer. Robinson's (2001) cognition hypothesis suggests that an increase in task complexity will actually lead to improved accuracy and complexity because task complexity will help learners focus their attention on those aspects of language production. Task complexity may affect written language differently because there are fewer demands on working memory. Furthermore, task differences may affect different parts of the writing process differently.

Research Questions

What are the lexical, syntactic, and cohesive differences between two types of written narrative tasks: one in which the content of the narrative is given and another in which students need to plan the content of their stories?

How does the performance of L1 and FL writers differ in terms of lexical, syntactic, and cohesive characteristics in two narrative tasks that make different cognitive complexity demands on the stages of writing? (p. 152)

Method

Forty-four secondary-level Hungarian EFL students and 10 UK university students wrote two narratives based on a set of pictures. In the cartoon condition, the pictures formed a coherent story, so the participants did not have to create the content but had to use some difficult vocabulary. Participants in the picture condition had a series of unrelated pictures that were to be used in a story. The students had to create their own story, but the task did not necessarily elicit difficult vocabulary. The narratives were assessed on lexical, syntactic complexity, accuracy, and cohesion measures.

Results

Despite all of the measures examined, little difference was found between the two tasks for the EFL students. One lexical and one cohesion measure showed a significant difference, but none of the other measures did. Differences were found between the native speakers and EFL students on some of the lexical measures and one of the complexity measures. No interaction effects for task and L1 were found.

Discussion of a Focal Study: Kormos (2011)

Kormos (2011) is one of several studies that have examined the effects of task complexity on learners' written texts. We chose this study to highlight because of the range of measures used to describe and evaluate the learners' texts. The study is an experimental study that manipulates the complexity of the writing task, but it is also a causal-comparative study (see Chapter 3) because it compares L1 and L2 writers. The L2 participants were secondary school Hungarian students of English, while the L1 students were British undergraduates who were slightly older than the Hungarian students.

After reviewing the related literature on the possible effects of task complexity and differences in L1 versus L2 writing processes, Kormos describes the two tasks that represent the independent variable. In the first task, students were given a series of pictures that told a story. This task was considered less complex because students did not need to conceptualize the plot, although they had to use potentially more difficult vocabulary. In the second task, the pictures did not tell a coherent story; instead, the students had to create one. It did, however, not require as difficult vocabulary. This latter task was considered to be more complex.

There are a variety of design issues that could be discussed, but the focus here is on the dependent variables measured through the analysis of the learners' texts. Recall that the goal of the study is to determine the effect of the different tasks on L1 and L2 writers' texts, but Kormos also needed to decide what constructs she wanted to focus on. In doing so, she drew on both theory and previous research. Robinson's (2001) cognition hypothesis suggests that the more complex task would lead to greater accuracy and complexity, while Skehan and Foster's (2001) model predicts the opposite. Thus, these two constructs were measured. Kormos also discussed other studies examining the influence of task type and writing conditions and noted that lexical variety and complexity were considered as well. Finally, she discussed studies that compared L1 and L2 writers and explained that previous research had shown that L2 writers may over- or underuse certain cohesive devices. Thus, she included cohesion as a dependent variable. One point of note is that Kormos, throughout her article, refers to the effect of the task on *text quality*. However, when talking about her own research, she avoids saying that her study is investigating quality. For example, she says, "The research presented in this paper aimed to investigate the linguistic and discourse characteristics of FL narratives produced by upper-intermediate foreign language learners in a bilingual secondary school" (p. 149). This is an important distinction because, as mentioned earlier, we cannot always equate specific text measures with increased quality, and in her study, she included only text measures and no measures of overall quality such as from a holistic or analytic rubric.

Once she chose to focus on lexical measures, syntactic complexity, accuracy, and cohesion, she had to decide on specific measures for each. The extent to which she justified each specific measure varied. For lexical measures, she chose the D-value and provided several references to support this choice, but she also acknowledged the possible problems regarding the influence of text length on the measure. She also chose two other measures that are less often used, vocabulary range and concreteness of the content words. The former was calculated with Nation's Range program (Heatley, Nation, & Coxhead, 2002) while the latter used Coh-Metrix. Although she did not explain her choice directly, these measures were likely used to cover a range of lexical competence issues as opposed to simply lexical diversity.

Kormos's choices for syntactic complexity and accuracy were not discussed either, but seem appropriate. For syntactic complexity, she chose a length of unit measure (clause length), a subordination measure (ratio of subordinate clauses), and a noun-phrase measure (modifiers per NP) as well as the number of words before the main verb, which she said reflects clausal complexity; however, it is not clear if this measure actually adds additional information. Accuracy was measured using the ratio of error-free clauses. This measure was not discussed, but recall that Polio and Shea (2014) did not find that any one measure of accuracy was better than any other. Cohesion was measured using a variety of measures from Coh-Metrix. Unlike with measures of complexity and accuracy, Kormos discussed at length her choice of measures for cohesion, relating her decisions to previous research as well as to more appropriate measures for shorter texts.

Many of the measures were calculated by a computer program, but for those that were done by hand, Kormos reported that the interrater agreement was .85. It seems that this was the average for all measures; reporting reliability for each measure would have been preferable.

Kormos did not find much difference in the two types of narratives and only some differences between the native and nonnative speaker narratives, with no interaction effects. The fact that not all measures of lexical competence nor all measures of complexity showed the same results suggests that they were not measuring the same construct. Kormos had many measures for each construct to choose from; she chose a range of measures and in most cases justified her choices well. Had she chosen fewer measures, we might have speculated that there were indeed differences in the narratives that she had not found. Having a range of measures thus strengthened the conclusions of her study.

Suggestions for Further Reading

Reviews of Various Text-Based Measures

- Bardovi-Harlig, K. (1992). A second look at T-unit analysis: Reconsidering the sentence. *TESOL Quarterly, 26,* 390–395.
- Housen, A., Kuiken, F., & Vedder, I. (2012). Complexity, accuracy and fluency: Definitions, measurement and research. In A. Housen, F. Kuiken, & I. Vedder (Eds.), *Dimensions of L2 performance and proficiency: Complexity, accuracy, and fluency in SLA* (pp. 1–20). Amsterdam and Philadelphia: John Benjamins.

- Jiang, W. (2013). Measurements of development in L2 written production: The case of L2 Chinese. *Applied Linguistics, 34*, 1–24.
- Norris, J. M. & Ortega, L. (2009). Measurement for understanding: An organic approach to investigating complexity, accuracy, and fluency in SLA. *Applied Linguistics, 30*, 555–578.
- Pallotti, G. (2009). CAF: Defining, refining, and differentiating constructs. *Applied Linguistics, 30*, 590–601.
- Polio, C. (2001). Research methodology in second language writing: The case of text-based studies. In T. Silva & P. K. Matsuda (Eds.), *On second language writing* (pp. 91–116). Mahwah, NJ: Erlbaum.
- Verspoor, M., Schmid, M. S., & Xu, X. (2012). A dynamic usage based perspective on L2 writing. *Journal of Second Language Writing, 21*, 239–263.
- Wolfe-Quintero, K., Inagaki, S., & Kim, H. Y. (1998). *Second language development in writing: Measures of fluency, accuracy, and complexity.* (Technical Report #17). Honolulu: National Foreign Language Resource Center.

Accuracy

- Evans, N. W., Hartshorn, K. J., Cox, T. L., & Martin de Jel, T. (2014). Measuring written linguistic accuracy with weighted clause ratios: A question of validity. *Journal of Second Language Writing, 24*, 33–50.
- Polio, C. (1997). Measures of linguistic accuracy in second language writing research. *Language Learning, 47*, 101–143.
- Polio, C. & Shea, M. (2014). An investigation into current measures of linguistic accuracy in second language writing research. *Journal of Second Language Writing, 24*, 10–27.

Complexity

- Biber, D., Gray, B., & Poonpon, K. (2011). Should we use characteristics of conversation to measure grammatical complexity in L2 writing development? *TESOL Quarterly, 45*, 5–35.
- Bulté, B. & Housen, A. (2012). Defining and operationalising L2 complexity. In A. Housen, F. Kuiken, & I. Vedder (Eds.), *Dimensions of L2 performance and proficiency: Investigating complexity, accuracy and fluency in SLA* (pp. 21–46). Amsterdam and Philadelphia: John Benjamins.
- Lu, X. (2012). A corpus-based evaluation of syntactic complexity measures as indices of college-level ESL writers' language development. *TESOL Quarterly, 45*, 36–62.
- Pallotti, G. (2014). A simple view of linguistic complexity. *Second Language Research, 31*, 117–134
- Rimmer, W. (2006). Measuring grammatical complexity: The Gordian knot. *Language Testing, 23*, 497–519.

Lexical Measures

- Jarvis, S. (2013). Capturing the diversity in lexical diversity. *Language Learning, 63*(Suppl. 1), 87–106.
- Lu, X. (2012). The relationship of lexical richness to the quality of ESL learners' oral narratives. *The Modern Language Journal, 96*, 190–208.
- McCarthy, P. M. & Jarvis, S. (2010). MTLD, vocd-D, and HD-D: A validation study of sophisticated approaches to lexical diversity assessment. *Behavior Research Methods, 42*, 381–392.
- Yu, G. (2010). Lexical diversity in writing and speaking task performances. *Applied Linguistics, 31*, 236–259.

Fluency

- Abdel Latif, M.M.M. (2012). What do we mean by writing fluency and how can it be validly measured? *Applied Linguistics, 34*, 99–105.

7

TARGET TEXT ANALYSIS

Much L2 writing research focuses not on learner texts but on target texts that are usually published in some appropriate venue and often, but not always, written by native speakers. A large portion of this work has been conducted using a Swalesian (e.g., Swales, 1990, 2004) approach to explain the discourse moves and accompanying language in genres such as research articles or business reports. For example, one might describe the various parts and subparts (i.e., *moves* and *steps*) of the literature review to a research article. With the growth of corpus methods, more and more research analyzes texts for specific grammatical structures, vocabulary, or phrases. Other research may analyze published articles or dissertations focusing on the function of certain structures such as integral citations (i.e., citations in which the author's name appears outside of the parentheses). What most of these analyses of nonlearner texts have in common is the goal of making features of specific genres explicit to L2 writers or to teachers of L2 writers. Some studies analyze genres without directly discussing teaching implications, but most of the research that we discuss in this chapter seems intended to benefit the teaching of writing (and reading) to L2 learners. In this chapter, we detail the purposes that researchers have for analyzing target texts, classify the various types of analyses that have been done, and discuss issues that researchers need to consider when planning such research. We end with a discussion of a focal study.

Purposes for Analyzing Target Texts

Much of the research discussed in this chapter is published in the *Journal of English for Academic Purposes* and *English for Specific Purposes*, so one would expect that the goal of analyzing nonlearner texts is to help students write, or read, those texts; however, exceptions, such as the analysis of suicide notes published in *Journal of*

English for Academic Purposes (Samraj & Gawron, 2015), can be found. Outside the field of L2 writing, texts are analyzed for a variety of features, but many of these analyses are not terribly useful to language students or teachers. For example, Paradis and Eeg-Olofsson (2013) examined the language used to express sensory perceptions in wine reviews. Of course, one could think of contexts where a second language learner might need to know how to talk or write about wine, but the researchers did not seem to have that audience in mind. Suicide notes and wine reviews aside, a great many descriptive studies of nonlearner texts are intended to benefit the field of L2 writing, either by asking a specific research question that attempts to describe some feature of the texts or by comparing different sets of text (see Table 7.1).

Studies that describe the target texts in some way may ask very different types of questions. For example, Yang and Allison (2003) investigated the relationship between the results, discussion, conclusion, and implications sections of 20 applied linguistics articles from four different journals. They argued that the distinction among sections is not always clear; for example, commentary may be included in the results sections of articles. (See the discussion of Lim, 2010 later in the chapter for more on this topic.) These types of studies simply describe a genre, in this case using a Swalesian move analysis, but Yang and Allison, like others, clearly had a pedagogical purpose in mind. They stated:

> Academic reading and writing courses for EFL postgraduates and novice teachers in applied linguistics could draw attention to the kind of flexibility involved in these stages of RA [research article] structure and encourage students to discuss the rationale behind this flexibility, as well as the adequacy or otherwise of our and others' attempts to describe it.
>
> *(p. 381)*

The running theme throughout much of the research on target texts is how to help draw learner and novice writers' attention to conventions and variations of specific genres.

Studies whose purpose is to describe texts vary, however, in the extent to which they consider pedagogy. Simpson-Vlach and Ellis (2010) created an academic formulas list based on a corpus of written (and oral) academic texts, and although they stated that such a list is pedagogically important, it is beyond the scope of their article and many others in this category to link the description of texts to actual ways to teach. Bloch (2009), however, went a step beyond describing and developed pedagogical materials that he tested to help students understand how reporting verbs are used in academic discourse.

A large number of the studies that describe target texts are in some ways causal-comparative studies (see Chapter 3). They ask questions that compare texts from different fields, genres or sections of a genre, journals, modalities, languages, or populations of writers, but they may or may not use inferential

TABLE 7.1 Sample Studies That Analyze Target Texts

Citation	Texts	Research questions	Comments
Yang & Allison (2003)	• 20 randomly chosen empirical articles from four applied linguistics journals published in 1996 and 1997	1. What is the relationship between the results, discussion, conclusion, and implication sections of applied linguistics articles?	• The journals were quite different in scope (e.g., *Applied Linguistics* vs. *ELT Journal*). • The segmenting of the articles into sections is clearly described. • No intercoder reliability was reported. • Problems with coding are noted in the article. • Chi-square was used.
Simpson-Vlach & Ellis (2010)	• Hyland (2004) research article corpus of 1.2 million words as British National corpus of academic article and textbooks (just below one million words) • Michigan Corpus of Spoken Academic English (1.7 million words) • British National Corpus of academic speech (431,000 words) • A comparison corpus of nonacademic writing and speech	1. How can a list of academic formulaic expressions be created using criteria other than only frequency?	• The corpora used are fully described. • Formulae were identified by frequency and mutual information scores. • Experienced teachers and test writers rated the formulae on their cohesiveness and importance of the phrases for teaching.
Bloch (2009)	• Articles from *Science* (600,000 words) • A set of student texts	1. How can one develop a concordance program from authentic texts to help students use reporting verbs in their writing?	• Sentences from the corpus were selected for the teaching materials. • The article mostly describes the creation of the materials but includes a short assessment of the program.

(Continued)

TABLE 7.1 (Continued)

Citation	Texts	Research questions	Comments
Samraj (2005)	• 12 articles each from *Animal Behaviour* and *Conservation Biology*	1. What are the similarities and differences between abstracts and research articles in two subfields of environmental science?	• The author includes an extensive discussion of why she chose the two fields that she did.
Millar, Budgell, & Fuller (2013)	• 297 reports of randomized clinical trials from the top five ranking medical journals	1. How does the frequency of passive constructions vary between journals and between the sections of articles? 2. What, if any, relationship exists between the frequency of use of the passive and the frequency of use of first-person pronouns? 3. Which verbs are most strongly associated with passive usage? (p. 397)	• The corpus and the retrieval of constructions are carefully described. • The authors looked at all occurrences of verbs and included the total frequency, not only passive tokens. • The number of reports containing each passive verb were noted, referred to here as *dispersion* but in other articles as *range*.
Yin (2015)	• A 21,623-word corpus of radio news broadcasts from New Zealand • A 21,101-word corpus of New Zealand newspaper articles	1. What are the forms of linking adverbials in news settings? What are the frequency patterns of the identified forms? Is there any difference in use of form between written and broadcast news? 2. How can linking adverbials be classified in terms of meaning in news settings? What are the frequency patterns of the identified meaning categories? Is there any difference in use of meaning between written and broadcast news? 3. How are linking adverbials positioned in news settings? What are the frequency patterns of the identified positions? Is there any difference in use of position between written and broadcast news? (p. 4)	• The data set is clearly described. • The author details why handcoding as opposed to automated coding was done. • The study includes a discussion of unit-of-analyses issues when comparing oral and written language. • No intercoder reliability is reported.

Study	Data	Research questions	Methodology notes
Hu & Wang (2014)	• Four parallel corpora in two languages (English and Chinese) and two fields (medicine and applied linguistics) consisting of 84 research articles	1. Are there differences/similarities in citation density, writer stance, textual integration, and author integration between RAs from applied linguistics and general medicine? 2. Are there differences/similarities in the aforementioned aspects of citation between RAs written in Chinese and English? 3. Is there a discipline/language interaction on the aforementioned aspects of citation? (pp. 17–18)	• The authors randomly sampled articles to ensure a range of research approaches in both fields. • The authors did not consider the background of the authors (i.e., they did not eliminate Chinese authors who had studied in English-speaking countries). • The comparability of journals across languages is discussed, including the authors' attempt to find parallel journals. • High-inference categories were used in coding, but acceptable intercoder reliability is reported.
Gil-Salom & Soler-Monreal (2014)	• The literature reviews from 10 Spanish and 10 English computing dissertations from Spain and England, respectively	1. How do Spanish and English writers of computing dissertations structure and position themselves in literature reviews?	• The authors used Kwan's (2006) model of research articles, which was adapted from Swales (1990). • Both moves and evaluative markers were coded. • No intercoder reliability is reported.
van Mulken & van der Meer (2005)	• Inquiries from a fake potential customer were sent to 40 Dutch and American companies by email. • 24 responses were received and used in the analysis.	1. Do American and Dutch companies differ in their replies to customer inquiries via email? (p. 97)	• The email replies were coded inductively to determine which moves emerged as common across emails. • The language used to achieve the moves is described without quantification.

(Continued)

TABLE 7.1 (Continued)

Citation	Texts	Research questions	Comments
Chen & Baker (2010)	• The British Academic Written English Corpus, consisting of a set of L1 Chinese and a set of L1 English essays • The Freiburg–Lancaster–Olso/Bergen corpus's subset of published academic English	1. How do student writers and L2 learners of English differ in their use of lexical bundles when compared to writers of published academic articles?	• The choice, composition, and size of the corpora are fairly well described. • Four-word lexical bundles that appeared at least four times in at least three texts were identified. • The authors included a fairly lengthy discussion of bundle identification. • The bundles are described with regard to structure and function, and no intercoder reliability is reported. • The authors used type frequencies as opposed to tokens in their results.
Gardner & Nesi (2012)	• A corpus of "assessed proficient university student writing" (p. 32) from undergraduate and graduate students across a wide range of fields • The 6.5 million-word corpus included 2,858 assignments from over 1,000 students.	1. How can student writing completed for university assignments be classified into genre families?	• The taxonomy of genres was created through researcher classification and interviews with faculty and students. • Few details are given about the interviews, and readers are referred to less accessible papers.

statistics in their comparisons. Samraj's (2005) study compared both two academic subfields within environmental science (conservation biology and wildlife behavior) and two subgenres (the abstracts and introductions of research articles). Using a Swalesian move analysis, she found that abstracts and introductions were more similar to each other in conservation biology than in wildlife behavior. Millar, Budgell, and Fuller (2013) described the use of the passive and active voice in medical journals. The goal of their study was not only to provide a quantitative description of medical articles but also to determine the influence of style guidelines from different journals on the articles.

Some studies also compare modalities or even languages. Yin (2015), whose concern was teaching EFL journalism majors, compared corpora of written and oral news stories from New Zealand and found differences in the number and function of linking adverbials in the two genres. Hu and Wang (2014) compared citations across two disciplines (applied linguistics and medicine) and across languages (Chinese and English), focusing on a variety of citation characteristics including citation density and writer stance. They found differences in some of the characteristics across both disciplines and languages. Gil-Salom and Soler-Monreal (2014) also looked across languages by comparing the literature reviews of dissertations in computer science written in Spanish and English. They found overall that the structure of the literature reviews, analyzed using a move analysis, was quite similar across the two languages, yet the English writers used more varied strategies to accomplish the moves. In a business setting, van Mulken and van der Meer (2005) studied how American and Dutch companies replied to email requests and were able to explicate both similarities and differences. These studies that compare writing across languages or cultures are part of the field of *contrastive rhetoric*. This field began with impressionistic comparisons of texts (e.g., Kaplan, 1966) and evolved to use more sophisticated techniques (see the volume by Belcher & Nelson, 2013). Many studies now go beyond text analyses (Connor, 2004) by including additional analyses, and some of these are discussed in the next section.

Studies may also compare nonnative or student texts to published texts. Chen and Baker (2010) compared *lexical bundles* (i.e., words that tend to co-occur) in the writing of L2 learners, native speaker students, and published British academic writing. They found the native speaker novice writers shared some similarities with the L2 learners and some with the writers of published texts. Considering both the frequency and function of the lexical bundles, the researchers were able to show that the two groups of novices' texts were distinct from the published texts.

Finally, in addition to describing and comparing target *texts*, studies may describe target *tasks* with the goal of determining what is important for writing instruction to focus on. There are a variety of approaches to describing target tasks, but most focus on a content analysis of the assignments (e.g., Hale, Taylor, Bridgeman, Carson, Kroll, & Kantor, 1996) or assessment tasks (e.g., Dunworth, 2008) as opposed to students' texts. Gardner and Nesi (2012), however, took a different approach and examined student texts from a database of student academic writing. They developed a classification system based on the purpose of the writing in which one genre family includes several different more traditional types (e.g., a narrative recount includes an accident report, an account of a website search, a plot synopsis, and an urban ethnography, among others).

Types of Target Text Analyses

The types of analyses used among researchers vary depending on the focus of their study; Table 7.2 summarizes the various approaches. A great many studies have taken a Swalesian approach to analyzing target texts, likely because this

TABLE 7.2 Types of Analyses

Technique	Sample foci of studies	Example
Move analysis		
Analysis of moves and steps only	The introduction to research articles across languages	Loi (2010)
Move analysis combined with lexical bundle analysis	The relationship between lexical bundles and the moves from research articles in which they occur	Cortes (2013)
Move analysis combined with a functional analysis of language	How stance is expressed in the conclusions of research articles	Loi, Lim, & Wharton (2016)
Move analysis combined with interviews	The relationship between texts and how knowledge is constructed	Kuteeva & McGrath (2013)
Move analysis combined with ethnography	The process of text construction	Flowerdew & Wan (2010)
Corpus analyses		
Word frequency counts	Words that exist in an academic field	Valipouri & Nassaji (2013)
Lexical bundle analysis	The differences in phrases across different academic fields	Ackermann & Chen (2013)
Analysis of co-occurring features in text types	How features group together in and across different genres	Biber & Conrad (2009)
Analysis of a specific feature	Citations	Kwan & Chan (2014)
	Specific structure	Zhang (2015)
Multimodal research	Translingual literacy practices on a social media site	Barton & Lee (2012)
Automated quantitative analysis of features	Cohesion and relativization	Hall, McCarthy, Lewis, Lee, & McNamara (2007) Hundt, Dennison, & Schneider (2012)

approach results in an analysis that can be used by teachers and students in teaching and learning how to write specific genres. Several studies have combined a Swalesian move analysis with additional data. Other schools of genre analysis, including the Sydney School and the New Rhetoric approaches (see Hyon, 1996, for a discussion of the different approaches to genre), are discussed later in this chapter. The second type of studies in Table 7.2 uses a corpus approach by quantitatively analyzing large amounts of data. The third type, which for lack of a better term we have categorized as a type of feature analysis, is more narrow and focuses on a particular feature. We end with an example of a multimodal study and two studies that use quantitative measures. Although these last studies may be of less interest to L2 writing instructors, they are included because they represent additional ways to analyze texts.

Move-Step Analyses

Swales (1990, 2004) approached the analysis of research articles not only by looking at the language used in the articles but also by analyzing the rhetorical moves and steps. Swales (2004) defines move as "a discoursal or rhetorical unit that performs a coherent communicative function in a written or spoken discourse" (p. 228). One example of this type of analysis is Loi (2010), who examined the introductions to research articles in Chinese and in English. Sampling 20 articles each from English and Chinese educational psychology journals, Loi first coded the moves into categories from Swales's (1990, 2004) *create a research space* (CARS) model: *establishing a territory, establishing a niche*, and *presenting the present work*. Within each of the three moves, steps were identified. For example, in *establishing a territory*, two of the steps included *defining terms/concepts* and *presenting the theoretical basis*. Through this analysis, Loi was able to determine that certain steps found in English articles were not found in Chinese articles. In presenting examples of the steps, Loi noted the language used but did not quantify the vocabulary or phrases in any way. In an additional step, she analyzed the sequence of moves across the two languages. As in many studies using move analysis, Loi did not report intercoder reliability or discuss coding problems, issues to which we return in the next section; however, she did provide clear examples of the steps that she coded. While this type of analysis is most commonly used in the study of research articles, it can be applied to other types of writing as well, including workplace writing, as in Flowerdew and Wan (2010, discussed later) or Ding (2007), who looked at application essays.

Move analyses can be combined with other types of analyses that focus either on the language used in the texts or on the participants who created the texts. For example, Cortes (2013) examined lexical bundles of four or more words found in the introduction to research articles from 13 different fields (with a corpus of just over a million words) and linked them to the moves and steps found in research article introductions. What sets Cortes's study apart from others is that she started by identifying lexical bundles through a corpus analysis and then looked at the functions of the bundles in terms of their moves and steps. For example, the bundles *has been shown to, has been shown to be, have been shown* to, and *it has been shown that* appeared only in Move 1, Step 2 (*making topic generalizations*). Cortes used the predetermined moves and steps from Swales and had a second coder identify the moves and steps. This paper is methodologically interesting because the bundles are identified first and are thus the primary *unit of analysis* (also discussed in Chapter 6), but then the functions are described using a Swalesian analysis.

Loi, Lim, and Wharton (2016) conducted a move-step analysis of the conclusions to English and Malay research articles. After identifying three moves containing various steps, they added a second-level analysis that focused on the writers' stance. In brief, they used Martin and Rose's (2003) appraisal theory, related to systemic functional linguistics (see Chapter 11), to examine the stance used in the various moves. They use a complex scheme with many categories and subcategories, but to give one example from their study, the clause *Hopefully, future researchers will jointly assess how people recall all the three classes of events we mentioned* . . . (p. 4) includes the word *hopefully*, which indicates an attitude (category) of appreciation (subcategory). Through the two analyses, they were able to present a more detailed description of the similarities and differences between English and Malay research articles. Unfortunately, the coding system is very complex and no intercoder reliability is given, a point addressed further in the next section, so it is difficult to determine if their coding could be used in other studies. Note also that drawing on systemic functional linguistics (which links structure and functions with contextual factors) to describe texts is an inherent part of the Sydney School of genre analysis (e.g., Martin & Rose, 2003).

One concern about move-step analyses is that they examine only texts and thus have to make assumptions about the writers' intentions, so the researchers cannot clarify the writers' reasons for making the various rhetorical choices that they do. Some studies have therefore combined a Swalesian analysis with qualitative data. Kuteeva and McGrath (2013), taking a somewhat novel departure in genre studies, examined articles from pure mathematics. Through a move analysis, they were able to determine which moves were and were not similar to research articles in other areas; for example, *establishing a niche* was optional. Yet their concern was not only the structure of the article but also the connection "between the rhetorical and organizational structure of the research articles and the knowledge making-practices of the pure mathematics academic community" (p. 218) Thus, the researchers interviewed five of the authors of the articles and shared their analyses with them for comments. Through these interviews, the authors of the articles confirmed, for example, Kuteeva and McGrath's finding that, instead of establishing a niche in the introduction, authors of mathematics articles state the results. Furthermore, the informants explained the process of writing a pure mathematics paper: One starts with a result that is known to be true. This method of combining text analysis with interviews seems particularly appropriate when investigating a field that is very different from one's own and helps confirm researchers' analyses.

Flowerdew and Wan (2010) conducted a genre analysis of audit reports written in Hong Kong, drawing on concepts from the New Rhetoric School (Hyon, 1996), including supplementing text analysis with ethnographic data (see Chapter 4) to better understand the construction of the texts. They conducted a genre analysis outlining the moves in the reports and observed the auditors conducting the audit and finalizing the report. Interviews were also conducted with auditors. Among the researchers' observations were the reliance on a template for the reports and reasons for diverging from the template.

Corpus Analyses

The various move studies involve some type of coding of texts, whereas other studies use large corpora and rely on a computational analysis of the data. In addition to Cortes (2013), discussed earlier, others have used large corpora to analyze texts with the hopes of improving instruction for L2 writing (and reading). Valipouri and Nassaji (2013) created a corpus of more than four million words from the introduction, methods, results, and discussion sections of chemistry articles from four subfields. Through their corpus analysis, they were able to determine words that appeared frequently in their corpus but did not appear in the general service list or academic word list. A different approach was taken by Ackermann and Chen (2013), who used a corpus of more than 25 million words to look at lexical bundles across 28 academic fields. Their study is noteworthy because of the detail and clarity with which they describe their method. In addition to explaining the quantitative calculation, they explained the other three stages of analysis, including a manual inspection of the bundle list, an expert review to determine pedagogical relevance, and systematizing the list (e.g., putting verbs into the infinitive form).

No discussion of corpus approaches would be complete without a discussion of the work of Douglas Biber and his colleagues. His approach to analyzing texts is best summarized in Biber and Conrad (2009). Briefly, their approach is to compare texts (both oral and written) on a variety of features that are related to functional differences; for example, a newspaper article uses the past tense more often than an academic article because reporting is one of the functions realized in the news story. Through statistical analysis, researchers show how these features bundle together to create *dimensions*. One dimension is *oral versus literate language*. With regard to academic written language, Biber and Conrad found that university institutional writing has more of the features associated with literate language than textbooks. They also reported on a study comparing the writing in English textbooks across fields and found that humanities textbooks contained more features associated with narrative discourse (e.g., past tense verbs and third-person pronouns) than natural science textbooks. This type of analysis, often called *a multidimensional analysis*, has also been applied to learner texts (e.g., Friginal & Weigle, 2014) as a way to examine students' linguistic development.

Feature Analyses

Some studies consider only one feature of a text and provide a detailed analysis of that feature. Zhang (2015) investigated one grammatical structure, extraposition. These are sentences that use an impersonal pronoun to introduce a that–clause or infinitive clause (e.g., *It is known that students have difficulty with citation. It is too easy to claim that this is the cause*). The main clause contains the writer's stance and the dependent or infinitive clause contains the proposition. Zhang used a corpus of 20 academic and 20 popular texts evenly spread among the humanities, social sciences, natural sciences, and technology. Each corpus was a little over 85,000 words. She found that extraposition was more common in academic texts than popular texts. She further analyzed the function of extraposition and found some differences in frequency across the two text types. In addition to grammatical features, many other studies have examined citations because citation practices are known to vary across fields (e.g., Hyland, 1999) in terms of both form and function. Kwan and Chan (2014) examined the results and discussion sections from 40 published information science articles. They noted that students often have difficulty relating the results of their studies to previous research and that while many have studied citation practices in literature reviews, few have looked at how citations are used to build knowledge in the results and discussions sections. They coded each citation segment according to the move it was carrying out (e.g., *demonstrating methodological rigor, qualifying the claims*). This descriptive study provides a framework for students to analyze articles from their own fields.

Other Types of Analyses

We end with two types of studies that are quite different than the ones discussed earlier and less common with regard to their types of analyses. Although they may be of less interest to L2 writing researchers because of the unclear relationship to pedagogy, they nevertheless represent new ways to analyze texts. Barton and Lee (2012) conducted an analysis of writing practices on Flickr in an examination of what they, and others, call *vernacular literacy*. They analyzed not only the written language used on Flickr but the layout, including fonts and tags, as well as how the participants categorized their photos. Barton and Lee also interviewed the Flickr authors and reported on their multilingual practices on Flickr. While most writing instruction does not focus on Flickr, there is an increasing interest in the use of social media in language teaching (e.g., Benson, 2015; Mompean & Fouz-González, 2016), and this study represents an example of multimodal text analysis (see also the discussion of multimodal discourse analysis in Chapter 11).

The final type of text analyses that we mention are studies that use complex automated analyses of texts. Such analyses can provide insight into text complexity and can be used to analyze learner texts (see Chapter 6), but at this point do not seem to offer any insight into teaching text features. One example is Hall, McCarthy, Lewis, Lee, and McNamara (2007) who used the computational tool Coh-Metrix to analyze British and American legal texts. This tool has been used to measure text readability as well as to measure developmental factors in learner texts. Hall et al. say that they hope the results will offer English for specific purposes materials developers useful information, but some of the indices they examine, such as the density of various parts of speech (i.e., incidence per 1,000 words) are not conducive to teaching. Hundt, Denison, and Schneider (2012) also used an automated analyzer to investigate relative clause complexity in British and American science texts (as well as their change over time) including the frequency of occurrence of different relative clause types as well as their contribution to syntactic complexity. Again, although the implications of their findings do not have obvious implications for teaching writing, the study provides an alternate way to analyze target texts.

Issues Involved in Analyzing Target Texts

Determining Representative Texts

In most target text research, there is a tacit assumption that published articles exemplify good writing or, at least, writing that we want L2 learners to approximate. However, in one of his analyses of research article introductions, Swales (1990) noted that some articles do not conform to his model, suggesting that not all published articles are of equal quality. In fact, he stated that his analysis highlighted some of the ambiguity in the introductions and claimed that had the authors followed the standard CARS model, the introduction would have been "tidier and easier to process" (p. 164). By rewriting a few sentences, Swales was able to show how a revised and improved version of the text better fit his model. Furthermore, among specific scholarly communities, the writing quality in some journals may be perceived to be better than the writing quality in other journals. Bloch (2009) stated that he chose *Science* because the articles were known to be of high quality, but other studies to not specifically mention the quality of the publications' research or writing. Furthermore, there is an assumption that the writers of published works are experts in their field. This raises the question as to the extent to which we should consider student texts when describing genres. Gardner and Nesi (2013), discussed earlier, looked at student texts to create a genre classification system. They stated that although the student essay is "a less valued genre" (p. 28), it represents a different purpose for writing (i.e., to demonstrate acquired knowledge) than the research article. Several studies have considered MA theses (e.g., Samraj, 2008) and PhD dissertations (e.g., Petrić, 2012), but note that Petrić separated low- and high-rated dissertations, with the high-rated dissertations being the target text. Connor and Mauranen (1999) conducted an analysis of grant proposals but did not distinguish between those that had been funded and those that had not been. Presumably, the assumption is that anyone submitting a grant proposal is an expert in his or her field.

When Swales (1990) found deviations in some of the research article introductions, he questioned whether the author might be inexperienced or did not see a need to establish a territory, presumably because the author was more experienced. It is obvious that many background factors will influence rhetorical style, but most of the studies discussed in this chapter, with the exception of those that use additional data sources such as interviews, do not consider the writers' backgrounds. It is interesting that Connor and Mauranen's (1999) study of grant proposals used only proposals in English from Finnish researchers, yet the characteristics of this specific population are not discussed. Loi (2010) is the only study discussed in this chapter that limited the authors of the articles studied to native speakers (both English and Chinese). Recall that she compared English and Chinese articles, so if she had included Chinese writers writing in English, such writers may have used some of the conventions found in Chinese writing. It is, however, inappropriate to assume that the writing of nonnative speakers is less likely to conform to discourse norms than the writing of native speakers when, in fact, expert nonnative speakers likely understand the writing conventions of their field better than most native-speaker novices.

For crosslinguistic comparisons, however, it seems important to consider the background and native language of the writers, as in Loi et al. (2016). Yet this study raises other issues related to crosslinguistic comparisons. Such comparisons could be very helpful if L2 writers could see explicated differences in writing between their L1 and L2, but finding appropriate comparisons may be challenging. The field of contrastive rhetoric developed from the idea different cultures write differently, yet the concern has been that there is as much variation within languages as across languages. Casanave (2004) provides an excellent review and explains, using an example from Hinds (1987) and citing Kubota (1997), that we cannot represent Japanese writing by analyzing only a single genre (newspaper columns); Japanese discourse structure, of course, will vary across genres. There might also be differences that make comparisons difficult even within that one genre: for example, letters to the editor in *the New York Times* and a local newspaper. Finding comparable genres *across* languages is likely to be even more challenging. Loi (2010) discussed this problem in relation to previous studies:

> Past studies which compared rhetorical organisation across two different cultures have been criticised for not considering the comparability of genres, authorships and journals under investigation. For instance, Ostler's (1987) study comparing Arabic native ESL speakers' essays and published English texts was criticised by Swales on the basis that the two genres were not compared equally across texts and expectations. Shim (2005) criticised Lee's (2001) study on the basis that Lee's corpora of published RAs and graduate students' writing were not comparable in terms of authorship and

also on the basis that Lee's corpora of experimental and theoretical papers were not comparable in terms of genre. Berkenkotter and Huckin's (1995) study also did not investigate comparable journals. They selected their corpus from specialised journals and interdisciplinary journals.

(p. 269)

Loi took detailed steps in her study to assure that her English and Chinese corpora were similar.

Coding and Reporting

Some of the studies discussed in this chapter used automated coding to examine certain features such as lexical bundles, which cannot be handcoded, or a relatively easy structure for the computer to identify using a syntactic parser. Nevertheless, many studies include human judgment as a follow up to automated analyses. In their construction of their academic phrase list, Simpson-Vlach and Ellis (2010) showed the list to EAP instructors to determine if the extracted lexical bundles constituted a perceivable phrase or not. Zhang (2015) used a syntactic parser to extract *it*-extraposition clauses but then manually checked the data and excluded a few of the examples tagged by the program.

Coding by hand is often a two-step process. First, one has to determine the structure or unit to be coded (i.e., *the unit of analysis*), and then one has to determine how to code the function of that structure. For some types of feature analyses, the unit of analysis is clear. Hu and Wang (2014) and Kwan and Chan (2014) examined citations, which are easily identifiable, but identifying moves and steps can be much more challenging. Swales's (2004) definition of a move as "a discoursal or rhetorical unit that performs a coherent communicative function in a written or spoken discourse" is somewhat difficult to operationalize, and it is even more difficult to determine how one breaks down a move into steps, which Swales says supports the function of the moves. In their move-step analysis, Loi et al. (2016) cited Swales and Feak's (2000) definition of a move, saying that it is a "defined and bounded communicative act that is designed to achieve one main communicative objective" (p. 3). The problem here is that communicative acts do not correspond to specific structures and can be as short as one word (e.g., as with a one-word hedge) or several pages long (e.g., when making references to past studies). This does not invalidate the notion of moves or steps but rather makes them difficult to delineate and count. Although the studies we reviewed did not directly discuss the issue of one function corresponding to a variety of units, one of the studies discussed the reverse: One unit can represent a variety of functions. Yang and Allison (2003) explained:

We were aware that a segment of text might have more than one function. In such a situation, it is analyzed in terms of the most salient purpose.

However, in some contexts, the salient purpose can still be difficult to identify. Hence, the analysis of the data involved repeated readings, making use not only of lexical signals, which include all the linguistic elements with signaling functions such as lexical items, metatextual expressions and discourse markers in the immediate context, but also of such clues in other parts of the RA, taking into account the overall purpose of the section and RA, and the propositional meaning of the text segment.

(p. 371)

Yang and Allison provided the most thorough discussion of the studies reviewed here related to problems quantifying moves and steps, discussing this issue in great detail. Nevertheless, they still provided quantitative data and referred to the number of times different moves and steps occur. One possible way to deal with this problem is to follow Samraj (2005), who counted the *types* of moves as opposed to each individual occurrence (i.e., the *tokens*). For example, one could consider whether or not one specific section of research article included at least one example of a specific move or step. Pho (2008) also addressed the problem of coding moves and steps, saying:

A major problem in most studies of abstracts (and also in studies of research articles following Swales's, 1990, approach) is that the identification of move seems to be based on both a bottom–up approach and a top–down approach. The description "bottom–up" means that researchers distinguish moves on the basis of certain linguistic signals. "Top–down" means they do this on the basis of content. For example, Anderson and Maclean (1997) identify the *Conclusion* move of the medical abstract by signals such as present tense and certain nouns and verbs. At the same time, they also rely on their intuitive interpretations of content. They then point to those particular lexical and grammatical items as characteristic of this move. This results in a circularity of the identification of rhetorical moves and linguistic realizations.

(p. 234)

She then said in a footnote that one reviewer commented that the process is cyclical and not circular in that researchers first identify content clues to code and then modify their judgments based on the language. Pho (2008) began by coding the types of moves found in article abstracts and reported a high reliability for coding, but this raises the question of which features can be reliably coded and whether or not all types of text analyses can be analyzed quantitatively with inferential statistics.

Some of the studies reviewed here reported intercoder reliability and some did not. We believe that if quantitative results, such as those comparing languages or academic fields, are presented, intercoder reliability needs to be established and reported (for a discussion of this issue in qualitative coding, see Chapter 10). Hu and Wang (2014) coded citations by assigning each citation three codes, one each for writer stance, textual integration, and author integration. They reported an overall acceptable intercoder reliability but did not report reliability for the individual codes. Whether a citation is integral requires no judgment, whereas determining the writers' stance does. Nevertheless, they were clearer than many studies in explaining their coding. Cortes (2013) reported a strong intercoder reliability, but she was not coding for total moves; rather, she coded each lexical bundle for the move and step it appeared in. Gil-Salom and Soler-Monreal (2014) coded for moves in the literature reviews of English and Spanish computer science dissertations without reporting any intercoder reliability. They did not provide many examples, and, like Samraj (2005), they reported only whether or not a move and step, which they called a *strategy*, was used at all. Their results were reported quantitatively along with many examples, but they did not do inferential statistics. Loi et al. (2016), who did not report reliability, also presented their results comparing English and Malay articles quantitatively without doing inferential statistics.

If one chooses to do inferential statistics, the choice of which to use is not always clear. Some studies (e.g., Yang & Allison, 2003) use a chi-square test to determine if difference across sections of research articles are significant, but one assumption of a chi-square test is that the observations (i.e., occurrences of a feature) are independent. Because several occurrences of a feature can come from one text, they cannot be considered independent. Thus, more corpus studies are opting to use *log-likelihood*, a statistic that compares the occurrences of a feature across corpora (http://ucrel.lancs.ac.uk/llwizard.html). In addition, log-likelihood is better for small sample sizes (Schmitt, 2010) and comparing different-sized corpora (Rayson, Berridge, & Francis, 2004).

Whether or not results are quantitatively analyzed, clear descriptions with examples of coding are essential (see also Chapter 10). Much of the research on target texts compares texts from different fields or authors, and we cannot compare studies unless we know that they are examining the same phenomenon. The issue of clear and reliable coding is often discussed in the context of replication (see Polio, 2012; Porte, 2012, and Chapter 12) in that another researcher has to know details of the coding process to be able to replicate a study.

Related to the issue of coding is that the reliance on one data source can sometimes be problematic. The addition of other data sources such as interviews or observations, as discussed in some of the studies already mentioned, can help researchers triangulate their data (see Chapter 4) and confirm findings determined from analyses of the target texts. A special issue of the *Journal of English for Academic Purposes* on 25 years of genre studies did not explicitly discuss the use of additional sources, but one study (Guinda, 2015) used interviews to supplement an analysis of graphic journal abstracts. Guinda's focus was on move trends and the communities' reactions to those trends, so the interviews were an essential part of the study. We highlight also Kuteeva and McGrath (2013), whose use of interviews allowed them to study a genre that was relatively unknown to them.

Overemphasis on Academic and English Texts

Given that many involved in language teaching work in academic contexts, it is not surprising that most of the studies reviewed in this chapter focus on academic texts. Furthermore, as the *Journal of English for Academic Purposes* focuses on academic English, there is a venue for publishing a large number of academic text analyses. *English for Specific Purposes* also publishes text analyses, including many that focus on academic contexts. In fact, when we searched for genre analysis articles in the journal, the large majority were related to academic English. Two exceptions included Hafner (2010), who looked at barristers' opinions, and Yeung (2007), who looked at business reports. It is possible that writing researchers' lack of familiarity with other contexts prevents them from looking more closely at workplace writing or that the logistics of collecting workplace target texts pose too many challenges. However, it is not impossible to collect examples of workplace texts. van Mulken and van der Meer (2005), discussed earlier, took a novel approach to obtaining target texts. Instead of asking companies for copies of emails, they constructed an email request that was sent to 40 companies and then analyzed the replies. Gimenez (2006) also analyzed emails and has a helpful discussion of his data collection procedure.

In addition, all of the studies reviewed here have been about English. Three studies discussed in this chapter included other languages (i.e., Chinese, Spanish, and Malay in Gil-Salom & Soler-Monreal, 2014; Hu & Wang, 2014; and Loi et al., 2016, respectively), but all the studies compared the features under investigation to English texts, presumably to benefit L2 writers of English. Studies outside of language teaching and learning no doubt describe texts in other languages but with less emphasis on teaching the genre under consideration. Parodi (2014), for example, conducted a genre analysis of Spanish textbooks across disciplines, and while the study could inform the teaching of Spanish reading, the study is likely of little benefit to L2 writers, given that most students will not become textbook writers. Much has been written about the genre-based Georgetown University German program by Heidi Byrnes and her colleagues (e.g., Byrnes, Maxim, & Norris, 2010), yet much of that research focuses on student writing (e.g., Ryshina-Pankova & Byrnes, 2013) and not a detailed analysis of the texts used in the program. Thus, we end this section with a call for more text-based studies of languages other than English, with the goal of benefitting L2 writers of other languages.

How to Design a Text Analysis Study

When analyzing target texts, the choice of texts and coding scheme or corpus analysis will be driven by the research question. Nevertheless, sampling a representative set of texts is not easy, and deciding the details of how to code can be even more difficult. In addition, some authors choose to supplement the text analysis with other types of data. Each of these issues is addressed here.

Selection of Target Texts

When deciding on the texts to use, one needs to consider each of the following: size of the data set, source of the data set, and the background and qualification of the writers. The size of the sample for text analysis will vary depending on whether one is doing, for example, a corpus analysis of lexical bundles or whether one is doing a move-type analysis where handcoding is needed. For the former, generally at least a million words are needed if one is trying to determine common academic phrases, for example, but that is a rule of thumb. Chen and Baker (2010) in their study comparing L2 writers with published text included a lengthy discussion of issues related to corpus size and their rationale for the size of their corpus.

For a move-step or feature analysis, the researcher has to decide whether depth or breadth is important. If a study attempts to generalize about texts across a broad field such as chemistry, the researcher might want to collect a limited number of articles in several subareas and then several journals within each of the subareas. On the other hand, if one were interested in the organization of qualitative empirical articles about second language writing, the researcher might choose a limited number of journals that publish such articles and try to find a reasonable number of qualitative articles, maybe around 30, to analyze. Samraj (2005) used 12 articles each from two journals, which were intended to represent two subfields within environmental science, while Loi et al. (2016) chose one journal to represent psychology. Trying to generalize across a broad field can be problematic because of the variations among journals even within one field. Thus, when working in an area outside of one's expertise, it is best to consult with experts about which journals are the most representative. Furthermore, if the goal of the study is to benefit teaching, it is important to distinguish target texts for reading versus writing. In other words, if medical students, for example, are going to be practitioners and not researchers, they probably do not need to deconstruct articles from *the Journal of the American Medical Association* if they can understand the content.

Analysis

Once the target texts are selected, the researcher has to determine a coding scheme and decide whether any automated analyses can be done. Let us take as an example a study that investigates the function of non-integral citations (i.e., where the authors' names appear with the year of publication in parentheses) in applied linguistics articles. Even with a large data set, such structures can easily be identified by hand, whereas a grammatical structure such as relative clauses might be more quickly identified by a tool such AntConc (see suggestions for further reading at the end of the chapter). But even with automated tools, examples often have to be double-checked because of the limitations of syntactic parsers used to identify grammatical structures. Once the structure is identified, the researcher would review previous studies of citation for sample coding schemes and try to adapt them to a new data set. We recommend writing coding guidelines with examples as the new coding schemes are being developed. They should then be tested with a second coder and modified further until intercoder reliability is established.

Of course, automated extraction of features is not appropriate for many target text studies, especially when the initial unit of analysis is not obvious, such as with moves and steps, and the functional categories require high inference judgments, such as those examining the authors' stances. In these cases, it is especially important to provide many examples in the discussion of the coding so that other researchers can try to conduct similar coding with other data sets. As a side note, Swales' (1990) CARS model has been tested and modified over the years, so despite the fact that researchers using this model do not report coding reliability, because of the accumulated research we have an understanding of how literature reviews work across a range of fields. Another option the researcher has when coding for high inference categories is to use other data sources such as interviews with experts in the field from which the texts were collected or, better yet, with the authors of the texts (e.g., Kuteeva & McGrath, 2013).

If copious examples from the coding description are provided in the method section, quantified results can be presented without too much explanation. There are, however, choices that need to be made about describing and analyzing the quantified data. First, the researcher should consider whether the texts are best described using type or token counts. As mentioned earlier, some move-step studies quantified the number of texts that included any occurrence of a move (type count) while some quantified the total number of moves in the texts (token count). Not only will a type count be easier for achieving reliability, but it also eliminates the possibility of one text skewing the results because it has a large number of one particular move. Because presenting the token data may provide a fuller picture of the texts, many researchers choose to present both type and token data in their tables.

Finally, the process of drawing conclusions from the data will vary depending on the sample size and type of data collected. Statistical tests can be done with large enough sample sizes; however, as stated earlier, inferential statistics can be challenging to do on text data. We recommend consulting some of the sources on statistics for corpus linguistics in the suggestions for further reading. Studies that claim to be qualitative studies and that draw conclusions using only examples from the texts without any statistics must nevertheless support their analyses through a systematic and detailed discourse analysis, incorporation of additional data (such as interviews), or, preferably, both (for a discussion of qualitative discourse analyses of written texts, see Chapter 11).

BOX 7.1   FOCAL STUDY

Lim, J. M. (2010). Commenting on research results in applied linguistics and education: A comparative genre-based investigation. *Journal of English for Academic Purposes, 9,* 280–294.

Background

Crossdisciplinary differences are common across academic journal articles, and one area where they may vary is the extent to which research results are commented on in the results sections of journal articles. In addition, graduate supervisors find it difficult to give feedback to novice writers on the results sections of their papers, and novice researchers even have difficulty in separating findings from commentary while reading. The fields of education and applied linguistics were chosen for this study because they overlap somewhat with regard to their area of inquiry yet they are often intended for different audiences. Research on the frequency and form of commentary could help novice writers in their respective fields.

Research Questions

1. What are the similarities and/or differences between researchers in applied linguistics and those in education with respect to the frequencies with which they provide comments on their findings in the results sections of quantitative, qualitative, and mixed method research papers?
2. What linguistic mechanisms do researchers in applied linguistics and education use to make comments on their findings in their results sections? (p. 282)

Design

Fifteen journal articles from education and 15 from applied linguistics were selected from three high-impact journals in each field. Two quantitative studies, two qualitative studies, and one mixed method study were chosen. The results sections of the articles were analyzed using a Swalesian move-step analysis in which presentation of research results and commentary on the results were identified. In addition, the language used in the commentaries was identified.

Results

Four steps were identified within the commentary move, and these steps and the frequency of commentary differed between the disciplines but less so among research methods. The language used in formulating the different steps was also described.

Discussion of a Focal Article: Lim (2010)

In this study Lim investigated the results sections of research articles because of the concerns among graduate supervisors who often help students with the results section of their papers. He cited Basturkmen and Bitchener (2005) as saying that supervisors find it difficult to give feedback on the results sections of students' theses. Specifically, it is not clear how much commentary should be in the results section and how much should be saved for the discussion. Lim carefully delineated the texts for his analysis by including only empirical studies that separated the results from the discussion in some way in the published article. For example, the articles used in the analysis all had a section called *results, findings,* or *analysis of data* but not *results and discussion.* The headings for these different results sections are included in a table in the article.

Lim wanted to compare two different academic fields because previous research has shown that academic writing is not monolithic; many researchers have written about various types of crossdisciplinary differences including the types of quotations used (Hyland, 1999) and involvement features such as first-person pronouns (Chang & Swales, 1999). Lim chose the fields of applied linguistics and education because although there is some overlap, education articles can have a different audience, such as policymakers. One issue that he did not address is the diversity of both applied linguistics and education in terms of subfields within each field and the range of types of research, and it appears that there was no attempt to limit the subfields. Furthermore, each field has a large number of journals that not only publish on different topics but also publish in different formats (e.g., the level of detail on study design). From applied linguistics Lim chose *TESOL Quarterly, English for Specific Purposes,* and *Applied Linguistics.* From education, he chose *Educational Research, International Journal of Education Research,* and *Studies in Educational Evaluation.* He did not say how he chose these journals other than to say that they are high-impact journals. While this limited choice of journals in what he calls applied linguistics is not a major flaw in his study, we need to keep in mind that they do not represent the full picture of applied linguistics, and the education journals likely do not either. The choice of fields and journals illustrate the breadth versus depth problem, namely, *Should we sample broadly or deeply?* In other words, Lim could have focused more on one subtopic of applied linguistics, for example, sampling a range of journals related to second language acquisition. Alternatively, he could have chosen one journal each from a range of applied linguistics journals. There is no one right way to sample, but one must clearly describe the sampling process. Other researchers can then replicate his analysis using a different set of journals to see if the results hold.

In addition to making choices with regard to journals, Lim had to choose which articles to sample. He chose five articles from each of the six journals (two quantitative, two qualitative, and one mixed methods) for a total of 30 articles. He also provided his criteria for differentiating among the three types of research, but as we noted in Chapter 5, classifying a mixed methods study can be problematic.

The results sections of the articles were then coded for each commentary move found. For example, a commentary might follow a finding and begin with a phrase such as *our interpretation is that. . . .* As noted earlier in this chapter, coding moves can be challenging because the unit of analysis is not always clear. For example, in this case, a commentary move could include one or more sentences. Lim, however, gave a clear explanation, stating:

> Hence, a step constituting a segment might consist of a main clause or even several sentences insofar as its occurrence was not interrupted by any other rhetorical step. In cases where another step (made up of at least a matrix clause) was inserted, the commentary steps appearing immediately before and after it were considered as two separate occurrences of the same step.
>
> *(p. 238)*

Two raters coded the data. It appears that Lim's two raters worked together to identify the moves but then coded the specific type separately on all of the data, reaching an agreement of .865 using a kappa statistic, which is excellent. The types of commentary (or steps) included *giving reasons for the findings, expressing views on the findings, comparing findings with the literature,* and *making recommendations for future research.* Lim provided clear examples of each of these steps (although in the results and not the methods section of his article) and the language used to express them, which should allow other researchers to follow the same analysis with other data sets.

Lim compared the number and types of commentary between the two fields and across the three types of research using nonparametric statistics. He found similarities across research types but differences between the two fields: Applied linguistics articles accounted for 84.5 percent of the number of commentary moves, showing the education articles were largely devoid of comments in the results sections of the papers. He also found that the applied linguistics articles were similar to articles from computer science, as described by Posteguillo (1999).

Such cross-study comparisons are important yet sometimes misleading. Lim carefully described his analysis and reports reliability; however, the Posteguillo study was less clear on the analysis, although it did include the same four steps as Lim's study.

To summarize, sampling and analysis are the two most challenging aspects of describing target texts, and Lim explained both carefully. His description will allow researchers to consider research articles in other fields or to attempt to replicate his research with a larger and broader sample. Although not truly a mixed methods study, a term Lim uses in his abstract, the various examples help readers, including teachers and students, to understand the language used in the different steps. While the article may seem to be of interest only to those in education and applied linguistics, Lim's analysis can help raise awareness of one particular move that students and teachers have found vexing.

Suggestions for Further Reading

Swalesian Genre Analysis

- Bitchener, J. (2010). *Writing an applied linguistics thesis or dissertation: A guide to presenting empirical research.* London and New York: Palgrave Macmillan.
- Lancaster, Z., Aull, L., & Perales Escudero, M. D. (2015). The past and possible futures of genre analysis: An introduction to the special issue. *Journal of English for Academic Purposes, 19*, 1–5.
- Swales, J. M. (1990). *Genre analysis: English in academic and research settings.* Cambridge: Cambridge University Press.
- Swales, J. M. (2004). *Research genres: Exploration and application.* Cambridge: Cambridge University Press.
- Swales, J. & Feak, C. (2000). *English in today's research world: A writing guide.* Ann Arbor: University of Michigan Press.

Other Approaches to Genre Analysis

- Hyland, K. (2004). *Genre and second language writing.* Ann Arbor: University of Michigan Press.
- Hyon, S. (1996). Genre in three traditions: Implications for ESL. *TESOL Quarterly, 30*, 693–722.
- Martin, J. R. & Rose, D. (2003). *Working with discourse: Meaning beyond the clause.* London: Continuum.
- Martin, J. R. & Rose, D. (2005). Designing literacy pedagogy: Scaffolding democracy in the classroom. In R. Hasan, C. Matthiessen, & J. Webster (Eds.), *Continuing discourse on language: A functional perspective* (Vol. 1, pp. 251–280). London: Equinox Publishing Ltd.

- Rose, D. (2012). Genre in the Sydney school. In J. Gee & M. Handford (Eds.), *The Routledge handbook of discourse analysis* (pp. 209–225). London: Routledge/ Taylor Francis.

Corpus Approaches

- Belcher, D. & Nelson, G. (Eds.). (2013). *Critical and corpus-based approaches to intercultural rhetoric.* Ann Arbor: University of Michigan Press.
- Biber, D. & Conrad, S. (2009). *Register, genre, and style.* Cambridge, UK: Cambridge University Press.

8

RETROSPECTIVE AND INTROSPECTIVE METHODS

Retrospective and *introspective* methods are often used to describe various aspects of L2 learners' writing processes and revisions as well as how raters, teachers, or editors respond to L2 learners' texts. The most common retrospective method is a *stimulated recall* task. Stimulated recall tasks (or *retrospective verbal protocols*) involve having participants reflect on their behavior while looking at some type of reminder (the *stimulus*) of their behavior such as a video of their actions or a screen capture of their writing. The most common introspective method is a *think-aloud* task (also called *concurrent verbal protocol*), which asks participants to talk about what they are doing as they do it. In addition, a very small number of studies have participants reflect on their behavior in writing rather than orally. All of these methods can be implemented in a variety of ways and in combination with a variety of other techniques. What retrospective and introspective techniques have in common is that they try to describe cognitive processes that are normally not observable.

We begin this chapter with a discussion of why researchers want to get into the minds of their participants when studying L2 writing and then outline the varieties of retrospective and introspective methods. We note that there has been much debate about what can be considered true stimulated recalls or think alouds, and these issues are addressed in the second section. In the first section, focusing on purposes for using retrospective and introspective methods, we include a range of studies that some would not consider true stimulated recalls or think alouds. We next discuss the issues related to collecting and analyzing retrospective and introspective data. We end with a discussion of how to conduct a study and provide a description of a sample study.

Purposes for Collecting Retrospective and Introspective Data

Two recent books discuss in detail the history of think alouds and stimulated recall, namely, Bowles (2010) and Gass and Mackey (2016), respectively, but neither focuses on L2 writing studies. In L2 writing, retrospective and introspective methods have been used for a variety of reasons, but most commonly to study and describe some aspect of the writing process. Yang and Shi (2003), for example, focused on MBA students. The researchers began with a very general research question simply asking how students wrote summaries for their courses and addressed this question by having students think aloud as they wrote. Yang and Shi classified the participants' verbalizations and were able to identify a variety of strategies (e.g., *reviewing task requirements, reviewing what was written,* and *evaluating what was written*). They also asked a second question (see Table 8.1) that is more causal-comparative in nature regarding how the various strategies used by the participants were related to their backgrounds. Sasaki's (2004) longitudinal study of 11 Japanese writers over 3.5 years looked at changes in the writing quality and writing processes of students who had and had not studied abroad. She used stimulated recall to focus on changes in the students' writing strategies (e.g., *local planning, rhetorical refining*) over the course of the study.

Other studies have chosen to focus on one or more specific aspects of the writing process. Roca de Larios, Manchón, and Murphy (2001) used think-aloud protocols to focus on *formulation* problems (i.e., how one actually produces words and sentences to reflect what one wants to say). Their study too began with a general research question followed by causal-comparative questions: They asked how much time participants spent solving formulation problems but were also interested in what variables (e.g., proficiency level) affected the amount of time spent on the different types of formulation problems. Plakans (2009) also examined how students wrote but in the context of an integrated reading-writing test. From think-aloud protocols, she was able to determine whether or not students used discourse synthesis strategies (e.g., *selecting information from the reading, connecting ideas in the reading with one's own ideas*).

Sometimes retrospective and introspective methods focus on the effects of external factors, such as instruction, feedback, or collaboration, on the writing process. Abbuhl (2012) examined the effects of explicit instruction on the use of authorial presence markers (i.e., first-person pronouns vs. third-person pronouns and phrases) as compared to exposure without an explicit focus. In her experimental study, she analyzed not only how often these features were used in the students' texts but also whether or not students in the experimental groups commented on the features that were taught. Although she did not code the stimulated recall protocols, she used examples from the protocols to help interpret her quantitative results. Zhao (2010) used stimulated recall to better understand how

TABLE 8.1 Sample Studies That Use Retrospective and Introspective Methods

Citation	Participants, context, and writing task	Research questions	Comments
Yang & Shi (2003)	• Three native English speakers and three Chinese MBA students studying in Canada wrote summaries of two business cases.	1. How do individual ESL and NES MBA students write summaries for their course assignments? 2. Can their various uses of writing strategies be traced to the participants' language backgrounds, previous writing experiences, and perceptions of the nature of the task? (p. 169)	• Both think alouds and interviews were included. • Details of the training were not provided. • The participants could use their L1 or L2. • A detailed coding scheme is provided along with intercoder reliability.
Sasaki (2004)	• 11 university Japanese EFL students were followed for 3.5 years; six had studied abroad during that time. • Timed argumentative essays	1. What changes could be identified in their L2 writing strategy use? (p. 534)	• Participants were videotaped to show their hands and body. • The researcher paused the video when the students paused for longer than 3 seconds to ask what they had been thinking. • Students could speak in Japanese or English. • Detailed explanation of the coding is given, and reliability is reported.
Roca de Larios, Manchón, & Murphy (2006)	• 21 Spanish speakers at three different English proficiency levels • Two timed argumentative writing tasks	1. How much of their total composition time do writers devote to solving formulation problems in L1 and L2 writing? 2. Is the time devoted to solving formulation problems proficiency-dependent? 3. Do writers devote different amounts of time to problem-solving formulation as a function of the type of problems they pose themselves? 4. Is there any interaction among the above-mentioned factors (language, proficiency, and type of problem) and the amount of time devoted by writers to problem-solving formulation? (p. 103)	• Participants had a chance to practice thinking aloud, but no modeling was done. • Students did the L2 task first. • Language of protocols is not stated. • Details on the transcription process are included. • The coding is described in detail. • Inferential statistics are used.

Plakans (2009)	• Six US university ESL students • An untimed reading-to-write task	1. Do L2 writers use discourse synthesis when composing reading-to-write tasks? 2. What language-related issues occur for L2 writers when responding to reading-to-write tasks? (pp. 564–565)	• A discussion of language choice is included; participants were instructed to use English. • Participants were trained to think aloud, but no details are given. • The transcripts were divided into idea units, which were then categorized into discourse synthesis subprocesses. • Reliability is reported.
Abbuhl (2012)	• 77 US university students at two levels of proficiency • Opinion essay to a fictitious audience	1. What effect does instruction have on the ability of L2 learners to employ two signals of authorial presence (first-person pronouns and self-referential third-person pronouns/phrases) while writing specially constructed essay types? 2. What effect does proficiency in the L2 have on the ability of L2 learners to employ these signals of authorial presence while writing specially constructed essay types? (p. 504)	• This was an experimental study looking at the effect of instruction. • Stimulated recall was used to check on what students learned during the treatment. • Recalls were not coded.
Zhao (2010)	• 18 English majors in China wrote a variety of assignments over three months. • Teacher and peer feedback were given.	1. Which type of written feedback did the learners understand better, peer feedback or teacher feedback? 2. What factors, if any, were reported to influence learners' decision-making process of dealing with peer and teacher feedback? (p. 5)	• Stimulated recalls were conducted in the students' L1. • Essays and revisions were used as stimuli, but the authors do not state how long after the writing the recalls were done. • Recalls were used to determine if a feedback instance was understood or not. • The coding scheme is given, and reliability was checked but not reported. • Semi-structured interviews were also conducted with a subset of students.

(Continued)

TABLE 8.1 (Continued)

Citation	Participants, context, and writing task	Research questions	Comments
Watanabe & Swain (2007)	• Four Japanese ESL students paired with students at two proficiency levels • A 30-minute TOEFL essay • Feedback provided as a reformulated version of their texts	1. What is the relationship between patterns of pair interaction and the frequency of LREs produced? (p. 124)	• Stimulated recalls were done of the writing and feedback interpretation stages. • Recalls were used mostly to check the researchers' interpretations of interaction patterns. • Follow-up interviews were also done.
Hirose (2003)	• 15 Japanese English majors • An argumentative essay in both English and Japanese with a suggested 30-minute time frame	1. How do the student-writers evaluate the organizational patterns they employed in L1/L2 argumentative writing? 2. What is the relation between rhetorical patterns and evaluation in L1/L2 argumentative texts? (pp. 186–187)	• Students commented in writing on their written texts. The full list of questions for the students to answer is given in the appendix. • The written comments were completed three months after the essays were written. • Follow-up interviews were done with students whose written comments needed clarification.
Yanguas & Lado (2012)	• 37 university heritage Spanish learners • A story based on a series of pictures	1. Does thinking aloud cause differences in students' writing with regard to fluency, accuracy, and lexical complexity?	• Students were told the purpose of the study was to understand their motivation and feelings about the writing task. • They were told to verbalize their thoughts but to try not to explain or justify them. • The process was modeled using a protocol from the pilot study. • Participants could use their L1, L2, or a combination.

Gebril & Plakans (2014)	• Two trained raters using a rubric evaluating source use • 21 essays from an integrated reading–writing task	1. What are the decision-making behaviors exhibited by raters while scoring reading-to-write tasks? 2. How do raters consider the source texts as they rate integrated writing tasks? 3. What features determine the ratings of integrated tasks at different proficiency levels? 4. What challenges do raters face in rating the written products from integrated tasks? (p. 59)	• Participants practiced thinking aloud on a math problem and then on an essay. • Participants listened to the practice think alouds with the researcher, who gave suggestions. • Follow-up interviews were conducted. • Details of coding are given; transcripts were divided into idea units. • Intercoder reliability is reported.
Willey & Tanimoto (2015)	• Five native or near-native English teachers teaching EFL in Japan • Editing of medical and engineering abstracts	1. What concerns are most on participants' minds while editing the scientific abstracts employed in this study? 2. What strategies do participants employ when faced with uncertainty while editing the scientific abstracts employed in this study? (pp. 65–66)	• A practice session was done. • Follow-up interviews were done to address issues of uncertainty from the think alouds or issues that were not addressed. • The full coding scheme and examples are given in the appendix, and intercoder reliability is reported. • No unit of analysis is mentioned.

students interpreted teacher and peer feedback. In addition to analyzing texts to determine if students used the feedback, Zhao conducted stimulated recall sessions to determine if students understood the feedback. Participants were specifically asked what they had been thinking about when they revised their texts. Stimulated recall can be used to understand what happens during collaborative writing or revision. Watanabe and Swain (2007) examined how the proficiency level of a peer affects collaborative writing and revision with regard *to language-related episodes* (i.e., discussions that focus on language). They analyzed the peer interactions but did not report in detail on the stimulated recall; rather, they used the recalls to confirm their classification of the interaction patterns as, for example, collaborative or dominant/passive (for more on these interaction patterns, see the discussion in Chapter 11).

Introspective and retrospective methods can also be used to supplement analyses of learner texts. Hirose (2003) conducted a study of Japanese students' text organization in their L1 and L2. After students wrote in English and Japanese, they were given a series of questions to answer about their two essays. Their responses helped Hirose to understand why the students organized the essays in the way that they did. This is similar to Abbuhl's (2012) use of stimulated recall to confirm the text data related to the effects of instruction; however, Hirose's written reflections were collected three months after the students wrote their essay, so their responses likely reflected information in their long-term memory related to writing in English versus Japanese as opposed to what they were thinking when they wrote the essays, a point discussed later.

In the case of think-aloud protocols, the introspective technique can actually be the focus of the study, or it can be the independent variable, as opposed to simply a way of investigating something about L2 writers. Such studies are experimental studies, including Yang, Hu, and Zhang (2014; see Chapter 2), in which the writing condition, with or without thinking aloud, was manipulated to examine the effects on the text. In a quasi-experimental study, Yanguas and Lado (2012) had two groups of heritage Spanish learners each write in a think-aloud and non-think-aloud condition. They found that the students in the think-aloud condition wrote more error-free T-units (see Chapter 6), which suggests that thinking aloud changed the writing process and outcome. This study is discussed more later in this chapter.

Finally, retrospective and introspective methods can be used to examine the thinking of teachers or raters of L2 writing. Gebril and Plakans (2014) used think alouds with raters as they rated essays with respect to source use on an integrated reading and writing task. The protocols were then coded into two dimensions: strategy (interpretation or judgment) and focus (language, content and organization, or self-monitoring). Willey and Tanimoto (2015) were interested in how EFL teachers in Japan went about editing written work from areas in which they were not experts, such as medicine or engineering. These teachers thought aloud while they edited, and Willey and Tanimoto coded their protocols to determine what their areas of concern were as well as their strategies for dealing with language and content that they did not understand.

Types of and Variations on Retrospective and Introspective Data Collection

Stimulated Recalls

Stimulated recalls are a type of interview, and the distinction between interviews and verbal protocols is not always obvious. For example, text-based interviews (see Chapter 9) are related to stimulated recall in that they use a stimulus (i.e., a text) as the focal point for the interview; however, they differ from stimulated recall in that they do not necessarily aim to study the writer's cognitive processes. For example, Lillis and Curry (2010) used text-based interviews to examine the resources the writer used as the text was constructed. Text-based interviews may also include general questions such as, "Any comments on the challenges in writing to include source information?" (Shi, 2008; see Box 9.1 in Chapter 9) as opposed to only specific questions such as, "What were you thinking when you wrote this?" True stimulated recalls attempt to limit the focus to the participants' thoughts as they were completing the task; however, some studies do not provide the exact questions, making it difficult to determine if the study was a true stimulated recall. In addition, some studies state that they use stimulated recall, but the verbal report (or *protocol*) is collected quite a bit of time after the participant completed the task. This issue is discussed more in the next section, but as noted by Gass and Mackey (2016) and others, a long delay can result in participants not having access to their cognitive processes used during the task. We have chosen to include in this chapter studies that use the term *stimulated recall* but note that they are not what Gass and Mackey would call a true stimulated recall. (Similarly, true think-aloud protocols, as defined by Ericsson and Simon (1993), do not ask participants to give reasons or explain their thoughts in which they have to access their long-term memory, and this issue is also discussed in this chapter.) With these caveats, we provide Table 8.2 as a summary of the different types of retrospective and introspective reports divided into three main categories: stimulated recall, think-aloud protocols, and written reflections. Variations within these categories are noted.

Although many L2 writing studies use some form of stimulated recall, we did not find any study that used only stimulated recall; all of the studies also collected some other type of data. In her study of the writing processes of South East Asian students, Bosher (1998) conducted what appeared to be a true stimulated recall in addition to structured interviews. She was interested in how the participants varied in their writing processes, particularly given that some had attended high school in the US and some had not. She videotaped eight students, but reported on three while their actions with the pen and paper were videotaped.

TABLE 8.2 Types of Retrospective and Introspective Methods

Type	Focus of study	Example
Stimulated recall		
True stimulated recall (with interview)	Writing processes	Bosher (1998)
Modified stimulated recall (with interview)	Students' goals for improving grammar and vocabulary	Zhou (2009)
Augmented stimulated recall	Collaborative writing and revision	Brooks & Swain (2009)
Stimulated recall with keystroke logging	Awareness of audience while writing	Lindgren, Leijten, & Van Waes (2011)
Stimulated recall after think aloud	Tutors' beliefs about feedback	Li & Barnard (2011)
Think-aloud protocols		
Think alouds (nonmetacognitive)	Children's test-taking strategies	Nikolov (2006)
	L1 use while writing	Wang & Wen (2002)
	Noticing of feedback	Sachs & Polio (2007)
Think aloud with modified stimulated recall	Rater behaviors	Lumley (2002)
	Self vs. peer revision	M. Suzuki (2008)
Write-aloud protocols	Rater behavior	Baker (2012)
Written reflection		
Reflective journals	Mental models of writing	Nicolas-Conesea, Roca de Larios, & Coyle (2014)
Reflective journals with stimulated recall	Corpus use	Park (2012)
Process logs with stimulated recall	Writing strategies	Lei (2008)
Written comments (languaging and metatalk)	Attention to feedback	W. Suzuki (2012)

The participants were observed from another room, and the researcher noted the timing of the pauses. During the stimulated recall interview, the researcher stopped the tape during the longer pauses and asked participants why they had stopped writing and what they had been thinking. She coded the responses according to what the students were paying attention to (e.g., *language use, discourse organization*) and how they solved (or did not solve) the problem (e.g., *assessing alternatives*), but no intercoder reliability is reported. This study is useful for those interested in using stimulated recall because of the level of detail in which the data collection and coding procedures are described, but we note two issues. First, even though the researcher may ask questions that focus on what the participants were thinking during the writing task, the participants may stray and talk about general processes, and when participants are reporting in their L2, the time frame may not be clear because of misuse of verb tenses. Bosher's examples included some in which participants talked in the present tense, so we cannot be sure if the participants were talking generally about writing or if they were focused on how they completed the task from the study. In addition, Bosher appears to have first interviewed students, and it is not clear how this interview may have affected the stimulated recall. The interview questions did, however, focus only on the immediately completed writing task and did not ask general questions about their writing processes.

Zhou (2009) and Brooks and Swain (2009) both used modified forms of stimulated recall combined with other data collection techniques for very different reasons. Zhou was interested in EAP students' goals and actions related to improving their grammar and vocabulary. After interviewing students, she conducted what we call a *modified stimulated recall*. Instead of asking students what they were thinking when they wrote, she asked students questions such as, "What was your purpose in writing this piece?" and "What did you find was a problem?" Furthermore, because she did not videotape the students writing and instead simply showed them their writing, the students had fewer cues to help them remember the process of composing. In addition, the recall was not conducted immediately after the students wrote and was preceded by an interview. Although these data were useful in answering her research questions, we need to understand they went beyond tapping into learners' cognitive processes as they wrote.

Brooks and Swain (2009) studied how learners talked about language while writing collaboratively and when comparing their writing to reformulated versions of their essays and how this talk was related to their revisions. The researchers wanted to determine what language issues the students focused on and, when they revised, what the source of that revision was, namely, their peer and/or the reformulated version. As a result, the collaborative writing sessions and reformulation comparison sessions were recorded and analyzed. What is somewhat unique about their study is that Brooks and Swain conducted what they termed an *augmented stimulated recall* both to find out about student learning *and* to use it as a teaching tool. They did this not only by asking about changes that the students made but also by assisting the students if they could not correct or understand a problem. As such, during the augmented stimulated recall, the researcher was yet another source of learning. Of course, it is possible that simply doing a stimulated recall will draw students' attention to language issues that they might not have noticed, thus resulting in learning of some type, but Brooks and Swain, by conducting an augmented stimulated recall, increased the chances of this happening. We return to this point later.

As stated earlier, stimulated recall is generally combined with other techniques including keystroke logging (Lindgren, Leijten, & Van Waes, 2011) and think alouds (Li & Barnard, 2011). Lindgren et al. (2011) reasoned that keystroke logging could record revisions and pauses and then be combined with verbalizations collected during stimulated recall. They were particularly interested in how writers at different levels of expertise adapted their texts for readers. Students wrote two essays for different audiences and then were asked to revise a piece of writing for a specific audience. This last task was used for the stimulated recall session. (Note that a screen-capturing video program, not the data from the keystroke logging program, was used for the recall.) The specific instructions for the stimulated recall were not provided, but the researchers said that the participants "commented on their revisions" and "were prompted to describe their actions as they appeared on the screen only when they fell silent" (p. 196). The researchers did not code the stimulated recall but instead combined information from the protocols with information from the keystroke logs and interviews to present profiles of the six writers.

Li and Barnard (2011) were interested in how tutors (i.e., graders) from New Zealand gave feedback and grades on essays. Nine of their participants thought aloud as they read student papers and provided written comments in addition to being interviewed, completing a questionnaire, and participating in a focus group. This study differs from most of the others, however, because the researchers' notes from the think alouds were used as the basis for the stimulated recall; it appears that the tutors did not listen to their think aloud. In their analysis, the researchers said the tutors commented on both the essays they were grading and on their experience more generally.

Think-Aloud Protocols

Think alouds, or concurrent verbal protocols, have been used extensively in L2 writing research to access learners' processes and strategies not only as they write but also as they apply and interpret feedback. They have also been used with teachers and raters as they read, comment on, and grade writing. Like stimulated recall, think alouds are often combined with other types of data collection methods. Also like stimulated recall, there are different types, and the type of think aloud used in a particular study is not always obvious. Ericsson and Simon (1993) explained that true think alouds (i.e., those that did not interfere with the cognitive processes required to complete a task) simply have participants report what is in their head without having to explain the reasons for their thoughts or actions by reporting from long-term memory. For example, compare:

1. This word sounds strange to me.
2. This word sounds strange to me. I am going to change this because I think when I looked it up once it had a different meaning.

The second statement includes a reason or explanation. Bowles (2008, 2010; Bowles & Leow, 2005) called think alouds that attempted to elicit explanations *metalinguistic* or *metacognitive*. However, as with stimulated recall, it is possible that the researcher will attempt to limit the nature of the participants' comments but that the writing or interpretation task completed by the participant will naturally elicit reasons or explanations.

Nikolov (2006) used think alouds with adolescents to understand their test-taking strategies. She had students say what they were thinking as they completed an integrated reading-writing task. Nikolov described the different strategies used but did not go into detail on the coding or participant instructions. The study appears to have elicited only nonmetacognitive information related to what the students were thinking as they composed. Similarly, Wang and Wen (2002) also used nonmetacognitive think alouds but instead aimed to find out about the language (i.e., L1 vs. L2) used for thinking while composing in the L2. They provided details on the instructions and training for their participants as well as a detailed description of their coding and intercoder reliability. Both of these studies seem to be nonmetacognitive think alouds because of the foci of the studies and the instructions given to participants. Also, it is difficult to imagine learners explaining the reasons for their choice of strategies or their choice of L1 versus L2, as learners probably do not have access to these thoughts.

Sachs and Polio (2007) used think alouds to find out what learners noticed in a reformulated version of their writing and to investigate the *reactivity* of the think alouds. (Reactivity, discussed in the next section, refers to how the think aloud might change the writing process.) The participants were asked simply to compare their original and reformulated essays and think aloud as they did this. In some cases where the participants noticed the difference, they simply stated that they noticed it, but sometimes they provided a reason or explained the difference. Nevertheless, these explanations were what were in their minds as they did the comparison; the nature of task elicited explanations. Lumley (2002), like Gebril and Plakans (2014), studied raters. His detailed description of the study included the exact instructions to the raters. He asked them to vocalize their thoughts and explain why they gave the score that they did. But note that unlike the composing process, explanations and rationales are likely a normal part of the rating process, as is interpreting feedback examined in Sachs and Polio. Thus, despite the request for explanations, the think-aloud technique likely tapped into only what was in the participants' minds at the time of the activity. We found no examples in the L2 writing research of studies that explicitly asked learners to give explanations as they wrote.

Think alouds can also be combined with other types of data such as stimulated recall. M. Suzuki (2012) examined Japanese EFL writers' self- versus peer revisions. Peer revisions elicit discussion, so researchers can observe the participants' focus, but in the self-revisions, M. Suzuki had to rely on think alouds to find out what was in the participants' minds as they revised. We include this study here as an example of a study that combined think alouds with stimulated recall, but we found only one example in her study where the stimulated recall data were used to confirm the researcher's interpretation. Furthermore, the stimulated recall was done several days after the writing task, and only the writing, not the think aloud or peer sessions, were used as the stimulus.

Finally, we refer to Baker (2012), who used a technique called *write-aloud protocols*. She had raters describe their decision processes as they rated. She argued that by writing, instead of talking, participants could stay in the same room and rate essays as they normally did. In addition, the data did not have to be transcribed. She also stated that a write aloud might require less training than an oral think aloud, although there is no evidence to confirm this. This technique was adapted from Gigerenzer and Hoffrage (1995), who used it as participants solved probability problems. Writing instead of speaking allowed participants to draw pictures and equations that might be more difficult to represent through language, but it is not clear that there are any advantages to using them in L2 writing research.

Written Reflection

Finally, a small set of studies used written reflections, as opposed to write-aloud protocols, to understand writers' processes. Nicolás-Conesa, Roca de Larios, and Coyle (2014) were interested in how writers' task representation (e.g., what they considered good writing) and goals for academic writing changed. The researchers had students complete written reflections at the beginning of the semester and then nine months later. The journals were coded according to the occurrence or nonoccurrence of specific themes determined by researchers. Intercoder reliability was reported, and quantitative results were given. Park (2012) investigated how students interacted with a corpus, using a variety of data collection methods including written reflection. Students were asked to write a page-long reflection focusing on which words and phrases they had looked up in the corpus and whether or not the corpus was helpful when they wrote. They also reflected, presumably more generally, on their experience with the corpus. Stimulated recall was also used in the study.

Lei (2008) investigated the strategies of proficient EFL students in China using an activity theory framework and considered the various sources that writers used to mediate their writing. In addition to stimulated recall and interviews, she had students write using what she called process logs, adapted from Wong (2000). Students completed the logs before and after writing. The logs included questions such as "What did you actually do to get ideas for the assignment?" (before writing) and "Did your perceptions of target readers change during the writing process?" (after writing). She did not code these separately but instead included them as another data source along with the interview and stimulated recall data.

Written reflective techniques can be used not only to understand what participants are doing and thinking but also as a type of treatment; in other words, they may help learners focus on some aspect of writing. W. Suzuki (2012) had Japanese EFL students write about grammar and vocabulary feedback on their essays and talk about why their language was corrected. He called this a *written languaging* activity. With this procedure, he obtained insight into the students' understanding of the feedback while at the same time drawing their attention to the feedback. He was able to both describe the type of language-related episodes found in the reflections and to relate those episodes to improvement on a revision task. We note, however, that the language-related episodes from the written reflections may have been a cause of what the students already knew or an effect of being asked to reflect on the feedback, but we cannot be sure which.

Issues Involved in Using Retrospective and Introspective Methods

The two major issues related to retrospective and introspective methods are *reactivity* (i.e., how the verbal report changes the process or outcome of the observed task) and *veridicality* (i.e., how accurate and complete the participants' reports of their thought processes are). How one goes about structuring the data collection session and giving directions to the participants will affect both of these issues. An additional concern is how the data are coded and reported.

Reactivity

A think-aloud verbal protocol can under certain circumstances be reactive. For example, imagine trying to drive a car and talk about the procedure while doing it. Talking about the activity might result in a crash. Conversely, for some people, solving an algebra problem while thinking aloud might cause them to focus better on the procedure and more easily solve the problem. In these scenarios, the think aloud can be said to have negative reactivity and positive reactivity, respectively. In addition, think alouds may be reactive for *latency*, which means that the process of thinking aloud can change the length of time needed to complete a task. In L2 writing, it is easy to see that thinking aloud could change how one goes about a process and what the outcome of the process is. For example, thinking aloud while writing may result in more planning of an essay (i.e., a change in the process) or it might result in an essay with fewer errors (i.e., a change in the outcome) because reading aloud may help writers catch problematic structures.

Both within and outside of the field of second language learning, the reactivity of think alouds has been studied extensively both with regard to the quality or accuracy of task performance and the time it takes to complete a task. There are a variety of factors that can affect reactivity including the nature of the task, the data collection procedure, and the instructions to the participant. Ericsson and Simon (1993) argued that nonmetacognitive think alouds, that is, those in which the participants simply report what they are thinking and do not try to explain their thinking, would not be reactive for task performance. Studies of reactivity on a variety of tasks are reviewed in Bowles (2010). With regard to studies of nonverbal tasks such as math problems, she explained that a number of studies have shown reactivity on complex cognitive tasks and that there is some evidence that metacognitive think alouds are more reactive. She also provided a meta-analysis of SLA studies. None of the studies had students write, but she included Sachs and Polio (2007), in which students reviewed feedback. Overall, Bowles found a very small effect for reactivity on task performance and a large effect for latency reactivity. She also investigated how certain factors affected reactivity including the type of think aloud, the nature of the task, and the participants, but with only 14 studies total in the meta-analysis, it was difficult to draw clear conclusions.

Since Bowles's (2010) meta-analysis, several studies focusing on the reactivity of think alouds in L2 writing have been published, and we discuss three here. Yanguas and Lado (2012), discussed earlier, found that heritage learners completing a picture narrative task wrote more grammatically accurate essays while thinking aloud. The authors provided examples of participants' speech produced while they wrote that showed how the think-aloud procedure may have helped them to consider sentences that did not sound right. It is important to consider here that heritage learners often have stronger oral skills than writing skills, so it is easy to see how speaking could have a facilitative effect on writing. We do note that students were allowed to verbalize their thoughts in either Spanish or English, and it appears that they used both.

Yang, Hu, and Zhang (2014) examined the effects of both metalinguistic and nonmetalinguistic think alouds on the writing of Chinese students. They examined several measures but found reactivity effects for only a few and none for accuracy. Thinking aloud in any form had a significant but very small effect on only one complexity measure, syntactic variety. We should interpret this finding cautiously because of the small effect size and lack of findings on other complexity measures, but if thinking aloud results in language that is more oral (i.e., less syntactically complex), this finding makes sense, as the Chinese participants, unlike the Spanish heritage speakers, likely had stronger written skills. Yang, Hu, and Zhang did find latency effects as expected: The metalinguistic think-aloud group took more time to complete the task. Furthermore, both think-aloud groups wrote less fluently, which is also expected since the process of thinking aloud results in slower task completion. Their study confirms previous research that found that think alouds are reactive for time.

Barkaoui (2011) included an excellent discussion on the use of think alouds to understand raters' rating processes. He reviewed 16 studies that used think alouds and presented the pros and cons of the technique. In his empirical study, he had novice and experienced raters rate on an analytic and holistic scale with and without thinking aloud. He found that some raters (six out of 25) were either more severe or less severe while rating aloud, but there was little relationship to the type of scale or experience of the rater. In interviews with the raters, however, 19 out of 25 reported that thinking aloud changed their rating process, and a few participants reported that they were not able to think aloud at all while rating.

Finally, Godfroid and Spino (2015) recently studied reactivity, but in a reading task. We discuss their study here because it raised an important issue related to studying reactivity, namely, the type of analysis one does to support findings of nonreactivity. They investigated the effect of thinking aloud (and eye tracking) on reading comprehension and vocabulary recognition, finding a small positive effect for thinking aloud on vocabulary recognition. However, instead of using traditional (i.e., *superiority*) statistical tests that are designed to reject the hypothesis that no difference exists, they used an *equivalence test*, which attempts to reject a hypothesis that states that a difference does exist. With a traditional superiority test, a finding of a significant difference between groups allows one to draw a conclusion, but a lack of difference does not indicate that there is no difference, simply that one has not been found. Because Godfroid and Spino used an equivalence test, their finding of reactivity in vocabulary learning is more noteworthy than studies that failed to find reactivity.

From the large amount of research on reactivity, we still cannot make clear claims about the effects of thinking aloud on writing other than we know that there is *a latency effect*: It takes longer to write while thinking aloud. It is also likely that the participant population (e.g., proficiency in oral vs. written language), instructions (e.g., metacognitive vs. nonmetacognitive), and task (e.g., writing vs. rating) may affect the reactivity of the think aloud. We also note that we know of no studies that have closely examined how individual differences in the think-aloud protocols affect task performance. In other words, no studies have examined how the quantity and quality of the verbal reports affect the outcome of the task.

At first glance, it might seem that reactivity is not an issue when using retrospective methods because the data collection is done after the task under investigation is completed. A stimulated recall or written reflection, however, can draw learners' attention to issues that they might not have noticed otherwise; thus, it can influence participants' performance on subsequent tasks. In fact, in at least one study (Brooks & Swain, 2009), the augmented stimulated recall was used to teach the students during a data collection phase of the study. Similarly, W. Suzuki (2012) argued that writing about feedback could be helpful in drawing learners' attention to the feedback and helping them process and retain it. We do not know of any studies that directly examined the reactivity of stimulated recall, but it is easy to imagine that they could be reactive on subsequent tasks. A few studies have used stimulated recall followed by interviews, and this complicates the interpretation of the data because the stimulated recall may cause learners to discuss issues that they had normally not been aware of (for a discussion of this issue in interviewing, see Chapter 9). Of course, depending on the interview questions, the opposite order can cause complications as well (i.e., the interview could affect what participants comment on in the stimulated recall). Egi (2007, 2008) conducted two studies on the reactivity of stimulated recall on the retention of responses to oral recasts and oral production. The results did not show a reactivity effect except on a delayed posttest among students who participated in a recall focused on recasts. We know of no studies that have directly examined the reactivity of stimulated recalls on writing, but the Brooks and Swain study showed that in an augmented stimulated recall, learning appeared to be taking place.

Veridicality

No one assumes that an introspective or retrospective protocol is a complete account of a participant's task performance. Given that some participants cannot do think alouds (as noted in Barkaoui, 2011) and that there are cognitive processes that cannot be articulated, the protocols cannot be complete, but they are assumed to be accurate: A participant probably would not or could not verbalize a false thought, at least not in a nonmetacognitive think aloud. Stimulated recalls, however, in addition to not being complete, may be inaccurate in that they may reflect what a participant is thinking at the time of the recall instead of what they were thinking while completing the task. For example, if a participant says, "That word does not sound right but I am not sure what it should be," it is not clear if the participant thought the word sounded wrong while writing or has just noticed a problem. This is particularly a problem if a participant is completing the recall in his or her second language and does not use verb tenses correctly. As discussed later, certain steps can be taken to increase the chance that the participants' stimulated recalls reflect their cognitive processes while completing the task as opposed to their thoughts while completing the recall.

Veridicality has been discussed in the L2 writing and applied linguistics literature. Barkaoui (2011), for example, summarized how the issue has been addressed in rater studies. He also interviewed his participants after a think aloud for their perspectives on why they were not able to verbalize all their thoughts. However, much less empirical research has been conducted on veridicality than on reactivity. One study outside of applied linguistics (Kuusela & Paul, 2000) had participants complete a task in which they had to choose among five insurance policies in either a think-aloud or stimulated recall condition. The researchers found that the amount of information produced by the participants was higher in the think-aloud condition. However, they also coded the protocols (e.g., categories included *discussion of features, pairwise comparisons*), and found that this trend was not consistent across all categories. The task used in their study did not focus on language and was done, presumably, by native speakers. We know of no studies in applied linguistics that have directly compared think alouds and stimulated recalls for degree of completeness; however, Chiu and Polio (2007) used think alouds from a writing task as the stimulus for a stimulated recall and found that the participants were able to add more information about what they had been thinking while writing. One participant even explained that he had been thinking about a particular soccer game when he wrote the name of a famous soccer player in his essay but had omitted these thoughts from the think aloud because they were not directly related to the essay that he was writing. Comparisons of think alouds and stimulated recalls are certainly an area for further research in second language writing.

Just as there are ways to reduce reactivity in think alouds, there are ways to improve the veridicality of verbal protocols described in the next section. Given that introspective or retrospective methods cannot provide a complete picture of writers' cognitive processes, many researchers have chosen to use verbal protocols with other data to triangulate their findings. Godfroid and Spino (2015) discussed triangulating eye-tracking data and think alouds during a reading task, and Gass and Mackey (2016) included examples of how stimulated recall can be used to supplement other data types. Appropriate triangulation can minimize the veridicality problem.

Finally, as discussed in Chapter 2 with regard to experimental research, most of the studies that use think alouds and stimulated recall have students write in timed situations. Because recording equipment is needed, such timed laboratory-based data collection is necessary, but the writing may not be a true representation of the participants' writing processes in other contexts. Park (2012), in her study of how students used a corpus while writing, was able to record students' writing and corpus search processes using screen capture software, and these screen videos were used as a basis for stimulated recall. Although the participants still had a limited amount of time to write, they were working toward major assignments such as a response paper and a research report. It is possible that such software might allow researchers to collect data outside the laboratory. This data could be used for stimulated recalls sessions, albeit not immediately after the students produced the text. Smagorinsky (1994) reported on an attempt to have students carry tape recorders for think alouds as they wrote outside of class, but most of the participants dropped out of the study.

Coding and Presenting the Data

Introspective and retrospective protocols can generate a massive amount of data, and accurately summarizing the data can be challenging. For studies that use multiple data sources, including qualitative case studies, fragments of the protocols may be extracted to verify or call into question interpretations of other data. In these cases, the full protocols may not be transcribed or coded. However, if researchers want to use the full verbal protocols to present a picture of what their participants were doing, the data has to be transcribed, segmented, and coded. When segmenting a protocol, a researcher has to be clear about what the unit of analysis is, and there is little consensus on this issue. For example, a certain writing strategy such as *consider the audience* may consist of a phrase or several sentences. It may be broken up by other thoughts or occur in the same sentence as other thoughts. In other words, should each sentence, each segment of connected speech, or each thought (if a thought can even be defined) be coded?

Even more problematic is that some studies do not clearly describe the process of segmenting the data.

Three of the studies from Table 8.1 included detailed descriptions of their units of analysis. Although these studies do not definitively solve the problem of how to segment the data, the researchers recognized the problem and explained their procedure. Roca de Larios, Manchón, and Murphy (2006) in their think-aloud study, stated, "Segmentation was carried out in our corpus by considering both implicit and explicit indicators of problems. Each individual problem-space was coded as a unit, regardless of the number and quality of behaviors interspersed between the initial and the final state" (p. 106). Their unit of analysis seems to be *problem space*, which is difficult to define, but seems reasonable given that the focus of their study was formulation problems. Although they reported reliability on their coding of the units, they, like others, did not report reliability on segmenting the data.

Lumley (2002), in his study of raters, gives the following account of transcribing and segmenting the data.

> Divisions of the TA protocols into text units for analysis were made according to the content of each unit. This is a pragmatic view, which recognizes that there is no single way to read a text and that division of the data into text units is ultimately an arbitrary act. The analyses conducted in this study attempt less to quantify instances of each behaviour, than to identify what range of behaviours can be observed, to consider whether or not raters demonstrate each behaviour, and to give a picture of the range of features that are examined by each rater.
>
> *(p. 253)*

Lumley acknowledged the problem, saying that divisions are arbitrary and went on to say the analysis was more about describing the raters' behaviors than quantifying them. In Willey and Tanimoto's (2015) study of editors, the researchers seemed to code for *areas of concern*. Each of these studies approached the unit of analysis issue differently depending on the focus of their study. Like the veridicality issue, the unit of analysis issue is more of a problem if the verbal protocols are the only data source and are quantified for presentation.

After segmenting the verbal protocols, some studies go on to code and quantify the results as opposed to using examples to triangulate with other data sources. The coding schemes to be used are related to the research questions. For example, Yang and Shi (2003) used a coding system based on the Hayes and Flower (1980) model of writing that included the macro-categories *planning, composing,* and *editing.* Their unit of analysis was a mention of any of the strategies within these categories. Plakans (2009) used categories related to discourse synthesis as she studied how participants wrote an essay in an integrated reading and writing task. She divided her data into *idea units* citing Green (2008) but does not discuss the segmentation process further. Both the Yang and Shi and Plakans studies reported acceptable intercoder reliability for their studies, but not all studies report reliability. Furthermore, because of the time-consuming data collection and transcription processes for verbal protocols, studies often have a very small sample size. Such small sample sizes call into question their use as the dependent variable in causal-comparative studies. Yang and Shi, for example, framed their research questions as causal-comparative (e.g., What are the differences between ESL students and native speakers?) but with only six participants, they did not report inferential statistics.

How to Conduct a Study Using Retrospective and Introspective Methods

Two comprehensive books on retrospective (Gass & Mackey, 2016) and introspective (Bowles, 2010) verbal protocols in second language research exist, and both go into detail about conducting research using these methods. We summarize the steps here with a focus on decisions that L2 writing researchers have to make but recommend readers see Chapters 3 in Gass and Mackey (2016) and Chapter 4 in Bowles (2010) for more details.

Deciding on the Appropriate Technique

The choice among stimulated recall, think alouds, or written reflection is related to one's research question, associated task, and the logistics of collecting data. True stimulated recall and nonmetacognitive think alouds usually both try to answer the same general question, namely, *What are the cognitive processes used to complete the task?* If one is interested in what the participant was thinking during the task, neither technique has an obvious advantage. One case where a think aloud is likely preferable is in studies where the researcher is interested in which language the participant is thinking in (e.g., van Weijen, van den Bergh, Rijlaarsdam, & Sanders, 2009; Wang & Wen, 2002). Whether or not participants can retrospectively recall which language they were thinking in an empirical and open question, but it seems unlikely that it can be done. On the other hand, it seems that the think-aloud task naturally lends itself to verbalizations that match the language of thought. If one is interested in collecting metacognitive data, it is more likely that a think aloud will be reactive, so a stimulated recall might be preferable. In addition, studies of raters and editors seem more conducive to think alouds because it is likely easier to think aloud while judging a text written in one's native language than while producing a text in one's second language.

The use of written reflection needs to be considered carefully for a few reasons. In particular, we do not recommend the use of written think alouds. They are logistically impossible to do when studying the writing process, but even when used with raters (as in Baker, 2012), they seem problematic because writing takes longer and is likely a more arduous task than speaking. Written reflections seem to offer no advantage over oral protocols in terms of tapping into learners' thought processes, and in fact may increase reactivity and decrease veridicality.

The logistics of data collection will also most certainly affect a researcher's choice of technique. For example, think alouds can be done in a group laboratory setting, whereas stimulated recalls are usually done with the researcher present to prompt the student. True stimulated recalls generally require that participants complete the task under investigation individually because the stimulated recall data are best collected immediately after the task is completed.

Procedures

Many procedural decisions need to be made when collecting verbal protocol data, and each of the decisions, while often related to logistics, can affect reactivity and veridicality. These include: the role of the researcher, the wording of the instructions and training provided for the participants, the timing of the data collection (for stimulated recall), and the language used in the protocol.

Ideally, we want to find out how participants behave when the researcher is not present, as discussed in relation to the observer's paradox in Chapter 4. At the same time, participants performing a think aloud may not speak unless the researcher is present to remind the participants to keep talking. Nevertheless, some studies have students record their think alouds in a laboratory with no researcher present (e.g., Roca de Larios et al., 2006). When researchers are present, they usually say something such as, "Please keep talking." It is possible to use other reminders; for example, in a reading study Block (1986) put black dots at the end of sentences to remind participant to keep talking. In stimulated recall, the researcher must be present to prompt the participant, but studies vary in how and when the prompting is done. Gass and Mackey (2016) explained that the researcher can prompt the participant by pausing the video when there is something the researchers want to focus on or during long pauses from the writing task. Alternatively, participants can be asked to pause the video of the writing task when they want to say what they were thinking. Gass and Mackey provide samples of questions that the researcher can ask to help participants focus on their thinking at the time of task completion as opposed to their thinking during the recall task. They also provide an example of a protocol that can be used or modified for use during the stimulated recall.

Instructions to the participants and training for verbal protocols are extremely important matters to consider. As discussed earlier, Ericsson and Simon's (1993) original definition of think alouds included the characteristic that participants report what is in their mind and not be asked to explain or give reasons for their thoughts. If participants give reasons, the think aloud becomes a metacognitive one with greater risk of reactivity (Bowles, 2010). In addition, one has to decide how much the participants should be told about the purpose of the study and what kind of training to include. Both of these decisions could affect how the participant completes the task. For example, if a researcher says, "We are interested in how you plan before you write an essay," the participant is more likely to plan before writing. A better, yet still honest, statement would be, "We are interested in how you go about writing an essay." Similarly, demonstrating a think aloud with the task under investigation can also influence participants' performances. If, while modeling the think aloud, the researcher says, "Now I need to edit this sentence and check for errors," the participant might be more likely to edit. Most studies demonstrate the think aloud procedure on a different task, such as an algebra problem, and then have participants practice on a shorter writing task. The extent to which studies report instructions varies greatly. Here is a lengthy excerpt from the Willey and Tanimoto (2015) study. We include it to show the various unresolved issues that may not be reported in other studies.

> The think-aloud methodology employed in this study was first explained to all participants separately. In order to reduce reactivity, or task interference, a non-metacognitive approach was employed (Bowles, 2010); participants were told that they did not need to explain reasons for each revision, but simply verbalize their thoughts while editing. Participants completed a practice task using a short text written by a university student to help them become accustomed to this method (Ericsson & Simon, 1993, p. 82); this practice session was audio-recorded and promptly received by the first author, who discussed the recording with participants in order to help them resolve difficulties they experienced while editing aloud. For instance, three participants noted that thinking aloud interfered with their concentration when reading and writing/typing in their revisions; to solve this problem we told participants that instances of silence were acceptable while they were reading or writing/typing. Moreover, the practice task indicated both pros and cons of a metacognitive approach: Two participants stated that they felt a need to explain revisions or else they would have little to say, but the other three preferred not having to explain revisions, as they often could not express reasons for revisions but simply felt something sounded wrong. As the slim majority appeared comfortable with not having to explain revisions, we did not alter our approach, and told the two participants who preferred to explain their revisions that they were free to do so, as our instructions had originally indicated.
>
> *(p. 67)*

With stimulated recall, there is generally no training done because the researcher can control, to some extent, what the participants say during the recall interview. Instead, the timing of the recall becomes an important matter. Specifically, the longer the time period between the task and the recall, the less valid the recall will be because of decays in short-term memory (Ericsson & Simon,

1993). Gass and Mackey (2016) point out that collecting the recall data immediately after a task is preferable, but that logistic issues may prevent immediate data collection. In any case, researchers need to clearly report their procedures.

The final issue in any L2 research using verbal protocols is to decide on the language in which the protocol is to be done (see Chapter 9 for a discussion of this issue in interviewing). In a foreign language setting where the researcher can communicate in the participants' L1, L1 interviews are possible. In an ESL setting, often the participants do not have the same L1, and it is logistically difficult to conduct the protocols in the participants' L1. Logistic issues aside, it may seem obvious that a verbal protocol will elicit better data with regard to both quantity and quality if done in the participants' L1. Participants must have the language needed to report their thoughts if one wants a full picture of their cognitive processes; reporting thoughts in a second language could prove challenging and result in less information. However, it is not necessarily true that using the L1 is always better; during think alouds, it could be extremely challenging to speak in one's first language but write in one's second language, particularly for advanced writers who may be thinking in their L2. In such cases, using the L1 could be cognitively taxing and reactive. Unfortunately, there is no empirical evidence to suggest which language is best for a think aloud, but it likely varies with the task and the participants. If one does have a choice, it is preferable to give participants the option of using their first language, second language, or a combination. Some studies do not specify which language was used, but it should be reported. For stimulated recalls, where reactivity is not a problem, the L1 can be used, but Gass and Mackey (2016) note that recall could be more difficult if the language of the task and the recall do not match. But again, there is no empirical research on this issue.

Analyzing and Reporting the Data

Researchers need to decide how much of the data should be transcribed and to what level of detail, and these decisions are related to how one analyzes and reports the results of the verbal protocols (for a discussion of transcription in qualitative research see Chapter 9 [on interviews] and Chapter 11 [on discourse analysis]). If the focus of research is on one aspect of the composing process, it may not be necessary to transcribe all of the data, and instead only the points of interest can be transcribed, as was done in Yang and Shi (2003), who were interested in only how their participants summarized and analyzed business cases. If the protocols are to be exhaustively coded, then the entire protocol needs to be transcribed.

One of the few studies that discusses transcription explicitly is Roca de Larios et al. (2006), who stated:

> [We] transcribed the participants' verbalizations in the ordinary writing system but including features of spoken discourse (hesitations, repetitions, paralinguistic features, and pauses), which are considered vital interpretive

resources (Ericsson & Simon, 1993; Kasper, 1998), and indicating the duration of the pauses in parentheses.

(p. 105)

The authors felt that more detailed transcription would help them understand how the writers in their study solved formulation problems, but most researchers do not transcribe at the same level of detail. What can be challenging is how to represent the task under investigation in the transcripts. With think alouds, researchers often underline any verbalizations that indicate that the participant was reading his or her text at the time. For stimulated recalls, it is helpful to have columns with the participants' verbalization in one column and the text that they are talking about in another. (Gass & Mackey, 2016, include some examples of coding sheets for stimulated recall.)

As discussed earlier, a decision about segmenting the data and deciding whether to quantify it or not has to be made. If the researcher is interested in only one particular issue or is using the verbal data to confirm hypotheses made on the basis of the quantitative data or other qualitative data, he or she may not need to segment and quantify the data. However, if the data is to be exhaustively coded, one needs to write clear coding guidelines for the coders, and these guidelines should be included in the appendix of the study. Bowles (2010) includes several excellent coding examples from different studies.

BOX 8.1 FOCAL STUDY

van Weijen, D., van den Bergh, H., Rijlaarsdam, G., & Sanders, T. (2009). L1 use during L2 writing: An empirical study of a complex phenomenon. *Journal of Second Language Writing, 19*, 235–250.

Background

Previous studies of L1 use during L2 writing described how writers used the L1 at various points in the writing process and how L1 use varied among writers. A few studies also tried to relate L1 use to text quality. It is not clear from these studies, however, if L1 use is related to proficiency level or what effect it has on text quality because of methodological problems and inconsistencies across studies. Furthermore, there has been little research linking L1 use to different parts of the writing process.

Research Questions

1. Do writers use their L1 to carry out conceptual activities while writing in L2?

2. To what extent does L1 use during L2 writing vary for individual writers?
3. Is L1 use while writing in L2 related to text quality?
4. Is this relation influenced by general writing proficiency and L2 proficiency? (p. 238)

Design

Twenty Dutch learners of English wrote eight texts while thinking aloud, four in Dutch and four in English. The prompts, which were randomized, required students to argue a point incorporating at least two of six short sources in either Dutch or English, and the order of the essays was randomized. Both the Dutch and English essays were scored to measure general writing proficiency and L2 writing proficiency, respectively. Students took a vocabulary test during the last session as a measure of general L2 proficiency.

Results

There was much variation among the writers in terms of the amount of L1 use, but writers were overall more likely to use the L1 for certain activities including self-instruction and metacomments. There was a negative correlation between L1 use and text quality only with regard to L1 use for metacomments. General writing proficiency, as opposed to L2 proficiency, had an effect on both text quality and L1 use during the writing process.

Discussion of a Focal Study: van Weijen, van den Bergh, Rijlaarsdam, and Sanders (2009)

van Weijen, van den Bergh, Rijlaarsdam, and Sanders (2009) explained that previous research on the use of L1 while writing in an L2 has not presented a clear picture of what writers do with regard to using the L1 to solve linguistic problems or for higher order strategies such as planning. It is also not clear how such use of the L1 affects text quality, although there is some sense that the use of the L1 can be helpful for some writers, depending on the writing task and characteristics of the writers. van Weijen et al. suggest that the conflicting findings are due to methodological problems and differences among the studies. For example, many studies use very small sample sizes, thus capturing the writing process of only a few participants. In addition, most studies have participants complete only one writing task, although L1 use likely varies with the writing task and topic. Finally, the researchers noted that most studies are not clear about defining or measuring what is meant by L1 use, nor do they link L1 use to specific parts of the writing process.

With these problems laid out, van Weijen et al. (2009) set out to determine which activities were completed in the L1, how individuals varied in their use of the L1, what the relationship between L1 use and text quality was, and how this relationship varied with writing proficiency and L2 proficiency. As such, this study attempted to not only describe the writing process but also examine relationships related to the use of the L1, which resulted in a causal-comparative study (see Chapter 3). Although van Weijen et al. thoroughly reviewed the previous research on L1 use during the writing process, they did not clearly articulate why such research might be useful to the field of L2 writing. For this study and other studies that use verbal protocols to describe the writing process, we need to consider the possible benefits of such a study. This study, like Wang and Wen (2002), discussed earlier, can help develop a model of the L2 writing process, but such models are complex because the writing process can be influenced by many individual and social factors that constantly change. Nevertheless, developing a model was likely the authors' goal.

Twenty Dutch English majors participated in the study. Four types of data were collected: scores on English texts, scores on Dutch essays, think-aloud protocols from two L2 writing sessions, and a general L2 proficiency test. Students wrote four essays in Dutch and four in English. The task in both languages involved having students write an essay for a fictitious essay contest in which they had to support a point of view while incorporating two of six short sources that were provided. The authors provided a sample of one full prompt. It appears that the eight prompts were counterbalanced in terms of the language of the essays, and the order of writing with regard to prompt and language was randomized. Both of these steps were important to avoiding topic and order effects. Students were given 30 minutes to write, with extra time given if needed to finish. The essays were scored by two separate sets of raters using first an analytic scale and then a holistic scale. Satisfactory reliability was reported.

The students participated in a think-aloud session for two of the English writing sessions. The participants were trained to think aloud on an algebra problem and a crossword puzzle before practicing on a short randomly assigned writing activity. Practice with a short writing activity was repeated before the second think-aloud session. The authors of this study detailed their procedure quite clearly but did not state the role of the researcher during the think-aloud sessions. Specific instructions to the students were not provided, but the study appears to be a true, or nonmetacognitive, think aloud. Also, the authors said that they did not ask the participants to think aloud in their L1 because they were interested in spontaneous language use, but it is not clear what happened in the practice session with regard to L1 use or if the participants asked about L1 use. One point to note is that students never had to think aloud while writing in Dutch, thus possibly making the Dutch writing task easier, but this does not appear to be a problem because no direct comparisons of Dutch and English scores were made.

Finally, a general L2 proficiency test was given in the form of a seven-minute vocabulary test. While such a test is certainly limited in the kinds of conclusions one can make about overall proficiency, the authors argued that vocabulary is a strong predictor of overall proficiency. We note that any study that collects eight writing samples, two of which involve thinking aloud, imposes much time on the participants, so it makes sense that the authors could use only a short test of proficiency.

The authors explained that the transcripts of the think aloud sessions were divided into segments based on the writers' behavior. For example, *formulating* would be one activity. If the writer then reread his or her text, that would be considered another activity. As stated earlier, segmenting protocol transcripts can be challenging. In this case, the categories of behavior and the segmenting seem to overlap, and it is not clear what was done when two categories of behavior occurred in the same segment. Once the transcripts were segmented, they were coded into categories according to the writers' cognitive activities: reading the assignment, three different types of planning, and evaluating the text. Six coders each coded 16 transcripts, with four overlapping between two raters so that intercoder reliability could be reported. Cohen's kappa of .95 was reached. The authors included a table describing each coding category with examples.

Because one goal of the study was to determine the quantity and quality of L1 use, the authors also needed a way to quantify L1 use, so they counted any segment containing at least one L1 word as L1 use. In other words, if one word of Dutch was used in an *evaluating-the-text* segment, then the segment was counted as L1 use. This decision is understandable but it may have overestimated the amount of L1 use.

The results of the study are complex because the study examined so many different variables and correlations among the variables. To summarize, the participants all used their L1 at least once while writing, but some activities were more likely to be conducted in the L1. With regard to the relationship among L1 use, L2 proficiency, general writing proficiency, and text quality, it is interesting to note that L1 use had a negative relationship with general writing proficiency but not L2 proficiency. This may be because lower writing proficiency taxed the students' cognitive processes while thinking aloud, so it was easier to use the L1. Alternatively, it may have been an artifact of the way L2 proficiency was measured.

This study is a good example for researchers to follow both because of the careful design and the detailed reporting. In addition, it used true nonmetacognitive think alouds to find out about learners' processes that likely cannot be determined any other way. What is not clear is how thinking aloud actually affected L1 versus L2 use while composing. In other words, it could be that thinking aloud caused students to use more of the L1, but this type of reactivity probably cannot be studied. We know of no studies that have used stimulated recall to assess L1 versus L2 use, but, as noted earlier, it remains an open question as to whether or not learners can retrospectively recall which language they were thinking in.

Suggestions for Further Reading

Books on Verbal Protocols

- Bowles, M. A. (2010). *The think-aloud controversy in second language research.* New York and London: Routledge.
- Ericsson, K. A. & Simon, H. A. (1993). *Protocol analysis: Verbal reports as data.* Cambridge, MA: MIT Press.
- Gass, S. M. & Mackey, A. (2016). *Stimulated recall methodology in second language research.* New York and London: Routledge.
- Green, A. (1998). *Verbal protocol analysis in language testing research: A handbook.* Cambridge: Cambridge University Press.
- Pressley, M. & Afflerbach, P. (1995). *Verbal protocols of reading: The nature of constructively responsive reading.* New York and London: Routledge/Taylor Francis.
- Smagorinsky, P. (Ed.). (1994). *Speaking about writing: Reflections on research methodology.* Thousand Oaks, CA: Sage.

Other Reactivity and Veridicality Studies

- Fox, M. C, Ericsson, K. A., & Best, R. (2011). Do procedures for verbal reporting of thinking have to be reactive? A meta-analysis and recommendations for best reporting methods. *Psychological Bulletin, 137,* 316–344.
- Godfroid, A. & Spino, L. (2015). Reconceptualizing reactivity research: Absence of evidence is not evidence of absence. *Language Learning, 65,* 896–928.
- Goo, J. (2010). Working memory and reactivity. *Language Learning, 60,* 712–752.
- Morgan-Short, K., Heil, J., Botero-Moriarty, A., & Ebert, S. (2012). Allocation of attention to second language form and meaning: Issues of think-alouds and depth of processing. *Studies in Second Language Acquisition, 34,* 659–685.
- Van den Haak, M., De Jong, M.D.T., & Schellens, P. J. (2003). Retrospective vs. concurrent think-aloud protocols: Testing the usability of an online library catalogue. *Behaviour & Information Technology, 22,* 339–351.

9

INTERVIEWS

Interviewing has become one of the most widely used qualitative data collection methods in L2 writing research; a search in the Linguistics and Language Behavior Abstracts (LLBA) database found 122 L2 writing articles using interviews that were published in major journals between 2000–2013, with the vast majority (103) appearing since 2008. Interviews commonly comprise one of several sources of data within a study, as in ethnographic or case study research, where they add an *emic* (insider) perspective to the researchers' *etic* (outsider) perspective and contribute to data triangulation (see Chapter 4). They may also be part of mixed methods studies (see Chapter 5); for example, quantitative analyses of survey data may be supplemented by interviews with a subset of respondents in order to probe more deeply into issues raised by the survey results. In many studies, however, interviews comprise the primary or sole source of data, particularly in those focused on opinions, goals, beliefs, or identity, in which participants' voices and perspectives take center stage.

The strength of interviewing lies in its potential to deepen understandings in many areas of interest to L2 writing researchers by adding voices of practitioners and other stakeholders to those of researchers and bringing out individual characteristics and perspectives that are lost in large-scale quantitative analyses. Nevertheless, interviewing as a research method raises a number of methodological and epistemological issues. This chapter will begin with an overview of how interviews have been employed in L2 writing research (see Table 9.1) and a summary of the challenges involved in using interviewing as a data collection method. It then proceeds step by step through the process of designing and conducting interviews as part of an L2 writing study and concludes with a discussion of a sample interview-based study.

TABLE 9.1 Representative Studies Using Interviews

Citation	Participants, context, and data	Research questions/focus	Comments
Hyland (2013)	• 20 faculty (11 Cantonese L1, nine English L1) from four disciplines (business, science, engineering, arts) at an English-medium university in Hong Kong • Semi-structured interviews, 20 student texts with feedback	1. What do they [faculty in the disciplines] focus on in their feedback? What is it they are looking for? (p. 242)	• Little information is given about data collection and analysis procedures. • Paper reports percentage of mentions of each theme within each discipline, illustrated with multiple quotations from interviews.
Li & Casanave (2012)	• Two first-year students (one Cantonese L1, one Mandarin L1), one instructor (English L1) at a Hong Kong university • Students' texts, source texts, text-based interviews with students and instructor about source use; notes from observation of one student as she wrote her paper	1. How do the students understand "plagiarism" at their university? 2. What strategies do they use as they write an assignment that requires sources? 3. What are the textual results of their strategies and the instructor's response to each text? (p. 167)	• There were five to six interviews with each student (in Cantonese or Mandarin) and two interviews with the instructor. • Analysis of students' texts is supplemented with examples from interviews to document how students approached assignments.
Pecorari & Shaw (2012)	• Eight instructors in natural science, engineering, and medicine at Swedish universities • Text-based interviews around five student texts and original sources	1. How do faculty from various disciplines interpret and respond to intertextuality in students' texts?	• There is a detailed description of text selection, but less about analysis. • Interview questions and sample texts are included.
Lo & Hyland (2007)	• 40 primary school students (age 10–11) in Hong Kong • Focus group interviews with nine participants, reflective student log entries, a questionnaire, student writing, and teacher-researcher journal	1. How did a new writing program affect students' motivation and the quality of their writing?	• Interview participants were selected to represent different proficiency levels. • Six interviews (in Cantonese) were conducted after completion of traditional and new programs. • Interview questions are included.

(Continued)

TABLE 9.1 (Continued)

Citation	Participants, context, and data	Research questions/focus	Comments
Zhou, Busch, & Cumming (2014)	• 15 (former) EAP students and their five ESL and nine content-area instructors at a Canadian university • Semi-structured interviews and stimulated recalls (i.e., text-based interviews) about a writing assignment of student's choice	1. How do ESL teachers' goals for improving grammar in their students' writing, or lack thereof, correspond with those of students? 2. How do university teachers' goals for improving grammar in their students' writing, or lack thereof, correspond with those of students? (p. 237)	• Data were collected over two years (before/after students' transition to regular courses). • Interview questions are included. • Analysis procedures and coding categories are clearly described.
Yayli (2011)	• Six advanced EFL students in an English Language Teaching program in Turkey • Pre- and postinstruction interviews; drafts of writing assignments; participants' written comments on their writing	1. How does genre awareness become embedded in the stances of EFL participants through genre-based writing instruction? 2. How viable is multigenre portfolio use in genre-based EFL writing instruction? (p. 122)	• Researcher was the instructor for the course. • The coding process is briefly described, but no coding scheme or interview questions are provided.
Lee (2013)	• Four students in an in-service writing teacher education course taught by the researcher at a Hong Kong university • Semi-structured interviews (in English); participants' classroom research reports completed for the course	1. How did teachers discursively construct their identities (in discourse and practice) as writing teachers? 2. What factors influenced the negotiation of their identities (identity-in-activity) in the process of becoming writing teachers? (p. 333)	• There were two interviews with each participant (after completion of the course and one year later). • Interview questions are included. • Findings are presented under common themes illustrated with quotations from each participant.
Costino & Hyon (2007)	• Nine L2 writers (US-born, immigrant, international) taking mainstream (2) and ESL (7) writing courses at a US university • Semi-structured interviews	1. How do our students understand and affiliate with various linguistic identity labels that are often institutionally ascribed to them? And how, if at all, are their responses to these labels related to their residency statuses? 2. Why do students prefer one type of composition course (mainstream or multilingual) over another? And how, if at all, are their preferences related to their label responses and/or residency statuses? (p. 65)	• Interview questions and coding scheme are included. • It is unclear if data were coded independently by each researcher. • Findings are presented based on coding categories and illustrated with examples from multiple interviews.

Li (2014)	• 14 management academics at seven business schools in China. • Interviews in Mandarin (face to face or via Skype)	1. What motivates the management academics to publish in English? 2. How do they collaborate with co-authors in international publication? 3. To what extent do they face an English language barrier? 4. How is their knowledge exchange with practitioners connected to their endeavor of international publication? (p. 43)	• There is a detailed description of data collection and analysis. • Report includes coding scheme, but not interview questions. • Findings are presented based on coding categories and illustrated with brief examples from multiple interviews.
Morton, Storch, & Thompson (2015)	• Part of a year-long longitudinal case study of 13 EAP students at an Australian university; article reports on three of these • Four to five semi-structured interviews per participant, background questionnaires, three writing tasks asking participants to reflect on various aspects of writing, written assignments with feedback	1. What are the students' understandings of what it means to "do" academic writing, and do these change over the year? 2. Do the students' perceptions of themselves as academic writers change? 3. What factors contribute to any changes? (p. 3)	• There is minimal discussion of analytical procedures; no coding scheme is provided. • Findings for each participant are presented separately, drawing primarily from interviews and writing tasks. • Interview questions are included.

Purposes for Using Interviews

One area of L2 writing research in which interviewing has begun to play a larger role is the extensive body of work on written corrective feedback, which has expanded beyond statistical analyses of feedback types and their efficacy to explorations of the beliefs, disciplinary expectations, and affective factors that shape how instructors give feedback and how L2 writers perceive it. One example is Hyland's (2013) study of the feedback practices of disciplinary faculty at a university in Hong Kong. Although Hyland triangulated his interview data with examples of faculty feedback on students' papers, the paper did not focus on the feedback itself, but on participants' accounts of their feedback practices and what this reveals about expectations for students' content knowledge or analytical skills. Interviews have similarly been used to examine student and faculty views on plagiarism and source use, thus illuminating the complexity of this controversial topic. In a study of two L2 writers writing from sources at a Hong Kong university, Li and Casanave (2012) analyzed instances of borrowing (or *patchwriting*) in the students' texts, supplementing this analysis with interviews in which the writers explain their choices (see also Shi, 2008, in Box 9.1). Taking another perspective on this issue, Pecorari and Shaw (2012) used interviews with faculty from various academic disciplines to document views on what constitutes plagiarism and the difficulty of establishing clear definitions and providing guidance to students.

Another use of interviews comes from research investigating instructors' and students' attitudes toward writing instruction. Lo and Hyland's (2007) study of a new program of writing instruction in Hong Kong schools included interviews with students in order to gauge the program's impact on students' motivation and engagement. In a study on attitudes toward grammar instruction, Zhou, Busch, and Cumming (2014) used interviews to compare and contrast the attitudes of EAP students and their instructors regarding the importance of grammar in writing. Researchers investigating genre-based pedagogies have also employed interviews with L2 writers to provide insider perspectives, as in Yayli's (2011) study of a writing course in Turkey for pre-service teachers, which drew on multiple interviews with six focal participants as well as their annotations on their own writing to document their increasing genre awareness and their evolving attitudes toward genre-based instruction.

Finally, emerging areas of L2 writing research, such as L2 writer or teacher identity, the challenges faced by international scholars writing for publication, and acquisition of L2 academic literacy, have drawn extensively upon interview data as a window onto the experiences of research participants (see Table 9.2). Using interviews with four writing teachers in Hong Kong, Lee (2013) examined how participants talked about themselves as writing teachers and the ways in which various social and institutional forces (e.g., the place of English in Hong Kong, the writing curriculum) shaped their self-identification. Costino

TABLE 9.2 A Typology of Interviews Used in L2 Writing Research

Type	Characteristics	Why use it	Example
Semi-structured	• Topics and some questions pre-determined; others emerge from the interview • Some variation in questions for each interviewee	• Allow for individual voices • Probe more deeply into responses • Provide flexibility	Costino & Hyon (2007)
Discourse-based (text-based)	• Interviewees are prompted to comment on a text (e.g., a sample of student writing, written feedback, etc.)	• Add perspectives of practitioners to text analysis • Explore processes behind the text	Pecorari & Shaw (2012)
Focus group	• Researcher proposes a set of topics for discussion among a group of participants • Researcher acts as moderator	• Generate in-group discussion • Create a supportive atmosphere for self-disclosure	Lo & Hyland (2007)

and Hyon (2007) similarly used interviews to explore how undergraduate students identified themselves (e.g., as *bilinguals, native English speakers*) and whether this self-identification influenced preferences for multilingual versus mainstream writing courses. Li's (2014) study of Chinese business academics' publishing practices is one of many in this growing area of L2 writing research, in which interviews are used to incorporate participants' voices on issues such as the pressure to publish internationally, their sense of community (or lack thereof) with other international scholars in their field, and how they deal with publishing in an L2. Finally, Morton, Storch, and Thompson's (2015) multiple case study of multilingual undergraduate students at an Australian university drew from a series of interviews conducted with participants over the course of their first year to document their varied experiences with and attitudes toward academic writing and how these evolved over time.

Types of Interviews

Research interviews can be classified based on elicitation methods; those that are most commonly found in L2 writing research are listed in Table 9.2. Most qualitative research interviews follow a *semi-structured* format that uses a pre-planned set of questions but may deviate from these questions when interviewers wish to pursue an interesting line of talk. The specific questions asked of each participant may therefore differ, although there is some consistency regarding the topics covered. The flexibility offered by this format, as well as the space it creates for interviewees to bring up points of importance to them (but that were not anticipated by the researcher), have made it the preferred choice for L2 writing researchers. Two other approaches to interviews found in L2 writing research are *discourse-based* (or *text-based*) interviews and *focus group* interviews. Each of these will be discussed briefly here; more information can be found in the list of suggested readings at the end of this chapter.

Discourse-Based (Text-Based) Interviews

In discourse-based or text-based interviews, participants are shown a piece of writing and prompted to comment on certain features. In some studies this technique is referred to as *stimulated recall* (e.g., Zhou et al., 2014), although in practice it does not always follow the strict protocols of stimulated recall (see Chapter 8). Originally, text-based interviews were proposed as a means of tapping into the implicit knowledge of expert writers in a discourse community (Odell, Goswami, & Herrington, 1983). However, they have also been used to explore participants' perspectives on topics such as paraphrasing and citation (see Li & Casanave, 2012; see also Shi, 2008, Box 9.1), writing development (e.g., Li & Schmitt, 2009), genre-based pedagogy (Yayli, 2011), writing processes (Seloni, 2014), and writer identity (Abasi, Akbari, & Graves, 2006). For example, in their case study of the acquisition of lexical phrases by a Chinese MA student, Li and Schmitt (2009; also discussed in Chapter 6) first identified lexical phrases in the student's writing assignments and then held text-based interviews in which they showed her the assignments with the phrases highlighted and asked how she had learned them. The information obtained through these interviews was used to supplement the researchers' analyses of the texts and to provide a fuller account of the focal student's acquisition process.

The first step in preparing for a discourse-based interview is the selection of sample texts and specific textual features that will be the focus of the interview (Odell et al., 1983). Sometimes the research participants themselves make this selection (e.g., Shi, 2008; see Box 9.1). More commonly, the researcher chooses a variety of texts that exemplify the target phenomenon; for example, in their study on student and faculty attitudes toward textual borrowing, Pecorari and Shaw (2012) chose student texts that represented different approaches to dealing with source text material and asked interviewees to comment on them. As for the questions themselves, Odell et al. recommend providing alternatives for the feature in question (e.g., *Dear Ron* vs. *Dear Mr. Bunch*) and asking writers to explain why they would (or would not) choose each one, an approach that they advocate as allowing a researcher to "create a cognitive dissonance that would enable a writer to become conscious of the tacit knowledge that justified the use of a particular alternative" (p. 229). However, most L2 writing researchers have taken a more direct approach with questions such as "Is this an example of a good way to use and refer to sources?" (Pecorari & Shaw, 2012, p. 162) or "Starting with this first [citation], could you tell me what each citation is helping you do?" (Harwood & Petrić, 2012, p. 91).

Focus Group Interviews

In focus group interviews individuals are brought together to discuss selected topics, with the researcher acting as a moderator. Originating in market research, focus group interviews have been taken up by social science researchers who believe that allowing interview participants to exchange ideas among peers leads to more in-depth discussions, openness, and willingness to self-disclose (Krueger & Casey, 2000). This format also presents an opportunity for researchers to draw insights through analysis of group dynamics, although this aspect has not been exploited in L2 writing research thus far. In L2 writing research, group interviews usually involve students exchanging opinions about a writing course or activity (Lo & Hyland, 2007) or sharing experiences as L2 or bilingual writers (Jarratt, Losh, & Puente, 2006; Parkinson & Crouch, 2011). Focus group interviews usually begin with an *opening question* designed to put participants at ease; it should be quick and easy to answer (e.g., asking each participant to give some background information about him- or herself). This is followed by an open *introductory question* (Krueger & Casey, 2000, p. 45) that gets participants thinking about a topic by asking them to talk about an experience related to the topic. For example, Lo and Hyland (2007) opened with the question "Do you enjoy writing in general? Why?" (p. 234). The core of the interview comprises several *key questions* (or *focus questions*) that elicit the specific information needed to answer the research questions; Krueger and Casey (2000) recommend preparing two to five such questions, although some L2 writing researchers employing this method use more. In Lo and Hyland's study, a separate set of key questions was developed to gauge students' feelings about the traditional writing program and the new program that replaced it, with questions asking participants about specific features of each program; for example, after the new program participants were asked "How did you feel about the pre-writing and post-writing activities?" (p. 234). Kruger and Casey also recommend *transition questions* that link introductory questions to key questions; to transition from their opening question about writing in general, Lo and Hyland asked participants to comment on topics that they like to write about, which eventually led to a key question about specific topics used in the course. Finally, *ending questions* ask participants to sum up their feelings or experience, for example, "Take a good look at your compositions. Tell me any other thoughts/feelings you had during or after the lessons" (Lo & Hyland, p. 234).

Issues Involved in Interview-Based Research

Subjectivity

The major issue confronting researchers who employ interviews is the fact that interviews are inherently subjective; that is, they constitute individuals' (usually post hoc) accounts of events, processes, or mental states that may or may not be accurate representations of the phenomena themselves. In his book on qualitative research methods, Patton (2002) points out some of the factors that may influence (or in his words, "distort") these accounts, including the interviewee's emotional state, biases, political ideology, inaccurate recall, lack of awareness of the phenomenon under discussion, or feelings about the interviewer, as well as the possibility that interviewees may be providing "self-serving responses" (p. 306). For example, if an interviewee explains why she chose to quote a passage from a source text in her essay, she may not actually remember (or never have been consciously aware of) why this choice was made but may feel compelled to provide a response to the interviewer's question. Alternatively, she might feel threatened by questions about her citation practices and endeavor to find a justification that she perceives to be acceptable to the interviewer, whether or not this accurately reflects her decision-making process at the time of composition.

Even in studies on attitudes, beliefs, or perceptions in which participants' subjective meanings rather than facts are the focus, one must be cautious about assuming that the views expressed represent beliefs that correspond to a reality outside the interview. Similar to *observer's paradox* or the *Hawthorne effect* in observational research (see Chapter 4), participating in a research interview may alter an individual's behavior. This phenomenon may be even more pronounced than it might be in an observational study, as interviews bring the researcher and the researched into close interpersonal contact to discuss matters that are often of a personal and delicate nature, thus heightening the face-threatening potential. Other factors, such as power imbalances between a professor-researcher and L2 student writer, whether participants are being interviewed in a first or second language, the status of the interviewer as an insider or outsider in the community being researched, the gender or race of participants, and possible cultural issues, such as the supposed tendency of Chinese students to show deference to teachers or other authority figures (e.g., Hu, 2002), may also have an impact on interviewee behavior and the quality of responses generated by interview questions.

L2 writing researchers have adopted a number of strategies to increase reliability of interview data. One common approach is to verify participants' accounts through some form of triangulation (see Chapter 4), usually methodological triangulation in which interviewees' accounts are compared with data collected through other methods; for example, Hyland (2013) triangulated instructors' comments about their written feedback practices with the actual feedback they provided on assignments. Other studies achieve data triangulation by comparing individuals' accounts across multiple interviews (Li & Casanave, 2012) or accounts of multiple individuals on the same topic (e.g., Li, 2014). Researchers may also increase the possibility of obtaining reliable interview data by structuring interviews so as to give interviewees space to answer freely without interference from the interviewer. For example, Li and Schmitt (2009) noted the need to have questions that are "fluid and asked in an unbiased manner" (p. 88), and Flowerdew and Li (2009), while acknowledging the possibility of interviewer influence in theory, claimed that this was not an issue in their study, since "the interviewer played the role of a facilitator who let the research participants lead the way" (p. 6). The wording of interview questions can also come under scrutiny, and interviewers often take care to avoid loaded terms (e.g., *plagiarism*) in order to allow interviewees to talk about a topic in their own way (e.g., Shi, 2008, Box 9.1). Transparency regarding the data collection process, such as how and by whom interviews were conducted and the questions that were asked, can also help readers to gauge potential external influences on interviewee responses and thus strengthen claims regarding the reliability of data.

However, even when interviewers take care to avoid leading interviewees, the relationship between them can affect how the interview unfolds. This issue may become particularly significant in studies in which researchers are instructors at the institution where the study is being conducted and interview colleagues or their own students, a not-uncommon situation in L2 writing research (e.g., Costino & Hyon, 2007; Lee, 2013; Lo & Hyland, 2007; Yayli, 2011). Some have emphasized the positive effects of such relationships, in particular, how they engender trust that makes interviewees more likely open up and speak frankly, especially on sensitive issues. However, pre-existing relationships can also complicate interpretations of interview data, particularly when researchers interview students about a class that they themselves created or taught. It is perhaps not surprising that students tend to report positive attitudes toward classroom activities when being interviewed by their current or former teacher; in such cases it is reasonable to ask whether expressed opinions were influenced by positive feelings about the teacher-interviewer (the so-called *halo effect*) or unwillingness to question the teacher's authority by commenting negatively on a practice that he or she had apparently endorsed. The related concern of unequal power relationships between an instructor-researcher and student interviewee has occasionally been brought up in terms of its ethical dimensions (Abasi et al., 2006) and potential effect on interviewees' readiness to discuss issues such as plagiarism (Li & Casanave, 2012; see also Shi, 2008, Box 9.1). However, the possible influence of other power-inflected social categories such as race, gender, or class (e.g., see Lee & Simon-Maeda, 2006; Norton & Early, 2011) is rarely addressed in L2 writing research, even by researchers who position themselves within a critical theory paradigm or who characterize L2 writers as marginalized. This is clearly an issue that deserves more consideration.

Interestingly, despite the field's focus on crosscultural communication, L2 writing researchers have paid relatively little attention to the effects of the language of the interview or cultural backgrounds of interviewers and interviewees. Yet these factors have implications not only in terms of interviewees' ability to communicate (and thus to provide useful data) but also in terms of potentially exacerbating existing power differentials (i.e., an interviewee using an L2 may be at a disadvantage vis-à-vis an interviewer using an L1). The language of the interview is most often mentioned in studies in which researchers share an

L1 (and usually a cultural background as well) with interviewees. In such cases, conducting interviews in this shared language is seen as allowing interviewees to more clearly express themselves, while a similar cultural background is thought to be advantageous in terms of establishing rapport. Sometimes participants choose the language of the interview (e.g., Li & Casanave, 2012); while offering certain advantages, this practice may also complicate crossparticipant comparisons if some interviewees choose to be interviewed in their L1 while others are interviewed in their L2. However, in many published reports the language of the interview is not mentioned, let alone discussed. In most cases it is presumed to be English, which may be an L2 for the interviewee, the interviewer, or both. This is not necessarily problematic; nevertheless, language proficiency and its potential effect on interviews need to be taken into account when devising questions, conducting interviews, and drawing conclusions from interview data.

Interpreting Interview Data

A second, closely related issue concerns interpretations of interview data; if they are subjective, what kind of conclusions can we draw from them? This has become a contentious topic in the social sciences, including applied linguistics (e.g., D. Atkinson, 2005; P. Atkinson & Silverman, 1997; Block, 2000; Freeman, 1996; Hammersley, 2003; Holstein & Gubrium, 1995; Pavlenko, 2007; Talmy, 2010; Talmy & Richards, 2011), with researchers tending to fall into one of two camps. The first, associated with a postpositivist paradigm (Chapter 1), sees interviewing as a method for obtaining (more or less) factual information regarding interviewees' personal experiences, opinions, beliefs, or practices. This approach, which Talmy (2010, p. 129) refers to as the *interview as a research instrument* orientation, rests on an assumption that one can get at the truth embedded in interview data as long as one asks the right questions, maintains an objective stance when asking them, and uses caution when interpreting the results. Researchers working from this perspective tend to "take them [interviewees] at their word" (Freeman, 1996, p. 733) and see interview data as an accurate reflection of reality, albeit subject to the limitations delineated here. The second perspective, adopted by some researchers working within postmodern paradigms, entails a radical rethinking of what an interview is and what interview data represent. Rather than seeing interviewing as a method for discovering pre-existing beliefs and meanings, the *interview as a social practice* orientation (Talmy, 2010 p. 131) views interviews as "reality-constructing, meaning-making occasions" (Holstein & Gubrium, 1995, p. 4) in which beliefs and meanings are co-constructed by interviewers and interviewees. Researchers working from this perspective are more likely to seek to understand *how* or *why* interviewees present themselves in particular ways during the interview and the role of the interviewer and the interview context in shaping this. In other words, the subjective aspects of interviewing are not seen as problems to overcome but as aspects of human behavior to be analyzed as part of the research.

The first position (i.e., interview as a research instrument) is by far the dominant one in L2 writing research and in applied linguistics research generally. To some extent this is understandable; an analysis of how interviewers and interviewees co-construct the interview would have little relevance to a study whose aims are to document teachers' feedback practices or students' approaches to paraphrasing. However, when researchers claim a postmodern orientation (e.g., in studies that investigate issues such as writer identity), failure to apply the basic assumptions of the paradigm to the interview itself is more questionable; if one takes the position that individuals construct, perform, or negotiate identities through writing, it is problematic to assume that this process of identity construction stops at the door to the interview room (see Talmy, 2010, for a critique on this point). Moreover, even if one rejects this position as inconsistent with one's overall approach or specific research aims, it raises important questions regarding interviewing as a research method. While defending more traditional views against what he calls "the radical critique of interviewing," Hammersley (2003) nevertheless concedes "to ignore it [the critique] would amount to complacency, since it points to some serious dangers in using interviews and especially in relying exclusively on data from that source" (p. 124).

Credibility of Findings

Hammersley's (2003) comment points to the third issue regarding use of interviews: how to establish credibility of findings in studies in which interviews comprise the sole source of data. In the absence of other data sources to support interpretations, researchers must take particular care regarding the claims they make. Investigator triangulation, in which more than one researcher codes data (e.g., Pecorari & Shaw, 2012), or member checking, in which interpretations are reviewed and verified by participants (e.g., Lee, 2013), can help overcome some of the limitations inherent in studies that rely primarily on interview data. Providing multiple quotations from interviews, thus giving readers direct access to the data and the opportunity to evaluate interpretations (e.g., Hyland, 2013), can also contribute to credibility. However, care must be taken that interviewees' words are represented accurately, especially when they have been translated. Interestingly, although some of the studies reviewed for this chapter include data from interviews that were conducted in a language other than English, none present quotations in the original language, meaning that readers must trust that translations accurately reflect interviewees' intended meanings.

Another concern is lack of sufficient contextualization when examples are presented as block quotations with no indication of the question or turn that prompted the response. Talmy (2010) has argued that removing interview data from the interactional context in which they were produced erases the role of the interviewer in their production, and as a result "a wide range of potentially important insights concerning the data, analysis, and interpretations of a given study can be lost" (p. 136). However, few L2 writing studies include both interviewer and interviewee turns when presenting examples (for exceptions, see Parkinson and Crouch, 2011; Zhou et al., 2014). Even when space constraints preclude including the full interactional context, basic information, such as the question that the interviewee was responding to or the topic under discussion when the words were uttered, can strengthen the credibility of interpretations.

Finally, insufficient transparency regarding how the data were analyzed and selected for presentation in the final report can lead to suspicions of cherry picking examples to support claims. Studies that present findings based on themes that emerge during thematic coding (see Chapter 10) can enhance transparency by explaining the coding scheme and specifying how many items were coded under each theme or how many interviewees mentioned it so that readers can evaluate the robustness of the findings (e.g., see Shi, 2008, Box 9.1). Similarly, while the volume of data generated in an interview study and the limited space available in journals requires researchers to be selective about the themes, participants, or examples to include in the final report, it is essential to be transparent regarding the criteria used during this selection process. For example, Morton et al. (2015), who reported on data from only three of their 13 participants, justify their sample as representative of the writing courses in the university EAP program (one student from each course) and various academic disciplines (business, science, and art) from which their larger sample was drawn.

Ethical Issues

In addition to the ethical issues common to qualitative research in general (see Chapter 4), interview-based research comes with its own set of ethical concerns that must be weighed against the requirements of research quality. For example, while establishing trust between an interviewer and interviewee is seen as an important element in a successful interview, Duncombe and Jessop (2002) have pointed to the dangers of what they call "doing rapport" and "faking friendship" (p. 110) in an attempt to encourage interviewees to open up and speak freely, as such strategies may deceive interviewees regarding a researcher's actual agenda and role (see also Kvale & Brinkmann, 2009, pp. 74–75). Researcher identity can become particularly problematic when the interviewer has a pre-existing relationship with the interviewees (e.g., as their instructor or colleague), as the ensuing "tension between a professional distance and a personal friendship" (Kvale & Brinkman, 2009, p. 75) may generate confusion regarding whether the interviewer is a researcher seeking information or a friend or sympathetic ear to whom interviewees might confess their innermost feelings (e.g., see Richards, 2003, pp. 93–97). While this tension may lead to revealing and potentially interesting disclosures, Duncombe and Jessop argue that it is "an ethically dubious substitute for more open negotiation of the interviewee's fully informed consent to participate in the interviewing process" (p. 112).

A related issue is how participants will be depicted in written reports. Although a primary reason for including interviews in research is to bring out the voices of research participants, ultimately it is the researcher who decides whose voices will be heard and how these will be represented. The frequently heard complaint of public figures that a controversial comment attributed to them was "taken out of context" is equally relevant to interview-based research. As Richards (2003) notes, "we must appropriate their [participants'] words, and in doing so the honesty we owe them is recognition of the interpretive act we are performing, even in so elementary an act as the selection and inevitable recontextualization of their utterances" (p. 93). Representation is also implicated in decisions regarding whether quotations from interviews should reflect features of imperfect speech. For example, if an L2 writing instructor says, "Yeah I shoulda went over that better in class," should this utterance be presented exactly as it was spoken, or should *shoulda went* be changed to *should have gone*? Although such grammatical and phonological features are not uncommon in informal speech, some maintain that rendering talk in this way stigmatizes interview participants, especially those who do not speak a standard language variety (e.g., Roberts, 1997). On the other hand, Bucholtz (2000) has argued that standardizing these features also constitutes a "political act" that "can imply that the original is inadequate" (p. 1453); it also risks privileging the voice of the researcher over that of the participant or altering the participant's original meaning. However one decides to handle this dilemma, one should be transparent in published reports regarding any alterations that were made and why they were made (for more on this issue, see Chapter 11).

Designing a Study Using Interviews

Preparing for Interviews

The first step before embarking on an interview project is selecting participants. Because of the time required to conduct, transcribe, and analyze interviews, interview studies tend to have relatively small sample sizes; in those reviewed for this chapter the number of participants ranged from as few as one in a case study (Li & Schmitt, 2009) to as many as 46 (19 teachers and 27 students) in Lee's (2004) study of corrective feedback in L2 writing classes in Hong Kong, with most falling into the low end (10–15 participants) of this range. As with qualitative research in general, there is no ideal number of participants that would apply in all contexts. Instead, this decision should be made based on the nature of the project, that is, how many participants are required to enable the researcher to answer research questions and substantiate claims. As Kvale and Brinkmann (2009) note, "If the purpose [of the interview] is to understand the world as experienced by one specific person . . . this one subject is sufficient" (p. 113).

For group interviews, the main decisions are (a) the size of the groups, (b) the number of groups, and (c) whether groups should be homogenous or heterogeneous. The literature on focus group interviews recommends using groups of 6–10 participants each to encourage group dynamics (Krueger & Casey, 2000; Kvale & Brinkmann, 2009, p. 150); however, groups used in L2 writing research tend to be smaller (two to three participants). Within-group homogeneity is also favored as a means of creating a more supportive and comfortable environment for sharing (Krueger & Casey, 2000). However, as Roulston (2010, p. 40) points out, one cannot necessarily assume that individuals whom the researcher places within the same category (e.g., Chinese L1 speakers) will necessarily see themselves as part of a homogenous group. In addition, Roulston cautions that when individuals in focus groups are already known to each other (as is often the case in L2 writing research), they may be reluctant to express views that diverge from those of peers or colleagues. She therefore recommends conducting a pilot study to determine whether the focus group format will generate the data needed to answer research questions or supplementing focus group data with individual interviews or other sources.

Once potential interviewees have been selected, researchers prepare what is variously referred to as an *interview protocol, interview schedule,* or *interview guide* (the preferred term for semi-structured interviews); that is, a list of topics and questions that will be used in the interview. For semi-structured interviews, the purpose of the interview guide is to provide enough structure so that useful information can be elicited across multiple interviews while still allowing for individual variation. Although a loosely structured guide consisting of little more than a set of topics can be a powerful instrument in the hands of an experienced interviewer, novices will benefit from preparing a list of main questions and possible follow-up questions, as long as this list is truly treated as a guide that can be deviated from when necessary and not as a checklist to be strictly followed.

Developing interview questions and organizing them into an interview guide that will enable collection of useful data requires careful thought and planning. Kvale and Brinkmann (2009) point out that interview questions must function both *thematically* to generate information relevant to the research and *dynamically* to encourage meaningful interaction (p. 131). If questions are to serve the latter function, they must be both comprehensible and relevant to interviewees. In addition to attending to surface features (e.g., avoiding academic terminology and complex syntax), interviewers must be careful not to assume that issues or concepts that are familiar or interesting to them are necessarily familiar or interesting to those whom they interview. For example, although writer identity has become an increasingly popular focus for L2 writing research, it is not clear that it is relevant or even salient to L2 writers themselves (Casanave, 2003, p. 94). In a study of L2 graduate student writers, Abasi et al. (2006) found that more experienced writers were able to speak about identities they constructed through their citation practices (although they never used the term *identity*); however, novice writers seemed to be baffled by questions asking them to "identify their own voice from those of others" (p. 106) in their writing and were unable to answer. Although this is an interesting finding that speaks to an understudied aspect of writing development, it also points to complications that can arise when interviewers and interviewees do not share a common set of assumptions. Since the goal of interviews is to explore interviewees' perspectives, it is necessary insofar as possible to see things from their perspective when framing interview questions.

Interview questions can be broadly classified as *closed* vs. *open* and *direct* vs. *indirect* (see Table 9.3), and methods texts offer various suggestions as to how each of these should be employed. Interviewers are usually advised to avoid closed questions as they may (a) generate short rather than elaborated responses and (b) push interviewees into taking an unequivocal stance that they may later feel obliged to defend, even though their actual position is more nuanced (Richards, 2003). Closed questions are also characterized as restricting responses to categories that have been pre-selected by the interviewer (Patton, 2002, p. 355). For example, a closed question such as "Do you think that peer review is useful?" may lead interviewees to adopt the interviewer's categories (i.e., useful vs. not useful), whereas an open question such as "What do you think of peer review?" could generate a greater range of stances toward the topic. However,

TABLE 9.3 A Typology of Interview Questions

Type	Characteristics	Why use it	Examples
Closed	• Limited set of responses (e.g., "yes" or "no")	• Target specific information • Verify understanding	• Do you think X is useful? • Did you mean X?
Open	• Potentially limitless set of responses • Framed as *wh*-questions, directives, or requests	• Allow participants to formulate response in their own words	• How do you feel about X? • Please describe X.
Direct	• Addresses topic directly	• Ask about topics in a straightforward manner	• What do you think of X? • Why did you do X?
Indirect	• Addresses topic indirectly • May use a prompt (e.g., text, story)	• Ask about sensitive or abstract issues • Avoid a generic or stock response	• Which of these examples best illustrates X?
Opening	• General question to open the interview	• Put participant at ease • Open up possible avenues to be explored through further questions	• Tell me about X.

some researchers (e.g., Kvale & Brinkmann, 2009) argue that closed questions may serve a useful function, such as verifying the interviewer's understanding or targeting specific information; if one is researching the usefulness of peer review (as opposed to students' feelings about peer review), the closed question given earlier would be a legitimate option. Nevertheless, a good rule of thumb is to build interviews around open questions and reserve closed questions for specific purposes, such as clarification.

The choice between direct and indirect questions will depend on one's judgment as to the best way to approach a topic. Direct questions, while straightforward, may not be the best option when a topic is sensitive ("Have you ever been accused of plagiarism?") or abstract ("How do you identify yourself as a writer?"). Kvale and Brinkmann (2009) suggest delaying direct questions until interviewees have brought up a topic, thus indicating a readiness to discuss it. Richards (2003) also points out that direct questions sometimes lead to a "stock response" (p. 73); for example, a question such as "What do you think of process writing?" might generate an answer that simply echoes received wisdom (e.g., "Oh, it's great. I always use it."). In such cases, it may be necessary to find an indirect means of eliciting desired information. Using prompts (such as pictures or texts) to make an abstract concept more concrete is one strategy; rather than asking disciplinary faculty to define plagiarism, Pecorari and Shaw (2012) showed interviewees examples of source use and asked whether they considered these to be appropriate. Similarly, Costino and Hyon (2007) explored L2 writers' self-identification by showing participants a list of conventionally used labels (e.g., *ESL, bilingual, native speaker*) and asking them to choose which ones best described themselves. One can also tell a story or create a scenario and ask interviewees to respond to it; instead of the direct question "What do you think of process writing?" one could ask, "If an instructor told you that she was using process writing, what activities would you expect to see in her classroom?" Framing the question in this way can push interviewees to go beyond generalizations and may elicit a more detailed and concrete response that will better illuminate how they understand a concept.

Finally, in creating an interview guide one must also consider how to sequence questions to ensure that interviews flow well and encourage free and open interaction. Patton (2002) recommends beginning with questions such as "What are you currently working on in school?" (p. 352) that are easy for interviewees to answer and will put them at ease; responses to these questions can also provide a context for the questions to follow. Spradley (1979, p. 86) recommends what he calls *grand tour questions* (e.g., "Tell me about your writing class") that allow interviewees considerable leeway in formulating responses and encourage them to respond at length, thus opening up possible avenues to be explored in more depth through follow-up questions.

Those with little to no prior experience in formulating interview questions will find it useful to use these criteria to review and evaluate interview questions that are often included in appendices to published articles. Trying out some of these questions in practice interviews would also provide some insight into what kind of data might be generated by different types of questions. In addition, before implementing any interview guide, one should pilot it, preferably with several individuals who are representative of the population that will be interviewed for the research. Piloting can provide invaluable information regarding how comprehensible and meaningful questions are to interviewees as well as how useful they are to the researcher in terms of generating data to address research questions. Piloting can also serve as a dress rehearsal that provides opportunities to practice interviewing techniques and to determine how much time should be allowed for the interview.

Conducting Interviews

Methods texts provide a wealth of advice on conducting interviews (e.g., Kvale & Brinkmann, 2009; Patton, 2002; Richards, 2003; Roulston, 2010). The main point to remember is that interviewing involves more than simply asking the questions on the interview guide; one must also listen attentively and respond appropriately to what interviewees are saying. Interviewer responses may include nodding or backchanneling (*uh-huh, yeah*) to indicate attentiveness and encourage further talk, verifying interpretations (e.g., "Do you mean X?" or "So you're saying X?"), or probing for further information through techniques such as reflecting the interviewee's words back to them ("Plagiarism?") or employing generic questions such as "Could you say a little more about that?" or "Could you give an example?" When used strategically, silence can also be a valuable interviewing technique, as it allows interviewees time to process questions and formulate responses, which may be especially important when interviewees are not fully proficient in the language of the interview. In addition, rather than moving quickly to the next question once an answer has been given, interviewers should remain silent for a short time to encourage interviewees to expand further; Kruger and Casey (2000) recommend "the five-second pause" (p. 110) as a technique to prompt additional contributions.

Beyond this general advice, the interview process and the role of interviewer in this process will vary depending on the approach to interviewing that one has adopted. While all researchers agree that interviewers should take care not to interfere with interviewee's responses, they differ in terms of what kind of behavior might be classified as interference. As research conducted from a postpositivist perspective aims to generate objective findings, a key concern is to avoid biasing what ideally should be an accurate account of the interviewee's beliefs or experiences. The interviewer's role may therefore be restricted to asking nondirective questions, probing when answers are unclear or insufficient, providing minimal responses (e.g., indicating that one is listening), and in general endeavoring to remain outside of the interview insofar as possible. On the other hand, assumptions regarding co-construction of knowledge that underlie postmodern approaches to interviewing presume a more active role for interviewers in generating (rather than simply eliciting) knowledge in partnership with interviewees. One of the more detailed explications of this approach is the *active interview* (Holstein & Gubrium, 1995) in which interviewers aim "to incite the production of meanings" (p. 17) through practices such as asking interviewees to try on different roles or to consider issues from different perspectives. For example, in an interview about attitudes toward peer review, interviewees might be asked to take the perspective of both givers ("What do you look for when you review a classmate's paper?") and recipients ("What kinds of peer comments are most useful for you?") of peer comments as well as that of the teacher who assigned the task ("Why do you think your teacher had you do peer review?") and to compare and reflect upon any differences that emerge. Although the responses may not necessarily reflect interviewees' thinking prior to the interview, this approach is not seen as interference but as assisting participants to "piece experiences together, before, during, and after occupying the respondent role" (p. 8).

Regardless of the approach that one takes, conducting interviews is a complex skill that takes considerable practice to master, and novice interviewers should develop their skills through piloting or role-playing before attempting the real thing. Richards (2003, p. 59) advises recording practice interviews (with permission, of course) for subsequent review and evaluation, and a number of methods texts contain useful checklists for evaluating interviewing techniques (e.g., Kvale & Brinkmann, 2009, p. 164; Richards, 2003, p. 59).

Analyzing Interview Data

Analysis of interview data can be approached in multiple ways, with the choice depending on research purpose, theoretical framework, and chosen paradigm. If the purpose of the interview is to uncover factual information (e.g., how a teacher gives feedback, why a student did not cite a source, how frequently an international scholar publishes in English), researchers may choose to give what Kvale and Brinkmann (2009, p. 252) call a *veridical* reading of the data; that is, one that focuses on content and treats that content as an accurate reflection of reality. However, other approaches are also possible. For example, Kvale and Brinkmann (2009, p. 252) note that one can also analyze interviews in terms of what they reveal about interviewees' personal perspectives and experiences (a *experiential* reading) or relationships to the topic (a *symptomatical* reading). Alternatively, one can analyze the language that interviewees use to represent the topic (or themselves), thus taking a *presentational* orientation (Freeman, 1996, p. 734). For example, imagine that an interviewee complains about a writing course that she took. One could treat this as a fact about the quality of instruction in the course (veridical reading), see it as indicative of the individual's personal experience in the course (experiential reading) or negative attitude toward the course or toward writing instruction in general (symptomatical reading), or consider how the interviewee uses terms such as *the writing process* or *voice* to represent herself as knowledgeable about writing instruction and thus qualified to offer a critique of the course (presentational reading). None of these approaches is inherently superior to the others, nor are they mutually exclusive. Rather, each provides different insights and answers different questions.

Interview data are typically analyzed using either some form of *thematic analysis*, in which data are coded to identify major themes, or *discourse analysis*, which focuses on the structures or functions of talk rather than (or in addition to) what is said. These methods will be discussed in more detail in Chapter 10 (thematic analysis) and Chapter 11 (discourse analysis); here we will briefly consider what each offers for interview analysis and how one might go about choosing between them. Thematic analysis is by far the most common method of analyzing interview data and was used in nearly all of the studies reviewed for this chapter. In thematic analysis, transcripts are read recursively and assigned *codes* that are subsequently refined and organized into a *coding scheme* comprising a hierarchy of major categories, themes, and subthemes. This method allows researchers to bring order to a disparate and unwieldy data set and to uncover patterns and make connections across interview participants or multiple data sources. Because researchers who employ it tend to be focused on the *whats* of interviews rather than on *hows* or *whys*, this method is often associated with the interview as a research instrument orientation (Talmy, 2010). It is sometimes criticized for reducing the complexities of interaction to a set of codes and isolating individual statements from the overall interview context, thus leading to facile or inaccurate interpretations (e.g., Pavlenko, 2007; Talmy, 2010). However, this need not necessarily be the case; it is possible to begin with a thematic analysis of the overall data set and to follow this by selecting representative examples for each theme and analyzing them through multiple interpretative frameworks, thus expanding beyond a veridical reading of the data.

Discourse analysis offers an alternative for those interested in taking a presentational view (Freeman, 1996) of interview data and analyzing interviews as "meaning-making occasions" (Holstein & Gubrium, 1995, p. 4; see also Roulston, 2010; Talmy, 2010; Talmy & Richards, 2011). Discourse analysts do not ignore content but are equally interested in how individuals construct talk in collaboration with others and may also consider the influence of cultural, social, or historical forces (e.g., interviewees' perception of the interviewer as a member of the dominant social class). While not suitable for addressing all research questions, this approach holds potential for research focused on areas such as writer identity, beliefs, or attitudes, as it allows analysts to go beyond the content of the talk to consider the significance of interviewees' linguistic choices and interactional behavior in terms of the issues under consideration. However, discourse analysis of interview data is not yet widely used in L2 writing research (for an exception, see the discussion of Pomerantz & Kearney, 2012, in Chapter 11). For example, although group interviews, in which participants respond to each other as well as to the interviewer, would lend themselves well to this approach, L2 writing researchers who have used this technique have tended to extract individual comments from transcripts and analyze them in isolation rather than as part of a larger interactional context.

Discussion of a Focal Study: Shi (2008)

BOX 9.1 FOCAL STUDY

Shi, L. (2008). Textual appropriation and citing behaviors of university undergraduates. *Applied Linguistics, 31*, 1–24.

Background

Noting that prior interview-based research on student source use has been limited to citation practices, Shi argues that a full understanding of this issue requires examination of textual borrowing that is not cited. She therefore designed her study to allow students to identify instances of textual borrowing in their own texts and to explain their reasons for citing or not citing the material.

Research Questions

1. Why do students appropriate source texts and cite them in their writing?
2. Why do students appropriate source texts but not cite them in their writing?
3. How do students apply principles of textual borrowing to quotations, paraphrases or summaries?

Method

Data collection comprised discourse-based interviews with 16 undergraduates at a North American university with a variety of majors and L1s (including English). Three of the L2 English speakers were recently arrived international students; the remainder were the children of immigrants and had received all or most of their education in North American schools. Participants were asked to bring a recently completed paper and a source text to the interview and to identify and comment on passages in which they had used the source text. A coding scheme was developed based on key words used by the students.

Results

Results are reported through descriptive statistics (frequency of mentions of each item from coding scheme) and illustrative quotations. The most commonly mentioned reasons for citing were (a) to provide support for claims and (b) to credit others' words or ideas. The primary reasons for not citing included (a) identification of information as common knowledge (although students differed in terms of the basis upon which they made this decision) and (b) avoiding over-citation. Shi concludes that even when seen as inappropriate to an outsider, students' citation choices seem to be principled. She proposes that acts of unintentional plagiarism are characteristic of an early stage of the process of becoming an academic writer.

In this study Shi uses discourse-based interviews to explore students' perspectives on citation. The primary strength of the study is its emic orientation, that is, its focus on students' explanations of their own borrowing and citation practices that Shi elicited by asking participants to bring in a sample paper and to identify and comment on instances of source use. By providing a window into students' rationales for citing or not citing, the study demonstrates that failure to cite appropriately may arise from many sources, including incomplete understanding of the conventions for citation operating in a particular discipline (e.g., what constitutes common knowledge). In addition, the study is unique in including both English L1 (3) and L2 (13) student writers with varying amounts of experience with the norms of the North American academic setting. Quotations from both L1 and L2 writers are included as examples and attributed to specific participants, and an interested reader can check these against the participant profiles provided in the methods section (p. 5) to get some basic background (e.g., L1, age of arrival in North America, etc.) about the speaker. However, Shi does not discuss the role that students' educational or linguistic backgrounds might have played in their citation practices or justification of these practices, meaning that this potential of the study is not exploited.

The study is somewhat handicapped by reliance on a single source of data, especially since participants were all students at the same university in Canada and were interviewed only once. Although Shi also collected sample texts from each participant, these were used as a stimulus for the discourse-based interviews rather than as an additional source of data. Excerpts from student texts and their original sources are presented in the paper to contextualize the students' comments, but not independently analyzed. Nevertheless, the fairly large sample size (16 participants) does allow for some data triangulation, and there was also investigator triangulation as a research assistant recoded a portion of the data to check reliability. In addition, although the sample was one of convenience (i.e., it comprised individuals who answered an advertisement), the fairly broad range of L1s (English, Cantonese, Mandarin, Polish, Japanese, Korean, and Romanian), majors (four science majors and 12 from humanities and social science), and lengths of residency (ranging from those born in North America to recent arrivals) of participants suggests that themes that emerged from this analysis might have relevance beyond this particular population. In addition, by comparing her results against those of similar studies throughout her analysis, Shi is able to extend (if not to generalize) her findings beyond the context of the study.

The study is also a model of transparency. Data collection and analysis procedures are thoroughly described, and the interview guide is available online as part of supplementary materials. Other than a few background questions (e.g., "What is your major?") the interview guide is comprised entirely of three open questions: (a) "Can you describe the assignment you just did?" (b) "Please point out words and ideas in your writing that were borrowed or appropriated from source texts (e.g., by quoting, paraphrasing or summarizing) and then explain, in each case, why you borrowed them and whether you decided to cite or not to cite" and (c) "Any comments on the challenges in writing to include source information?" By allowing participants a great deal of leeway in formulating responses, these questions contribute to the achievement of Shi's stated aim of privileging students' view of source use rather than those of the researcher. The paper also includes a coding scheme that is exemplary in its level of detail, including definitions and examples for each theme. Frequency counts allow readers to see how often each item on the coding scheme was mentioned, and provision of quotations from two different interviews in support of each theme provides a reasonably strong basis on which to make claims.

One potential issue is the fact that participants were asked to provide a retrospective account of their citation practices and to do so in front of an authority figure (unfortunately, Shi does not mention the nature of her relationship with her participants, although they were presumably students at the university where she is an associate professor). While Shi acknowledges possible outside influences that could have impacted the reliability of her data (e.g., attempts by students to provide explanations that would be acceptable to the interviewer), this is simply mentioned as a limitation rather than incorporated into the analysis. Nevertheless, through careful attention to the conduct and documentation of her research, Shi is able to overcome some of the limitations of interview-only studies and to add a useful perspective on citation practices that adds to the growing literature on source use.

Suggestions for Further Reading

General Guides to Interviewing

- Holstein, J. A. & Gubrium, J. F. (1995). *The active interview.* Thousand Oaks, CA: Sage.

- Kvale, S. & Brinkmann, S. (2009). *InterViews: Learning the craft of qualitative research interviews* (2nd edn.). Thousand Oaks, CA: Sage.
- Patton, M. Q. (2002). Qualitative interviewing. In M. Q. Patton (Ed.), *Qualitative research and evaluation methods* (3rd edn., pp. 339–428). Thousand Oaks, CA: Sage.
- Richards, K. (2003). Interviewing. In K. Richards (Ed.), *Qualitative inquiry in TESOL* (pp. 47–103). London: Palgrave Macmillan.
- Roulston, K. (2010). *Reflective interviewing: A guide to theory and practice.* Thousand Oaks, CA: Sage.
- Spradley, J. P. (1979). *The ethnographic interview.* Belmont, CA: Wadsworth/ Thomson Learning.

Specialized Interview Types

- Krueger, R. A. & Casey, M. A. (2000). *Focus groups: A practical guide for applied research* (3rd edn.). Thousand Oaks, CA: Sage.
- Odell, L., Goswami, D., & Herrington, A. (1983). The discourse-based interview: A procedure for exploring the tacit knowledge of writers in nonacademic settings. In P. Mosenthal, L. Tamor, & S. A. Walmsley (Eds.), *Research on writing: Principles and methods* (pp. 221–226). New York: Longman.

Methodological and Ethical Issues

- Bucholtz, M. (2000). The politics of transcription. *Journal of Pragmatics, 32,* 1439–1465.
- Duncombe, J. & Jessop, J. (2002). "Doing rapport" and the ethics of "faking friendship". In M. Mauthner, M. Birch, J. Jessop, & T. Miller (Eds.), *Ethics in qualitative research* (pp. 107–122). London: Sage.
- Lee, E. & Simon-Maeda, A. (2006). Racialized research identities in ESL/EFL research. *TESOL Quarterly, 40,* 573–594.
- Norton, B. & Early, M. (2011). Researcher identity, narrative inquiry, and language teaching research. *TESOL Quarterly, 45,* 415–439.

Interpreting Interview Data

- Atkinson, D. (2005). Situated qualitative research and second language writing. In P. K. Matsuda & T. Silva (Eds.), *Second language writing research: Perspectives on the process of knowledge construction* (pp. 49–64). Mahwah, NJ: Lawrence Erlbaum.
- Block, D. (2000). Problematizing interview data: Voices in the mind's machine? *TESOL Quarterly, 34,* 757–763.
- Freeman, D. (1996). "To take them at their word": Language data in the study of teachers' knowledge. *Harvard Educational Review, 66,* 732–761.

- Hammersley, M. (2003). Recent radical criticism of interview studies: Any implications for the sociology of education? *British Journal of Sociology of Education, 24*, 119–126.
- Talmy, S. (2010). Qualitative interviews in applied linguistics: From research instrument to social practice. *Annual Review of Applied Linguistics, 30*, 128–148.
- Talmy, S. & Richards, K. (Eds.). (2011). Qualitative interviews in applied linguistics: Discursive perspectives. [Special Issue]. *Applied Linguistics, 32*(1).

10

THEMATIC ANALYSIS

Analysis of qualitative data often involves systematic coding in order to discover patterns or *themes* that can subsequently become the basis for interpretation. Because of its wide applicability and versatility, thematic analysis is commonly used in qualitative L2 writing research to analyze data from sources such as observational field notes, interviews (see Chapter 9), stimulated recall, open-ended responses to questionnaires, and various types of written texts (see Table 10.1). Unlike in studies in which researchers apply a pre-determined coding scheme to the data (see Chapter 7), coding in qualitative research tends to be *emergent*; that is, the codes are derived *from* the data rather than being imposed *on* them. Qualitative coding can also be distinguished from quantitative coding in that instead of reducing the data to numeric codes for the purpose of statistical analysis, it aims to bring order to what might otherwise seem to be a large and unwieldy data set and to facilitate deeper understandings and interpretations of what the data represent. In other words, qualitative coding is not an end in itself but "a first step to somewhere else" (L. Richards, 2009, p. 93).

In this chapter we will outline some of the most common approaches to thematic analysis and review how these have been used in L2 writing research. We will also discuss some of the major issues related to this form of data analysis, such as coding dependability and analytical transparency. The chapter continues with a general discussion of the coding process and the potential advantages and disadvantages of carrying out this process using qualitative data analysis software. We conclude with a discussion of a sample study that uses thematic coding.

Purposes for Using Thematic Analysis

Thematic analysis is used whenever there is an interest in the content of a text; for example, *what* research participants say in an interview or write in a journal

TABLE 10.1 Representative Studies Using Thematic Analysis

Citation	Participants, context, and data	Research questions/focus	Comments
Cho (2010)	• Part of a larger study of 25 Koreans residing in U.S.; paper focuses on four who attended graduate school in Korea • Interviews (in Korean) about learning to read and write in L1 and L2, relevant historical documents	1. How do the Korean scholars negotiate their multilingual identities? 2. What macro factors do they associate with their academic biliteracy development? 3. How do their views of academic writing in Korean and English relate to each other? (p. 84)	• Thematic coding is used to identify common themes across the data set. • List of codes is not provided. • Emergent themes are triangulated with information about the Korean educational system to situate the narratives within a larger social context.
Abasi (2012)	• 10 students in a course on Iranian media in an advanced-level intensive Persian program at a US university • Students given two editorials to summarize; one from an Iranian paper and one from *NY Times* translated by researcher into Persian • Summaries, students' posttask written responses to questions about the tasks, transcript of posttask discussion, instructor/researcher's reflective journal	1. How do the [L2 Persian] students perceive two argumentative "Persian" texts while attempting to summarize them without knowing that one is a loyal translation of an American text? 2. How do the students summarize the two texts, and are there any differences between their written summaries of the texts? (p. 197)	• Initial coding was based on key words (in vivo coding). • Themes were crosschecked with another researcher. • Coding procedures are briefly but clearly described. • Multiple examples illustrate themes.
Matsuda & Tardy (2007)	• Graduate student (author of the manuscript) and two professors of rhetoric and composition (reviewers); all NS of English • Simulated blind peer review • Manuscript, two reviews, posttask interviews with reviewers, confirmatory interviews with reviewers about results, interview with author	1. Do readers construct the author's voice when reading an academic text? 2. If so, what are some of the discursive and nondiscursive features that readers draw upon when constructing this voice? (p. 239)	• Coding was done separately by each researcher and compared; results were confirmed with reviewers. • There is little description of coding procedures, and a list of categories or themes is not provided.

Weigle & Nelson (2004)	• Three MATESOL candidates in a graduate course on L2 writing paired with three ESL grad students who volunteered for 10 hours of tutoring • Online discussions from the writing course, videotapes of six tutoring sessions, tutors' and students' retrospective interviews using videos for stimulated recall, tutors' final reflective papers	1. What factors affected the tutor-tutee relationship? 2. How did these factors affect the success of the tutoring sessions and the tutor–tutee relationship? 3. How did the tutoring context influence tutor roles? (p. 205)	• Data were coded on Atlas.ti qualitative data analysis software using grounded theory (but without theoretical sampling). • Categories for each participant were summarized on a matrix and subsequently turned into narratives; narratives were member-checked with tutors.
Kuteeva (2013)	• 32 participants from the four most represented disciplines in an English for academic research course in Sweden • Online genre-analysis tasks, personal statements from participants	1. What kind of variation can be traced in the way that students in a multidisciplinary humanities faculty approach "examine-and-report-back" genre-analysis tasks? (p. 85)	• Course used genre-based pedagogy and was taught by the researcher. • Detailed description of analysis process given. • Paper includes table listing major themes; numerous examples provide rich description. • Coding was checked with another researcher.
Liao & Chen (2009)	• Six high school textbooks used to teach writing in Taiwan (three English, three Chinese)	1. What is the purpose of argumentative writing in Chinese and English? 2. How do writers properly express their position? 3. What are the strategies used for organizing the overall essay, including where to place the thesis statement and how to sequence the supporting ideas? 4. What are the strategies for writing the introduction and the conclusion? 5. What are the strategies for supporting writers' argumentation?	• Analysis is based on key words (in vivo coding) related to RQs. • Themes were compared across textbooks and across languages. • There is minimal description of coding procedures.

(*Continued*)

TABLE 10.1 (Continued)

Citation	Participants, context, and data	Research questions/focus	Comments
		6. What are the suggested techniques of logical reasoning?	
		7. What are the suggested rhetorical strategies apart from logical reasoning?	
		8. What is the role of the audience and addressing opposing views?	
		9. What are the rhetorical similarities and differences between Chinese and English argumentative writing? What are the possible factors that could account for the similarities and differences in the rhetorical elements? (p. 699)	
Negretti (2012)	• 17 students in three classes at a community college in the US; all classified as "beginning academic writers" (NS, NNS, Gen 1.5) • 20 journal entries for each student, "initial and final self-descriptions as writers" (p. 148)	1. What is the nature of beginning academic writers' perceptions of task, and how do these perceptions develop over time? 2. What is the nature of beginning academic writers' metacognitive awareness of strategies, and how does this awareness develop over time? 3. How do beginning academic writers use this metacognitive awareness to monitor, self-regulate, and evaluate their writing? (p. 147)	• Analysis is based on constructivist grounded theory (but without theoretical sampling). • There is a detailed description of analysis procedures and a full list of codes, including frequencies and examples.

Study	Data and participants	Research questions	Analysis notes
James (2010)	• 11 students in a two-semester first-year EGAP [English for general academic purposes] writing course at a US university from a range of L1s and majors • 2–4 audio-recorded text-based interviews with each participant over the course of 1–2 semesters, writing samples from each participant, demographic questionnaires • Instructor interviewed for background info, but this data not analyzed	1. Does learning transfer from EAP writing instruction to other academic courses? 2. If so, what transfers, and to where? (p. 186)	• Analysis uses deductive coding based on a start list derived from RQs and relevant prior literature. • There is a detailed discussion of coding procedures.
Harwood & Petrić (2012)	• Two students and their two lecturers in a business program in Britain • Two discourse-based interviews with each participant	1. How do the students enact performance by means of their citing behavior? 2. What impressions do the students attempt to convey about themselves to their lecturers who are reading their work? (p. 63)	• Analysis is based on Miles and Huberman (1994). • Paper focuses on a single code (*performance*). • Data were coded separately by each researcher, and differences were resolved through discussion. • Full coding scheme is provided, but there is little discussion of how codes were developed.
Hasrati & Street (2009)	• 13 Iranian doctoral students and six of their supervisors in different universities in Britain • Email responses from 30 students regarding origins of PhD topics; semi-structured interviews with 13 of them (in Persian) and their supervisors (in English)	1. How were participating PhD students initiated into their courses? 2. How were their PhD topics arranged? 3. What is the role of their supervisors and other students in their PhD work? (p. 17)	• Analysis uses constructivist grounded theory. • Final RQs emerged from process of data collection and analysis.

rather than on *how* they say or write it. A primary purpose is to identify themes that can be compared across multiple sources of data or multiple participants, thus facilitating discovery of trends that characterize the overall data set. Cho's (2010) thematic analysis of narratives told by four Korean scholars working in the US uncovered some common features characterizing her participants' academic literacy experiences in both Korean and English, which allowed her to draw broader conclusions regarding the impediments to developing biliteracy that are faced by Korean-English bilingual scholars. In a study investigating students' awareness of intercultural rhetorical differences, Abasi (2012) asked advanced-level students in his Persian foreign language class to summarize and comment upon two editorials on the same topic, one from an Iranian newspaper and one from *The New York Times* that he had translated into Persian. His thematic analysis of students' post-task written comments and a transcript of a whole class discussion about the assignment revealed consistent themes across 10 participants, thus providing support for his argument regarding the salience of crosscultural differences in text organization.

On the other hand, crossdata comparisons that are facilitated by thematic analysis may call attention to important differences as well as similarities. Motivated by ongoing debates regarding the role of voice in readers' assessments of writing (see Matsuda, 2015), Matsuda and Tardy (2007) designed a study in which two professors of rhetoric and composition were asked to do a simulated blind peer review of a manuscript written by a graduate student writer. The reviews and posttask interviews with each reviewer were coded for common themes related to voice, defined as "the reader's impression [of the writer] derived from the particular combination of the ways in which both discursive and non-discursive features are used" (p. 239). The researchers found that the reviewers constructed very similar images of the writer (whom they did not know personally); however, each reviewer pointed to different features of the text as influencing his or her impressions. Weigle and Nelson's (2004) thematic analysis of stimulated recall data (using video recordings of peer tutoring sessions as the stimulus) allowed them to identify several common factors that shaped how these tutoring sessions unfolded but also revealed the unique ways in which these factors played out across the three dyads that they studied. Kuteeva (2013) coded genre-analysis tasks produced by students in her English for academic research course in order to identify features that students most often focused on in their analyses of research articles. She found significant individual differences in terms of how each student approached the analyses, which she traces to the level of disciplinary knowledge that they brought to the task (see also Cheng, 2011, Box 10.1). Liao and Chen (2009) compared textbooks used in Taiwanese high schools to teach argumentative writing in Chinese and English to determine if there was any basis for assumptions that argumentative writing is approached differently in these two academic communities. Using a thematic analysis based on key words derived from their research questions, they compared how each textbook described the purpose of argumentative writing and how it taught students to organize their writing and support their arguments, finding both similarities and differences.

When applied to longitudinal data, thematic analysis allows researchers to document how patterns change over time. Negretti (2012) examined beginning L1, L2, and Generation 1.5 student writers' development of metacognitive awareness of tasks and writing strategies through a thematic analysis of reflective journals that students produced throughout a semester-long writing course. Comparing themes and categories both within and across participants over time enabled Negretti to identify which aspects of metacognitive awareness showed the most development as well as how these interacted. In another longitudinal study, James (2010) drew on thematic analyses of interviews with 11 students in an EAP writing course and examples of papers collected over one to two semesters to identify learning outcomes that were applied to students' writing both in the EAP course and in other courses. Comparison of categories generated from the analysis across time and settings demonstrated how some of the learning outcomes that were evident in students' EAP writing did not necessarily transfer to other contexts.

Finally, thematic analysis can sometimes uncover anomalies or unexpected themes worthy of further investigation. One example comes from Harwood and Petrić's (2012) study of the citation practices of international students enrolled in a business program in Britain. Among the themes that emerged from their initial coding of interview data was one that they labeled *performance*, defined as "instances where student writers describe engaging in an activity which serves to influence their lecturers in any way" (p. 97); this theme subsequently became the focus for an extended analysis. Hasrati and Street's (2009) study of how dissertation topics were chosen among a group of Iranian graduate students at several British universities provides another example of how a research focus can evolve based on findings from initial coding. After an analysis of email responses to the researchers' questions on this topic indicated variation across disciplines (i.e., topics were assigned by supervisors in engineering but chosen by students in social sciences and humanities), a subgroup of students and their supervisors from each discipline was selected to participate in face-to-face interviews to investigate discipline-specific factors that might account for this variation.

Approaches to Thematic Analysis

Types of Coding

Qualitative codes can be divided into two broad categories, those that describe data (*descriptive codes*) and those that reflect the researcher's interpretations of data (*interpretative codes*). The former comprises codes consisting of explanatory labels (usually a noun or short phrase) that are used to organize material and provide a means of accessing information in a systematic way. For example, a researcher might use descriptive codes to identify interview participants' gender, first language, and language proficiency in order to be able to classify participants into groups based on these variables for a subsequent comparative analysis. Another use of descriptive codes is to indicate the topic of a passage, for example, what an interview participant is talking about (*favorite writing teacher* or *vocabulary problems*) or what is going on at a certain point in a recording of classroom interaction (*warm up activity* or *group work*). In interpretative coding, the researcher goes beyond the surface level of what the text says to interpret what the text means. The difference between these two types of codes can be seen in the following excerpt from Harwood and Petrić (2012). As she talks about how she tries to create an extensive list of references, an interviewee says, "[S]ometimes I borrow books and I just read through like this [leafs pages]. To see if 'Oh, OK this person also talks about X.' And I remember it's in my essay, I'll just, I'll take the person's [laughs]" (p. 73). Harwood and Petrić coded this passage with both a descriptive code (*literature searching*) and an interpretative code (*performance*), with the latter indicating their interpretation of the student's action as a performance of a good student identity for her instructor. However, this distinction is not always so clear-cut; for example, assigning descriptive codes often involves some degree of interpretation. In addition, some researchers, such as Miles, Huberman, and Saldaña (2014), stress that when done thoughtfully rather than mechanically, any type of coding may involve "deep reflection about and, thus, deep analysis and interpretation of the data's meanings" (p. 72).

Beyond these broad categories, coding in thematic analysis can be classified in a number of ways (see Table 10.2). One useful distinction is between *deductive* and *inductive* coding. Deductive coding begins with a *start list* (Miles et al., 2014, p. 81) of codes derived from research questions, hypotheses, interview topics, or specific variables that the study is investigating. These codes are then applied to the data, evaluated in terms of how well they fit, and revised and refined. This approach is best suited for studies in which researchers have a clear sense of what they are looking for prior to beginning the analysis or have formed a hypothesis about what they may find. For example, in order to investigate transfer of learning from EAP writing courses to other writing contexts, James (2010) created a coding scheme based on several points that were relevant to his research questions, including the topics and learning outcomes from the EAP course syllabus (e.g., *using temporal transitions*), Horowitz's (1986) classification of academic writing tasks (e.g., *summary, synthesis of multiple sources*), and a model of academic language use developed by Chapelle, Grabe, and Berns (1997); for example, references to paraphrasing were coded as *using resources*. Codes from the start list were then applied to interview data and student papers and revised as needed; for instance, the start list code *annotated bibliography* (from Horowitz, 1986) was dropped as none of the examples fit this category, while others (e.g.,

TABLE 10.2 Approaches to Thematic Analysis Used in L2 Writing Research

Type	Characteristics	Why use it	Example
Deductive coding	• Start list of codes developed prior to beginning analysis. • Initial codes may be refined or discarded during analysis.	• Examine data for specific concepts or themes based on research questions, hypotheses, or prior research	James (2010)
Inductive coding	• Codes not pre-determined but emerge from analysis.	• Allow for discovery of themes that do not fit a pre-existing coding scheme	
In vivo coding	• Based on key words or phrases in the text being analyzed • Used for first round of coding	• Capture an emic perspective through participants' own words or concepts	Abasi (2012)
Constant comparative method	• Cycles of *open coding, focused coding,* and *axial coding* • Action codes (e.g., gerunds) to describe what is happening in the data • Codes compared against the data and against each other to identify most important themes	• Generate valid findings through a rigorous approach to qualitative analysis	Negretti (2012)
Grounded theory	• Coding follows the constant comparative method (see previous type) • Additional data are collected to further develop emerging theory (theoretical sampling)	• Create theory from data	Lee & Schallert (2008a)
Miles & Huberman (1994) Miles, Huberman, & Saldaña (2014)	• Codes are assigned to data (first cycle coding) and then grouped into categories or themes (second cycle coding) • Use of visual displays to identify relationships across themes	• Reduce data to a manageable set of themes • Identify recurring patterns	Harwood & Petrić (2012)

explanation of calculations) were added to account for examples that did not fit into any existing categories (see James, 2010, pp. 188–190).

In inductive coding (sometime referred to as *emergent coding*), the researcher begins without any predetermined categories and allows the themes to emerge from the data. This approach allows the researcher to be open to themes that may not fit pre-existing hypotheses. Inductive coding is the most common approach adopted by L2 writing researchers employing thematic analysis and was used in the majority of studies reviewed for this chapter. For example, in contrast with James's (2010) deductive approach, Canagarajah (2011) took an inductive approach to coding to identify the rationale and strategies behind a student's *codemeshing* (i.e., use of multiple languages) in an autobiographical essay about her literacy experiences. Having codes and themes emerge *from* the data (i.e., essay drafts, journals, and interviews) rather than imposing them *on* the data allowed Canagarajah to build an account of the student's codemeshing practices that reflected the student's emic perspective.

Among the many possible methods of inductive coding (e.g., see Miles et al., 2014), one that is commonly found in L2 writing research is *in vivo* coding (not to be confused with the software program NVivo), which is based on key words and phrases in the text being analyzed. This method is used in studies in which the actual words, perspectives, voices, or cultural categories (e.g., terms unique to a specific academic discipline or social group) used by research participants or focal texts are central to the analysis. For example, Abasi (2012) began his analysis by coding students' written and oral reflections on a summary writing task based on key words such as *lay-out, packaging, main idea*, and *better organized* (p. 200). Using the students' own words for the initial round of coding allowed Abasi to stay close to the emic perspective that was crucial to his analysis.

Thematic coding may also take place within an established approach to qualitative data analysis; those most frequently referenced in L2 writing studies include the *constant comparative method* (Corbin & Strauss, 2008), *grounded theory* (Glaser & Strauss, 1967), and Miles and Huberman's (unnamed) approach (Miles & Huberman,1994; Miles et al., 2014). However, labels such as *grounded theory* or the *constant comparative method* often seem to be applied rather loosely to designate any analytical method involving multiple cycles of coding, even when the study does not strictly follow the procedures outlined by the originators and practitioners of these methods. Researchers intending to use any of these approaches are encouraged to become more familiar with its procedures and overarching philosophy as well as its suitability for the proposed research design through a careful reading of the suggested readings listed at the end of this chapter.

The Constant Comparative Method

The constant comparative method is an approach to coding developed by grounded theorists Julie Corbin and Anselm Strauss (2008) that has also been taken up by researchers who do not otherwise follow a grounded theory approach (for a discussion of grounded theory, see the next section). It involves multiple rounds of coding during which codes, categories, and patterns are generated, compared, evaluated, and refined. The first stage is *initial* (or *open*) *coding*, during which the researcher reads through the data line-by-line (or paragraph-by-paragraph or incident-by-incident) keeping in mind questions such as "What is actually happening in the data?" (Glaser, 1978, p. 57). Charmaz (2006) suggests using gerunds as codes to keep the focus on actions and processes. Through a process of constantly comparing "data with data, data with codes, and codes with codes" (Thornberg & Charmaz, 2012, p. 78), the researcher will come to identify the most important or frequent codes, which then become the basis for the next phase of *focused* (or *selective*) *coding*. Focused codes, which may come directly from initial coding or be developed through combining several initial codes, are then applied to the same data; when appropriate, they may also be subsequently "raised" to the level of categories (Thornberg & Charmaz, 2012, p. 81). Categories that result from focused coding are then refined by comparing data within and across cases (e.g., different accounts of the same incident by different participants, different points in time for a single participant), relating larger categories to subcategories, and establishing connections between categories, a process that in some versions of grounded theory is referred to as *axial coding* (Corbin & Strauss, 2008; see also Thornberg & Charmaz, 2012, p. 82).

An example of the constant comparative method as applied in L2 writing research can be found in Negretti's (2012) study of student writers' awareness of writing strategies. The data comprised writing journals written by students (L1 English, Generation 1.5, and ESL) in a community college composition class. Negretti began with open coding of journal entries using action codes; for example, the passage "[I used] the box strategy to pin-point the main idea that I thought the author was trying to message out to his readers, giving my explanation" (p. 156) was coded as *describing strategies*, while the passage "Requires lots thinking, reading, more reading and lots of editing. . . . I will be a little stress out. . . . I don't understand what I need to do or write about" (p. 151) was coded as *expressing emotions*. As these codes were applied across the data set during focused coding, they were further refined; for example, *describing strategies* was broken down into more specific codes such as *describing personal writing strategies to tackle task* and *describing personal writing strategies [not task specific]* (p. 156). As these codes were compared across multiple participants during axial coding, they were merged into larger categories, such as *metacognitive awareness of strategies and self-regulation*, which then became the basis for the final analysis.

Grounded Theory

Grounded theory was first formulated by social scientists Barney Glaser and Anselm Strauss (1967; see also Corbin & Strauss, 2008; Glaser, 1978) as a means of providing a rigorous and systematic way of generating valid findings based on a qualitative analysis. More recently, researchers critical of grounded theory's postpositivist orientation have developed an alternative version known as *constructivist grounded theory* (e.g., Charmaz; 2006; Thornberg & Charmaz, 2012) that aims to incorporate consideration of the social construction of both data and analysis into a grounded theory approach. Grounded theory seeks to generate theory that is grounded in data through recurrent cycles of data collection and analysis. For example, in a study of how the teacher-student relationship affects students' response to written feedback, Lee and Schallert (2008a; see also Lee & Schallert, 2008b) used the constant comparative method to code data from interviews, student papers, classroom observations, and transcripts of teacher-student conferences. Through multiple cycles of coding and reviewing the data (see pp. 514–516), they looked for interrelationships between categories, eventually constructing a model (i.e., theory) to represent how various factors, such as the teacher's goals, students' writing ability, and degree of trust between teacher and students, interacted in this particular context (see p. 517).

In the classic approach to grounded theory, the theory that begins to emerge from initial stages of coding is further developed through *theoretical sampling*, the selective collection of additional data motivated by the emergent theory. Data collection and analysis end when the analysis reaches *saturation*, that is, "when gathering fresh data no longer sparks new theoretical insights, nor reveals new properties of your core theoretical categories" (Charmaz, 2006, p. 113). However, despite the centrality of theoretical sampling in grounded theory, the studies reviewed for this chapter that referenced grounded theory as the chosen analytical approach showed no evidence that any data were collected subsequent to coding and, with a few exceptions, did not necessarily aim to generate theory. That is, L2 writing researchers have tended to reduce grounded theory to a coding method rather than treating it as an overall approach to qualitative research at the level of ethnography or case study, as it is commonly described in the methodological literature (e.g., Creswell, 2013).

Miles and Huberman

The (unnamed) approach to qualitative data coding outlined in Matthew Miles and Michael Huberman's methods sourcebook (1994, revised and updated in Miles et al., 2014), has been widely used by researchers in multiple disciplines. Unlike approaches such as grounded theory, Miles and Huberman's approach does not adhere to any particular philosophical or theoretical position but rather seeks to provide a flexible and practical guide to qualitative coding. Similar to the approaches described earlier, these coding procedures involve a recursive process in which codes are developed, evaluated, and revised; in the latest edition (Miles et al., 2014) these are referred to as *first cycle coding*, in which codes are used to summarize the contents of data, and *second cycle coding*, in which these codes are aggregated into categories in order to identify patterns (p. 73). First cycle coding may be based on any of a number of features, including topics, key words (in vivo coding), processes (what actions are being performed), emotions (what individuals are feeling), values (what attitudes and beliefs are reflected in the passage), or evaluations (how individuals assess a topic or situation), among other possibilities (Miles et al., 2014, pp. 73–81; see also Saldaña, 2013). For example, Harwood and Petrić's (2012) coding scheme for interviews with students about their citation practices included topic codes (*parties consulted*), process codes (*literature searching*), evaluation codes (*self-evaluation*), and values codes (*beliefs about citing*) (see pp. 95–97 for the full coding scheme). In second cycle coding, the researcher assigns *pattern codes*, which Miles, Huberman, and Saldana (2014) define as "explanatory or inferential codes, ones that identify an emergent theme, configuration, or explanation" (p. 86). These pattern codes may comprise categories, themes, or *clusters* (p. 90) that characterize multiple codes from the first cycle of coding. Although Harwood and Petrić (2012) do not describe the process through which initial codes were developed into their final coding scheme, a number of these final codes appear to be pattern codes or larger categories subsuming a number of subcodes; for example, the category "Advice" comprises the subcodes *advice before writing, advice during writing, written advice,* and *advice given orally* (p. 95).

Issues Involved in Qualitative Coding

Dependability

A major issue in thematic analysis is dependability (also called *reliability* or *trustworthiness*) of coding. As noted in Chapter 4, dependability refers to consistency, and in the case of coding usually concerns whether the categories derived through the analysis are applied uniformly across the data set. The most common means of checking for coding dependability is to have all or part of the data coded independently by another researcher who has been trained in the coding procedure. Studies using deductive coding may report *interrater reliability* (see also the discussion in Chapters 6 and 7), a percentage that expresses the degree of agreement between coders (e.g., James, 2010). However, in inductive coding there is no expectation that multiple coders will independently achieve identical results. For this reason, studies using inductive coding usually do not report interrater reliability but instead follow a procedure in which two (or more) researchers code all or part of the data separately and then meet to compare codes, negotiate any discrepancies until agreement is reached, and revise the coding scheme accordingly (e.g., Abasi, 2012; Harwood & Petrić, 2012; Weigle & Nelson, 2004). A variant of this approach is *collaborative coding* (Smagorinksy, 2008, p. 401), in which researchers code together rather than working independently. The aim of using multiple coders in inductive coding is not only to strengthen dependability but also to use the ensuing negotiation as a means of generating more insightful interpretations of the data. Coding categories can also be checked with research participants; for example, Matsuda and Tardy (2007) conducted what they called *confirmatory interviews* (p. 248) in which they shared the themes identified in their coding with the two individuals who had acted as manuscript reviewers in the study, and Weigle and Nelson (2004) shared their narrative summaries of the data with the three tutors in their study. For those operating within a postmodern paradigm (see Chapter 1), inconsistent results from different coders are not necessarily seen as problematic, as it is assumed that each individual will bring his or her own unique experiences and perspectives to the data. However, these different interpretations need to be documented and their implications discussed as part of the final analysis (L. Richards, 2009, p. 108). In addition, some approaches, such as grounded theory, reject use of outside researchers as additional coders as contrary to the principle that a researcher's immersion in the data is central to producing a viable grounded theory.

Another type of dependability involves consistency of coding across time, which can be established when the same researcher codes the data at different points in the research process (L. Richards, 2009, p. 108), as is the norm in approaches such as the constant comparative method. Again, unlike in studies reporting interrater reliability, there is no assumption that a researcher will necessarily code the same data in the same way each time. Rather, the aim is to treat each set of codes as hypotheses that are subsequently tested, refined, and possibly rejected along the way as the analyst deepens his or her understanding of the data.

Data Reduction and Credibility

Data reduction (not to be confused with reductionism discussed in Chapter 2), also referred to as *data condensation* (Miles et al., 2014, p. 12), is an inevitable part of qualitative analysis through which a large collection of data is transformed into a more manageable set of themes and patterns. However, insufficient transparency in documenting this process can lead to questions regarding how representative these themes are of the larger data set and thus threaten credibility of findings. In a pointed critique of the quality of methods sections in social science research reports, Smagorinsky (2008) laments the failure of many researchers to provide a description of their analytical procedures, noting, "If I don't know pretty clearly how the researcher is conducting the study, then it doesn't matter much to me what the results are because I have no idea of how they were produced" (p. 393). Miles, Huberman, and Saldana (2014) echo this complaint and suggest that, among other things, readers need to know how the data were "aggregated, condensed, partitioned, displayed, analyzed, and interpreted" (p. 317). Simply stating that one used grounded theory or providing a generic account of coding procedures (e.g., "I coded the data several times, refining the categories until I arrived at a final set of themes") does not provide readers with sufficient information to evaluate the quality of the analysis.

An account of coding procedures should ideally detail the steps involved, examples of codes that were generated during the initial analysis, and how initial codes were subsequently refined, merged, or discarded, as well as a description of the final coding scheme. If space limitations do not permit this level of detail, at a minimum there should be some indication of what the final categories are and how the researcher arrived at them (Smagorinsky, 2008). By making the researcher's coding decisions transparent, documentation of analytical procedures and the codes that they engender can both contribute to the dependability of coding and strengthen the credibility of the resulting claims. A number of the studies discussed in this chapter provide good examples of analytical transparency (e.g., James, 2010; Kuteeva, 2013; Negretti, 2012; see also Cheng, 2011, Box 10.1). However, it is all too common to find instances in which it is impossible to judge how categories were generated or applied based on the brief (or in some cases nonexistent) descriptions of analytical procedures given in the methods section. Neglect of this vital aspect of thematic analysis constitutes a major threat to establishing credibility in the eyes of readers.

Doing Thematic Analysis

Methods texts often stress that analysis is not a stage of qualitative research but part of a cycle that begins during data collection and continues throughout the research process (e.g., Miles et al., 2014; K. Richards, 2003; L. Richards, 2009). Although this may not be possible in all research designs, beginning to analyze data while data collection is still in progress has a number of advantages. First, spreading out the job of coding over a longer period of time somewhat eases the burden of analyzing large amounts of data. More importantly, it also allows the researcher to use preliminary findings and insights to shape subsequent data collection and fill in any gaps. For example, a thematic analysis of interviews conducted during an early stage of the research may cause the researcher to revise the interview guide for subsequent interviews or to expand the pool of participants in order to explore themes that have unexpectedly emerged from the analysis.

Thematic analysis involves querying the data, that is, asking questions that will lead to deeper understanding and insights through multiple rounds of coding during which an initial set of codes is refined and reduced to a smaller set of themes. This process can be performed manually by highlighting text, writing codes in the margins, and cutting up the paper into strips or recording notes on index cards to be sorted and categorized (for examples, see Miles & Huberman, 1994; K. Richards, 2003). More recently, however, researchers have been turning to computer-assisted qualitative data analysis software (CAQDAS) to assist in this task (see the section on Using Software later in the chapter). Regardless of whether one takes on this task manually or uses software, the basic procedures remain the same. Here we offer a sketch of the process of thematic analysis; more detailed accounts can be found in the suggested readings listed at the end of this chapter.

Generating and Refining Codes

A basic version of thematic analysis can be found in King and Horrocks (2010) and L. Richards (2009), both of which recommend beginning with descriptive coding in order to get a sense of what the data set contains. The key question at this stage is "What is this about?" (L. Richards, p. 101). The next stage involves *interpretive* (King & Horrocks) or *analytical* (L. Richards) coding during which the descriptive codes developed in the first stage are gathered together into categories. L. Richards (2009) suggests approaching the task of analytical coding by first identifying interesting passages in the data and then asking "Why is it interesting?" and "Why am I interested in that?" (p. 103), using the answer to the latter question as a category. For example, given Abasi's (2012) research questions (see Table 10.1), we can assume that students' comments about text organization were interesting because they pointed to perceptions of crosscultural differences between the original Persian and original English texts, thus leading him to create a category, "Cultural Explanation of Text Organization," for in vivo codes such as *arrangement is Western.*

Thematic analysis involves continual review, reflection, evaluation, and refinement of the codes and categories that one is creating. Two codes may turn out to be different labels for the same (or very similar) phenomenon and can thus be merged into a single overarching code, some may subsequently appear to be overly general and thus require breaking down into smaller subcodes, and others may apply to only a small portion of the overall data set and might therefore be discarded. Drawing from grounded theory, K. Richards (2003, p. 276) offers a useful set of criteria for evaluating coding categories that involve asking whether a category is *empirically relevant* (fits the data), *practically useful* (is clearly defined), *conceptually coherent* (is suitable for the chosen theoretical or conceptual framework), and *analytically useful* (helps the researcher understand the data). Similarly, L. Richards (2009) suggests that researchers "constantly tidy up" (p. 123) the category system that they are developing by reviewing categories to check that none are redundant or otherwise not useful (e.g., they can be applied to only one passage of text) and merging categories together when they seem to represent the same meaning. For example, Abasi eventually collapsed two categories, "Text Organization" and "Cultural Explanation of Text Organization," into a single theme, "Culturally Familiar Macrostructure" (see p. 200).

As the process of thematic analysis is interpretive, there is no single correct set of codes or categories that can capture everything about the data set. There may also be cases in which more than one code can be assigned to the same piece of data in what Miles, Huberman, and Saldana (2014, p. 81) call *simultaneous coding.* For example, Harwood and Petrić (2012) note that some comments from interview participants, such as "Smith was supposed to be a very important book, so I used it. And that's what I'm saying, I know what they [the instructors] want to read" (p. 72), might be coded as both *motivation to cite* and *performance* if the participant expressly noted an intention to influence their instructor as a primary reason to cite a particular source. In such cases, they assigned both codes to the passage. In addition, categories developed during coding can vary depending on the research focus or the researcher's perspective. As Miles, Huberman, and Saldana note, assigning pattern codes is "an interpretative act" (2014, p. 90), and many configurations are possible. This does not mean, however, that the coding is unreliable or invalid. Rather, one must recognize that any segment of text may contain multiple meanings; the job of the researcher is to draw out those aspects that are most relevant for the project or that seem to lead in the most promising directions.

Recording and Reflecting

All methods texts on thematic analysis emphasize the importance of recording one's thoughts and reflections about the data and what it means throughout the research process. L. Richards (2009) recommends keeping what she calls a *log* (p. 25), beginning from the initial phases of a project, in which the researcher records things such as changes to the research design that occur during data collection, memos about how and why coding categories were created or revised, and reflections on the implications of decisions made during data collection and analysis. The purpose of a log is both to document the research process (which, as noted in Chapter 4, is an important element in establishing credibility in interpretative research) as well as to provide a space in which to try out ideas and explanations for emerging findings that can subsequently be supported (or rejected) through further data collection and analysis (pp. 49–50). Similarly, K. Richards (2003, p. 272) argues for keeping a *research diary* to record ideas, thoughts, and plans regarding the project as it progresses; he further notes that by encouraging reflection on the research process, a research diary can help the researcher work through difficulties, discover new insights, and identify problematic areas.

Miles, Huberman, and Saldana (2014) advocate using both *jottings* (short notes scribbled in the margins of hard copy texts or attached to the data in qualitative analysis software) as well as more extended and formal *analytic memos*. Jottings can include information such as the researcher's personal reactions to something in the data, notes about something that needs to be followed up on later, reflections on the inadequacy of interview questions or other data collection methods and ways that this might be dealt with in future rounds of data collection, and so on (see Miles et al., 2014, pp. 93–95). The aim of jottings is to capture "fleeting and emergent reflections and commentary" (p. 93) while working through the data in order to identify possible issues that require further consideration or to mark features that could later turn out to have significance. Analytic memos, on the other hand, represent the researcher's interpretations of the data at various stages of analysis and may include topics such as how the data relate to the research questions, possible connections among codes and categories, or what a code or category means or why it has been selected (Miles et al., 2014, p. 96; see also Saldaña, 2013, pp. 49–50). These analytic memos may subsequently become the basis for the final write up of the research.

Memos are also central in grounded theory approaches to analysis, where they are used during all phases of coding to note down "ideas about codes and their relationships as they strike the analyst while coding" (Glaser, 1978, p. 83). Thornberg and Charmaz (2012) characterize memos as a means of "conversing with ourselves" (p. 55) in order to raise questions, make comparisons, elaborate ideas, and test assumptions. In a memo a researcher might define codes, outline the processes behind the coding, try out hypotheses, or identify gaps in the analysis that require further data collection. Like codes and categories, memos in grounded theory are also compared and integrated through the process of *memo sorting* (Charmaz, 2006) in order to further refine the developing theory.

Moving From Coding to Theory

Simply compiling a list of codes and categories does not in itself constitute an analysis. At some point the researcher must move from coding to theory, that is, begin to construct an overall account of the data that is adequate to address the project's research questions or research focus and, ideally, contribute to the field of L2 writing. This may involve synthesizing the themes, patterns, and insights that have been emerging from the analysis into some sort of coherent whole or, alternatively, using them to identify contrasts across cases or changes over time (see the studies in Table 10.1 for examples of these possible outcomes). It may also involve moving outside of the data itself to situate one's findings within a larger field by, for example, comparing them with results of other studies or framing interpretations within relevant theory.

In moving from coding to theory the researcher may engage in a number of activities. One possibility is to conduct searches and queries (tasks greatly simplified by use of software) to identify relationships across codes, categories, and data sources; for example, one might search for all instances of the emotion code *anxious* to see if these diminish over time or examine passages that were coded for both *anxious* and the category "Past Experiences of Writing" to see if there is any connection between the two (e.g., L. Richards, 2009, pp. 158–168). Another option is creating visual displays such as *matrices* (i.e., charts or tables) or *networks* (flow charts in which items are connected by lines to indicate processes), a practice strongly advocated by Miles, Huberman, and Saldana (2014), who devote an entire section of their sourcebook to this topic. These displays are derived from pattern codes and enable the researcher to see connections and relationships. After developing a list of categories based on their coding of stimulated recalls with learners and writing tutors, Weigle and Nelson (2004) used matrix displays to summarize these categories for each dyad, which allowed them to better understand the patterns of interaction within each dyad as well as the similarities and differences across them. Changes across time might be visualized through a network display that traces how a particular emotion evolved, for example, from *feeling incompetent* to *somewhat anxious* to *confident*.

During these final stages of analysis, researchers must constantly review, reflect upon, and test the developing theory to ensure that it provides a good fit with the data. One useful technique is to adopt a skeptical approach to one's own analysis by deliberately questioning one's findings and looking for gaps, deviant cases, or other forms of disconfirming evidence that are incongruent with the developing theory (K. Richards, 2003, p. 283; L. Richards, 2009, p. 173). In addition, researchers working from a postmodern perspective have also argued for the need to attend to "the sociohistoric and cultural influences on the researcher's conceptual lens" (Pavlenko, 2007, p. 167), that is, to consider how one's analytical categories are shaped by one's identity as a researcher and the context in which the research is being conducted.

Using Software

In recent years, computer-assisted qualitative data analysis software (CAQDAS) has become increasingly common in qualitative research and has occasionally been employed in L2 writing studies (e.g., Weigle & Nelson, 2004). The primary purpose of using such software is to simplify the mechanical aspects of analysis, such as managing, integrating, and searching large amounts of qualitative data. Of the many software packages available, those most commonly used in L2 writing research include Atlas.ti, MAXQDA, and NVivo. While differing in some respects, these share a number of common features, which will be briefly outlined here. More information on CAQDAS, including detailed specifications for various software packages, can be found in the suggested readings at the end of this chapter (for a description of Transana, a software package designed for discourse analysis, see Chapter 11).

One of the benefits of CAQDAS is the ability to consolidate data from multiple sources, including text, spreadsheets, graphics, and media (voice or video) into a single location, thus facilitating comparison and triangulation across the data set. Some packages also allow importing of data from online sources, such as web pages, Twitter, Facebook, and Google Earth. Once data have been imported into the program, researchers create codes by highlighting a portion of text or a segment of a picture or media file and typing in a label (for a new code) or choosing an already-created code from a drop-down menu. As the coding scheme develops, initial codes can easily be renamed, gathered under larger themes, ordered into hierarchies, and re-sorted and recategorized as needed. Codes and key words can then be searched across the data set; for example, one could search for and gather together all instances of the word *plagiarism* from classroom and interview transcripts, syllabi, and the university website or all instances of the category "Vocabulary Problems" from multiple interviews. CAQDAS programs also allow writing comments and memos that are linked to specific points in the data as well as generation of visual displays, including word clouds, charts, and matrices, that can facilitate identification of patterns and relationships among data points.

Despite the many potential contributions of CAQDAS, some cautions are in order. One issue that has frequently arisen involves what is called *closeness to data* (e.g., Gilbert, 2002; Serór, 2005), a term that is variously used to refer to the higher levels of engagement that are assumed to result from physical contact with data (e.g., writing codes on hard copies of transcripts, manipulating and sorting index cards by hand) as well as the need to remain connected to the original data (e.g., the interview from which a segment has been extracted for coding). It is not uncommon for researchers new to CAQDAS to express a sense of distance from their data when working on a screen, although this sensation appears to dissipate as one becomes accustomed to the software (Gilbert, 2002, p. 217) and may be less of a concern for a new generation of researchers for whom computer-mediated activity has become part of everyday experience. There is also debate about the potential distancing effect resulting from the ease with which CAQ-DAS makes it possible to generate lists of codes that have been detached from their original contexts (e.g., Serór, 2005). To some extent this problem has been alleviated by improved versions of the software, which now routinely include features such as hyperlinks, which allow researchers to shift quickly between search results and the original data from which they came, or multiple windows that permit viewing of both codes and source text simultaneously. Gilbert (2002, p. 218) reported that for many users, such features created a stronger sense of closeness to data than what would be possible if the researcher had to manually search through a set of papers to locate the original source of a code. However, it is incumbent on the researcher to make use of these features and to guard against the tendency to see codes *as* data rather than as a means of accessing the deeper meanings *in* data.

The ease of coding in CAQDAS may also lead to the opposite problem of staying *too* close to the data, in what L. Richards (2009) calls "the coding trap" (p. 109); that is, the researcher becomes so engrossed in coding or so intent on coding everything that he or she loses sight of the bigger picture and fails to advance to the crucial level of interpretation and analysis. Richards provides a number of suggestions on how to avoid the coding trap, including (a) continually asking "Why is that interesting?" and not coding if you cannot answer the question, (b) regularly reviewing and revising codes and categories to be sure they are useful, and (c) "dropping out of the document" (p. 110) from time to time to reflect on the categories one has generated and what they mean. Ultimately, it is important to remember that CAQDAS simply provides a set of tools; the responsibility for producing (or failing to produce) a quality piece of research resides with the researcher who uses them.

BOX 10.1 FOCAL STUDY

Cheng, A. (2011). Language features as the pathways to genre: Students' attention to non-prototypical features and its implications. *Journal of Second Language Writing 20*, 69–82.

Background

This study is framed around theoretical arguments regarding a perceived dichotomy between the English for specific purposes (ESP) school of genre (in which contexts of text production are used to understand how texts are constructed) and New Rhetoric (in which texts are used to understand social contexts). Cheng notes that what is missing from these arguments is the perspective of student writers on the text-context relationship and proposes to fill this gap by examining students' genre-analysis tasks.

Research Questions

1. When engaging in genre-focused learning, in particular written analysis of genre exemplars, how do students approach the relationship between text and context?
2. How do their approaches to the relationship compare with theorists' characterization of the relationship?

Method

Data comprise four genre-analysis (GA) tasks produced by four male international graduate students in EAP courses taught by the researcher at two US universities. In these tasks students analyzed research articles (RAs) that they had selected from their own disciplines (urban planning, marketing, chemistry, and electrical engineering) as class assignments. The written analyses were coded using the constant comparative method (Strauss & Corbin, 1998) and compared across tasks, students, and language features that the students commented upon. One category that emerged from the coding was "Non-Prototypical Features," which Cheng defines as "words, phrases, sentence patterns, and other language features that may not overtly index the rhetorical organization of the targeted genre" (p. 73), and this category subsequently became the focus of the analysis.

Results

Four examples of nonprototypical features (one per student) are presented alongside the original texts of the RAs. Examples are closely analyzed in order to determine how and why each student understood the feature to be significant in terms of the RA genre within his own discipline. The analysis leads Cheng to suggest that in doing their analyses, students drew upon their disciplinary knowledge (however limited) to identify features of the texts that served specific communicative purposes, even though these features did not necessarily correspond to what is found in the genre literature on RAs; that is, these analyses were situated within particular contexts. He further argues that doing an ESP textual analysis enabled these students to better understand their disciplinary contexts. Cheng concludes that the complex interrelationships between text and context evidenced in these tasks seemed to occupy a middle ground between the theoretical positions of ESP and New Rhetoric.

Discussion of a Focal Study (Cheng, 2011)

This study represents one piece of a larger research program (Cheng, 2006, 2007, 2008a, 2008b) that aimed to fill a perceived gap in genre research by examining how L2 writers (rather than genre researchers) understand relationships between text and context. Rather than using interviews (see Chapter 9) or think-aloud protocols (see Chapter 8), Cheng chose to investigate "the learners' side of genre-based instruction" (p. 70) through an examination of classroom genre-analysis (GA) tasks in which L2 graduate students analyzed research articles in their own disciplines. Data were collected in two graduate-level EAP courses taught by the researcher at two different universities. From a total of 36 students (14 in one course and 22 in the other) and eight GA tasks, Cheng selected four students (all male, from different L1s and academic disciplines) and four tasks (one per student) to present in this paper.

A major strength of the paper lies in Cheng's detailed account of the analytical process that led to the emergence of the focal theme "Non-Prototypical Features," that is, features of target texts that students identified as salient to them but that have not been accounted for in the genre literature or in pedagogical materials. Cheng identified his chosen analytical approach as the constant comparative method (Glaser, 1978; Strauss & Corbin, 1998). During the process of open coding, Cheng noted key words and phrases that students identified as important in their genre-analysis tasks (e.g., the phrase "within the literature" as a useful way to begin a literature review) and began to look for patterns across the data set, creating initial codes such as *students marking some ordinary features as carrying genre-specific meanings through attention to concrete details in text* (p. 71). A table listing selections from the texts, researcher's notes, and preliminary codes provides documentation of this phase of analysis (p. 72). Inclusion of the notes (or *jottings*, in Miles et al.'s 2014 parlance) is especially useful as a window into the analytical processes; for example, the researcher's note accompanying the reference to "within the literature" asks, "Is 'within the literature' a common feature for opening the literature review section? Why did she [the student] mark this feature as interesting?" (p. 72). The second phase, axial coding, was described in less detail, but Cheng briefly noted how a comparison between the code *students marking some ordinary features as carrying genre-specific meanings* and the code *some students highlighting textual features that are often recognized by experts as carrying genre-specific meanings* showed that not all of the instances of the first could be accounted for by the second, which in turn led him to recognize the presence of nonprototypical features in the students' analyses as a theme worthy of further exploration. Making the coding process visible in this way affords a clear sense of how Cheng arrived at the focal theme and adds to dependability, as does use of two other researchers to crosscheck the coding.

Because the paper focuses on this single theme, Cheng did not provide a full coding scheme. However, the focal theme "Non-Prototypical Features" was clearly specified through the definition given earlier as well as a brief discussion in which Cheng contrasted it with examples of more prototypical features identified by students in these tasks (e.g., use of the phrase "remain poorly understood" to designate a gap in prior research). The focal theme was further illustrated through the detailed discussion of multiple examples from different students. In each case, Cheng provided a rationale for the students' choice of this feature of the text in terms of the function that this feature seems to be performing; for example, a student's commentary on the noun phrase *polarized society* as indicative of a key element of the article author's analytical focus was interpreted by Cheng as having the function *entry into authorial intentions* (pp. 73–74). One or more examples from students' GA tasks are provided for each function, which are also clearly illustrated through a side-by-side comparison of an excerpt from the original research article text and the student's comments on the excerpt, thus allowing the reader direct access to these comments and an opportunity to evaluate the researcher's interpretations. However, these interpretations were not member checked with the students themselves, meaning that Cheng had to hedge his claims regarding what the students might have intended by their choices.

The lack of students' perspectives also somewhat weakens Cheng's final conclusions. His first point, that, despite the focus of the courses on conventional features of genre, each student seemed to take an individual approach to identifying salient features of the specific texts that they were working on, is well grounded in his detailed thematic analysis. However, Cheng further interpreted these findings as indicative of a middle ground between the text-focused ESP approach to genre and the context-focused approach of rhetoric; that is, he claimed that students' understanding of context influenced their interpretation of texts, while their interpretation of texts influenced their understanding of contexts. These claims, although intriguing, are necessarily more speculative and are further limited by the selective nature of the data presented in the article. Some explanation of why these particular students and particular tasks were selected for inclusion in the paper would have strengthened the credibility of findings, as would further clarity regarding how widespread the focal category was across the larger data set (i.e., whether similar nonprototypical features were also found in GA tasks beyond the four analyzed here). Nevertheless, the study's careful documentation of procedures and distinctive focus on an emic (L2 writer) perspective on genre represents a welcome addition to the literature on target text analysis (see Chapter 7) and genre-based pedagogy and might serve as a model for those interested in using a thematic analysis of learner texts as a means of bringing learners' voices into such research.

Suggestions for Further Reading

General Guides to Qualitative Coding

- King, N. & Horrocks, C. (2010). An introduction to interview data analysis. In N. King & C. Horrocks (Eds.), *Interviews in qualitative research* (pp. 142–174). Thousand Oaks, CA: Sage.
- Merriam, S. B. (2009). Qualitative data analysis. In S. B. Merriam (Ed.), *Qualitative research: A guide to design and implementation* (3rd ed., pp. 169–207). San Francisco: Jossey-Bass.
- Miles, M. B., Huberman, A. M., & Saldaña, J. (2014). *Qualitative data analysis: A methods sourcebook* (3rd edn.). Thousand Oaks, CA: Sage.
- Richards, K. (2003). Analysis and representation. In K. Richards (Ed.), *Qualitative inquiry in TESOL* (pp. 263–296). London: Palgrave Macmillan.
- Richards, L. (2009). *Handling qualitative data: A practical guide* (2nd ed.). Thousand Oaks, CA: Sage.
- Saldaña, J. (2013). *The coding manual for qualitative researchers* (2nd ed.). Thousand Oaks, CA: Sage.

Computer-Assisted Qualitative Data Analysis Software (CAQDAS)

- Atlas.ti Scientific Software Development GmbH. ATLAS.ti, http://www.atlasti.com
- Baralt, M. (2012). Coding qualitative data. In A. Mackey & S. M. Gass (Eds.), *Research methods in second language acquisition* (pp. 222–244). Malden, MA: Wiley Blackwell.
- Bazeley, P. & Jackson, K. (2013). *Qualitative data analysis with NVivo* (2nd edn.). Thousand Oaks, CA: Sage.
- QSR International. NVivo. http://www.qsrinternational.com/
- Silver, C. & Lewins, A. (2014). *Using software in qualitative research: A step-by-step guide* (2nd edn.). Thousand Oaks, CA: Sage.

- University of Surrey CAQDAS networking project (n.d.). Retrieved from http://www.surrey.ac.uk/sociology/research/researchcentres/caqdas/
- VERBI GmbH. MAXQDA. http://www.maxqda.com/

Grounded Theory and the Constant Comparative Method

- Charmaz, K. (2006). *Constructing grounded theory: A practical guide through qualitative analysis*. Thousand Oaks, CA: Sage.
- Corbin, J. & Strauss, A. (2008). *Basics of qualitative research: Techniques and procedures for developing grounded theory* (3rd ed.). Thousand Oaks, CA: Sage.
- Glaser, B. G. & Strauss, A. L. (1967). *The discovery of grounded theory: Strategies for qualitative research*. Chicago: Aldine.
- Thornberg, R. & Charmaz, K. (2012). Grounded theory. In S. D. Lapan (Ed.), *Qualitative research: An introduction to methods and designs*. San Francisco: Jossey-Bass.

Issues in Thematic Analysis and CAQDAS

- Crowley, C., Harré, R., & Tagg, C. (Eds.). (2002). Qualitative research and computing: Methodological issues and practices using QSR NVivo and NUD*IST. [Special issue]. *International Journal of Social Research Methodology, 5*(3).
- Gilbert, L. S. (2002). Going the distance: "Closeness" in qualitative data analysis software. *International Journal of Social Research Methodology, 5,* 215–228.
- Séror, J. (2005). Computers and qualitative data analysis: Paper, pens, and highlighters vs. screen, mouse, and keyboard. *TESOL Quarterly, 39,* 321–328.
- Smagorinsky, P. (2008). The method section as conceptual epicenter in constructing social science research reports. *Written Communication, 25,* 389–411.

11

QUALITATIVE DISCOURSE ANALYSIS

Discourse analysis (DA) is an umbrella term for a variety of approaches to analyzing texts, whether spoken, written, or computer-mediated. At the most basic level, *discourse* refers to any instance of meaningful language use, and *discourse analysis* is the study of how individuals use language to construct and interpret meaning (Cook, 2011, p. 431; Johnstone, 2008, pp. 2–3). However, the term *discourse* (or *discourses*) may be extended beyond language to encompass meaning-making more broadly. Gee (2015) distinguishes what he calls *little d discourse*, defined as any instance of language in use, and *big D Discourse*, which incorporates not only language, but also actions, tools, beliefs, and so on that are related to how participants perform and recognize social identities. For example, being recognized as a member of a scholarly discourse community may involve not only using language in particular ways (little d discourse), but also activities such as following a specific citation format, publishing in certain journals, and displaying certain kinds of knowledge or beliefs (big D Discourse). Other scholars use the term in Foucault's sense to refer to "conventional ways of talking that both create and are created by conventional ways of thinking" (Johnstone, 2008, pp. 2–3); for example, one can speak of *the discourse of plagiarism* with reference to institutional policies that frame it as a breach of moral order (e.g., Li & Casanave, 2012).

The concern of DA is what a text *does*; that is, the social actions (agreeing, making a counterargument, claiming authority) that are performed through language and how these actions are realized (Bazerman & Prior, 2004). In L2 writing research, it has been used to analyze both the practices involved in text production and the texts themselves (see Table 11.1). It entails an array of methodologies and foci, ranging from corpus-based analyses of academic registers and genres (see Chapter 7) to microanalyses of talk around writing (e.g., Waring,

TABLE 11.1 Representative Studies Using Discourse Analysis

Citation	Participants, context, and data	Research questions/focus	Comments
Tan, Wigglesworth, & Storch (2010)	• Six dyads in a Chinese class • Seven writing tasks in two versions, face to face (FTF) and computer mediated (CMC) • FTF interactions audio recorded; CMC interactions were logged	1. Does the modality (CMC vs. FTF) affect the nature of peer interaction during collaborative writing?	• Analysis is based on Storch's (2002) model of dynamic interaction. • Patterns are illustrated through examples from both FTF and CMC and compared within and across dyads.
Waring (2005)	• American tutor and an Indian graduate student in a graduate school of education in the US • Audiotapes of tutor–tutee interaction	1. How and why does a graduate student writer resist the advice provided by her writing center tutor?	• Conversation analysis (CA) is used to examine sequential organization and linguistic resources used to resist advice.
de Guerrero & Villamil (2000)	• Part of a project involving 40 dyadic interactions; focus on two male intermediate ESL college learners (Spanish L1) • Audio recording of pair discussion; first and revised drafts of text	1. What is the nature of the interaction between two ESL college students who are collaboratively revising a text?	• Selected segments focusing on revision are taken from different points in the interaction and discussed in detail. • Students' texts were collected but are not analyzed in the paper.
Young & Miller (2004)	• Vietnamese intermediate ESL learner and his writing instructor at US university • Videotapes of four weekly writing conferences	1. How does a novice learn to participate in *revision talk* during writing conferences?	• The paper outlines structure of *revision talk* and provides evidence of its status as a routine practice in the focal community. • Both verbal and nonverbal features (e.g., eye gaze) are taken into account.

(Continued)

TABLE 11.1 (Continued)

Citation	Participants, context, and data	Research questions/focus	Comments
de Oliveira & Lan (2014)	• Part of a four-year project in a fourth-grade classroom in which English language learners (ELLs) were mainstreamed • Focus on ELL from Korea (Ji-Soo) during second phase of the project • Data for this phase comprised 11 days of observation and audio recording of the class over three months; collection of students' writing before and after instruction	1. How does a fourth-grade teacher incorporate genre-based pedagogy into her teaching of science writing? 2. What is the nature of a fourth-grade teacher's guidance through interaction in the context of writing a procedural recount about a science inquiry activity? 3. Over the course of the teacher's implementation of genre-based pedagogy, how did Ji-Soo's ability to produce a procedural account in science change? (p. 29)	• Paper uses systemic functional linguistics (SFL) to examine specific linguistic features (e.g., scientific vocabulary, temporal markers) in focal student's texts, which are traced to their use in the teacher's genre-based instruction. • There is a clear description of SFL and its application to the data.
Bunch & Willet (2013)	• Six middle-school social studies classrooms in a program to promote academic language and content development of language-minority students • Corpus of essays written by 40 students	1. How did the curriculum and instruction provide dialogic opportunities for students to engage with, and produce, multimodal texts for meaning-making? (p. 145)	• Analysis is built around a model of "meaning-meaning resources" (p. 145) that draws from several theoretical frameworks. • Description of model and procedures are clear and comprehensive. • Concepts outlined in the model are applied to multiple examples of students' essays to show how students made use of these resources.
Ivanič & Camps (2001)	• Six Mexican graduate students at a British university from a variety of disciplines • Written assignments and dissertations; 3–5 interviews with each student	1. How is voice expressed in writing? 2. How can L2 writing pedagogy raise students' awareness of voice?	• The article provides a detailed explication of the analytical framework. • The framework is applied to multiple examples from each student to illustrate different types of positioning.

Study	Data	Research questions	Analysis
Hafner (2015)	• 52 students in an English for science course at a Hong Kong university • Student-created videos, focus group interviews (18 students)	1. How is the practice of remix evidenced in the multimodal compositions of English language learners? 2. How does remix either promote or compromise the expression of learner voice? (p. 493)	• Researcher was the coordinator for the course. • Report focuses on a detailed analysis (including illustrations) of two student videos. • Based on the analysis, the author creates a theoretical model of remix practices.
Ouellette (2008)	• Freshman student from Taiwan in an ESL composition course at a US university • Essay drafts; student's journal assignments	1. What happens to writer identity in successive essay drafts written by an NNES student identified as a "plagiarist"? More concretely, what discourse choices does the writer make in borrowing textual material from other sources? 2. To what extent do other strands of identity (i.e., autobiographical self and discourse self) shape those choices in her attempt to convey, or mitigate, the self as author?	• The analysis compares student's texts to original sources and examines linguistic features that signal stance. • Student is not interviewed, but her perspective is presented through her journals. • Analysis of multiple drafts show how student's ability to distinguish her voice from that of her sources developed over time.
Matsuda (2003)	• Texts on process and postprocess writing (both L1 and L2) published from the mid–20th century to the early 21st century	1. How did key texts on process and postprocess writing shape understandings of these models within the field of L2 writing?	• Analysis focuses on use of key terms (e.g., *process, postprocess*) and associated concepts (e.g., *freewriting, prescriptive*) in the literature on writing. • Paper includes numerous quotations from focal texts with extensive commentary.

2005) and critical analyses of the discourses *of* writing (Ivanič, 2004; Matsuda, 2003). Despite their differences, these approaches share an interest in how social contexts, both macrolevel and microlevel, shape writing, and it is this that distinguishes DA from text analyses that focus solely on linguistic features.

DA studies can be quantitative, qualitative, or both. In this chapter we will focus on qualitative approaches, drawing upon Lazaraton's (2002, p. 33) distinction between studies that use frequency counts and statistical analyses to determine *how often* something happens (quantitative) and those that take an interpretive approach to examine *why* and *how* something happens in specific instances (qualitative). The emphasis will be on methods used to analyze oral interaction; however, we will also review studies that employ DA methodology to qualitatively analyze written texts (for a discussion of quantitative analyses of L2 writers' texts, see Chapter 6). We will then summarize the major approaches to DA that have been used in L2 writing research and discuss some issues that need to be considered by researchers employing this methodology. The final sections will outline some basic steps involved in doing a study utilizing DA and discuss a sample study.

Purpose for Using Qualitative Discourse Analysis

Analysis of Spoken Discourse

Interest in interconnections between speaking and writing (e.g., Belcher & Hirvela, 2008; Weissberg, 2006) has stimulated a growing number of L2 writing studies that use DA to examine how writing is shaped by talk around text in settings such as pair and group work, writing center tutorials, teacher-student conferences, and writing classrooms. One area of research has been pair interaction during collaborative writing tasks (Storch, 2011; Wigglesworth & Storch, 2012). Much of this work has drawn upon Storch's (2002) *model of dyadic interaction*, which comprises four distinct patterns, *collaborative, dominant/dominant, dominant/passive,* and *expert/novice.* Using this model, Tan, Wigglesworth, and Storch (2010) compared computer-mediated communication (CMC) and face-to-face (FTF) interaction between the same dyads in a Chinese as a foreign language class in order to determine which environment is more likely to generate collaboration and equal participation. Another body of work has investigated the nature of talk around writing in the university writing center. Waring (2005) focuses on the sometimes-heated discussions between an American tutor and an Indian graduate student around a paper that the student is writing. Using the tools of conversation analysis (see "Approaches to Discourse Analysis" later in the chapter), she analyzed the sequential organization and linguistic resources used by the tutee to resist her tutor's advice.

Other DA work in L2 writing is grounded in social theories of learning, such as sociocultural theory (Vygotsky, 1978) and situated learning (Lave & Wenger,

1991). Using frameworks developed in research on adult-child interaction (Lidz, 1991; Wood, Bruner, & Ross, 1976) and Aljaafreh and Lantolf's (1994) regulatory scale of writing conference feedback, de Guerrero and Villamil (2000) analyzed scaffolding in a dialogue between two L2 writers revising a text originally written by the less proficient of the two (the Writer) as a window into *microgenetic development*, that is, development that occurs "right before one's eyes" (Vygotsky, 1978, p. 61). Young and Miller (2004) drew from situated learning, which posits that learning can be observed in novices' increasing levels of participation in socially valued activities, to trace the progress of a Vietnamese L2 writer as he learned to participate in the practice of *revision talk* during teacher-student writing conferences through a microlevel analysis of four writing conferences over the course of one month.

Finally, studies in the Sydney School of genre-based pedagogy (e.g., Martin & Rose, 2007) incorporate discourse analyses of classroom interaction and students' texts in order to investigate how specific pedagogical practices support learning. One example is de Oliveira and Lan's (2014) case study that followed a fourth-grade English language learner as he became more skilled in the genre of *procedural recount*, detailing steps of a scientific experiment. Focusing on specific linguistic forms, such as connectors and scientific vocabulary, the researchers analyze excerpts from teacher talk in which these forms were taught and compare the student's work before and after instruction for evidence of these forms in his writing.

Analysis of Written Discourse

The primary concern of qualitative DA of written texts is how these texts create meaning. When applied to the texts of L2 writers, this approach moves beyond a focus on accuracy, complexity, or fluency (see Chapter 6) to encompass other elements that contribute to the effectiveness of a text. The study by de Oliveira and Lan (2014) discussed earlier offers one example of how a qualitative discourse analysis of written texts can link linguistic forms to larger issues, in this case acquisition of thinking, doing, and writing science. Another example is Bunch and Willet's (2013) analysis of essays produced by L2 middle school students in a school program designed to develop high-level academic language and literacy skills. Drawing on a range of theoretical frameworks, the researchers analyzed what they called *meaning-making resources* (e.g., register, genre, positioning, and intertextuality) that students employed as they responded to a somewhat confusing writing prompt.

A major area for written DA in L2 writing research has investigated how voice, stance, and identity are enacted in writing (e.g., Hyland, 2012; Hyland & Sancho Guinda, 2012; Ivanič, 1998; Matsuda, 2001, 2015; Prior, 2001). An early and influential example of this research is Ivanič and Camps (2001), who proposed a framework for analyzing writer self-representation built around Halliday's

(1985) *metafunctions* of language (see the discussion of systemic functional linguistics in "Approaches to Discourse Analysis"). Using a corpus of academic writing produced by six Mexican graduate students in Britain and interviews with the writers, they analyzed how lexical choices, pronouns, modality, and other linguistic features functioned as resources for writers to position themselves in various ways. In a study of writer voice in multimodal compositions, Hafner (2015) analyzed two videos created by students in an English for science course in Hong Kong with a focus on the practices of *remixing*, that is, drawing from and reusing images and music from online sources in their compositions. His analysis considers whether these practices, which are quite common in multimodal creative work, serve to obscure or promote students' individual voices as content creators. A related area of research investigates the process through which L2 writers acquire the linguistic and rhetorical means to create an authorial identity that meets the expectations of their academic community. Ouellette's (2008) study of a Taiwanese ESL student accused of plagiarism traces the student's gradually increasing skill in constructing an authorial identity across multiple drafts as she moves from heavy reliance on source texts to a more clearly articulated distinction between the original author's words and opinions and her own.

Finally, DA has informed the genre of *metadisciplinary narrative* (Casanave, 2005; Matsuda, 2005), which details the evolution of thinking in a particular disciplinary field. Matsuda's (2003) review of the discourses surrounding the emergence and critiques of process writing examines the terms and concepts used by proponents and critics of process and postprocess composition pedagogy as they engaged in "discursively constructing" (p. 71) narratives that positioned these approaches in opposition to current-traditional (i.e., product-oriented) approaches and to each other.

Approaches to Discourse Analysis

Schiffrin (1994) has described DA as "one of the most vast, but also one of the least defined, areas of linguistics" (p. 5). It borrows from many disciplines, including linguistics, sociolinguistics, anthropology, sociology, critical studies, rhetoric, education, and pragmatics, and is employed by scholars in these disciplines in diverse ways for diverse purposes. A glance at the table of contents of any DA handbook illustrates this vastness and diversity; for example, the *Routledge Handbook of Discourse Analysis* (Gee & Handford, 2012) covers 13 approaches, each of which has its own characteristics and methodologies that can lead to different insights when applied to the same set of data (for examples, see Richards, 2003, pp. 208–220; Schiffrin, 1994). Here we briefly summarize four approaches that have been employed in L2 writing research (see Table 11.2). Readers interested in more information on these or other types of DA should consult the suggested readings at the end of this chapter.

TABLE 11.2 Qualitative Approaches to Discourse Analysis Used in L2 Writing Research

Type	Characteristics	Why use it	Example
Conversation analysis	• Microanalysis of naturally occurring talk • Emic perspective on what talk means to participants • Focus on local interactional context	• Examine how actions are performed through talk • Analyze how talk is organized through sequences and conversational turn-taking	Waring (2005)
Systemic functional linguistics (SFL)	• Based on Halliday's (1985) approach to linguistics • Focus on *metafunctions* of language (i.e., ideational, interpersonal, textual)	• Analyze the social functions of language	de Oliveira & Lan (2014)
Multimodal analysis	• Incorporation of both linguistic and nonlinguistic features in analysis of text or talk	• Analyze the multimodal resources in production and interpretation of texts • Examine how gesture, body positioning, and other nonverbal features are integrated with talk to perform social actions	Nelson (2006) Nishino & Atkinson (2015)
Narrative analysis	• Analysis of structure of personal stories and how narrators position themselves and others within those stories	• Understand how individuals use stories to make sense of events • Investigate the emergent nature of storytelling in conversation	Pavlenko (2001)

Conversation Analysis

Conversation analysis (CA) was developed in the late 1960s and early 1970s by sociologists Harvey Sacks, Emmanuel Schegloff, and Gail Jefferson to analyze talk in interaction as a primary locus of social organization. Much work in CA has focused on the structure of conversation, such as how turns are built, how individuals get (and hold) a turn at talk, and how each turn is constructed (and heard) to be relevant to a prior turn. A key unit of analysis is the *sequence*, which minimally consists of two turns that implement a course of action, such as question-answer, invitation-(non)acceptance, or request-(non)compliance. CA-based research in L2 writing has drawn from work on institutional talk (e.g., Drew & Heritage, 1992; Heritage, 1997), which considers how these basic features of conversation are instantiated within institutional contexts, such as classrooms or workplaces. One example is Waring's (2005) analysis of advice-giving sequences in writing center tutor-student interaction. It centers on the CA concept of *preference*, which refers to whether the second turn in a sequence fur-thers the action initiated by the first turn; for example, giving advice initiates an action (a request to have someone do something in accordance with that advice), and the next turn either furthers that action (acceptance of the advice) or blocks it (nonacceptance). The first response is said to be *preferred*, while the second is *dispreferred* (see Schegloff, 2007, pp. 58–96). Noting that the student's frequent rejection of her tutor's advice violated the preference for advice acceptance, War-ing conducted a line-by-line analysis of advice sequences. She identified five distinct practices used by the student to resist the tutor's suggestions, for example *assert own agenda* (reject the tutor's advice as irrelevant) or *invoke authority* (reject the advice as contrary to what her professor wants), and further noted when each tended to occur (e.g., *invoke authority* was used after an extended exchange failed to resolve the conflict). Based on this analysis, Waring interpreted the students' resistance as a means of "exercising control over where the tutoring is going" (p. 161), thus recalibrating the exchange from one involving an expert tutor and novice writer to one of negotiation between peers.

Systemic Functional Linguistics

Systemic functional linguistics (SFL), developed by Michael Halliday (1985; Hal-liday & Matthiessen, 2014), emphasizes the meaning-making functions of lan-guage and how these functions are embedded in larger social systems. SFL posits that all instances of language use involve three *metafunctions*—*ideational* (related to content), *interpersonal* (related to stance and relationships), and *textual* (related to the wording and structure of the text)—which operate in conjunction to construct meaning. These metafunctions are related to three aspects of the con-text in which a text is produced: *field* (situation), *tenor* (participants), and *mode* (channel of communication). In L2 writing research, SFL has been applied to the analysis of research articles (e.g., see the discussion of Loi, Lim, & Wharton, 2016 in Chapter 7) as well as to the analysis of text and talk in K–12 contexts. An example of the latter is de Oliveira and Lan's (2014) study of an L2 stu-dent acquiring facility in the genre of scientific procedural recount. The study focused on the ideational metafunction, which the researchers broke down into *participants* (expressed through nouns), *processes* (expressed through verbs), and the temporal connectors (e.g., *then, first*) that indicate the sequence in which these processes take place. These categories were applied to an analysis of the focal student's texts and to teacher talk in which these forms were taught. For example, in his first effort to describe an experiment in which different liquids were poured into a cup, the student used vague nouns such as *soapy thingy* to describe dishwashing liquid and basic temporal markers such as *then* or *when* (e.g., "then when I mixed it with red water . . .," p. 32) that did not indicate the order in which the liquids were added to the cup. After presenting an analysis of classroom genre instruction in which the teacher explicitly taught temporal markers and gave examples of how to organize a procedural recount, de Oliveira and Lan examined subsequent examples of the student's work and found evidence of more precise vocabulary and more appropriate use of temporal markers; for example, "First we poured corn syrup. Then we poured dishwater soap and it made 2 layers" (p. 36).

Halliday's three metafunctions were also incorporated into Ivanič and Camps's (2001) framework for analyzing how individuals position themselves in their writing, which comprises *ideational positioning* ("ways of representing the world"), *interpersonal positioning* ("relative authoritativeness or tentativeness and in terms of the writers' relationship with their readers"), and *textual positioning* ("preferred ways of turning meanings into text") (p. 4). Ideational positioning concerns how the writer takes a position toward a topic and is realized through linguistic features such as word choice and syntax; for example, the phrase "natural resources *are being exploited*" is semantically similar to "natural resources *are disappearing*," but the first conveys a more value-laden stance both through the verb *exploited* as well as the passive voice, which suggest that some unnamed agent is carrying out this action (p. 14). Interpersonal positioning involves the writer's degree of certainty and relationship with the reader; for example, use of present tense ("The big auto companies *have* a huge influence," p. 21) conveys a high degree of confidence that a statement is factual, whereas use of a modal ("It *could* be said," p. 23) expresses the writer's uncertainty. Textual positioning refers to how writers position themselves relative to writing itself and is reflected in features such as adoption of a formal academic style (long noun phrases, multisyllabic words) versus a more conversational style.

Multimodal Analysis

Multimodal analysis refers to approaches that incorporate nonlinguistic as well as linguistic features to analyze text or talk. One form of multimodal analysis is *multimodal discourse analysis* (MMDA), which is based on systemic functional linguistics (SFL, see the previous section). MMDA expands the SFL category of *mode* to encompass a range of sign systems, including language, gesture, music, images, objects, formatting, and fonts, that together create meaning in a text (see Kress, 2012; Kress & Bezemer, 2009). In L2 writing research, MMDA is most often found in work on digital literacies. Using MMDA, Hafner (2015) analyzed the remixing practices evident in videos produced by two students in his English for science class in Hong Kong, such as blending original and borrowed video footage with original commentary, snippets of popular music, and content from Hong Kong television advertising. Nelson (2006) used MMDA to analyze multimodal texts on topics related to language, culture, and identity produced by L2 writers in a course on multimedia writing. Combining his analysis with the students' comments on their work during post-assignment interviews, Nelson shows how these texts achieved their meanings through a juxtaposition of multiple modalities, including words, images, fonts, colors, and music. For example, he notes how repeated use of an image (a photo of the student's parents) took on different meanings (or as Nelson puts it, was *resemiotized*) depending on the accompanying spoken text; the first two times the image appeared in conjunction with the word *parents*, while the third time it was accompanied by the word *motivation*. Nelson further argues that it is the multimodality of these texts that makes resemiotization possible.

Another approach to multimodal analysis, *embodiment* (Goodwin, 2000, 2001), focuses on face-to-face interaction. Grounded in the methodology of conversation analysis, embodiment goes beyond CA's traditional focus on the structure of talk to encompass the full range of *semiotic fields* (e.g., language, activity, participation frameworks, participants' bodies, tools, and objects) oriented to by participants as they engage in social activities. An application of this approach in L2 writing research can be found in Nishino and Atkinson's (2015) analysis of an interaction between two Japanese doctoral students co-writing an article in English for publication. Arguing that the study of cognition in L2 writing research needs to take into account the full array of resources available in the "ecosocial" (p. 38) setting in which writing occurs, the researchers analyzed how language choice (Japanese and English), eye gaze, orientation to objects (e.g., books, the computer on which the participants were composing), and gestures contributed to the achievement of *alignment*, defined as "the complex means by which human beings effect coordinated interaction, and maintain that interaction in dynamically adaptive ways" (Atkinson, Nishino, Churchill, & Okada, 2007, p. 169) as the participants negotiated the text that they were collaboratively producing.

Narrative Analysis

Analysis of narrative data has been generating increasing interest in applied linguistics (e.g., Barkhuizen, 2011, 2013, 2014; Benson, 2014; Pavlenko, 2007) and has been advocated in the field of L2 writing for those "who are interested more in the text-related experiences of teachers and writers than in the formal analysis of the text that writers produce" (Casanave, 2005, p. 21). Narratives in L2 writing research are often analyzed thematically to examine research participants' accounts of "what happened" (see Chapter 10); however, some have argued for a discourse analytic approach that attends to the structure of narratives (e.g., how the teller orders events, chooses words or presents him- or herself as a character in the story) and how the telling is shaped by the context of the telling (e.g., De Fina, 2009; Kasper & Prior, 2015; Pavlenko, 2007). One example of this approach is Pavlenko's (2001) analysis of autobiographies (13 books and 15 essays) written by bilingual writers. Using Davis and Harré's (1990) *positioning approach*, she examined how these writers make connections between writing and identity; situate themselves (or are situated by others) relative to a range of ethnic, linguistic, racial, class, and gendered identities; and negotiate transitions between their L1, L2, and multilingual selves. Her analysis considered not only explicit claims of identity (e.g., "Because all of my formal training as a writer took place in an American setting, and because I only write in English, I always thought of myself as an American writer," Mori, 2000, p. 141 cited in Pavlenko, p. 329), but also linguistic features such as metaphors (e.g., [re]*invention, imagining,* and *translation*) used by these writers to describe their experiences and their struggles to create new multilingual and multicultural identities (see also Pomerantz & Kearney, 2012, Box 11.1 for another approach to narrative analysis).

Issues Involved in Discourse Analysis

Transcription

Analysis of oral data involves transcription, a process in which speech is rendered into a written form. Many have argued that transcription is not a preliminary step before analysis, but constitutes a stage *of* analysis, as decisions made during transcription will impact how data are interpreted (Bucholtz, 2000; Green, Fránquiz, & Dixon, 1997; Ochs, 1979; Oliver, Serovich, & Mason, 2005). As is the case with transcription of retrospective and verbal protocols (see Chapter 8), transcription in qualitative discourse analysis is a hidden aspect of the research process that receives relatively little attention in DA methods texts and is rarely discussed in published accounts, leaving an impression that it is simply a technical matter. However, although researchers may aim to create objective and complete transcripts that accurately represent talk, transcription is an interpretative process involving multiple theoretical and methodological decisions that are shaped by research aims, theoretical orientations, and ethical concerns. As a result, no transcript can truly be objective or disinterested. Practical aspects of transcription will be discussed in the section "Doing Qualitative Discourse Analysis"; here we will focus on several theoretical and methodological issues regarding transcription that can affect analyses (see also Chapter 9 on transcribing interviews).

First, a discourse analysis of spoken interaction requires a transcript that is sufficiently detailed to allow the researcher to produce an analysis that addresses the research questions or research focus. However, there is no simple model of what such a transcript might include. Although it may be sufficient to transcribe only the words spoken by participants for a transcript that will be subject to a thematic analysis (see Chapter 10), a discourse analysis of interaction typically requires a finer level of detail and may include elements such as pauses, speech delivery (e.g., words spoken with strong emphasis or notably louder, softer, slower, or quicker than surrounding talk), intonation, audible expressions of emotion such as laughter or sighs, sound stretches (i.e., when a sound is held longer than usual), and overlapping talk between speakers. Deciding whether to transcribe any or all of these features depends on the aims of the research and the overall theoretical and analytical frameworks that govern it. For example, CA requires highly detailed transcripts, as researchers using this methodology take the position that even seemingly minor features of talk (e.g., an audible intake or exhalation of breath) may be of import (see the transcripts in Waring, 2005). On the other hand, studies that focus on more global concerns, such as scaffolding moves or characteristics of peer interaction, typically use transcripts with a lower level of detail, as such nuances are not seen as relevant to the issues that they are investigating (see the transcripts in de Guerrero & Villamil, 2000; Tan et al., 2010).

Another question involves how (or whether) to render pronunciation. Phonetic transcription, which can represent pronunciation with a high degree of precision, is difficult to use and interpret for those who lack training in phonetics (a group that is likely to include most writers and readers of L2 writing research) and is therefore probably best reserved for instances in which pronunciation becomes the focus of the talk. Another option is using nonstandard spelling that reflects how a word sounds (e.g., *becuz* for *because* or *sez* for *says*). Nonstandard orthography has been advocated by some analysts, who argue that it allows the researcher to capture small but potentially significant variations in pronunciation both within and across speakers (e.g., Jefferson, 1983), and some L2 writing researchers have employed it on the grounds that participants' differing language proficiencies or membership in different speech communities may be relevant to an analysis (e.g., Kibler, 2010). Nevertheless, the rendering of speech using nonconventional spelling is a controversial issue, as it may inadvertently convey an image of the speaker as uneducated and can be particularly sensitive when the individual is a speaker of a nonstandard or nonnative variety (Bucholtz, 2000; Roberts, 1997; see also the discussion in Chapter 9). Using standard orthography may seem to be the safest choice, but it risks homogenizing speech and erasing the distinctiveness of speech styles that may be important to the speaker as well as to the analyst. There is no simple solution to this dilemma; however, all discourse analysts would do well to attend to Bucholtz's (2000) call for "a reflexive discourse analysis in which the researcher strives not for an unattainable self-effacement [i.e., a supposedly neutral transcript], but for vigilant self-awareness" (p. 1461).

Supporting Claims

DA is an inherently interpretive (and thus subjective) approach to data analysis that often involves making inferences that go beyond the surface level of what is said or written. Although many discourse analysts take a postmodern perspective that acknowledges the possibility of multiple understandings of a given text, this does not mean that anything goes when making claims, and a common flaw in the work of novice discourse analysts is going beyond what the data can reasonably support. Presenting the results of a discourse analysis essentially involves making an argument in favor of one's interpretation of the data, even while acknowledging that other interpretations are possible, and, as in any formal argument, this requires providing evidence to support claims. Depending on the approach that one is using, this evidence may be external to the text (provided through triangulation), internal to the text (provided through reference to features of the text that support the analysis), or both.

Any or all of the four types of triangulation discussed in Chapter 4 (data triangulation, investigator triangulation, theoretical triangulation, and methodological triangulation) can be applied to support a discourse analysis. Many studies employ methodological triangulation in which interpretations are checked against perspectives of participants derived through interviews (de Oliveira & Lan, 2014) or journals (Ouellette, 2008). Analyses of talk around writing during instruction, peer revision, or tutor-student interactions can be triangulated with students' papers to determine how or whether these interactions shaped the resulting texts (de Oliveira & Lan, 2014). In studies that rely primarily (or entirely) on a single method or source, data triangulation can strengthen claims. For example, although de Guerrero and Villamil (2000) reported on only one interaction, examples from different points in the interaction allowed them to show how the level of participation of the less proficient writer developed over a relatively brief period of time. Bunch and Willet (2013) focused on a single assignment but achieved data triangulation through analysis of essays of different students.

Some approaches, such as CA, eschew methods such as interviews on the grounds that they provide participants' post hoc accounts rather than what they were actually thinking or feeling at the time. In the absence of these external sources of support, CA analysts rely on careful and detailed analyses of interactional sequences, with particular attention to how participants themselves orient to the talk; for example, Waring (2005) demonstrated how certain turns by the student were treated by the tutor as "doing advice resisting" (p. 147) by analyzing his response to these turns. In addition, unlike analytical methods that largely take place behind the scenes, CA and other microlevel DA approaches make the analysis visible in the report through a detailed, step-by-step examination of interactional turns and how they relate to each other, thus allowing readers to judge the quality of the analysis.

Transparency in documenting the research process can also strengthen credibility. For example, a DA study invariably involves selection of participants, texts, specific features, or excerpts from a larger data set, and researchers may be vulnerable to accusations that they have foregrounded data that fit their interpretations and ignored what did not. It is therefore essential that data selection be principled and that researchers be transparent regarding how they made these decisions. Supporting claims also requires a clear definition of the phenomenon being investigated as well as key constructs (e.g., *scaffolding, voice, identity, collaboration, alignment*) and how these are being applied to the data. For example, de Guerrero and Villamil (2000) provided a detailed explanation of the scaffolding frameworks that they used and described how these frameworks had been used in prior research, thereby establishing a basis for their analysis. Young and Miller (2004), whose central claim involved an L2 writer's increasing participation in what they called *revision talk*, explained what revision talk consisted of and how it could be distinguished from other types of talk that occurred during teacher-student conferences. They also offered a well-supported argument for why it could be considered an established discursive practice within the community that they studied.

Doing Qualitative Discourse Analysis

Recording Interaction

The first step for studies that aim to analyze spoken discourse is the collection of data through audio or video recordings. Recording interaction involves matters ranging from seemingly mundane but essential tasks such as choosing and learning to use equipment to the many crucial decisions that must be made before and during recording. A number of methods texts and articles provide guidance on the technical, methodological, and ethical issues involved in this process (e.g., DuFon, 2002; Heath, Hindmarsh, & Luff, 2010; Richards, 2003, pp. 174–180; ten Have, 2007, pp. 67–92; Zuengler, Ford, & Fassnacht, 1998). Here we will point out some of the major issues that need to be considered before embarking on this method of data collection.

The first decision is whether to use audio or video. Video recording provides a more detailed picture of the interactional event and allows the analyst to incorporate features such as participants' eye gaze, orientation to objects during the talk, or gestures, any or all of which could potentially be significant. Young and Miller's (2004) analysis depended in part on how participants oriented toward the paper being discussed as well as to each other, thus necessitating access to visual information (such as pointing or eye gaze) captured through video recording. On the other hand, the presence of a camera can be distracting to participants and may not be feasible in all settings. Most studies reviewed for this chapter were based on audio recordings, which offer practical advantages such as ease of use and relative unobtrusiveness, thus reducing potential effects of observer's paradox (see Chapter 4).

Although many approaches to DA emphasize the importance of collecting data in natural (vs. experimental) settings, natural settings often present less than ideal conditions for recording, such as poor lighting, background noise, or tight spaces that make it impossible to position a camera far enough away to capture the entire scene. Most of these problems have technical fixes (e.g., providing additional sources of light, miking individual participants, using a wide-angle lens), but these need to be assessed against other considerations, particularly the need to avoid overly interfering with the event that one is supposed to be observing. For example, Waring (2005) explains that she chose audio over video recording because her participants (a graduate student and her writing tutor) often met in off-campus settings such as cafés, and asking them to relocate to a site more conducive to video recording might have disrupted the natural flow of conversation that was essential to her analytical approach. Similarly, manipulating the setting to create conditions more favorable to recording (e.g., asking participants to sit so that everyone is facing the camera, to move where the light is better, or to lean closer to the audio-recorder when speaking) adds an air of artificiality that risks making participants more self-conscious and compromising the supposed naturalness of the ensuing talk. As is the case with many methodological decisions, making recordings requires striking a balance between the kind of data needed to answer research questions, the comfort of participants, and the affordances and limitations of the research setting.

Transcribing Recorded Data

Unfortunately, speech recognition software has yet to reach a level of sophistication that would permit computerized transcription of multiparty interaction, leaving manual transcription as the only viable option. The task of transcribing hours of audio or video data can be daunting, with demands on time and energy increasing exponentially the more detail one includes in the transcript. Those with sufficient resources can outsource this task; however, given the centrality of transcription as part of (not preliminary to) analysis, reliance on transcripts produced by others risks distancing the researcher from the data and negatively impacting the quality of the analysis. If outside transcribers are used, the resulting transcripts should be taken as a first step and not as a final product; for example, researchers might use such transcripts to get an overview of the data but then do their own transcription of segments that will be used for the analysis. Those doing their own transcription may choose to transcribe only selected portions of the recorded data following a review of the recordings or doing it in "rounds," beginning with a rough transcript of the words spoken and adding details later (ten Have, 2007, p. 111).

Rendering nonverbal aspects of spoken discourse (e.g., pauses, restarts, overlapping speech) into writing requires some sort of transcription symbols. Although there are established transcription systems in widespread use, such as the one developed by Gail Jefferson for conversation analysis (e.g., Hepburn & Bolden, 2013; Markee & Kasper, 2004, pp. 499–500; Ochs, Schegloff, & Thompson, 1996, pp. 461–465; ten Have, 2007, pp. 93–115), even a cursory review of the transcripts included in published L2 writing studies will lead one to agree with Johnstone's (2008) observation that "there are almost as many ways to transcribe speech as there are researchers who do so" (p. 23). Most published articles using transcripts include a list of transcription conventions in an appendix or endnote, and newcomers to transcription are encouraged to review these to determine if they can be adopted or adapted to their own purposes.

When transcripts are based on video recordings, transcribers will also have to decide how much of the wealth of available visual information (e.g., gestures, eye gaze, facial expressions, body positioning, pointing to a specific passage in a written text) to incorporate and how to translate this information onto the printed page. Although a detailed discussion of this issue cannot be included here, options for transcribing visual data can be found in several of the references included at the end of this chapter (Goodwin, 1981, 2001; Heath et al., 2010; Hepburn & Bolden, 2013). Researchers are increasingly incorporating drawings or frame grabs (i.e., still frames taken from a video) into transcripts, which provide readers with direct access to visual data (e.g., Nishino & Atkinson, 2015; Young & Miller, 2004).

Given that the vast majority of research on L2 writing is conducted in English-speaking settings, transcribing talk in languages other than English is less of an issue than it might be in other contexts. However, researchers working outside of the English-speaking world or in multilingual settings face an additional set of questions if they intend to present their transcripts to an English-speaking audience, for example, how to represent a language that does not use the Roman alphabet (e.g., Russian, Japanese, Arabic), how to represent tones in languages such as Chinese, and whether the symbols used to indicate intonation in standard transcription systems (which are based on English) can adequately represent talk in languages with different prosodic systems (see Hepburn & Bolden, 2013 for a brief discussion of these questions from a CA perspective). Some L2 writing researchers have chosen to present transcripts in English translation, sometimes using typefaces (e.g., boldfacing) to indicate words spoken in different languages (de Guerrero & Villamil, 2000). Others present both the original language and an English translation, using transliteration to render languages such as Chinese into Roman script (Tan et al., 2010), a technique that allows readers with knowledge of the original language to access the actual words that were spoken. Regardless of the option one choses, the decision should be a reasoned one based on the imperatives of the research. For example, an English-only transcript may be a viable option if language choice is not the primary focus of analysis, although it means that readers will have to trust that the researchers have provided an accurate translation.

Developing an Analysis

Once a researcher has collected and (if using spoken data) transcribed the data, the next step is to get a general picture of what it contains. Many discourse analysts take an *inductive* approach, in which themes and patterns emerge from the data rather than being predetermined. That is, the researcher approaches the data without any particular focus in mind and chooses one based on what looks interesting. Given that much of the talk and texts of L2 writing are likely to be quite familiar and routine to L2 writing researchers, finding something interesting may at first seem impossible; however, a number of methods texts offer guidance to help novice discourse analysts develop the ability to see the significant in the everyday. One useful approach comes from K. Richards (2003, pp. 185–191), who suggests a four-step process to the analysis of oral data consisting of (a) *providing a general characterization* (reviewing data and labeling episodes), (b) *identifying grossly apparent features* (making some general observations about each episode), (c) *focusing in on structural elements* (considering features such as who dominates the floor or how the talk is organized), and (d) *developing a description* (expanding on the preliminary analysis developed in the first three steps).

Other DA methods texts offer recommendations that can be applied to both oral and written data. For example, Gee's (2011) discourse analysis toolkit includes 27 tools, such as *the making strange tool* (look at the text as if you were an outsider with no background knowledge) and *the cohesion tool* (examine how different parts of the text are connected and the significance of these connections). Johnstone's (2008) heuristic comprises six broad categories (the world, language, participants, prior discourse, medium, and purpose) that can guide a preliminary analysis and lead to areas that are worth a closer look. This exploratory phase may also be guided by one's chosen analytical approach; for example, both Ochs and Capps's (2001) multidimensional framework for analyzing narratives (see Pomerantz & Kearney, 2012, Box 11.1) and Ivanič and Camps's (2001) framework for analyzing writer positioning outline specific features to examine.

Another way to begin to make sense of a large data set is to divide it into smaller, more manageable segments or specific foci. In their study of two L2 writers engaged in a collaborative revision task de Guerrero and Villamil (2000) segmented their transcripts into *episodes*, defined as "units of discourse during which the students were on task, that is, dealing with one discrete troublesource or a connected series of troublesources, or talking about the task, that is, discussing task procedures" (pp. 55–56), and subsequently analyzed several of these episodes in more detail. Other studies target specific linguistic features; for example, Ouellette (2008), drawing from Hyland's (2005) work on stance and engagement, examined the focal student's texts for elements such as hedges (*possibly, maybe*), boosters (*clearly, obviously*), and personal pronouns (*I, we, you*).

Once one has determined an area of interest, the next step is to look for recurring patterns. Some studies seek to trace patterns across source texts, teacher talk, and students' essays (Bunch & Willet, 2013; de Oliveira & Lan, 2014). Others look for patterns that characterize specific types of interaction and the factors that shape them; for example, Tan et al. (2010) used Storch's (2002) model of dynamic interaction to identify patterns of collaboration in student dyads and examined whether the modality (face to face vs. computer mediated) affected how students interacted with each other. Identifying patterns may also lead one to notice disruptions or unexpected events that may subsequently become the focus of analysis; for example, Waring's (2005) focus on advice resisting during peer tutoring sessions arose from her observation that the focal student's response to her tutor's advice frequently violated a supposed preference for advice acceptance.

Finally, throughout the process of analysis it is essential to reflect on one's interpretations of the data with a critical eye. Initial impressions of a particular stretch of text or talk may not hold up under further scrutiny, and researchers must always be ready to look for examples that do not fit patterns (what CA analysts call *deviant cases*) or that disconfirm the analysis that they have been developing. The presence of counterexamples does not necessarily mean that the analysis should be discarded, but these counterexamples need to be accounted for. Giving due consideration to counterexamples not only strengthens credibility but can also lead to deeper insights and may open up new avenues for exploration.

Using Software

As noted in Chapter 10, a wide range of software is now available to facilitate qualitative data management and analysis. Among these, the one with the most direct relevance to discourse analysis of oral data is Transana, originally developed by Chris Fassnacht and now maintained at the Wisconsin Center for Education Research, University of Wisconsin-Madison (http://www.transana.org). Unlike the software packages described in Chapter 10, Transana was specifically designed to work with audio and video recorded data and offers a number of advantages for researchers who work extensively with such data. For example, video or audio recordings can be uploaded to Transana, where they can be played, paused, rewound, and even slowed down while the researcher is simultaneously transcribing in another window. While basic transcription is possible in other software, Transana is unique in supporting symbols used in transcription systems such as CA, thus allowing for more detailed transcripts that go beyond the words spoken. It also allows use of non–Latin orthographic systems as long as the necessary fonts are available on the computer. Transana also permits insertion of time codes that link a point in the transcript to a corresponding point in the media file. This allows the analyst to move easily between the two and to synchronize data across multiple media sources, such as audio and video recordings of the same interaction, video recordings from different cameras, or multiple transcripts (e.g., separate transcripts of multiple interactions occurring simultaneously or a transcript in the original language and one in translation). In addition, one can incorporate frame grabs from video recordings or still photos into the transcripts, a useful feature for multimodal analyses.

Similar to other CAQDAS packages (see Chapter 10), Transana allows researchers to apply descriptive codes (*keywords*) to the data in order to identify episodes, sequences, or other relevant analytical units and to organize them into units that can subsequently be searched or gathered into *collections*. For example, one could bring together all incidents of corrective feedback, mentions of topic sentences, or pointing gestures that occur in recordings of tutor-student writing conferences. Another useful feature allows the researcher to write *notes* (i.e., comments or analytical memos) that are linked to specific points in a transcript or to collections.

One possible disadvantage of Transana for L2 writing researchers is its primary focus on audio- and video-recorded data. Although written texts can be imported into Transana, they must be in Rich Text (*.rtf) or plain text (*.txt) formats; formats such as MS-Word (*.doc) or Portable Document Format (*.pdf) are not supported. Those engaged in projects in which analysis of documents in these formats is central might be better served by one of the other CAQDAS packages described in Chapter 10, which also allow importing of audio and video files and in-software transcription, albeit with a lesser degree of functionality than what is supplied by Transana.

BOX 11.1 FOCAL STUDY

Pomerantz, A. & Kearney, E. (2012). Beyond 'write-talk-revise-(repeat)': Using narrative to understand one multilingual student's interactions around writing. *Journal of Second Language Writing, 21*, 221–238.

Background

Observing that L2 writers in their program engaged in numerous conversations about writing both inside and outside of class, the researchers wondered what role such conversations were playing in L2 writers' development. Rather than focusing on how these conversations shaped L2 writers' texts (what they call the "write-talk-revise" model, p. 223), they chose to investigate the writers' perspectives by examining their own accounts of these interactions.

Research Focus

The overall project sought "to understand how multilingual writers make sense of and respond to the multiple conversations they engage in around specific pieces of writing in English" (p. 225). The specific aim of the paper is to demonstrate how a narrative analysis can provide alternative perspectives on the connections between talk and writing.

Method

The focal participant, an international graduate student from Taiwan (Victoria), was part of a study of six multilingual students in a TESOL program at a US university. Data include three interviews with Victoria conducted over the course of one year, recordings of two tutoring sessions and three lessons from an academic writing class in which she was enrolled, her journal entries for the writing course, her emails about her writing, five written assignments from the writing course and another course on the sociology of language (including all drafts and notes), and "story-like diagrams" (p. 226) that Victoria spontaneously created to illustrate her thoughts and feelings about writing. The narratives that emerged from this data set were analyzed using a framework proposed by Ochs and Capps (2001).

Results

The results revolve around three questions derived from one of Victoria's diagrams entitled "My Writing": (1) What is "good academic writing" in this English language discourse community? (2) What is a "normal" writing process? (3) Who am I as a multilingual writer? (p. 229). Five narratives from the interviews and diagrams are analyzed in detail and triangulated with other sources, such as Victoria's journal. The analysis of narratives from different points over one year trace Victoria's evolving understandings of what constitutes "good" writing and her increasing confidence in herself as a writer. The researchers conclude with a reflection on how narrative analysis can expand research beyond the "write-talk-revise" model and argue for its further application in research on L2 writers.

Discussion of a Focal Study (Pomerantz & Kearney, 2012)

This study offers an illustration of how a DA approach can be applied to analysis of *small stories* (Georgakopoulou, 2006) that emerge in interviews. The data came from a larger project investigating how L2 writers engage with, make sense of, and appropriate (or resist) the many voices (instructors, tutors, peers) that surround the act of composition. From the six multilingual students who participated in this larger project, the researchers selected one, a Taiwanese student whom they call Victoria, as the focal participant. Although data collection included recordings of writing classroom and tutoring sessions involving Victoria, these data were not included in this paper. Instead, the analysis focused on Victoria's accounts of these interactions as evidenced in interviews and journal entries. In choosing this focus, the researchers' stated aim was to provide an emic perspective on the relationships between talk and text as an alternative to the emphasis on what they call "write–talk–revise" (p. 223) found in other studies on talk around writing and to make an argument in favor of narrative analysis as an approach to researching this topic. Consistent with their overall emic perspective, they organized the paper around three questions that they saw as central to Victoria's own concerns about writing as evidenced in a "story-like diagram" that she brought to the first interview: "(1) What is 'good academic writing' in this English language discourse community? (2) What is a 'normal' writing process? (3) Who am I as a multilingual writer?" (p. 229).

Arguing that "narratives are constructions, not reflections of reality" (p. 224), Pomerantz and Kearney explored these questions through a *dimensional approach* to narrative analysis proposed by Ochs and Capps (2001) that comprises five dimensions: *tellership* (who tells the story), *tellability* (what makes a story worth telling from the participants' perspective), *embeddedness* (how stories are embedded in ongoing talk and activity), *linearity* (how the story is organized), and *moral stance* (attitude toward the moral implications of the story). This framework was applied to an analysis of five stories (four oral, one written) told by Victoria at different points over the course of one year that illustrated how she appropriated or resisted the voices of others as she developed as a writer.

Adoption of a narrative analysis framework allowed for a deeper and more insightful exploration of these stories than what would have resulted from a thematic analysis (see Chapter 10). For example, attention to *linearity* demonstrated how these stories frequently shifted between a sequentially ordered account of events and Victoria's commentary on those events, which suggests that they were less a straightforward recounting of experience than an attempt to make sense of that experience through the narratives. In examining the *moral stance* that Victoria took toward herself as a writer in some of the excerpts, the researchers noted her tendency to be critical of perceived failures to live up to a "Platonic ideal" (p. 229) of good academic writing. However, they also analyzed these critiques as *embedded* within the interactional context of an interview (a context that also contributed to the *tellability* of these stories) as well as the larger context of American academia. Finally, expanding the notion of *tellership* from the actual narrator (Victoria) to include the audience for the stories (the interviewer, Pomerantz, who was also the lead instructor of the writing course in which Victoria was enrolled, but not Victoria's instructor) allowed for consideration of how these narratives were shaped by relationships among the research, the researcher, and the researched. In other words, rather than seeing this moral stance as simply reflecting Victoria's identity as an L2 writer, Pomerantz and Kearney interpreted it as one of many possible writer identities that Victoria may have seen as appropriate to display when being interviewed by a writing instructor.

Consistent with their analytic approach, the researchers presented excerpts from interviews within their interactional context (i.e., with interviewer as well as participant turns), which allowed the reader to see the extent to which the interviewer may have contributed to how narratives unfolded. However, for the most part the interviewer's role in tellership was taken into account in the analysis only when it was clearly evident (e.g., when the interviewer's comments were explicitly taken up by Victoria in a subsequent turn). The researchers did note that even minimal responses (such as "mmhm") may at times have shaped the moral stance that Victoria demonstrated in her stories (p. 232), but this insight was not further developed.

Although relying heavily on interviews with a single participant, the analysis was triangulated through examples taken from multiple types of data collected from Victoria (methodological triangulation) at different points over one year (data triangulation). The longitudinal perspective also allowed the researchers to document how Victoria's views of writing and herself as a writer evolved over time. The detailed description of Ochs and Capps's (2001) framework and its application across multiple examples gives readers a strong foundation for judging the credibility of the researchers' interpretations. There was also a high degree of transparency regarding data selection; for example, the researchers frankly admitted that Victoria was chosen as the focal participant for the paper because her proficiency in English and her enthusiasm and high degree of reflexivity regarding her own writing made her "a narrative researcher's dream subject" (p. 225). Appropriately, they did not attempt to generalize from Victoria's experiences but rather sought to use her case to illustrate what a narrative approach can contribute to L2 writing research.

Suggestions for Further Reading

General Guides to Discourse Analysis

- Bazerman, C. & Prior, P. (Eds.). (2004). *What writing does and how it does it: An introduction to analyzing texts and textual practices.* Mahwah, NJ: Lawrence Erlbaum.
- Cook, G. (2011). Discourse analysis. In J. Simpson (Ed.), *The Routledge handbook of applied linguistics* (pp. 431–444). New York: Routledge.
- Gee, J. P. (2010). *How to do discourse analysis: A tool kit.* New York: Routledge.
- Gee, J. P. & Handford, M. (Eds.). (2012). *The Routledge handbook of discourse analysis.* New York: Routledge.
- Johnstone, B. (2008). *Discourse analysis* (2nd edn.). Oxford: Blackwell.
- Jones, R. H. (2016). Discourse analysis. *TESOL Quarterly, 50,* 54–56.
- Kaplan, R. B. & Grabe, W. (2002). A modern history of written discourse analysis. *Journal of Second Language Writing, 11,* 191–223.
- McGroarty, M. (Ed.). (2002). Discourse and dialogue. *Annual Review of Applied Linguistics, 22.*
- Richards, K. (2003). Collecting and analyzing spoken interaction. In K. Richards (Ed.), *Qualitative inquiry in TESOL* (pp. 172–230). London: Palgrave Macmillan.
- Schiffrin, D. (1994). *Approaches to discourse.* Cambridge, MA: Blackwell.

- Zuengler, J. & Mori, J. (Eds.). (2002). Microanalyses of classroom discourse: A critical consideration of method. [Special issue]. *Applied Linguistics, 23*(3).

Conversation Analysis

- Kasper, G. & Wagner, J. (2014). Conversation analysis in applied linguistics. *Annual Review of Applied Linguistics, 34*, 171–212.
- Schegloff, E. A. (2007). *Sequence organization in interaction: A primer in conversation analysis.* Cambridge: Cambridge University Press.
- Seedhouse, P. (2005). Conversation analysis and language learning. *Language Teaching, 38*, 165–187.
- Stivers, T. & Sidnell, J. (Eds.). (2013). *The handbook of conversation analysis.* Malden, MA: John Wiley & Sons.
- ten Have, P. (2007). *Doing conversation analysis: A practical guide* (2nd edn.). Thousand Oaks, CA: Sage.

Multimodal Discourse Analysis

- Early, M., Kendrick, M., & Potts, D. (Eds.). (2015). Multimodality: Out from the margins of English language teaching. [Special issue]. *TESOL Quarterly, 49*(3).
- Goodwin, C. (2000). Action and embodiment within situated human interaction. *Journal of Pragmatics, 32*, 1489–1522.
- Goodwin, C. (2001). Practices of seeing: Visual analysis: An ethnomethodological approach. In T. van Leeuwen & C. Jewitt (Eds.), *Handbook of visual analysis* (pp. 157–182) London: Sage.
- Kress, G. (2012). Multimodal discourse analysis. In J. P. Gee & M. Handford (Eds.), *The Routledge handbook of discourse analysis* (pp. 35–50). New York: Routledge.
- Kress, G. & Bezemer, J. (2009). Writing in a multimodal world of representation. In R. Beard, D. Myhill, & J. Riley (Eds.), *Sage handbook of writing development* (pp. 167–181). Thousand Oaks, CA: Sage.
- Norris, S. (2004). *Analyzing multimodal interaction.* New York: Routledge.

Narrative Analysis

- Benson, P. (2014). Narrative inquiry in applied linguistics research. *Annual Review of Applied Linguistics, 34*, 154–170.
- Casanave, C. P. (2005). Uses of narrative in L2 writing research. In P. K. Matsuda & T. Silva (Eds.), *Second language writing research: Perspectives on the process of knowledge construction* (pp. 17–32). Mahwah, NJ: Lawrence Erlbaum.
- De Fina, A. (2009). Narratives in interview—The case of accounts: For an interactional approach to narrative genres. *Narrative Inquiry, 19*, 233–258.

- Kasper, G. & Prior, M. T. (2015). Analyzing storytelling in TESOL interview research. *TESOL Quarterly, 49*, 226–254.
- Ochs, E. & Capps, L. (2001). *Living narrative: Creating lives in everyday storytelling*. Cambridge, MA: Harvard University Press.
- Pavlenko, A. (2007). Autobiographic narrative as data in applied linguistics. *Applied Linguistics, 28*, 163–188.

Systemic Functional Linguistics

- Halliday, M.A.K. & Matthiessen, C.M.I.M. (2014). *Halliday's introduction to functional grammar* (4th ed.). New York: Routledge.
- Martin, J. R. & Rose, D. (2007). *Working with discourse: Meaning beyond the clause* (2nd edn.). New York: Continuum.
- Schleppegrell, M. J. (2012). Systemic functional linguistics. In J. P. Gee & M. Handford (Eds.), *The Routledge handbook of discourse analysis* (pp. 21–34). New York: Routledge.

Recording and Transcription

- Bucholtz, M. (2000). The politics of transcription. *Journal of Pragmatics, 32*, 1439–1465.
- DuFon, M. A. (2002). Video recording in ethnographic SLA research: Some issues of validity in data collection. *Language Learning and Technology, 6*, 40–59.
- Goodwin, C. (1993). Recording human interaction in natural settings. *Pragmatics, 3*, 181–209.
- Green, J., Fránquiz, M., & Dixon, C. (1997). The myth of the objective transcript: Transcribing as a situated act. *TESOL Quarterly, 31*, 172–176.
- Heath, C., Hindmarsh, J., & Luff, P. (2010). *Video in qualitative research: Analysing social interaction in everyday life*. Thousand Oaks, CA: Sage.
- Hepburn, A. & Bolden, G. (2013). The conversation analytic approach to transcription. In J. Sidnell & T. Stivers (Eds.), *The handbook of conversation analysis* (pp. 57–76). Oxford: Wiley-Blackwell.
- Leung, C. & Hawkins, M. R. (2011). Video recording and the research process. *TESOL Quarterly, 45*, 344–354.
- Ochs, E., Schegloff, E. A., & Thompson, S. A. (1996). Transcription conventions. In E. Ochs, E. A. Schegloff, & S. A. Thompson (Eds.), *Interaction and grammar* (pp. 461–465). Cambridge: Cambridge University Press.
- Roberts, C. (1997). Transcribing talk: Issues of representation. *TESOL Quarterly, 31*, 167–172.
- Zuengler, J., Ford, C., & Fassnacht, C. (1998). *Analyst eyes and camera eyes: Theoretical and technological considerations in "seeing" the details of classroom interaction*. CELA Technical Report. Albany, NY: SUNY, Center for English Learning and Achievement.

Software

- Transana 3.00 [Computer software]. (2015). Madison, WI: The Board of Regents of the University of Wisconsin System. Available: http://www.transana.org
- University of Surrey CAQDAS networking project. (2014). *Transana 2.60: Distinguishing features and functions.* Retrieved from http://www.surrey.ac.uk/sociology/research/researchcentres/caqdas/files/Transana%202_6%20-%20Distinguishing%20features%20FINAL.pdf

Conclusion

12

EMERGING METHODS AND CURRENT ISSUES

In our concluding chapter, we take a look at emerging trends and future directions in L2 writing research. We begin with a review of some technologies, approaches, and techniques that are still not well represented in L2 writing research but which we feel have potential for greater use. We have included sections on both quantitative cognitively oriented research and qualitative socially oriented research. This is followed by a discussion of using research syntheses in L2 writing research (both quantitative and qualitative). Finally, we conclude with a summary of what we see as overall issues related to study quality that we believe need to be addressed to move the field of L2 writing research forward.

Emerging Approaches and Techniques in Quantitative and Cognitively Oriented Research

Eye Tracking

Chapter 8 discussed methods for studying writers' and raters' cognitive processes through their verbalization, but, as explained, not all cognitive processes can be verbalized. Researchers in the area of reading have long tracked participants' eye movements with eye tracking devices in an attempt to better understand how they process individual parts of sentences. To give a simple example, readers' eyes will pause longer on a new word or on a grammatical error. Also, they may reread parts of a sentence if there is an ambiguity to be resolved. Dussias (2010) provides a clear description of eye tracking research and its applications to written and oral sentence processing research, and Anson and Schwegler (2012) present a very readable discussion of its application to L1 reading and writing research.

However, we know of no studies that have studied L2 composing processes using eye trackers as learners write or produce sentences. Currently, eye tracking is used in cognitive psychology to study L1 writers' processes within cognitive models of writing such as the Flower and Hayes model (1980), which is widely cited, as well as Kellogg (1996). Because eye tracking studies are by definition laboratory studies, they are limited in the types of writing that can be studied.

Several studies of various aspects of the L1 composing process have been conducted. Alamargot, Chesnet, Dansac, and Ros (2006) used technology called *eye and pen*, a device that can record handwriting and eye movement to indicate how writers look at text that they have already produced as well as other sources in the task environment. This technology was also used in Alamargot, Plane, Lambert, and Chesnet (2010) to study five writers at a range of expertise levels who were asked to read the beginning of a story and finish it. The researchers analyzed the pausing behaviors and eye movements of the participants and were able to hypothesize on how the writing process changed as the participants developed increasing expertise.

Another eye tracking study focused on how writers read their developing texts as they composed and how the behavior related to text quality (Beers, Quinlan, & Harbaugh, 2010), while others have focused on single sentence production (Nottbusch, 2010; Van Waes, Leitjten, & Quinlan, 2010). A study by Paulson, Alexander, and Armstrong (2007) may be particularly interesting to L2 writing researchers because it examined peer-review processes. Participants read an essay that included a holistic problem, specifically, a mismatch between the prompt and essay, as well as 10 surface-level errors. Participants were given peer-review type questions to answer that did not focus on surface errors. Among the findings were that the reviewers fixated on the surface level errors but only glanced at the prompt for the assignment.

In L2 writing research, Shintani and Ellis (2013) supplemented their experimental study of different types of L2 corrective feedback with an eye-tracking and stimulated recall component with a few additional participants. Three students each from the direct corrective feedback and the metalinguistic explanation groups reread their essays in an eye tracker. There was no obvious difference between the groups, but one finding was that some of the students did focus on their errors but could not correct them. Winke and Lim (2015) used eye tracking to study where raters looked on a rubric when they scored essays. They found that higher interrater reliability on the subcategories was associated with attention to those categories, but noted that the order of the subcategories on the rubric were not randomized, so it is possible that raters simply looked to the left of the rubric more often. While neither of these studies tracked L2 writers as they composed, they illustrate the range of research that can be conducted using eye tracking technology. Although it is not accessible to all researchers, it holds promise for investigating previously unobservable cognitive processes.

Keystroke Logging

Keystroke logging tracks participants' actions on a computer as they compose. Like the eye-tracking studies, these studies are situated within cognitive models of writing from the L1 literature. Many of the writing research studies use Inputlog, free software developed by Mariëlle Leijten and Luuk Van Waes, who have published much of the research using this technology (but see Leijten & Van Waes, 2013, for a description of other software). Their web site (www.inputlog. net) includes instructional videos and announcements about workshops. This program produces information about where and how long writers pause and which keys they hit. Note that the program is different from screen capturing software, such as Camtasia, which simply records a video of the screen. As one might imagine, such software produces a large amount of data that might be difficult to interpret. The developers address this in Leijten and Van Waes (2013), specifically explaining how the data can be combined with other methods including eye tracking and verbal protocols.

Many studies using keystroke logging have been conducted with L1 writers. Some are experimental, such as De Smet, Brand-Gruwel, Leijten, and Kirschner (2014), who researched the effect of electronic outlining on the writing process, while others describe aspects of the writing process, such as Leijten, Janssen, and Van Waes (2010), who investigated writers' use of speech recognition software and how they corrected the software's production errors. In a more unusual study, Deane and Zhang (2015) analyzed over 2,500 essays from a language arts test given to students in grades six to nine and the associated keystroke data to determine, among other things, how well such data could predict human scores. Analyzing 10 behaviors such as pause length between sentences and the duration of cut-and-paste events, they were able to determine, using regression, how much the writers' process behaviors contributed to their final score. What is particularly interesting is that the specific processes did not contribute to the final scores in the same way across genres, which seems particularly relevant for those who compare the effect of tasks and genres.

We highlight here two studies with L2 writers, since the research frameworks are more accessible to those interested in L2 writing research. Miller, Lindgren, and Sullivan (2008) conducted a longitudinal study of Swedish high school students' writing processes and products, collecting data three times over three years. They were interested in how the students' writing behavior changed with regard to revising, pausing, and fluency and whether or not these process variables were related to text improvement. The measures calculated by the software (in this case, JEdit) included fluency (i.e., the number of words written per minute), bursts (the number of typed characters written between pauses or revisions, and revisions (deletions or insertions). It is interesting to note that they did not find an improvement in text quality, but fluency and bursts increased over time. Using regression, they showed that fluency and fluency during bursts were related to text quality. While none of these findings are surprising, the study illustrates more sophisticated methods of assessing fluency than simply counting the number of words (a concern noted in Chapter 6).

Barkaoui (2016) focused on revisions made during a timed writing task. He wanted to determine when and how students revised and whether or not the revisions were affected by task type, L2 proficiency, and keyboarding skills. He used Inputlog as well as screen capturing software (Morae). Using a detailed and well described coding scheme, he coded all revisions along several dimensions including whether the revision was made just as part of a text was written (precontextual) or if the student went back to revise previously written text (contextual). Among the findings were that both the low and high proficiency level writers made more precontextual changes and that the low proficiency students made more precontextual changes than the high proficiency students. Keyboarding skills and task type did not have strong effects. This study is a helpful example for anyone wanting to code revision processes. As noted in Chapter 6, coding revisions can be challenging, but keystroking logging data combined with a detailed coding scheme can facilitate the process. The software also collects temporal data (i.e., when the revision was made), which is not available when coding writers' texts.

Overall, keystroke logging software seems to have great potential for L2 writing research. In particular, it is unobtrusive and therefore nonreactive, unlike think-aloud protocols. Data can also be collected in large groups and does not need to be transcribed. One caution is that the software generates a huge amount of data, and one needs principled reasons for examining various aspects of the writing process, but all of the studies mentioned here on both L1 and L2 writing are solidly situated in research on cognitive models of writing or revision.

Emerging Approaches and Techniques in Qualitative and Socially Oriented Research

Reflective Narratives and Autoethnography

Reflective narratives, in which individuals reflect upon their experiences as L2 researchers, learners, or instructors, are becoming increasingly visible in the field of applied linguistics; recent examples include Nunan and Choi's (2010) edited volume in which applied linguistic researchers reflect upon their identities as language learners or teachers, De Costa's (2015) collection of narratives in which researchers reflect upon the ethical issues that they have encountered in the field, and Duff, Anderson, Ilnyckyj, VanGaya, Wang, and Yates's (2013) account of learning Chinese, which includes participants' personal narratives (as well as *metanarrative* accounts of how these narratives evolved). This use of narratives is distinct from other forms of narrative inquiry (see Chapter 11) in that narrative is used as a research method rather than as a source of data; that is, writing an account of one's experience of language learning, acquisition of academic literacy, or development as a language teaching professional is seen as an occasion for reflection that can lead to insights not available through traditional research methods (e.g., Benson, 2014). In addition, unlike other types of narrative inquiry, in which a researcher analyzes narratives told by others, in reflective narratives the researcher is part of (indeed, central to) the story that is presented. That is, the writer of the narrative is simultaneously the researcher and the subject of the research.

Personal narrative has a long history in the field of L2 writing, for example, Bell's (1997) autobiography of her acquisition of Chinese literacy, Casanave's (1997) reflections on her sometimes fraught relationship with academic discourse as a student, scholar, and educator, Belcher and Connor's (2001) collection in which scholars from a range of academic disciplines discuss the processes and emotions involved in becoming multiliterate, and Casanave and Li's (2008) edited volume comprising stories of academic enculturation written by individuals who successfully negotiated the literacy demands of English-medium graduate education (in either their L1 or L2). However, whether such narratives count as (or even aspire to be) research is an open question. For example, Casanave and Li (2008) describe their volume as "an inspirational resource book" (p. 4) for current and aspiring graduate students and their mentors that intentionally avoids the theorizing and methodology expected in research studies (e.g., there is no formal description of data collection or explanation of analytical procedures), although many of the contributors make reference to theory in order to frame and understand their experiences. Nunan and Choi (2010), on the other hand, expressly classify the narratives in their volume as research on the grounds that contributors were asked to theorize about their experiences in relation to some aspect of culture, identity, or language learning (p. 1). For example, in his chapter recounting his memories of growing up as a Chinese American in Los Angeles and his encounters (and struggles) with academic writing, Luke (2010), who refers to his narrative as an "autotheoretic account" (p. 131), filters and interprets his experience through the critical perspectives that are part of his current scholarly identity. Similarly, Vandrick (2009), whose collection of personal essays documenting her experiences as a TESOL professional include several on academic writing, argues for the value and legitimacy of personal narrative as a research method (pp. 10–17).

The related genre of *autoethnography* is more firmly situated within the scope of research, although the lines between autoethnography and other forms of personal narrative are often blurred. Ellis and Bochner (2000) define autoethnography as "an autobiographical genre of writing and research that displays multiple layers of consciousness, connecting the personal to the cultural" (p. 739). It arose in part in reaction to ethnographic accounts in which an outsider researcher claimed the right to assign meaning to the cultural practices of an Other (i.e., a people whom we perceive to be radically different from ourselves). Auto-ethnography has been advocated as a means of restructuring the relationship between the researcher and the researched, allowing alternative voices that are often silenced in traditional representational research to emerge. It is also seen as a means of humanizing the research process by acknowledging and highlighting the involvement of the researcher as a person and possibly providing therapeutic benefits to the narrator (e.g., Ellis & Bochner, 2000). The approach shares with traditional ethnography an emphasis on culture (see Chapter 4); that is, it expressly focuses on the narrator's experience as a member of a particular cultural or social group (e.g., L2 writers, language educators) and seeks to provide cultural explanations for experience, and it is this emphasis that distinguishes autoethnography from other introspective methods, such as diary studies. However, autoethnography stresses researcher reflexivity to a greater extent than traditional ethnography and, in at least some versions (e.g., *evocative autoethnography*), also puts a premium on exploration of the researcher's emotional responses (Ellis & Bochner, 2000). That is, in autoethnography, the researcher is not a dispassionate observer, but an individual who is fully emotionally engaged with the phenomena or experience being described, and this emotional engagement is on full display in the narrative itself.

Autoethnographies can vary in the extent to which they adopt the methodology of ethnography, such as observation, field notes, and interviews with other group members (see Chapter 4). For example, as an alternative to evocative autoethnography, Anderson (2006) has proposed what he calls *analytic autoethnography*, which includes characteristics such as (a) a researcher who is a full member of the community being studied (what Anderson calls *complete member researcher* [CMR] status, p. 378), (b) use of methods such as interviews to bring in other voices and avoid the "self-absorption" (p. 385) that Anderson feels is an ever-present threat in evocative autoethnography, and (c) an analysis that goes beyond mere description of personal experience. Other scholars (e.g., Ellis & Bochner, 2000, 2006), however, appear to be more open to a less prescriptive methodological approach, for example, acknowledging the possibility of using recollected past experiences (vs. current observation and field notes) as data for an autoethnography and reaffirming the value of emotional rather than analytical interpretations. This ongoing debate illustrates the lack of clarity as to what autoethnography actually is (or should be).

Unlike reflective narratives, which appear to be fairly common in L2 writing (see the previous discussion), there are as yet very few examples of studies in the field that are expressly labeled autoethnography, although some of the reflective narratives on writing described earlier might fit into this category (e.g., Luke, 2010; Vandrick, 2009). One of the few self-described (analytic) autoethnographic studies published in a mainstream applied linguistics journal is Canagarajah's (2012) account of his development as a TESOL professional, which provides a thoughtful reflection on the author's experience as a nonnative speaker in the field and offers a template for how this genre might be realized. Despite Canagarajah's extensive experience as a teacher and researcher on L2 writing, this aspect of his professional experience does not figure prominently in his narrative. Nevertheless, analytic autoethnography holds promise as a methodology through which a writing teacher-researcher might explore his or her own practice, while evocative ethnography might serve as a means of encouraging L2 writers or pre-service teachers to think more deeply about their experiences and how these relate to larger social and theoretical issues related to writing instruction.

Critical Discourse Analysis

Critical discourse analysis (CDA) is a type of research that uses discourse analytic methods (see Chapter 11) to analyze how social power and inequality are enacted, reproduced, or resisted through text and talk. CDA is not a method per se but an approach to doing discourse analysis that may employ a variety of discourse analytic methods, such as systemic functional linguistics or conversation analysis, to achieve its aims. Lin (2014) has proposed a set of criteria for evaluating applied linguistics CDA research that includes (a) social commitment, (b) a problem-orientation that has practical implications and is accessible to the public, (c) diversity and interdisciplinarity in methods and approaches, (d) attention to the agency of readers and subjects of the discourses being critiqued, and (e) researcher reflexivity (pp. 214–215). There are a number of approaches to CDA (see Blommaert & Bulcaen, 2000; Lin, 2014), each of which approaches analysis in a somewhat different way. For example, Fairclough (1992, 2012), whose work has been particularly influential in applied linguistics, proposes a three-dimensional framework that includes (a) *discourse as text* (analysis of linguistic features such as metaphors, use of passive voice to obscure agency, pronouns such as *we* vs. *they*, etc.), (b) *discourse as discursive practice* (how texts are produced, circulated, and consumed and how they are intertextually linked to other texts), and (c) *discourse as social practice* (the relation of discourse to ideology and hegemony). Drawing from the methodological literature on CDA, Flowerdew (2008) provides several lists of linguistic features (e.g., syntax, metaphor, modality), guiding questions (e.g., Are sentences positive or negative?), and other foci (e.g., genre conventions) that might be used to structure an analysis (pp. 199–203). However, some CDA researchers have also emphasized the need to go beyond texts to incorporate ethnographic methods into CDA studies in order to examine how these texts are used, interpreted, adopted, or resisted (e.g., Blommaert & Bulcaen, 2000; Lin, 2014).

While it is not unusual for L2 writing researchers to take a critical stance, use of CDA as a method is less common. One example is Gebhard (2002), who embeds a critical discourse analysis of the discourses of school reform within a two-year classroom ethnographic study of English language learners in a magnet school in Silicon Valley. The addition of observation and interviews allowed her to show how these discourses, which encouraged use of technology, being organized, and demonstrating effort and initiative, were enacted in everyday classroom literacy practices in ways that disadvantaged L2 students; for example, an emphasis on having students take responsibility for their own learning meant that L2 students received minimal guidance from teachers on their writing. Adapting Fairclough's (1992) three-dimensional model, Ivanič (2004) analyzed the discourses of writing found in policy documents, textbooks, and teacher discourses in the United States and Britain, identifying six distinct discourses that embodied very different beliefs about what writing is and how it should be learned. Her framework might serve as the basis for future CDA work on the discourses of writing in commonly used ESL/EFL writing texts and how these are instantiated (or resisted) in L2 writing programs and classrooms. Another CDA study from outside of the field of L2 writing but quite relevant to it is Sutherland-Smith (2011), who used Fairclough's model to analyze plagiarism policies at 20 top universities in Australia, Britain, and the United States. Among her findings was the preponderance of legal (e.g., plagiarism as a type of theft or fraud of which a student may be found *innocent* or *guilty*) and ethical (e.g., *moral responsibility, ethical practice*) discourses used in these policies. The paper also includes a thoughtful discussion of the potential effect of such policies on student writers that draws in part from research on L2 writing. Expanding such a study to other university settings (the US sample used here was limited to top-tier private institutions, such as Harvard and Yale, which are not representative of the type of institutions that ESL writers typically attend) or other sites of plagiarism discourses (e.g., media, L2 writing programs) is an area for future CDA research in the field.

Computer Mediated Discourse Analysis

Computer mediated discourse analysis (CMDA) is an approach to discourse analysis that examines how language is used in computer-mediated environments (e.g., Internet chat, email, blogs, wikis, Internet gaming). There is some overlap between CMDA and multimodal discourse analysis (MMDA, see Chapter 11) in that both approaches can be used to study digital texts; however, CMDA has tended to be more squarely focused on language versus MMDA's broader focus on interfaces across words, pictures, and sound. Indeed, one area of abiding interest for CMDA has been how communication and other coordinated activity is managed in text–only environments (e.g., Internet chat) in the absence of other channels of communication such as prosody, eye gaze, facial expressions, and gestures that are available in face-to-face interaction (Herring, 2001). More recently, however, as computer-mediated communication has become more multimodal through Web 2.0 technologies such as video chat and voice-over Internet protocols (VoIP), the field of CMDA has been moving toward encompassing a more multimodal perspective as well (see Herring, 2015).

In L2 writing research, CMDA can be classified into two broad areas. The first comprises studies that compare face-to-face versus computer-mediated communication (CMC) during activities such as peer review or collaborative writing with the aim of determining whether the affordances of the CMC environment (e.g., availability of planning time, the presence of visual text that can facilitate comprehension, the possibility of editing before posting) facilitate or hinder L2 students' participation in such activities. For example, Chang (2012) compared peer review in face-to-face, synchronous, and asynchronous CMC, examining features such as frequency of on-task episodes (to measure the level of student engagement) and the types of feedback provided. Li and Zhu (2013), drawing from Storch (2002), analyzed the different patterns of collaboration evident during small group work among EFL students in China who were using wikis (see also the discussion of Tan et al., 2010 in Chapter 11).

The second area of CMDA research in L2 writing involves analysis of the texts produced in CMC environments. Many of these studies have focused on out-of-class writing, for example, Lam's (2000) study of an English-language website about a Japanese pop singer created by a Chinese immigrant teenager and Yi's (2010) study of a Korean immigrant student's composing practices (in her L1 and L2) on various out-of-class sites, both on- and offline. Black (2005, 2009) analyzed several L2 English writers' experiences on a fan fiction site, considering how the writers identified themselves on the site as well as the multilingual practices (e.g., use of Romanized Japanese in stories based on anime characters) they employed in their stories. For the most part, this research has been focused on issues such as writer identity rather than on writing development per se, although some, such as Lam (2000), have made claims regarding possible positive effects of these online writing experiences on L2 writers' confidence in their abilities as writers and thus on their overall writing development. Studies of in-class computer-mediated writing are less common and have mainly examined use of wikis as a collaborative tool. For example, Mak and Coniam's (2008) analysis of students' use of wikis in a Hong Kong secondary school writing program examined the texts that students produced and how these evolved over time through the contributions of various group members. However, despite much discussion about the value of alternative forms of literacy afforded by digital genres for L2 writers (e.g., Lotherington & Jenson, 2011), we found relatively little research that incorporates an analysis of the texts that L2 writers produce in this environment or that attends to how its specific affordances (e.g., the ability of readers to comment on or revise online texts) shape the eventual product and the potential for learning in these spaces. This is clearly a rich area for future work.

Research Syntheses

In Norris and Ortega's (2010) timeline on research synthesis, they noted the increase of meta-analyses, one type of synthesis discussed in this chapter, but they also said:

> [W]e also hope that researchers will avail themselves of the full potential of systematic research synthesis, which considerably transcends the narrower

domain of meta-analysis and includes other quantitative as well as qualitative methods that more fully enable the task of synthesizing accumulated knowledge in the increasingly diverse research landscape of applied linguistics.

(p. 461)

Several research syntheses in the area of L2 writing can be found. For example, Hyland and Hyland (2006) published a review of feedback on L2 writing in what is called a *state-of-the-art article* in the journal *Language Teaching*. This type of article can be found in various journals, but *Language Teaching* includes detailed and specific guidelines for such articles (http://assets.cambridge.org/LTA/LTA_ifc.pdf). Authors are asked not only to synthesize the research but also to critically examine it and suggest directions for future research. In their synthesis, Hyland and Hyland divided the foci of the feedback research into four broad categories (teacher written feedback, teacher oral feedback, peer and self-evaluation, and computer-mediated feedback). Another example that focused primarily (but not exclusively) on qualitative research is Pecorari and Petrić's (2014) recent state-of-the-art article on plagiarism and L2 writing in which the authors reviewed various perspectives on plagiarism (e.g., as cheating, as developmental, as appropriation) and discussed the varied foci that have characterized L2 writing research in this area (e.g., student views, instructor views, disciplinary differences). This type of review is generally intended to be comprehensive but not necessarily exhaustive, and neither Hyland and Hyland nor Pecorari and Petrić detailed their literature search. This approach can be compared to Manchón, Murphy, and Roca's (2007) review of research on lexical retrieval during writing. They used the term *narrative review* and detailed their search process, which suggests that their review was intended to be exhaustive. They too classified and summarized the research. Ortega's (2003) synthesis of studies of syntactic complexity in academic writing systematically reviewed the literature and summarized the statistical results by graphically presenting differences in complexity measures across proficiency levels but did not use meta-analytic statistics.

Meta-analyses have been used recently in the field of L2 writing. A meta-analysis is distinct from other types of research syntheses because it includes statistical methods for summarizing results across studies. It is a principled method that involves defining the scope of the research to be reviewed and explaining how the search was conducted and why studies were included or excluded. The studies are then coded according to several features such as context and measures. Plonsky and Oswald (2012) provided a detailed discussion of how the coding can be done. This is followed by calculating the effect sizes for the studies and weighting them according to sample size. Plonsky and Oswald provide a discussion of how to do this, as do some of the suggestions for further reading at the end of this chapter.

In L2 writing research, there have been several meta-analyses done, all on written corrective feedback: Kang and Han (2015), Kao and Wible (2014), Russell and

Spada (2006), and Truscott (2007). What is interesting about the meta-analyses is that they do not all come to the same conclusions about the effects of corrective feedback, suggesting that meta-analyses require some amount of judgment and decision making. We compare these meta-analyses here to illustrate this point and to emphasize that they must be carefully read and evaluated.

Truscott (2007) conducted a meta-analysis with only a small number of studies. He focused on studies of corrective feedback over time and specifically excluded studies that involved only one treatment. Although van Beuningen et al. (2012), the study of corrective feedback discussed in Chapter 2, was published later, his decision would have excluded such a study that did find an effect for written corrective feedback. Reviewing experimental studies from five articles, he concluded that there was a small negative effect for error correction. Interestingly, he also conducted an analysis that included studies without control groups and studies with noncomparable control groups to calculate overall gains in accuracy. He found a very small increase in accuracy measures but explained that the increase could have been due to a number of factors other than corrective feedback. These results contrast with Russell and Spada (2006), who argued that their meta-analysis showed a positive effect for corrective feedback; however, their study included oral feedback, omitted some studies that Truscott included, and included studies that measured accuracy on grammar tests or revisions. These two meta-analyses show how different results can be obtained when researchers make different decisions, and they highlight how important an accompanying narrative description of the tests and measures used in the studies is.

As a coda, Kao and Wible (2014) used Truscott's (2007) inclusion criteria, expanding the scope of studies examined to 26, and found a small positive effect for unfocused feedback and a large effect for focused feedback. Kang and Han (2015) also found a positive effect for corrective feedback but no significant difference for focused versus unfocused feedback. Again, although these two new meta-analyses were well done, they illustrate that one has to critically examine the methodology and results when evaluating meta-analyses. We return here to points made in Chapter 2, namely that experimental research can be reductionist. Studies of focused feedback often examine only the effects of a treatment on a specific grammatical feature and not the overall accuracy or complexity of the writing (cf. Xu, 2009), and this needs to be kept in mind when interpreting any meta-analysis.

Although meta-analyses of the type described here are not possible in qualitative research, the related procedure called *metasynthesis* can be done from a qualitative perspective. Similar to a meta-analysis, a metasynthesis involves a meticulous approach to selecting and evaluating studies for inclusion and aims to analyze and synthesize the results of these studies in order to draw broader conclusions about the focal phenomenon. There are a number of types of and approaches to qualitative metasynthesis (see Finfgeld, 2003; Timulak, 2014), many of which use some sort of thematic coding (often following grounded theory methodology; see Chapter 10) in order to consolidate the results of multiple studies and identify larger themes. While becoming more common in the field of education, qualitative metasyntheses are still rare in the field of applied linguistics. One example from education with relevance to the language teaching field is Téllez and Waxman's (2006) metasynthesis of qualitative studies on the effectiveness of various teaching practices for English language learners (ELLs) in K–12 settings. Through the metasynthesis of 25 studies primarily drawn from education journals (along with a few from applied linguistics journals, such as *TESOL Quarterly*), the authors identified four teaching practices deemed to be effective for ELLs. Although the conclusions are somewhat weakened by the lack of discussion on how the key construct of *effectiveness* was defined and determined in the focal studies, Téllez and Waxman provide a useful overview of the place of metasynthesis in qualitative research and an informative account of their data collection and analysis procedures. Another study from education is Graham, Harris, and Santangelo's (2015) review of studies related to K-12 writing instruction, which combined a meta-analysis of quantitative (experimental, quasi-experimental, and single-subject) studies and a metasynthesis of what the authors refer to as "qualitative studies of the writing practices of exceptional teachers of literacy" (p. 502). Results from both quantitative and qualitative analyses were combined to produce a final set of recommendations for writing instruction. Unfortunately, the authors report that they were unable to find sufficient numbers of studies on L2 writers to enable them to draw conclusions on the most effective approaches for this student population.

One last type of research synthesis is typified by Liu and Brown (2015), who conducted an exhaustive methodological review of research on written corrective feedback. They used meta-analytic search methods but did not conduct a meta-analysis. Instead, they coded studies for methodological features to address questions about sampling and design features, statistical methods, reporting procedures, and design changes over time. They came to several conclusions, finding, for example, much use of intact classes with no random sampling, a lack of studies reporting effect sizes, and inconsistent reporting of interrater reliability. Their study is an important one for quantitative L2 writing researchers, and we hope that other such methodological reviews will be conducted for other areas of L2 writing research such as task complexity or peer review.

Reporting L2 Writing Research

Replication

Replication has long been discussed in the quantitative social sciences, and it is widely agreed that replication is necessary in quantitative research, although, as we will discuss later, it is much more controversial in qualitative research. In the field of applied linguistics, replication was brought to light by Santos (1989) in a commentary in *TESOL Quarterly* when she argued:

> What is considered standard procedure in other disciplines that hypothesize, quantify, and generalize is ignored in ours. . . . Research is an accretive process; it is the accumulation and consolidation of knowledge over time. Replication of research confirms or calls into question existing findings; without it, a discipline consists of scattered hypotheses and insufficiently substantiated generalizations.
>
> *(p. 700)*

Since then, there has been a focus on definitions of replication and what types of replications are possible (e.g., Polio, 2012; Porte, 2012), the importance of detailed reporting practices (Polio & Gass, 1997; Porte, 2010), and when studies should be replicated (Mackey, 2012). Note that in these discussions, there is also widespread agreement that an *exact replication*—one in which nothing is changed—is impossible in applied linguistics, whereas an *approximate* or *systematic replication*—where one variable, such as learners' proficiency or L1, is changed—is the goal.

Polio (2012) summarized the history of replication in the broader field of applied linguistics and highlighted the case of written error correction studies. She concluded that although all the studies addressed the same general research question, none could be considered approximate replications of any other study. She also singled out Hartshorn et al. (2010), discussed in Chapter 2, as a good candidate for replication, and it has now been replicated (Evans, Hartshorn, & Strong-Krause, 2011) with the same findings.

As the commentary in the debate on replication published in the *Journal of Second Language Writing* (Atkinson, 2012) makes clear, replication is a highly contentious topic among qualitative researchers in L2 writing. On the one hand, some have argued that replication is incompatible with qualitative research, whose aim is to identify the effects of local contextual factors (including the researcher him- or herself) on results rather than to generate findings that might be generalized (or replicated) across settings. In other words, the expectation is that research conducted in different settings or by different researchers, even when following similar procedures, will generate different results, meaning that replication in the strict sense is not possible (e.g., Matsuda, 2012). In addition, there has been concern that the inability to replicate findings in qualitative research may lead to claims that such research is invalid or unscientific, and thus of no value (e.g., Casanave, 2012). On the other hand, others feel that replication, at least in a limited sense, has a role to play in qualitative L2 writing research (e.g., Porte & Richards, 2012). For example, it would be possible to use the same set of questions to conduct interviews with students and instructors regarding views on plagiarism across multiple academic disciplines and sociocultural settings and to compare these to look for patterns of differences as well as similarities. The idea would not be to test or validate the findings of one study by comparing it to another but to build upon the first study's results so as to expand knowledge production beyond what can be accomplished by a single study. Although we are reluctant to label such research as *replication* (as it has very different purposes), we agree with Cumming (2012) that such comparative research, which has a well-established history in qualitative research in the social sciences, has a place in qualitative L2 writing research and should be encouraged.

Documentation of the Research Process

Discussions of replication in the field of L2 writing have in part revolved around the problem of insufficient information about methodology; that is, one cannot replicate a study if one does not know how the study was conducted. For example, Polio (2012) noted that none of the 16 studies she reviewed on written error correction contained enough information that would allow another researcher to replicate the study. In the past, journal space was limited, but now, most journals have online appendices that can be used for study details, such as data collection and analysis procedures, data collection instruments, and coding schemes. In addition, open repositories, such as *Instruments for Research Into Second Languages*, or IRIS (https://www.iris-database.org/iris/app/home/index), exist where researchers can post their instruments used for data collection, along with any other information or documents they wish (e.g., data, analysis tools, reliability coefficients, notes about usage). IRIS was created, in part, because of the need for greater transparency in publishing research (Marsden, Mackey, & Plonsky, 2015). IRIS currently makes over 2,000 data collection tools available and is supported by 34 journals in the field. Recently, Derrick (2016) coded 385 L2 studies published in three journals between 2009 and 2013. She noted that 62 percent of the studies did not make their instruments available and only 17 percent made their complete materials available either online or in an appendix. Thus, IRIS is an important development in providing access to study details, and it can also serve as a helpful resource for researchers as they design their own studies.

In addition to common research instruments, shared data might facilitate replication as well (Connor-Linton & Polio, 2014). In other words, researchers can run the same analysis from their study on a freely available data set. For example, many of the studies discussed in Chapter 6 related to learners' texts could be replicated with new data sets. Learner corpora are now widely available for L2 writing researchers (https://www.uclouvain.be/en-cecl-lcworld.html), but it is important to note how the data were collected in these corpora. Another approach to replication is *registered replication*. The Association for Psychological Science has a helpful description of this process (http://www.psychological science.org/index.php/replication) for the journal *Perspectives on Psychological Science*. In a registered replication, the researchers submit a study proposal before collecting data, and then the protocol is posted for others to follow. Through this process, the studies can be published together, and in the case of *Perspectives on Psychological Science*, the journal will publish a meta-analytic effect size analysis. In the area of second language acquisition, Morgan-Short, Heil, and Marsden (https://osf.io/tvuer/) established a site through Open Science Framework (https://osf.io/) in which they registered their protocols to replicate two studies on the effects of attention to form. This multisite project will produce studies from seven sites that can then be analyzed together.

We further note that taking a position that qualitative research cannot and should not be replicated does not excuse a qualitative researcher from providing a full and transparent account of methodological procedures. As we have noted in several places in these chapters, the fact that qualitative research is interpretative puts an onus on researchers to demonstrate that their interpretations of the data are credible (if not necessarily the only possible interpretations). This in turn requires transparency in accounting for how these interpretations were arrived at. Nevertheless, in many qualitative L2 writing studies, discussions of methodology, especially sampling and data analysis procedures, are often woefully inadequate. Providing direct links to data sources, discussed earlier for quantitative research, has also been advocated by some researchers for qualitative research (e.g., Porte & Richards, 2012) and has occasionally been done; for example, some conversation analysts offer links to sound files so that readers of articles can access the actual data and evaluate the adequacy of the transcriptions and interpretations presented in the articles. Although potentially useful, this practice does raise some ethical as well as methodological concerns; for example, posting video clips of classroom interaction on a website might violate confidentiality or privacy pledges and should never be done without prior informed consent from participants. In addition, researchers in some qualitative research traditions, such as ethnography and grounded theory, contend that an understanding of the data requires a level of immersion and engagement with the data and setting that is not possible for an outsider to achieve. The potential benefits of allowing open access to data must therefore be weighed against these considerations.

Reflexivity and Credibility in Qualitative Research

Another issue related to transparency in qualitative research is reflexivity, that is, the role of the researcher in the research (see Chapter 4). The concept is central to ethnographic research (e.g., Starfield, 2013), but is equally relevant to other forms of qualitative research. For example, in interviews, various factors related to the interviewee-interviewer relationship (language of the interview, power relationships, etc.) can play a crucial role, while in discourse analysis the researcher's personal background or agenda can affect the data that is collected (e.g., as a potential audience for the talk or text that is being produced), how the data are transcribed, what is noticed in the data, and how data are interpreted. Yet it is rare to find examples of reflexivity in interview or discourse analytic studies in the L2 writing field beyond a brief statement (usually in the section on limitations) that some aspect of the study (e.g., the researcher's relationship with the participant) may have had an influence. We believe that the field of L2 writing would benefit from a deeper engagement with researcher reflexivity in all forms of qualitative research, one that does not simply acknowledge possible effects but that directly takes these possible effects into consideration in the analysis, a crucial but often missing step.

Finally, a critical but often overlooked aspect of establishing credibility of findings in qualitative research involves demonstrating expertise in the particular approach that one is using. In reviewing studies for this volume, it was unfortunately all too common to find instances in which the researcher displayed little familiarity with the designated approach (e.g., grounded theory, conversation analysis) or failed to apply it in ways consistent with its methodological or philosophical foundations. In such circumstances, the credibility of the researcher's interpretations can be called into question. Avoiding this outcome requires deep background reading on the chosen approach, preferably including some of its foundational literature (see the references in relevant chapters). In addition, the decision to adopt a specific qualitative research approach, such as grounded theory, systemic functional linguistics, or critical discourse analysis, should be made only after careful consideration of its suitability for the research project and the researcher's readiness to implement it in a way consistent with its underlying principles. For example, given that the goal of conversation analysis is "not to explain *why* people act as they do, but rather to explicate *how* they do it" (ten Have, 2007, p. 9), it would not be a viable choice for a study that seeks to uncover participants' motivations or beliefs or otherwise to explicate their behavior. Providing an informed discussion of the chosen approach and how it has been used in other research can also help establish one's credentials and contribute to credibility.

Conclusion

This book has been challenging to write not only because of the wide range of research methods used in L2 writing studies, which we nevertheless see as a positive phenomenon, but also because of constant addition of new approaches, techniques, and technologies. Thus, we see this book as only a beginning for further discussion of research methods in L2 writing research. In particular, we encourage more methodological reviews, such as Liu and Brown (2015), reviews of study quality (cf. Plonsky, 2013, regarding SLA studies), as well as more mixed methods research that can better capture both the cognitive and social aspects of writing. We also hope to see the field of L2 writing engaging more directly in discussions of methodological issues that have animated related fields such as applied linguistics, education, psychology, and anthropology, for example, interpretation of interview data and research ethics. Finally, as we have emphasized throughout this book, researchers need to provide and editors need to require detailed reporting of study designs, instruments, and coding procedures. It is only through such detail that we can evaluate studies and prevent the proliferation of unreliable or insufficiently supported findings, thus allowing the field to continue to advance our knowledge of the complex processes involved in L2 writing.

Suggestions for Further Reading

Research Syntheses

- Finfgeld, D. L. (2003). Meta-synthesis: The state of the art—So far. *Qualitative Health Research, 13*, 893–904.
- Ortega, L. & Norris, J. M. (Eds.). (2006). *Synthesizing research in language learning and teaching.* Amsterdam and Philadelphia: John Benjamins.
- Plonsky, L. & Oswald, F. L. (2012). How to do a meta-analysis. In A. Mackey & S. M. Gass (Eds.), *Research methods in second language acquisition: A practical guide* (pp. 275–295). London: Basil Blackwell.
- Plonsky, L. & Oswald, F. L. (2015). Meta-analyzing second language research. In L. Plonsky (Ed.), *Advancing quantitative methods in second language research* (pp. 106–128). New York: Routledge.
- Timulak, L. (2014). Qualitative meta-analysis. In U. Flick (Ed.), *The Sage handbook of qualitative data analysis* (pp. 481–495). Thousand Oaks, CA: Sage.

Eyetracking

- Alamargot, D., Chesnet, D., Dansac, C., & Ros, C. (2006). Eye and pen: A new device for studying reading during writing. *Behavior Research Methods, 38*, 287–299.
- Anson, C. M. & Schwegler, R. A. (2012). Tracking the mind's eye: A new technology for researching twenty-first-century writing and reading processes. *College Composition and Communication, 64*, 151–171.
- Dussias, P. E. (2010). Uses of eye-tracking data in second language sentence processing research. *Annual Review of Applied Linguistics, 30*, 149–166.

Keystroke Logging

- Leijten, M. & Van Waes, L. (2013). Keystroke logging in writing research: Using inputlog to analyze and visualize writing processes. *Written Communication, 30*, 358–392.
- Van Waes, L., Leijten, M., Wengelin, A., & Lindgren, E. (2012). Logging tools to study digital writing processes. In V. W. Berninger (Ed.), *Past, present, and future contributions of cognitive writing research to cognitive psychology* (pp. 507–533). New York and Sussex: Taylor & Francis.

Replication and Reporting Research

- Atkinson, D. (Ed.). (2012). Disciplinary dialogues. *Journal of Second Language Writing, 21,* 298–305.
- Porte, G. (Ed.). (2012). *Replication research in applied linguistics.* Cambridge: Cambridge University Press.
- Starfield, S. (2013). Researcher reflexivity. In C. A. Chapelle (Ed.), *Encyclopedia of applied linguistics* (pp. 1–7). Malden, MA: Wiley-Blackwell.

Reflective Narrative and Autoethnography

- Anderson, L. (2006). Analytic autoethnography. *Journal of Contemporary Ethnography, 35,* 373–395.
- Benson, P. (2014). Narrative inquiry in applied linguistics research. *Annual Review of Applied Linguistics, 34,* 154–170.
- Duff, P. A., Anderson, T., Ilnyckyj, R., VanGaya, E., Wang, R. T., & Yates, E. (2013). Narrative and metanarrative perspectives on learning, researching, and theorizing Chinese as an additional language. In Duff et al. (Eds.), *Learning Chinese: Linguistic, sociocultural, and narrative perspectives* (pp. 141–179). Boston: De Gruyter Mouton.
- Ellis, C. & Bochner, A. P. (2000). Autoethnography, personal narrative, reflexivity: Researcher as subject. In N. Denzin & Y. Lincoln (Eds.), *Handbook of qualitative research* (2nd ed., pp. 733–768). Thousand Oaks, CA: Sage.
- Ellis, C. S. & Bochner, A. P. (2006). Analyzing analytic autoethnography: An autopsy. *Journal of Contemporary Ethnography, 35,* 429–449.

Critical Discourse Analysis

- Blommaert., J. & Bulcaen, C. (2000). Critical discourse analysis. *Annual Review of Anthropology, 29,* 447–466.
- Fairclough, N. (1992). *Discourse and social change.* Cambridge, UK: Polity.
- Fairclough, N. (2012). Critical discourse analysis. In J. P. Gee & M. Handford (Eds.), *Routledge handbook of discourse analysis* (pp. 9–20). New York: Routledge.
- Flowerdew, J. (2008). Critical discourse analysis and strategies of resistance. In V. K. Bhatia, J. Flowerdew, & R. H. Jones (Eds.), *Advances in discourse studies* (pp. 195–210). New York: Routledge.
- Kumarivadivelu, B. (1999). Critical classroom discourse analysis. *TESOL Quarterly, 33,* 453–484.
- Lin, A. (2014). Critical discourse analysis in applied linguistics: A methodological review. *Annual Review of Applied Linguistics, 34,* 213–232.
- van Dijk, T.A. (2001). Critical discourse analysis. In D. Schiffrin, D. Tannen, & H. E. Hamilton (Eds.), *The handbook of discourse analysis* (pp. 352–371). Malden, MA: Blackwell.

Computer-Mediated Discourse Analysis

- Georgakopoulou, A. & Spilioti, T. (2015). *The Routledge handbook of language and digital communication.* New York: Routledge.
- Herring, S. C. (2001). Computer-mediated discourse. In D. Schiffrin, D. Tannen, & H. E. Hamilton (Eds.), *The handbook of discourse analysis* (pp. 612–634). Malden, MA: Blackwell.
- Herring, S. C. (2004). Computer-mediated discourse analysis: An approach to researching online behavior. In S. A. Barab, R., Kling, & J. H. Gray (Eds.), *Designing for virtual communities in the service of learning* (pp. 338–376). New York: Cambridge University Press.

REFERENCES

Abasi, A. R. (2012). The pedagogical value of intercultural rhetoric: A report from a Persian-as-a-foreign-language classroom. *Journal of Second Language Writing, 21,* 195–220.

Abasi, A. R., Akbari, N., & Graves, B. (2006). Discourse appropriation, construction of identities, and the complex issue of plagiarism: ESL students writing in graduate school. *Journal of Second Language Writing, 15,* 102–117.

Abbuhl, R. (2012). Using self-referential pronouns in writing: The effect of explicit instruction on L2 writers at two levels of proficiency. *Language Teaching Research, 16,* 501–518.

Abdel Latif, M. M. (2013). What do we mean by writing fluency and how can it be validly measured? *Applied Linguistics, 34,* 99–105.

Ackermann, K. & Chen, Y. H. (2013). Developing the Academic Collocation List (ACL)–A corpus-driven and expert-judged approach. *Journal of English for Academic Purposes, 12,* 235–247.

Alamargot, D., Chesnet, D., Dansac, C., & Ros, C. (2006). Eye and pen: A new device for studying reading during writing. *Behavior Research Methods, 38,* 287–299.

Alamargot, D., Plane, S., Lambert, E., & Chesnet, D. (2010). Using eye and pen movements to trace the development of writing expertise: Case studies of a 7th, 9th and 12th grader, graduate student, and professional writer. *Reading and Writing, 23,* 853–888.

Aljaafreh, A. & Lantolf, J. (1994). Negative feedback as regulation and second language learning in the zone of proximal development. *The Modern Language Journal, 78,* 465–483.

Anderson, L. (2006). Analytic autoethnography. *Journal of Contemporary Ethnography, 35,* 373–395.

Anson, C. M. & Schwegler, R. A. (2012). Tracking the mind's eye: A new technology for researching twenty-first-century writing and reading processes. *College Composition and Communication, 64,* 151–171.

Atkinson, D. (2003). Writing and culture in the post-process era. *Journal of Second Language Writing, 12,* 49–63.

Atkinson, D. (2004). Contrasting rhetorics/contrasting cultures: Why contrastive rhetoric needs a better conceptualization of culture. *Journal of English for Academic Purposes, 3,* 277–289.

Atkinson, D. (2005). Situated qualitative research and second language writing. In P. K. Matsuda & T. Silva (Eds.), *Second language writing research: Perspectives on the process of knowledge construction* (pp. 49–64). Mahwah, NJ: Lawrence Erlbaum.

Atkinson, D. (2012). Disciplinary dialogues: Introduction. *Journal of Second Language Writing, 21*, 298–305.

Atkinson, D. (2014). Language learning in mindbodyworld: A sociocognitive approach to second language acquisition. *Language Teaching, 47*, 467–483.

Atkinson, D., Nishino, T., Churchill, E., & Okada, H. (2007). Alignment and interaction in a sociocognitive approach to second language acquisition. *The Modern Language Journal, 91*, 169–188.

Atkinson, D. & Ramanathan, V. (1995). Cultures of writing: An ethnographic comparison of L1 and L2 university writing/language programs. *TESOL Quarterly, 29*, 539–568.

Atkinson, P. & Silverman, D. (1997). Kundera's immortality: The interview society and the invention of the self. *Qualitative Inquiry, 3*, 304–325.

Baba, K. & Nitta, R. (2014). Phase transitions in development of writing fluency from a complex dynamic systems perspective. *Language Learning, 64*, 1–35.

Baker, B. A. (2012). Individual differences in rater decision-making style: An exploratory mixed-methods study. *Language Assessment Quarterly, 9*, 225–248.

Bardovi-Harlig, K. (2002). A new starting point? Investigating formulaic use and input in future expression. *Studies in Second Language Acquisition, 24*, 189–198.

Barkaoui, K. (2010). Do ESL essay raters' evaluation criteria change with experience? A mixed-methods, cross-sectional study. *TESOL Quarterly, 44*, 31–57.

Barkaoui, K. (2011). Think-aloud protocols in research on essay rating: An empirical study of their veridicality and reactivity. *Language Testing, 28*, 51–75.

Barkaoui, K. (2016). What and when second-language learners revise when responding to timed writing tasks on the computer: The roles of task type, second language proficiency, and keyboarding skills. *The Modern Language Journal, 100*, 320–340.

Barkhuizen, G. (2011). Narrative knowledging in TESOL. *TESOL Quarterly, 45*, 391–414.

Barkhuizen, G. (2013). *Narrative research in applied linguistics*. Cambridge: Cambridge University Press.

Barkhuizen, G. (2014). Narrative research in language teaching and learning. *Language Teaching, 47*, 450–466.

Barton, D. & Lee, C. K. (2012). Redefining vernacular literacies in the age of Web 2.0. *Applied Linguistics, 33*, 282–298.

Basturkmen, H. & Bitchener, J. (2005). The text and beyond: Exploring the expectations of the academic community for the discussion of results section in master's theses. *New Zealand Studies in Applied Linguistics, 11*, 1–19.

Bazerman, C. & Prior, P. (Eds.). (2004). *What writing does and how it does it: An introduction to analyzing texts and textual practices*. Mahwah, NJ: Lawrence Erlbaum.

Beers, S. F., Quinlan, T., & Harbaugh, A. G. (2010). Adolescent students' reading during writing behaviors and relationships with text quality: An eyetracking study. *Reading and Writing, 23*, 743–775.

Belcher, D. & Connor, U. (Eds.). (2001). *Reflections on multiliterate lives*. Clevedon, UK: Multilingual Matters.

Belcher, D. & Hirvela, A. (2008). *The oral-literate connection: Perspectives on L2 speaking, writing, and other media interactions*. Ann Arbor, MI: University of Michigan Press.

Belcher, D. & Nelson, G. (Eds.). (2013). *Critical and corpus-based approaches to intercultural rhetoric*. Ann Arbor: University of Michigan Press.

Bell, J. S. (1997). *Literacy, culture and identity.* New York: Peter Lang.

Benevento, C. & Storch, N. (2011). Investigating writing development in secondary school learners of French. *Assessing Writing, 16*, 97–110.

Benson, P. (2014). Narrative inquiry in applied linguistics research. *Annual Review of Applied Linguistics, 34*, 154–170.

Benson, P. (2015). Commenting to learn: evidence of language and intercultural learning in comments on YouTube videos. *Language Learning & Technology, 19* (3), 88–105.

Berg, E. C. (1999). The effects of trained peer response on ESL students' revision types and writing quality. *Journal of Second Language Writing, 8*, 215–241.

Bergman, M. M. (Ed.). (2008). *Advances in mixed methods research.* Thousand Oaks, CA: Sage.

Biber, D. (2006). *University language: A corpus-based study of spoken and written registers.* Amsterdam: John Benjamins Publishing.

Biber, D. & Conrad, S. (2009). *Register, genre, and style.* Cambridge: Cambridge University Press.

Black, R. W. (2005). Access and affiliation: The literacy and composition practices of English-language learners in an online fanfiction community. *Journal of Adolescent & Adult Literacy, 49*, 118–128.

Black, R. W. (2009). Online fan fiction, global identities, and imagination. *Research in the Teaching of English, 43*, 397–425.

Bloch, J. (2009). The design of an online concordancing program for teaching about reporting verbs. *Language Learning & Technology, 13*, 59–78.

Block, D. (1996). Not so fast: Some thoughts on theory culling, relativism, accepted findings and the heart and soul of SLA. *Applied Linguistics, 17*, 63–83.

Block, D. (2000). Problematizing interview data: Voices in the mind's machine? *TESOL Quarterly, 34*, 757–763.

Block, D. (2003). *The social turn in second language acquisition.* Edinburgh, Scotland: Edinburgh University Press.

Block, E. (1986). The comprehension strategies of second language readers. *TESOL Quarterly, 20*, 463–494.

Blommaert. J. & Bulcaen, C. (2000). Critical discourse analysis. *Annual Review of Anthropology, 29*, 447–466.

Bosher, S. (1998). The composing processes of three Southeast Asian writers at the postsecondary level: An exploratory study. *Journal of Second Language Writing, 7*, 205–241.

Bowles, M. A. (2008). Task type and reactivity of verbal reports in SLA: A first look at an L2 task other than reading. *Studies in Second Language Acquisition, 30*, 359–387.

Bowles, M. A. (2010). *The think-aloud controversy in second language research.* New York: Routledge.

Bowles, M. A. & Leow, R. P. (2005). Reactivity and type of verbal report in SLA research methodology: Expanding the scope of investigation. *Studies in Second Language Acquisition, 27*, 415–440.

Brooks, L. & Swain, M. (2009). Languaging in collaborative writing: Creation of and response to expertise. In A. Mackey & C. Polio (Eds.), *Multiple perspectives on interaction: Second language research in honor of Susan M. Gass* (pp. 58–89). New York: Routledge.

Brown, J. D. (2014). *Mixed methods research for TESOL.* Edinburgh, UK: Edinburgh University Press.

Bryman, A. (2008). Mixed methods research: Combining quantitative and qualitative research. In A. Bryman (Ed.), *Social research methods* (3rd edn., pp. 602–626). Oxford: Oxford University Press.

Bucholtz, M. (2000). The politics of transcription. *Journal of Pragmatics, 32*, 1439–1465.

Bulté, B. & Housen, A. (2012). Defining and operationalising L2 complexity. In A. Housen, F. Kuiken, & I. Vedder (Eds.), *Dimensions of L2 performance and proficiency—Investigating complexity, accuracy and fluency in SLA* (pp. 21–46). Amsterdam: John Benjamins.

Bulté, B. & Housen, A. (2014). Conceptualizing and measuring short-term changes in L2 writing complexity. *Journal of Second Language Writing, 26,* 42–65.

Bunch, G. C. & Willet, K. (2013). Writing to mean in middle school: Understanding how second language writers negotiate textually-rich content-area instruction. *Journal of Second Language Writing, 22,* 141–160.

Busse, V. (2013). How do students of German perceive feedback practices at university? A motivational exploration. *Journal of Second Language Writing, 22,* 406–424.

Byrnes, H., Maxim, H. H., & Norris, J. M. (2010). Realizing advanced foreign language writing development in collegiate education: Curricular design, pedagogy, assessment. *Modern Language Journal, 94.*

Canagarajah, S. (2011). Codemeshing in academic writing: Identifying teachable strategies of translanguaging. *The Modern Language Journal, 95,* 401–417.

Canagarajah, S. (2012). Teacher development in a global profession: An autoethnography. *TESOL Quarterly, 46,* 258–279.

Caracelli, V. J. & Greene, J. C. (1993). Data analysis strategies for mixed-method evaluation designs. *Educational Evaluation and Policy Analysis, 15,* 195–207.

Carreira, M. (2004). Seeking Explanatory Adequacy: A Dual Approach to Understanding the Term "Heritage Language Learner." *Heritage Language Journal, 2,* 1–25.

Carson, J. G. & Nelson, G. L. (1996). Chinese students' perceptions of ESL peer response group interaction. *Journal of Second Language Writing, 5,* 1–19.

Casanave, C. P. (1997). Body mergings: Searching for connections with academic discourse. In C. Casanave & S. Schecter (Eds.), *On becoming a language educator* (pp. 187–200). Mahwah, NJ: Erlbaum.

Casanave, C. P. (2002). *Writing games: Multicultural case studies of academic literacy practices in higher education.* Mahwah, NJ: Erlbaum.

Casanave, C. P. (2003). Looking ahead to more sociopolitically-oriented case study research in L2 writing scholarship (But should it be called "post-process"?). *Journal of Second Language Writing, 12,* 85–102.

Casanave, C. P. (2004). *Controversies in second language writing: Dilemmas and decisions in research and instruction.* Ann Arbor: University of Michigan Press.

Casanave, C. P. (2005). Use of narrative in L2 writing research. In P. K. Matsuda & T. Silva (Eds.), *Second language writing research: Perspectives on the process of knowledge construction* (pp. 17–32). Mahwah, NJ: Lawrence Erlbaum.

Casanave, C. P. (2012). Heading in the wrong direction? A response to Porte and Richards. *Journal of Second Language Writing, 21,* 296–297.

Casanave, C. & Li, X. (Eds.). (2008). *Learning the literacy practices of graduate school: Insiders' reflections on academic enculturation.* Ann Arbor: University of Michigan Press.

Chan, A. Y. W. (2010). Toward a taxonomy of written errors: Investigation into the written errors of Hong Kong Cantonese ESL learners. *TESOL Quarterly, 44,* 295–319.

Chang, C. F. (2012). Peer review via three modes in an EFL writing course. *Computers and Composition, 29,* 63–78.

Chang, Y. Y. & Swales, J. (1999). Informal elements in English academic writing: Threats or opportunities for advanced non-native speakers? In C. Candlin & K. Hyland (Eds.), *Writing: Texts, processes and practices* (pp. 145–167). London: Longman.

Chapelle, C. A. & Duff, P. A. (Eds.). (2003). Some guidelines for conducting quantitative and qualitative research in TESOL. *TESOL Quarterly, 37,* 163–178.

Chapelle, C. A., Grabe, W., & Berns, M. (1997). *Communicative language proficiency: Definition and implications for TOEFL 2000*. Princeton, NJ: Educational Testing Service.

Charmaz, K. (2006). *Constructing grounded theory: A practical guide through qualitative analysis*. Thousand Oaks, CA: Sage.

Chen, Y. H. & Baker, P. (2010). Lexical bundles in L1 and L2 academic writing. *Language Learning & Technology, 14*, 30–49.

Cheng, A. (2006). Analyzing and enacting academic criticism: The case of an L2 graduate learner of academic writing. *Journal of Second Language Writing, 15*, 279–306.

Cheng, A. (2007). Transferring generic features and recontextualizing genre awareness: Understanding writing performance in the ESP genre-based literacy framework. *English for Specific Purposes, 26*, 287–307.

Cheng, A. (2008a). Analyzing genre exemplars in preparation for writing: The case of an L2 graduate student in the ESP genre-based instructional framework of academic literacy. *Applied Linguistics, 29*, 50–71.

Cheng, A. (2008b). Individualized engagement with genre in academic literacy tasks. *English for Specific Purposes, 27*, 387–411.

Cheng, A. (2011). Language features as the pathways to genre: Students' attention to non-prototypical features and its implications. *Journal of Second Language Writing, 20*, 69–82.

Cheng, Y. S. (2002). Factors associated with foreign language writing anxiety. *Foreign Language Annals, 35*, 647–656.

Chiu, C. H. & Polio, C. (2007). *Veridicality, reactivity, and language choice in L2 writing think aloud protocols*. Presented at the American Association for Applied Linguistics. Costa Mesa, CA.

Cho, S. (2010). Academic biliteracy challenges: Korean scholars in the United States. *Journal of Second Language Writing, 19*, 82–94.

Cohen, L., Manion, L., & Morrison, K. (2000). *Research methods in education* (5th ed.). New York: RoutledgeFalmer.

Connor, U. (2004). Intercultural rhetoric research: Beyond texts. *Journal of English for Academic Purposes, 3*, 291–304.

Connor, U. & Mauranen, A. (1999). Linguistic analysis of grant proposals: European Union research grants. *English for Specific Purposes, 18*, 47–62.

Connor-Linton, J. & Polio, C. (2014). Comparing perspectives on L2 writing: Multiple analyses of a common corpus. *Journal of Second Language Writing, 26*, 1–9.

Cook, G. (2011). Discourse analysis. In J. Simpson (Ed.), *The Routledge handbook of applied linguistics* (pp. 431–444). New York: Routledge.

Corbin, J. & Strauss, A. (2008). *Basics of qualitative research: Techniques and procedures for developing grounded theory* (3rd ed.). Thousand Oaks, CA: Sage.

Cortes, V. (2004). Lexical bundles in published and student writing in disciplinary writing: Examples from history and biology. *English for Specific Purposes, 23*, 397–423.

Cortes, V. (2013). The purpose of this study is to: Connecting lexical bundles and moves in research article introductions. *Journal of English for Academic Purposes, 12*, 33–43.

Costino, K. A. & Hyon, S. (2007). "A class for students like me": Reconsidering relationships among identity labels, residency status, and students' preferences for mainstream or multilingual composition. *Journal of Second Language Writing, 16*, 63–81.

Creswell, J. W. (2013). *Qualitative inquiry and research design: Choosing among five approaches*. Thousand Oaks, CA: Sage.

Creswell, J. W. & Plano Clark, V. L. (2007). *Designing and conducting mixed methods research*. Thousand Oaks, CA: Sage.

Creswell, J. W. & Plano Clark, V. L. (2011). *Designing and conducting mixed methods research* (2nd ed.). Thousand Oaks, CA: Sage.

Creswell, J. W., Plano Clark, V. L., & Garrett, A. L. (2008). Methodological issues in conducting mixed methods research designs. In M. M. Bergman (Ed.), *Advances in mixed methods research* (pp. 66–83). Thousand Oaks, CA: Sage.

Crossley, S. A. & McNamara, D. S. (2009). Computational assessment of lexical differences in L1 and L2 writing. *Journal of Second Language Writing, 18,* 119–135.

Crossley, S. A. & McNamara, D. S. (2014). Does writing development equal writing quality? A computational investigation of syntactic complexity in L2 learners. *Journal of Second Language Writing, 26,* 66–79.

Crossley, S. A., Weston, J. L., Sullivan, S. T. M., & McNamara, D. S. (2011). The development of writing proficiency as a function of grade level: A linguistic analysis. *Written Communication, 28,* 282–311.

Cumming, A. (1992). Instructional routines in ESL composition teaching: A case study of three teachers. *Journal of Second Language Writing, 1,* 17–35.

Cumming, A. (2012). Comparative research, research syntheses, and adopting instruments in second language writing. *Journal of Second Language Writing, 21,* 298–299.

Cumming, A. (2016). Theoretical orientations to L2 writing. In R. Manchón & P. K. Matsuda (Eds.), *Handbook of second and foreign language writing.* Berlin: De Gruyter Mouton.

Curry, M. J. & Lillis, T. (2004). Multilingual scholars and the imperative to publish in English: Negotiating interests, demands, and rewards. *TESOL Quarterly, 38,* 663–688.

Davis, B. & Harré, R. (1990). Positioning: The discursive production of selves. *Journal for the Theory of Social Behavior, 20,* 43–63.

De Costa, P. (Ed.). (2015). *Ethics in applied linguistics research: Language researcher narratives.* New York, NY: Routledge.

De Fina, A. (2009). Narratives in interview—The case of accounts: For an interactional approach to narrative genres. *Narrative Inquiry, 19,* 233–258.

de Guerrero, M. C. M. & Villamil, O. S. (2000). Activating the ZPD: Mutual scaffolding in L2 peer revision. *The Modern Language Journal, 84,* 51–68.

de Oliveira, L. C. & Lan, S.-W. (2014). Writing science in an upper elementary classroom: A genre-based approach to teaching English language learners. *Journal of Second Language Writing, 25,* 23–39.

De Smet, M. J., Brand-Gruwel, S., Leijten, M., & Kirschner, P. A. (2014). Electronic outlining as a writing strategy: Effects on students' writing products, mental effort and writing process. *Computers & Education, 78,* 352–366.

Deane, P. & Zhang, M. (2015). Exploring the feasibility of using writing process features to assess text production skills. *ETS Research Report Series, 2,* 1–16.

Denzin, N. K. (1978). *The research act: A theoretical introduction to sociological methods.* New York: McGraw-Hill.

Derrick, D. (2016). Instrument reporting practices in second language research. *TESOL Quarterly, 50,* 132–153.

Ding, H. (2007). Genre analysis of personal statements: Analysis of moves in application essays to medical and dental schools. *English for Specific Purposes, 26,* 368–392.

Doolan, S. M. & Miller, D. (2012). Generation 1.5 written error patterns: A comparative study. *Journal of Second Language Writing, 21,* 1–22.

Dörnyei, Z. (2007). *Research methods in applied linguistics: Quantitative, qualitative, and mixed methodologies.* Oxford: Oxford University Press.

Dörnyei, Z. & Csizér, K. (2012). How to design and analyze surveys in second language acquisition research. In A. Mackey & S. Gass (Eds.), *Research methods in second language acquisition: A practical guide* (pp. 74–94). Malden, MA: Wiley-Blackwell.

Drew, P. J. & Heritage, J. (1992). *Talk at work: Interaction in institutional settings*. Cambridge: Cambridge University Press.

Duff, P. A. (2006). Beyond generalizability: Contextualization, complexity, and credibility in applied linguistics research. In M. Chalhoub-Deville, C. A. Chapelle & P. Duff (Eds.), *Inference and generalizability in applied linguistics* (pp. 65–95). Amsterdam: John Benjamins.

Duff, P. A. (2008). *Case study research in applied linguistics*. New York: Lawrence Erlbaum Associates.

Duff, P. A. (2010). Language socialization into academic discourse communities. *Annual Review of Applied Linguistics, 30*, 169–192.

Duff, P. A. (2014). Case study research on language learning and use. *Annual Review of Applied Linguistics, 34*, 233–255.

Duff, P. A., Anderson, T., Ilnyckyj, R., VanGaya, E., Wang, R. T., & Yates, E. (2013). Narrative and metanarrative perspectives on learning, researching, and theorizing Chinese as an additional language. In P. A. Duff et al. (Eds.), *Learning Chinese: Linguistic, sociocultural, and narrative perspectives* (pp. 141–179). Boston: De Gruyter Mouton.

DuFon, M. A. (2002). Video recording in ethnographic SLA research: Some issues of validity in data collection. *Language Learning and Technology, 6*, 40–59.

Duncombe, J. & Jessop, J. (2002). "Doing rapport" and the ethics of "faking friendship". In M. Mauthner, M. Birch, J. Jessop, & T. Miller (Eds.), *Ethics in qualitative research* (pp. 107–122). London: Sage.

Dunworth, K. (2008). A task-based analysis of undergraduate assessment: A tool for the EAP practitioner. *TESOL Quarterly, 42*, 315–323.

Durrant, P. & Schmitt, N. (2009). To what extent do native and nonnative writers make use of collocations? *International Review of Applied Linguistics in Language Teaching, 47*, 157–177.

Dussias, P. E. (2010). Uses of eye-tracking data in second language sentence processing research. *Annual Review of Applied Linguistics, 30*, 149–166.

East, M. (2007). Bilingual dictionaries in tests of L2 writing proficiency: Do they make a difference? *Language Testing, 24*, 331–353.

Edge, J. & Richards, K. (1998). May I see your warrant, please? Justifying outcomes in qualitative research. *Applied Linguistics, 19*, 334–356.

Egi, T. (2007). Recasts, learners' interpretations, and L2 development. In A. Mackey (Ed.), *Conversational interaction in second language acquisition: A series of empirical studies* (pp. 249–267). Oxford: Oxford University Press.

Egi, T. (2008). Investigating stimulated recall as a cognitive measure: Reactivity and verbal reports in SLA research methodology. *Language Awareness, 17*, 212–228.

Eisenhart, M. (2001). Educational ethnography past, present, and future: Ideas to think with. *Educational Researcher, 30*, 16–27.

Ellis, C. & Bochner, A. P. (2000). Autoethnography, personal narrative, reflexivity: Researcher as subject. In N. Denzin & Y. Lincoln (Eds.), *Handbook of qualitative research* (2nd edn., pp. 733–768). Thousand Oaks, CA: Sage.

Ellis, C. S. & Bochner, A. P. (2006). Analyzing analytic autoethnography: An autopsy. *Journal of Contemporary Ethnography, 35*, 429–449.

Ellis, N. C. (2012). Formulaic language and second language acquisition: Zipf and the phrasal teddy bear. *Annual Review of Applied Linguistics, 32*, 17–44.

Ellis, R. & Loewen, S. (2007). Confirming the operational definitions of explicit and implicit knowledge in Ellis (2005): Responding to Isemonger. *Studies in Second Language Acquisition, 29,* 119–126.

Ellis, R. & Yuan, F. (2004). The effects of planning on fluency, complexity, and accuracy in second language narrative writing. *Studies in Second Language Acquisition, 26,* 59–84.

Engeström, Y. (2015). *Learning by expanding: An activity-theoretical approach to developmental research* (2nd edn.). New York: Cambridge University Press.

Erickson, F. (1986). Qualitative methods in research on teaching. In M. Wittrock (Ed.), *Handbook of research on teaching* (3rd edn., pp. 119–161). Washington, DC: American Educational Research Association.

Ericsson, K. A. & Simon, H. A. (1993). *Protocol analysis: Verbal reports as data.* Cambridge, MA: MIT Press.

Evans, N., Hartshorn, K. J., & Strong-Krause, D. (2011). The efficacy of dynamic written corrective feedback for university-matriculated ESL learners. *System, 39,* 229–239.

Evans, S. & Green, C. (2007). Why EAP is necessary: A survey of Hong Kong tertiary students. *Journal of English for Academic Purposes, 6,* 3–17.

Faigley, L. & Witte, S. (1981). Analyzing revision. *College Composition and Communication, 32,* 400–414.

Fairclough, N. (1992). *Discourse and social change.* Cambridge, UK: Polity.

Fairclough, N. (2012). Critical discourse analysis. In J. P. Gee & M. Handford (Eds.), *Routledge handbook of discourse analysis* (pp. 9–20). New York: Routledge.

Ferris, D. (2014). Responding to student writing: Teachers' philosophies and practices. *Assessing Writing, 9,* 6–23.

Ferris, D., Brown, J., Liu, H., & Stine, A. (2011). Responding to L2 students in college writing classes: Teacher perspectives. *TESOL Quarterly, 45,* 207–234.

Ferris, D. & Roberts, B. (2001). Error feedback in L2 writing classes: How explicit does it need to be? *Journal of Second Language Writing, 10,* 161–184.

Finfgeld, D. L. (2003). Meta-synthesis: The state of the art—So far. *Qualitative Health Research, 13,* 893–904.

Flower, L. & Hayes, J. (1980). The cognition of discovery: Defining a rhetorical problem. *College Composition and Communication, 310,* 21–32.

Flowerdew, J. (2008). Critical discourse analysis and strategies of resistance. In V. K. Bhatia, J. Flowerdew, & R. H. Jones (Eds.), *Advances in discourse studies* (pp. 195–210). New York: Routledge.

Flowerdew, J. & Li, Y. (2009). English or Chinese? The trade-off between local and international publication among Chinese academics in the humanities and social sciences. *Journal of Second Language Writing, 18,* 1–16.

Flowerdew, J. & Wan, A. (2010). The linguistic and the contextual in applied genre analysis: The case of the company audit report. *English for Specific Purposes, 29,* 78–93.

Fránquiz, M. E. & Salinas, C. S. (2011). Newcomers developing English literacy through historical thinking and digitized primary sources. *Journal of Second Language Writing, 20,* 196–210.

Frear, M. W. & Bitchener, J. (2015). The effects of cognitive task complexity on writing complexity. *Journal of Second Language Writing, 30,* 45–57.

Freeman, D. (1996). "To take them at their word": Language data in the study of teachers' knowledge. *Harvard Educational Review, 66,* 732–761.

Friginal, E., Li, M., & Weigle, S. C. (2014). Revisiting multiple profiles of learner compositions: A comparison of highly rated NS and NNS essays. *Journal of Second Language Writing, 23,* 1–16.

Friginal, E. & Weigle, S. C. (2014). Exploring multiple profiles of L2 writing using multi-dimensional analysis. *Journal of Second Language Writing, 26*, 80–95.

Galbraith, D. & Torrance, M. (2004). Revision in the context of different drafting strategies. In L. Allal, L. Chanquoy, & P. Largy (Eds.), *Studies in writing: Vol. 13. revision: Cognitive and instructional processes* (pp. 63–85). Dordrecht, the Netherlands: Kluwer Academic.

Gardner, S. & Nesi, H. (2013). A classification of genre families in university student writing. *Applied Linguistics, 34*, 25–52.

Gass, S. M. & Mackey, A. (2016). *Stimulated recall methodology in second language research.* New York and London: Routledge.

Gass, S., Mackey, A., & Ross-Feldman, L. (2005). Task-based interactions in classroom and laboratory settings. *Language Learning, 55*, 575–611.

Gebhard, M. (2002). Fast capitalism, school reform, and second language literacy practices. *The Canadian Modern Language Review, 59*, 15–52.

Gebril, A. & Plakans, L. (2013). Toward a transparent construct of reading-to-write tasks: The interface between discourse features and proficiency. *Language Assessment Quarterly, 10*, 9–27.

Gebril, A. & Plakans, L. (2014). Assembling validity evidence for assessing academic writing: Rater reactions to integrated tasks. *Assessing Writing, 21*, 56–73.

Gee, J. P. (2011). *How to do discourse analysis: A tool kit.* New York: Routledge.

Gee, J. P. (2012). *Social linguistics and literacies: Ideology in discourses* (4th ed.). New York: Routledge.

Gee, J. P. (2015). Discourse, small d, big D. In K. Tracy, C. Ilie, & T. Sandel (Eds.), *The international encyclopedia of language and social interaction* (pp. 418–422). Malden, MA: Wiley Blackwell.

Gee, J. P. & Handford, M. (Eds.). (2012). *Routledge handbook of discourse analysis.* New York: Routledge.

Geertz, C. (1973). Thick description: Toward an interpretive theory of culture. In C. Geertz (Ed.), *The interpretation of cultures: Selected essays by Clifford Geertz* (pp. 3–30). New York, NY: Basic Books.

Gentil, G. (2005). Commitments to academic biliteracy: Case studies of Francophone university writers. *Written Communication, 22*, 421–471.

Gentil, G. (2011). A biliteracy agenda for genre research. *Journal of Second Language Writing, 20*, 6–23.

Georgakopoulou, A. (2006). Thinking big with small stories in narrative and identity analysis. *Narrative Inquiry 16*, 122–130.

Gigerenzer, G. & Hoffrage, U. (1995). How to improve Bayesian reasoning without instruction: Frequency formats. *Psychological Review, 102*, 684–704.

Gilbert, L. S. (2002). Going the distance: "Closeness" in qualitative data analysis software. *International Journal of Social Research Methodology, 5*, 215–228.

Gil-Salom, L. & Soler-Monreal, C. (2014). Writers' positioning in literature reviews in English and Spanish computing doctoral theses. *Journal of English for Academic Purposes, 16*, 23–39.

Gimenez, J. (2006). Embedded business emails: Meeting new demands in international business communication. *English for Specific Purposes, 25*, 154–172.

Glaser, B. G. (1978). *Theoretical sensitivity.* Mill Valley, CA: Sociology Press.

Glaser, B. G. & Strauss, A. L. (1967). *The discovery of grounded theory: Strategies for qualitative research.* Chicago: Aldine.

Godfroid, A. & Spino, L. (2015). Reconceptualizing reactivity research: Absence of evidence is not evidence of absence. *Language Learning, 65*, 896–928.

Goodwin, C. (1981). *Conversational organization: Interaction between speakers and hearers.* New York: Academic Press.

Goodwin, C. (2000). Action and embodiment within situated human interaction. *Journal of Pragmatics, 32,* 1489–1522.

Goodwin, C. (2001). Practices of seeing: Visual analysis: An ethnomethodological approach. In T. van Leeuwen & C. Jewitt (Eds.), *Handbook of visual analysis* (pp. 157–182). London: Sage.

Graham, S., Harris, K. R., & Santangelo, T. (2015). Research-based writing practices and the Common Core: Meta-analysis and meta-synthesis. *The Elementary School Journal, 115,* 498–522.

Green, J., Fránquiz, M., & Dixon, C. (1997). The myth of the objective transcript: Transcribing as a situated act. *TESOL Quarterly, 31,* 172–176.

Greene, J. C. (2007). *Mixed methods in social inquiry.* San Francisco, CA: Jossey-Bass.

Greene, J. C. (2008). Is mixed methods social inquiry a distinctive methodology? *Journal of Mixed Methods Research, 2,* 7–22.

Greene, J., Caracelli, V. J., & Graham, W. F. (1989). Toward a conceptual framework for mixed-method evaluation designs. *Educational Evaluation and Policy Analysis, 11,* 255–274.

Guest, G. (2013). Describing mixed methods research: An alternative to typologies. *Journal of Mixed Methods Research, 7,* 141–151.

Guillemin, M. & Gillam, L. (2004). Ethics, reflexivity, and "ethically important moments" in research. *Qualitative Inquiry, 10,* 261–280.

Guinda, C. S. (2015). Genres on the move: Currency and erosion of the genre moves construct. *Journal of English for Academic Purposes, 19,* 73–87.

Hafner, C. (2010). A multi-perspective genre analysis of the barrister's opinion: writing context, generic structure, and textualization. *Written Communication, 27,* 410-441.

Hafner, C. A. (2015). Remix culture and English language teaching: The expression of learner voice in digital multimodal compositions. *TESOL Quarterly, 49,* 486–509.

Hale, G., Taylor, C., Bridgeman, B., Carson, J., Kroll, B., & Kantor, R. (1996). *A study of writing tasks assigned in academic degree programs* (Research Report 54). Princeton, NJ: Educational Testing Service.

Hall, C., McCarthy, P. M., Lewis, G. A., Lee, D. S., & McNamara, D. S. (2007). Using Coh-Metrix to assess differences between English language varieties. *Coyote Papers: Working Papers in Linguistics, Linguistic Theory at the University of Arizona, 15,* 40–54.

Halliday, M. A. K. (1985). *Introduction to functional grammar.* London: Edward Arnold.

Halliday, M. A. & Matthiessen, C. M. (2014). *Halliday's introduction to functional grammar* (4th ed.). New York: Routledge.

Hammersley, M. (2003). Recent radical criticism of interview studies: Any implications for the sociology of education? *British Journal of Sociology of Education, 24,* 119–126.

Hammersley, M. (2007). *Ethnography: Principles in practice* (3rd edn.). New York: Routledge.

Haneda, M. (2006). Classrooms as communities of practice: A reevaluation. *TESOL Quarterly, 40,* 807–817.

Harman, R. (2013). Literary intertextuality in genre-based pedagogies: Building lexical cohesion in fifth-grade L2 writing. *Journal of Second Language Writing, 22,* 125–140.

Hartshorn, K. J., Evans, N. W., Merrill, P. F., Sudweeks, R. R., Strong-Krause, D., & Anderson, N. J. (2010). Effects of dynamic corrective feedback on ESL writing accuracy. *TESOL Quarterly, 44,* 84–109.

Harwood, N. & Petrić, B. (2012). Performance in the citing behavior of two student writers. *Written Communication, 29,* 55–103.

Hashemi, M. R. (2012). Reflections on mixing methods in applied linguistics research. *Applied Linguistics, 33*, 206–212.

Hashemi, M. R. & Babaii, E. (2013). Mixed methods research: Toward new research designs in applied linguistics. *The Modern Language Journal, 97*, 828–852.

Hasrati, M. & Street, B. (2009). PhD topic arrangement in 'D'iscourse communities of engineers and social sciences/humanities. *Journal of English for Academic Purposes, 8*, 14–25.

Hayes, J. R. & Flower, L. S. (1980). Identifying the organization of writing processes. In L. W. Gregg & E. R. Steinberg (Eds.), *Cognitive processes in writing* (pp. 3–30). Hillsdale, NJ: Erlbaum.

Heath, C., Hindmarsh, J., & Luff, P. (2010). *Video in qualitative research: Analysing social interaction in everyday life.* Thousand Oaks, CA: Sage.

Heatley, A., Nation, I. S. P., & Coxhead, A. (2002). *RANGE and FREQUENCY programs.* Retrieved from http://www.victoria.ac.nz/lals/resources/range.aspx.

Hepburn, A. & Bolden, G. (2013). The conversation analytic approach to transcription. In J. Sidnell & T. Stivers (Eds.), *The handbook of conversation analysis* (pp. 57–76). Oxford: Wiley-Blackwell.

Heritage, J. (1997). Conversation analysis and institutional talk: Analysing data. In D. Silverman (Ed.), *Qualitative research: Theory, method, and practice* (pp. 161–182). Thousand Oaks: Sage.

Herring, S. C. (2001). Computer-mediated discourse. In D. Schiffrin, D. Tannen, & H. E. Hamilton (Eds.), *The handbook of discourse analysis* (pp. 612–634). Malden, MA: Blackwell.

Herring, S. C. (2015). New frontiers in interactive multimodal communication. In A. Georgakopoulou & T. Spilioti (Eds.), *The Routledge handbook of language and digital communication* (pp. 398–402). New York: Routledge.

Hinds, J. (1987). Reader versus writer responsibility: A new typology. In U. Connor & R. B. Kaplan (Eds.), *Writing across languages: Analysis of L2 texts* (pp. 141–152). Reading, MA: Addison-Wesley.

Hirose, K. (2003). Comparing L1 and L2 organizational patterns in the argumentative writing of Japanese EFL students. *Journal of Second Language Writing, 12*, 181–209.

Holliday, A. (1999). Small cultures. *Applied Linguistics, 20*, 237–264.

Holstein, J. A. & Gubrium, J. F. (1995). *The active interview.* Thousand Oaks, CA: Sage.

Hornberger, N. H. (1989). Continua of biliteracy. *Review of Educational Research, 59*, 271–296.

Hornberger, N. H. (2003). Continua of biliteracy. In N. H. Hornberger (Ed.), *Continua of biliteracy: An ecological framework for educational policy, research, and practice in multilingual settings* (pp. 3–34). Clevedon, UK: Multilingual Matters.

Horowitz, D. M. (1986). What professors actually require: Academic tasks for the ESL classroom. *TESOL Quarterly, 20*, 445–462.

Hu, G. (2002). Potential cultural resistance to pedagogical imports: The case of communicative language teaching in China. *Language, Culture and Curriculum, 15*, 93–105.

Hu, G. & Lei, J. (2012). Investigating Chinese university students' knowledge of and attitudes toward plagiarism from an integrated perspective. *Language Learning, 62*, 813–850.

Hu, G. & Wang, G. (2014). Disciplinary and ethnolinguistic influences on citation in research articles. *Journal of English for Academic Purposes, 14*, 14–28.

Hulstijn, J. H. (1997). Second language acquisition research in the laboratory. *Studies in Second Language Acquisition, 19*, 131–143.

Hundt, M., Denison, D., & Schneider, G. (2012). Relative complexity in scientific discourse. *English Language and Linguistics, 16,* 209–240.

Hyland, K. (1999). Academic attribution: Citation and the construction of disciplinary knowledge. *Applied Linguistics, 20,* 341–367.

Hyland, K. (2004). *Disciplinary discourses: Social interactions in academic writing.* Ann Arbor, MI: Michigan University Press.

Hyland, K. (2005). Stance and engagement: A model of interaction in academic discourse. *Discourse Studies, 7,* 172–192.

Hyland, K. (2009). *Teaching and researching writing.* London and New York: Routledge/Taylor and Francis.

Hyland, K. (2012). *Disciplinary identities: Individuality and community in academic discourse.* Cambridge: Cambridge University Press.

Hyland, K. (2013). Faculty feedback: Perceptions and practices in L2 disciplinary writing. *Journal of Second Language Writing, 22,* 240–253.

Hyland, K. & Hyland, F. (2006). Feedback on second language students' writing. *Language Teaching, 39,* 83–101.

Hyland, K. & Sancho Guinda, C. (Eds.). (2012). *Stance and voice in written academic genres.* New York: Palgrave Macmillan.

Hyon, S. (1996). Genre in three traditions: Implications for ESL. *TESOL Quarterly, 30,* 693–722.

Isemonger, I. M. (2007). Operational definitions of explicit and implicit knowledge: Response to R. Ellis (2005) and some recommendations for future research in this area. *Studies in Second Language Acquisition, 29,* 101–118.

Ivanič, R. (1998). *Writing and identity: The discoursal construction of identity in academic writing.* Philadelphia, PA: John Benjamins.

Ivanič, R. (2004). Discourses of writing and learning to write. *Language and Education, 18,* 220–245.

Ivanič, R. & Camps, D. (2001). I am how I sound: Voice as self-representation in L2 writing. *Journal of Second Language Writing, 10,* 3–33.

Jackson, D. O. & Suethanapornkul, S. (2013). The cognition hypothesis: A synthesis and meta-analysis of research on second language task complexity. *Language Learning, 63,* 330–367.

Jacobs, H. L., Zinkgraf, S. A., Wormuth, D. R., Hartfiel, V. F., & Hughey, J. B. (1981). *Testing ESL composition: A practical approach.* Rowley, MA: Newbury House.

James, M. A. (2010). An investigation of learning transfer in English-for-general-academic-purposes writing instruction. *Journal of Second Language Writing, 19,* 183–206.

Jang, E. E., Wagner, M., & Park, G. (2014). Mixed methods research in language testing and assessment. *Annual Review of Applied Linguistics, 34,* 123–153.

Jarratt, S. C., Losh, E., & Puente, D. (2006). Transnational identifications: Biliterate writers in a first-year humanities course. *Journal of Second Language Writing, 15,* 24–48.

Jarvis, S. (2013). Capturing the diversity in lexical diversity. *Language Learning, 63,* 87–106.

Jarvis, S., Grant, L., Bikowski, D., & Ferris, D. (2003). Exploring multiple profiles of highly rated learner compositions. *Journal of Second Language Writing, 12,* 377–403.

Jefferson, G. (1983). Issues in the transcription of naturally occurring talk: Caricature versus capturing pronunciational particulars. *Tilburg Papers in Language and Literature, 34,* 1–12.

Jiang, N. (2012). *Conducting reaction time research in second language studies.* London and New York: Routledge.

Jiang, W. (2013). Measurements of development in L2 written production: The case of L2 Chinese. *Applied Linguistics, 34*, 1–24.

Johnson, R. B. & Onwuegbuzie, A. J. (2004). Mixed methods research: A research paradigm whose time has come. *Educational Researcher, 33*, 14–26.

Johnson, R. B., Onwuegbuzie, A. J., & Turner, L. A. (2007). Toward a definition of mixed methods research. *Journal of Mixed Methods Research, 1*, 112–133.

Johnstone, B. (2008). *Discourse analysis* (2nd edn.). Oxford: Blackwell.

Kang, E. & Han, Z. (2015). The efficacy of written corrective feedback in improving L2 written accuracy: A meta-analysis. *Modern Language Journal, 99*, 1–18.

Kang, J. Y. (2009). Referencing in a second language: Korean EFL learners' cohesive use of references in written narrative discourse. *Discourse Processes, 46*, 439–466.

Kao, C. W. & Wible, D. (2014). A meta-analysis on the effectiveness of grammar correction in second language writing. *English Language Teaching & Learning, 38*, 29–69.

Kaplan, R. B. (1966). Cultural thought patterns in inter-cultural education. *Language Learning, 16*, 1–20.

Kasper, G. & Prior, M. T. (2015). Analyzing storytelling in TESOL interview research. *TESOL Quarterly, 49*, 226–255.

Keck, C. (2006). The use of paraphrase in summary writing: A comparison of L1 and L2 writers. *Journal of Second Language Writing, 15*, 261–278.

Keck, C. (2014). Copying, paraphrasing, and academic writing development: A re-examination of L1 and L2 summarization practices. *Journal of Second Language Writing, 25*, 4–22.

Kellogg, R. T. (1988). Attentional overload and writing performance: Effects of rough draft and outline strategies. *Journal of Experimental Psychology: Learning, Memory, and Cognition, 14*, 355–365.

Kellogg, R. T. (1996). A model of working memory in writing. In C. M. Levy & S. Ransdell (Eds.), *The science of writing: Theories, methods, individual differences and applications* (pp. 57–72). Mahwah, NJ: Lawrence Erlbaum.

Kibler, A. (2010). Writing through two languages: First language expertise in a language minority classroom. *Journal of Second Language Writing, 19*, 121–142.

Kibler, A. K. (2014). From high school to the *noviciado*: An adolescent linguistic minority student's multilingual journey in writing. *The Modern Language Journal, 2*, 629–651.

Kim, S. H. O. (2012). Learner background and the acquisition of discourse features of Korean in the Australian secondary school context. *Australian Review of Applied Linguistics, 35*, 339–358.

King, N. & Horrocks, C. (2010). An introduction to interview data analysis. In N. King & C. Horrocks (Eds.), *Interviews in qualitative research* (pp. 142–174). Thousand Oaks, CA: Sage.

Kobayashi, H. & Rinnert, C. (2013). L1/L2/L3 writing development: Longitudinal case study of a Japanese multicompetent writer. *Journal of Second Language Writing, 22*, 4–33.

Kokhan, K. (2012). Investigating the possibility of using TOEFL scores for university ESL decision-making: Placement trends and effect of time lag. *Language Testing, 29*, 291–308.

Kormos, J. (2011). Task complexity and linguistic and discourse features of narrative writing performance. *Journal of Second Language Writing, 20*, 148–161.

Kress, G. (2012). Multimodal discourse analysis. In J. P. Gee & M. Handford (Eds.), *Routledge handbook of discourse analysis* (pp. 35–50). New York: Routledge.

Kress, G. & Bezemer, J. (2009). Writing in a multimodal world of representation. In R. Beard, D. Myhill, & J. Riley (Eds.), *Sage handbook of writing development* (pp. 167–181). Thousand Oaks, CA: Sage.

Krueger, R. A. & Casey, M. A. (2000). *Focus groups: A practical guide for applied research* (3rd edn.). Thousand Oaks, CA: Sage.

Kubanyiova, M. (2008). Rethinking research ethics in contemporary applied linguistics: The tension between macroethical and microethical perspectives in situated research. *The Modern Language Journal, 92*, 503–518.

Kubota, R. (1997). A reevaluation of the uniqueness of Japanese written discourse implications for contrastive rhetoric. *Written Communication, 14*, 460–480.

Kubota, R. (1999). Japanese culture constructed by discourses: Implications for applied linguistics research and ELT. *TESOL Quarterly, 33*, 9–35.

Kuiken, F. & Vedder, I. (2008). Cognitive task complexity and written output in Italian and French as a foreign language. *Journal of Second Language Writing, 17*, 48–60.

Kunnan, A. J. (2013). *Validation in language assessment.* New York, NY: Routledge.

Kuteeva, M. (2013). Graduate learners' approaches to genre-analysis tasks: Variations across and within four disciplines. *English for Specific Purposes, 32*, 84–96.

Kuteeva, M. & McGrath, L. (2013). The theoretical research article as a reflection of disciplinary practices: The case of pure mathematics. *Applied Linguistics, 31*, 1–22.

Kuusela, H. & Paul, P. (2000). A comparison of concurrent and retrospective verbal protocol analysis. *The American Journal of Psychology, 113*, 387–404.

Kvale, S. & Brinkmann, S. (2009). *InterViews: Learning the craft of qualitative research interviews* (2nd edn.). Thousand Oaks, CA: Sage.

Kwan, B. (2006). The schematic structure of literature reviews in doctoral theses of applied linguistics. *English for Specific Purposes, 25*, 30–55.

Kwan, B. S. C. & Chan, H. (2014). An investigation of source use in the results and the closing sections of empirical articles in information systems: In search of a functional-semantic citation typology for pedagogical purposes. *Journal of English for Academic Purposes, 14*, 29–47.

Labov, W. (1972). *Sociolinguistic patterns.* Philadelphia: University of Pennsylvania Press.

Lam, W. S. E. (2000). L2 literacy and the design of the self: A case study of a teenager writing on the internet. *TESOL Quarterly, 34*, 457–482.

Lantolf, J. P. & Thorne, S. L. (2006). *Sociocultural theory and the genesis of second language development.* New York: Oxford University Press.

Larsen-Freeman, D. (2006). The emergence of complexity, fluency, and accuracy in the oral and written production of five Chinese learners of English. *Applied Linguistics, 27*, 590–619.

Lave, J. & Wenger, E. (1991). *Situated learning: Legitimate peripheral participation.* New York: Cambridge University Press.

Lavolette, E., Polio, C., & Kahng, J. (2015). The accuracy of computer-assisted feedback and students' responses to it. *Language, Learning & Technology, 19*, 50–68.

Lazaraton, A. (1995). Qualitative research in applied linguistics: A progress report. *TESOL Quarterly, 29*, 455–472.

Lazaraton, A. (2002). Quantitative and qualitative approaches to discourse analysis. *Annual Review of Applied Linguistics, 22*, 3–51.

Lazaraton, A. (2003). Evaluative criteria for qualitative research in applied linguistics: Whose criteria and whose research? *The Modern Language Journal, 87*, 1–12.

Lee, E. & Simon-Maeda, A. (2006). Racialized research identities in ESL/EFL research. *TESOL Quarterly, 40*, 573–594.

Lee, G. & Schallert, D. L. (2008a). Constructing trust between teacher and students through feedback and revision cycles in an EFL writing classroom. *Written Communication, 25*, 506–537.

Lee, G. & Schallert, D. L. (2008b). Meeting in the margins: Effects of the teacher–student relationship on revision processes of EFL college students taking a composition course. *Journal of Second Language Writing, 17*, 165–182.

Lee, I. (2004). Error correction in L2 secondary writing classrooms: The case of Hong Kong. *Journal of Second Language Writing, 13*, 285–312.

Lee, I. (2013). Becoming a writing teacher: Using "identity" as an analytical lens to understand EFL writing teachers' development. *Journal of Second Language Writing, 22*, 330–345.

Lee, I. & Coniam, D. (2013). Introducing assessment for learning for EFL writing in an assessment of learning examination-driven system in Hong Kong. *Journal of Second Language Writing, 22*, 34–50.

Lei, X. (2008). Exploring a sociocultural approach to writing strategy research: Mediated actions in writing activities. *Journal of Second Language Writing, 17*, 217–236.

Leijten, M., Janssen, D., & Van Waes, L. (2010). Error correction strategies of professional speech recognition users: Three profiles. *Computers in Human Behavior, 26*, 964–975.

Leijten, M. & Van Waes, L. (2013). Keystroke logging in writing research using inputlog to analyze and visualize writing processes. *Written Communication, 30*, 358–392.

Leki, I. (1999). "Pretty much I screwed up": Ill-served needs of a permanent resident. In L. Harklau, K. Losey, & M. Siegal (Eds.), *Generation 1.5 meets college composition* (pp. 17–43). Mahwah, NJ: L. Erlbaum.

Leki, I. (2007). *Undergraduates in a second language: Challenges and complexities of academic literacy development*. New York: Lawrence Erlbaum Associates.

Leki, I., Cumming, A., & Silva, T. (2008). *A synthesis of research on second language writing in English*. New York: Routledge.

Leontiev, A. N. (1981). The problem of activity in psychology. In J. V. Wertsch (Ed.), *The concept of activity in Soviet psychology: An introduction* (pp. 37–71). Armonk, NY: M. E. Sharpe.

Li, J. & Barnard, R. (2011). Academic tutors' beliefs about and practices of giving feedback on students' written assignments: A New Zealand case study. *Assessing Writing, 16*(2), 137–148.

Li, J. & Schmitt, N. (2009). The acquisition of lexical phrases in academic writing: A longitudinal case study. *Journal of Second Language Writing, 18*, 85–102.

Li, M. & Zhu, W. (2013). Patterns of computer-mediated interaction in small writing groups using wikis. *Computer Assisted Language Learning, 26*, 61–82.

Li, Y. (2000). Linguistic characteristics of ESL writing in task-based e-mail activities. *System, 28*, 229–245.

Li, Y. (2006). A doctoral student of physics writing for publication: A sociopolitically-oriented case study. *English for Specific Purposes, 25*, 456–478.

Li, Y. (2007). Apprentice scholarly writing in a community of practice: An intraview of an NNES graduate student writing a research article. *TESOL Quarterly, 41*, 55–79.

Li, Y. (2014). Seeking entry to the North American market: Chinese management academics publishing internationally. *Journal of English for Academic Purposes, 13*, 41–52.

Li, Y. & Casanave, C. P. (2012). Two first-year students' strategies for writing from sources: Patchwriting or plagiarism? *Journal of Second Language Writing, 21*, 165–180.

Liao, M. T. & Chen, C. H. (2009). Rhetorical strategies in Chinese and English: A comparison of L1 composition textbooks. *Foreign Language Annals, 42*, 695–720.

Lidz, C. S. (1991). *Practitioner's guide to dynamic assessment*. New York: Guilford Press.

Lillis, T. (2008). Ethnography as method, methodology, and "deep theorizing": Closing the gap between text and context in academic writing research. *Written Communication, 25*, 353–388.

Lillis, T. & Curry, M. J. (2006). Professional academic writing by multilingual scholars: Interactions with literacy brokers in the production of English-medium texts. *Written Communication, 23,* 3–35.

Lillis, T. & Curry, M. J. (2010). *Academic writing in a global context: The politics and practices of publishing in English.* New York: Routledge.

Lim, J. M. H. (2010). Commenting on research results in applied linguistics and education: A comparative genre-based investigation. *Journal of English for Academic Purposes, 9,* 280–294.

Lin, A. (2014). Critical discourse analysis in applied linguistics: A methodological review. *Annual Review of Applied Linguistics, 34,* 213–232.

Lincoln, Y. S. & Guba, E. G. (2000). Paradigmatic controversies, contradictions, and emerging confluences. In N. K. Denzin & Y. S. Lincoln (Eds.), *Handbook of qualitative research* (2nd edn., pp. 182–185). Thousand Oaks, CA: Sage.

Lindgren, E., Leijten, M., & Van Waes, L. (2011). Adapting to the reader during writing. *Written Language & Literacy, 14,* 188–223.

Liu, M. & Braine, G. (2005). Cohesive features in argumentative writing produced by Chinese undergraduates. *System, 33,* 623–636.

Liu, Q. & Brown, D. (2015). Methodological synthesis of research on the effectiveness of corrective feedback in L2 writing. *Journal of Second Language Writing, 30,* 66–81.

Lo, J. & Hyland, F. (2007). Enhancing students' engagement and motivation in writing: The case of primary students in Hong Kong. *Journal of Second Language Writing, 16,* 219–237.

Lockhart, C. & Ng, P. (1995). Analyzing talk in ESL peer response groups: Stances, functions, and content. *Language Learning, 45,* 605–651.

Loewen, S., Lavolette, E., Spino, L. A., Papi, M., Schmidtke, J., Sterling, S., & Wolff, D. (2014). Statistical literacy among applied linguists and second language acquisition researchers. *TESOL Quarterly, 48,* 360–386.

Loi, C. K. (2010). Research article introductions in Chinese and English: A comparative genre-based study. *Journal of English for Academic Purposes, 9,* 267–279.

Loi, C. K., Lim, J. M. H., & Wharton, S. (2016). Expressing an evaluative stance in English and Malay research article conclusions: International publications versus local publications. *Journal of English for Academic Purposes, 21,* 1–16.

Long, M. H. (1980). Inside the "black box": Methodological issues in classroom research on language learning. *Language Learning, 30,* 1–42.

Lotherington, H. & Jenson, J. (2011). Teaching multimodal and digital literacy in second language settings: New literacies, new basics, new pedagogies. *Annual Review of Applied Linguistics, 31,* 226–246.

Lu, X. (2010). Automatic analysis of syntactic complexity in second language writing. *International Journal of Corpus Linguistics, 15,* 474–496.

Lu, X. (2011). A corpus-based evaluation of syntactic complexity measures as indices of college-level ESL writers' language development. *TESOL Quarterly, 45,* 36–62.

Luke, A. (2010). On this writing: An autotheoretic account. In D. Nunan & J. Choi (Eds.), *Language and culture: Reflective narratives and the emergence of identity* (pp. 131–139). New York: Routledge.

Lumley, T. (2002). Assessment criteria in a large-scale writing test: What do they really mean to the raters? *Language Testing, 19,* 246–276.

Lundstrom, K. & Baker, W. (2009). To give is better than to receive: The benefits of peer review to the reviewer's own writing. *Journal of Second Language Writing, 18,* 30–43.

Mackey, A. (2012). Why (or why not), when, and how to replicate research. In G. Porte (Ed.), *Replication research in applied linguistics* (pp. 21–46). Cambridge: Cambridge University Press.

Mak, B. & Coniam, D. (2008). Using wikis to enhance and develop writing skills among secondary school students in Hong Kong. *System, 36,* 437–455.

Manchón, R. (Ed.). (2011). *Learning-to-write and writing-to-learn in an additional language.* Philadelphia, PA: John Benjamins Publishing.

Manchón, R. & Matsuda, P. K. (Eds.). (2016). *The handbook of second and foreign language writing.* Berlin: De Gruyter Mouton.

Manchón, R., Murphy, L., & Roca, J. (2007). Lexical retrieval processes and strategies in second language writing: A synthesis of empirical research. *International Journal of English Studies, 2,* 149–174.

Markee, N. & Kasper, G. (2004). Classroom talks: An introduction. *The Modern Language Journal, 88,* 491–500.

Marsden, E., Mackey, A., & Plonsky, L. (2015). The IRIS repository: Advancing research practice and methodology. In A. Mackey & E. Marsden (Eds.), *Advancing methodology and practice: The IRIS repository of instruments for research into second languages* (pp. 1–22). New York: Routledge.

Martin, J. R. & Rose, D. (2007). *Working with discourse: Meaning beyond the clause* (2nd edn.). New York: Continuum.

Matsuda, P. K. (2001). Voice in Japanese written discourse: Implications for second language writing. *Journal of Second Language Writing, 10,* 35–53.

Matsuda, P. K. (2003). Process and post-process: A discursive history. *Journal of Second Language Writing, 12,* 65–83.

Matsuda, P. K. (2005). Historical inquiry in second language writing. In P. K. Matsuda & T. Silva (Eds.), *Second language writing research: Perspectives on the process of knowledge construction* (pp. 33–46). Mahwah, NJ: Lawrence Erlbaum.

Matsuda, P. K. (2012). On the nature of second language writing: Replication in a postmodern field. *Journal of Second Language Writing, 21,* 300–302.

Matsuda, P. K. (2015). Identity in written discourse. *Annual Review of Applied Linguistics, 35,* 140–159.

Matsuda, P. K. & Tardy, C. M. (2007). Voice in academic writing: The rhetorical construction of author identity in blind manuscript review. *English for Specific Purposes, 26,* 235–249.

McCarthy, P. M. & Jarvis, S. (2007). vocd: A theoretical and empirical evaluation. *Language Testing, 24*(4), 459–488.

McCarthy, P. M. & Jarvis, S. (2010). MTLD, vocd-D, and HD-D: A validation study of sophisticated approaches to lexical diversity assessment. *Behavior Research Methods, 42*(2), 381–392.

McNamara, D. S., Graesser, A. C., McCarthy, P. M., & Cai, Z. (2014). *Automated evaluation of text and discourse with Coh-Metrix.* New York, NY: Cambridge University Press.

Merriam, S. B. (1998). *Qualitative research and case study applications in education* (2nd edn.). San Francisco: Jossey-Bass.

Mertens, D. M. (2007). Transformative paradigm: Mixed methods and social justice. *Journal of Mixed Methods Research, 1,* 212–225.

Miles, M. B. & Huberman, A. M. (1994). *Qualitative data analysis: An expanded sourcebook* (2nd edn.). Thousand Oaks, CA: Sage.

Miles, M. B., Huberman, A. M., & Saldaña, J. (2014). *Qualitative data analysis: A methods sourcebook* (3rd edn.). Thousand Oaks, CA: Sage.

Millar, N., Budgell, B., & Fuller, K. (2013). 'Use the active voice whenever possible': The impact of style guidelines in medical journals. *Applied Linguistics, 34*, 393–414.

Miller, K. S., Lindgren, E., & Sullivan, K. P. (2008). The psycholinguistic dimension in second language writing: Opportunities for research and pedagogy using computer keystroke logging. *TESOL Quarterly, 42*, 433–454.

Molle, D. & Prior, P. (2008). Multimodal genre systems in EAP writing pedagogy: Reflecting on a needs analysis. *TESOL Quarterly, 42*, 541–566.

Mompean, J. A. & Fouz-González, A. (2016). Twitter-based EFL pronunciation instruction. *Language Learning & Technology, 10*, 166–190.

Morgan, D. L. (2007). Paradigms lost and pragmatism regained: Methodological implications of combining qualitative and quantitative methods. *Journal of Mixed Methods Research, 1*, 48–76.

Morton, J., Storch, N., & Thompson, C. (2015). What our students tell us: Perceptions of three multilingual students on their academic writing in first year. *Journal of Second Language Writing, 30*, 1–13.

Negretti, R. (2012). Metacognition in student academic writing: A longitudinal study of metacognitive awareness and its relation to task perception, self-regulation, and evaluation of performance. *Written Communication, 29*, 142–179.

Nelson, M. E. (2006). Mode, meaning, and synaesthesia in multimedia L2 writing. *Language Learning and Technology, 10*, 56–76.

Neumann, H. (2014).Teacher assessment of grammatical ability in second language academic writing: A case study. *Journal of Second Language Writing, 24*, 83–107.

Nicolás-Conesa, F., Roca de Larios, J., & Coyle, Y. (2014). Development of EFL students' mental models of writing and their effects on performance. *Journal of Second Language Writing, 24*, 1–19.

Nikolov, N. (2006). Test-taking strategies of 12- and 13-year-old Hungarian learners of EFL: Why whales have migraines. *Language Learning, 56*, 1–55.

Nishino, T. & Atkinson, D. (2015). Second language writing as sociocognitive alignment. *Journal of Second Language Writing, 27*, 37–54.

Norris, J. M. (2015). Statistical significance testing in second language research: Basic problems and suggestions for reform. *Language Learning, 65*(Suppl.), 97–126.

Norris, J. M. & Ortega, L. (Eds.). (2006). *Synthesizing research on language learning and teaching.* Amsterdam: John Benjamins Publishing.

Norris, J. M. & Ortega, L. (2009). Towards an organic approach to investigating CAF in instructed SLA: The case of complexity. *Applied Linguistics, 30*, 555–578.

Norris, J. M. & Ortega, L. (2010). Timeline: Research synthesis. *Language Teaching, 43*, 61–79.

Norton, B. & Early, M. (2011). Researcher identity, narrative inquiry, and language teaching research. *TESOL Quarterly, 45*, 415–439.

Norton, B. & McKinney, C. (2011). An identity approach to second language acquisition. In D. Atkinson (Ed.), *Alternative approaches to second language acquisition* (pp. 73–94). New York: Routledge.

Nottbusch, G. (2010). Grammatical planning, execution, and control in written sentence production. *Reading and Writing, 23*, 777–801.

Nunan, D. & Choi, J. (2010). *Language and culture: Reflective narratives and the emergence of identity.* New York: Routledge.

Ochs, E. (1979). Transcription as theory. In E. Ochs & B. B. Schieffelin (Eds.), *Developmental pragmatics* (pp. 43–72). New York: Academic Press.

Ochs, E. & Capps, L. (2001). *Living narrative: Creating lives in everyday storytelling* Cambridge, MA: Harvard University Press.

Ochs, E., Schegloff, E. A., & Thompson, S. A. (1996). Transcription conventions. In E. Ochs, E. A. Schegloff, & S. A. Thompson (Eds.), *Interaction and grammar* (pp. 461–465). Cambridge: Cambridge University Press.

Odell, L., Goswami, D., & Herrington, A. (1983). The discourse-based interview: A procedure for exploring the tacit knowledge of writers in nonacademic settings. In P. Mosenthal, L. Tamor, & S. A. Walmsley (Eds.), *Research on writing: Principles and methods* (pp. 221–236). New York: Longman.

Oliver, D. G., Serovich, J. M., & Mason, T. L. (2005). Constraints and opportunities with interview transcription: Towards reflection in qualitative research. *Social Forces, 84,* 1273–1289.

Ong, J. (2014). How do planning time and task conditions affect metacognitive processes of L2 writers? *Journal of Second Language Writing, 23,* 17–30.

Ong, J. & Zhang, L. J. (2013). Effects of the manipulation of cognitive processes on EFL writers' text quality. *TESOL Quarterly, 47,* 375–398.

Onwuegbuzie, A. J. & Collins, K. M. T. (2007). A typology of mixed methods sampling designs in social science research. *The Qualitative Report, 12,* 281–316.

Onwuegbuzie, A. J. & Johnson, R. B. (2006). The validity issue in mixed research. *Research in the Schools, 13,* 48–63.

Ortega, L. (2003). Syntactic complexity measures and their relationship to L2 proficiency: A research synthesis of college-level L2 writing. *Applied Linguistics, 24,* 492–518.

Ortega, L. (2012). Epistemological diversity and moral ends of research in instructed SLA. *Language Teaching Research, 16,* 206–226.

Oswald, F. L. & Plonsky, L. (2010). Meta-analysis in second language research: Choices and challenges. *Annual Review of Applied Linguistics, 30,* 85–110.

Ouellette, M. A. (2008). Weaving strands of writer identity: Self as author and the NNES "plagiarist". *Journal of Second Language Writing, 17,* 255–273.

Paltridge, B. (2008). Textographies and the researching and teaching of writing. *Ibérica, 15,* 9–24.

Paradis, C. & Eeg-Olofsson, M. (2013). Describing sensory experience: The genre of wine reviews. *Metaphor and Symbol, 28,* 22–40.

Park, K. (2012). Learner–corpus interaction: A locus of microgenesis in corpus-assisted L2 writing. *Applied Linguistics, 33,* 361–385.

Parkinson, J. & Crouch, A. (2011). Education, language, and identity amongst students at a South African university. *Journal of Language, Identity, and Education, 10,* 83–98.

Parodi, G. (2014). Genre organization in specialized discourse: Disciplinary variation across university textbooks. *Discourse Studies, 16,* 65–87.

Patton, M. Q. (2002). Qualitative interviewing. In M. Q. Patton (Ed.), *Qualitative research and evaluation methods* (3rd edn., pp. 339–428). Thousand Oaks, CA: Sage.

Paulson, E. J., Alexander, J., & Armstrong, S. (2007). Peer review re-viewed: Investigating the juxtaposition of composition students' eye movements and peer-review processes. *Research in the Teaching of English, 41,* 304–335.

Pavlenko, A. (2001). "In the world of the tradition, I was unimagined": Negotiation of identities in cross-cultural autobiographies. *International Journal of Bilingualism. 5,* 317–344.

Pavlenko, A. (2007). Autobiographic narratives as data in applied linguistics. *Applied Linguistics, 28,* 163–188.

Pearl, J. (2012). The causal foundations of structural equation modeling. In R. H. Hoyle (Ed.), *Handbook of structural equation modeling* (pp. 68–91). New York: Guilford Press.

Pecorari, D. & Petrić, B. (2014). Plagiarism in second-language writing. *Language Teaching, 47*, 269–302.

Pecorari, D. & Shaw, P. (2012). Types of student intertextuality and faculty attitudes. *Journal of Second Language Writing, 21*, 149–164.

Petrić, B. (2012). Legitimate textual borrowing: Direct quotation in L2 student writing. *Journal of Second Language Writing, 21*, 102–117.

Pho, P. D. (2008). Research article abstracts in applied linguistics and educational technology: A study of linguistic realizations of rhetorical structure and authorial stance. *Discourse Studies, 10*, 231–250.

Plakans, L. (2009). Discourse synthesis in integrated second language writing assessment. *Language Testing, 26*, 561–587.

Plakans, L. & Gebril, A. (2012). A close investigation into source use in integrated second language writing tasks. *Assessing Writing, 17*, 18–24.

Plonsky, L. (2013). Study quality in SLA: An assessment of designs, analyses, and reporting practices in quantitative L2 research. *Studies in Second Language Acquisition, 35*, 655–687.

Plonsky, L. & Oswald, F. L. (2012). How to do a meta-analysis. In A. Mackey & S. M. Gass (Eds.), *Research methods in second language acquisition: A practical guide* (pp. 275–295). London: Basil Blackwell.

Plonsky, L. & Oswald, F. L. (2015). Meta-analyzing second language research. In L. Plonsky (Ed.), *Advancing quantitative methods in second language research* (pp. 106–128). New York: Routledge.

Polio, C. (1997). Measures of linguistic accuracy in second language writing research. *Language Learning, 47*(1), 101–143.

Polio, C. (2001). Research methodology in second language writing research: The case of text-based studies. In T. Silva & P. K. Matsuda (Eds.), *On second language writing* (pp. 91–115). Mahwah, NJ: Lawrence Erlbaum.

Polio, C. (2012). Replication in published applied linguistics research: An historical perspective. In G. Porte (Ed.), *Replication in applied linguistics: A practical guide* (pp. 47–91). Cambridge: Cambridge University Press.

Polio, C. & Gass, S. (1997). Replication and reporting. *Studies in Second Language Acquisition, 19*, 499–508.

Polio, C. & Park, J. H. (2016). Language development in second language writing. In R. Manchón & P. K. Matsuda (Eds.), *Handbook of second and foreign language writing*. Berlin: De Gruyter Mouton.

Polio, C. & Shea, M. C. (2014). An investigation into current measures of linguistic accuracy in second language writing research. *Journal of Second Language Writing, 26*, 10–27.

Pomerantz, A. & Kearney, E. (2012). Beyond 'write-talk-revise-(repeat): Using narrative to understand one multilingual student's interactions around writing. *Journal of Second Language Writing, 21*, 221–238.

Porte, G. (2010). *Appraising research in second language learning: A practical approach to critical analysis of quantitative research*. Amsterdam: John Benjamins.

Porte, G. (2012). Introduction. In G. Porte (Ed.), *Replication research in applied linguistics* (pp. 1–18). Cambridge: Cambridge University Press.

Porte, G. & Richards, K. (2012). Focus article: Replication in second language writing. *Journal of Second Language Writing, 21*, 284–293.

Posteguillo, S. (1999). The schematic structure of computer science research articles. *English for Specific Purposes, 18,* 139–160.

Prior, P. (1995). Redefining the task: An ethnographic examination of writing and response in graduate seminars. In D. Belcher & G. Braine (Eds.), *Academic writing in a second language: Essays in research and pedagogy* (pp. 47–82). Norwood, NJ: Ablex.

Prior, P. (2001). Voices in text, mind, and society: Sociohistoric accounts of discourse acquisition and use. *Journal of Second Language Writing, 10,* 55–81.

Ramanathan, V. & Atkinson, D. (1999). Ethnographic approaches and methods in L2 writing research: A critical guide and review. *Applied Linguistics, 20,* 44–70.

Rayson, P., Berridge, D., & Francis, B. (2004). *Extending the Cochran rule for the comparison of word frequencies between corpora.* In 7th International Conference on Statistical Analysis of Textual Data (JADT 2004) (pp. 926–936). Retrieved from http://eprints.lancs.ac.uk/12424/1/rbf04_jadt.pdf (Last accessed on 28 March 2016).

Riazi, A. M. & Candlin, C. N. (2014). Mixed-methods research in language teaching and learning: Opportunities, issues and challenges. *Language Teaching, 47,* 135–173.

Richards, K. (2003). *Qualitative inquiry in TESOL.* London: Palgrave Macmillan.

Richards, K. (2009). Trends in qualitative research in language teaching since 2000. *Language Teaching, 42,* 147–180.

Richards, L. (2009). *Handling qualitative data: A practical guide* (2nd edn.). Thousand Oaks, CA: Sage.

Roberts, C. (1997). Transcribing talk: Issues of representation. *TESOL Quarterly, 31,* 167–172.

Robinson, P. (Ed.). (2001). *Cognition and second language instruction.* Cambridge: Cambridge University Press.

Robinson, P. (Ed.). (2011). *Second language task complexity: Researching the cognition hypothesis of language learning and performance.* Amsterdam, the Netherlands: John Benjamins Publishing.

Roca de Larios, J. R., Manchón, R. M., & Murphy, L. (2006). Generating text in native and foreign language writing: A temporal analysis of problem solving formulation processes. *The Modern Language Journal, 90,* 100–114.

Roulston, K. (2010). *Reflective interviewing: A guide to theory and practice.* Thousand Oaks, CA: Sage.

Ruiz-Funes, M. (2015). Exploring the potential of second/foreign language writing for language learning: The effects of task factors and learner variables. *Journal of Second Language Writing, 28,* 1–19.

Russell, J. & Spada, N. (2006). The effectiveness of corrective feedback for the acquisition of L2 grammar: A meta-analysis of the research. In J. M. Norris & L. Ortega (Eds.), *Synthesizing research on language learning and teaching* (pp. 133–164). Philadelphia: John Benjamins.

Ryshina-Pankova, M. & Byrnes, H. (2013). Writing as learning to know: Tracing knowledge construction in L2 German compositions. *Journal of Second Language Writing, 22,* 179–197.

Sachs, R. & Polio, C. (2007). Learners' uses of two types of written feedback on a L2 writing revision task. *Studies in Second Language Acquisition, 29,* 67–100.

Saldaña, J. (2013). *The coding manual for qualitative researchers* (2nd edn.). Thousand Oaks, CA: Sage.

Samraj, B. (2005). An exploration of a genre set: Research article abstracts and introductions in two disciplines. *English for Specific Purposes, 24,* 141–156.

Samraj, B. (2008). A discourse analysis of master's theses across disciplines with a focus on introductions. *Journal of English for Academic Purposes, 7,* 55–67.

Samraj, B. & Gawron, J. M. (2015). The suicide note as a genre: Implications for genre theory. *Journal of English for Academic Purposes, 19*, 88–101.

Santos, T. (1989). Replication in applied linguistics research. *TESOL Quarterly, 23,* 699–702.

Sasaki, M. (2004). A multiple-data analysis of the 3.5-year development of EFL student writers. *Language Learning, 54,* 525–582.

Sasaki, M. (2007). Effects of study-abroad experiences on EFL writers: A multiple-data analysis. *The Modern Language Journal, 91,* 602–620.

Schegloff, E. A. (2007). *Sequence organization in interaction: A primer in conversation analysis.* Cambridge: Cambridge University Press.

Schiffrin, D. (1994). *Approaches to discourse.* Cambridge, MA: Blackwell.

Schmitt, N. (2010). *Researching vocabulary: A vocabulary research manual.* New York: Palgrave Macmillan.

Schoonen, R., van Gelderen, A., Stoel, R. D., Hulstijn, J., & de Glopper, K. (2011). Modeling the development of L1 and EFL writing proficiency of secondary school students. *Language Learning, 61,* 31–79.

Segalowitz, N. (2010). *Cognitive bases of second language fluency.* London and New York: Routledge.

Seloni, L. (2014). "I'm an artist and a scholar who is trying to find a middle point": A textographic analysis of a Columbian art historian's thesis writing. *Journal of Second Language Writing, 25,* 79–99.

Séror, J. (2005). Computers and qualitative data analysis: Paper, pens, and highlighters vs. screen, mouse, and keyboard. *TESOL Quarterly, 39,* 321–328.

Severino, C. & Cogie, J. (2016). The writing center. In R. Manchón and P. K. Matsuda (Eds.), *The handbook of second and foreign language writing.* Berlin: De Gruyter Mouton.

Shi, L. (2003). Writing in two cultures: Chinese professors return from the West. *Canadian Modern Language Review/La Revue Canadienne des Langues Vivantes, 59,* 369–392.

Shi, L. (2008). Textual appropriation and citing behaviors of university undergraduates. *Applied Linguistics, 31,* 1–24.

Shintani, N. & Ellis, R. (2013). The comparative effect of direct written corrective feedback and metalinguistic explanation on learners' explicit and implicit knowledge of the English indefinite article. *Journal of Second Language Writing, 22,* 286–306.

Short, D. J., Fidelman, C. G., & Louguit, M. (2012). Developing academic language in English language learners through sheltered instruction. *TESOL Quarterly, 46,* 334–361.

Shoukri, M. M. (2010). *Measures of interobserver agreement and reliability.* Boca Raton, FL: CRC Press.

Simpson-Vlach, R. & Ellis, N. C. (2010). An academic formulas list: New methods in phraseology research. *Applied Linguistics, 31,* 487–512.

Skehan, P. (1996). A framework for the implementation of task-based instruction. *Applied Linguistics, 17,* 38–62.

Skehan, P. (1998). *A cognitive approach to language learning (Oxford Applied Linguistics).* Oxford: Oxford University Press

Skehan, P. & Foster, P. (2001). Cognition and tasks. In P. Robinson (Ed.), *Cognition and second language instruction* (pp. 183–205). Cambridge: Cambridge University Press.

Smagorinsky, P. (1994). Think-aloud protocol: Beyond the black box. In P. Smagorinsky (Ed.), *Speaking about writing: Reflections on research methodology* (pp. 3–19). Thousand Oaks, CA: Sage.

Smagorinsky, P. (2008). The method section as conceptual epicenter in constructing social science research reports. *Written Communication, 25,* 389–411.

Spack, R. (1997). The acquisition of academic literacy in a second language: A longitudinal case study. *Written Communication, 14*, 3–62.

Spradley, J. P. (1979). *The ethnographic interview.* Belmont, CA: Wadsworth/Thompson Learning.

Stake, R. E. (2000). Case studies. In N. K. Denzin & Y. S. Lincoln (Eds.), *Handbook of qualitative research* (2nd ed., pp. 435–454). Thousand Oaks, CA: Sage.

Starfield, S. (2013). Researcher reflexivity. In C. A. Chapelle (Ed.), *Encyclopedia of applied linguistics* (pp. 1–7). Malden, MA: Wiley-Blackwell.

Starfield, S. (2016). Ethnographic research. *TESOL Quarterly, 50*, 51–54.

Storch, N. (2002). Patterns of interaction in ESL pair work. *Language Learning, 52*, 119–158.

Storch, N. (2005). Collaborative writing: Product, process, and students' reflections. *Journal of Second Language Writing, 14*, 153–173.

Storch, N. (2011). Collaborative writing in L2 contexts: Processes, outcomes, and future directions. *Annual Review of Applied Linguistics, 31*, 275–288.

Strauss, A. & Corbin, J. (1998). *Basics of qualitative research* (2nd edn.). Newbury Park, CA: Sage.

Street, B. V. (1995). *Social literacies: Critical approaches to literacy in development, ethnography, and education.* New York: Longman.

Sutherland-Smith, W. (2011). Crime and punishment: An analysis of university plagiarism policies. *Semiotica 187*, 127–139.

Suzuki, M. (2008). Japanese learners' self-revisions and peer revisions of their written compositions in English. *TESOL Quarterly, 42*, 209–233.

Suzuki, W. (2012). Written languaging, direct correction, and second language writing revision. *Language Learning, 62*, 1110–1133.

Swain, M. & Deters, P. (2007). "New" mainstream SLA theory: Expanded and enriched. *The Modern Language Journal, 91*, 820–836.

Swales, J. M. (1990). *Genre analysis: English in academic and research settings.* Cambridge: Cambridge University Press.

Swales, J. M. (1998a). Textography: Toward a contextualization of written academic discourse. *Research on Language and Social Interaction, 3*, 109–121.

Swales, J. M. (1998b). *Other floors, other voices: A textography of a small university building.* Mahwah, NJ: Laurence Erlbaum.

Swales, J. M. (2004). *Research genres: Exploration and application.* Cambridge: Cambridge University Press.

Swales, J. & Feak, C. (2000). *English in today's research world: A writing guide.* Ann Arbor: University of Michigan Press.

Talmy, S. (2010). Qualitative interviews in applied linguistics: From research instrument to social practice. *Annual Review of Applied Linguistics, 30*, 128–148.

Talmy, S. & Richards, K. (Eds.). (2011). Qualitative interviews in applied linguistics: Discursive perspectives. [Special Issue]. *Applied Linguistics, 32*(1).

Tan, L. L., Wigglesworth, G., & Storch, N. (2010). Pair interactions and mode of communication: Comparing face-to-face and computer-mediated communication. *Australian Review of Applied Linguistics, 33*, 27.1–27.24.

Tardy, C. M. (2006). Researching first and second language genre learning: A comparative review and a look ahead. *Journal of Second Language Writing, 15*, 79–101.

Tashakkori, A. & Teddlie, C. (2003). *Sage handbook of mixed methods research in social and behavioral research.* Thousand Oaks, CA: Sage.

Tashakkori, A. & Teddlie, C. (2008). Quality of inferences in mixed methods research: Calling for an integrative framework. In M. M. Bergman (Ed.), *Advances in mixed methods research* (pp. 101–119). Thousand Oaks, CA: Sage.

Tashakkori, A. & Teddlie, C. (2010). *Sage handbook of mixed methods research in social and behavioral research* (2nd edn.). Thousand Oaks, CA: Sage.

Téllez, K. & Waxman, H. C. (2006). A meta-synthesis of qualitative research on effective teaching practices for English language learners. In J. M. Norris, & L. Ortega (Eds.), *Synthesizing research on language learning and teaching* (pp. 245–277). Philadelphia, PA: John Benjamins.

ten Have, P. (2007). *Doing conversation analysis: A practical guide* (2nd edn.). Thousand Oaks, CA: Sage.

TESOL International Association. (2014, November). *TESOL research agenda 2014.* Alexandria, VA: TESOL. Retrieved from http://www.tesol.org/advance-the-field/research.

Thompson, C., Morton, J., & Storch, N. (2013). Where from, who, why and how? A study of the use of sources by first year L2 university students. *Journal of English for Academic Purposes, 12*, 99–109.

Thornberg, R. & Charmaz, K. (2012). Grounded theory. In S. D. Lapan (Ed.), *Qualitative research: An introduction to methods and designs* (pp. 73–99). San Francisco: Jossey-Bass.

Thyer, B. A. (2012). *Quasi-experimental research designs.* New York, NY: Oxford University Press.

Timulak, L. (2014). Qualitative meta-analysis. In U. Flick (Ed.), *The Sage handbook of qualitative data analysis* (pp. 481–495). Thousand Oaks, CA: Sage.

Truscott, J. (1996). The case against grammar correction in L2 writing classes. *Language Learning, 46*, 327–369.

Truscott, J. (2007). The effect of error correction on learners' ability to write accurately. *Journal of Second Language Writing, 16*, 255–272.

Truscott, J. & Hsu, A. Y. P. (2008). Error correction, revision, and learning. *Journal of Second Language Writing, 17*, 292–305.

Valipouri, L. & Nassaji, H. (2013). A corpus-based study of academic vocabulary in chemistry research articles. *Journal of English for Academic Purposes, 12*, 248–263.

van Beuningen, C. G., De Jong, N. H., & Kuiken, F. (2012). Evidence on the effectiveness of comprehensive error correction in second language writing. *Language Learning, 62*, 1–41.

Vandrick, S. (2009). *Interrogating privilege: Reflections of a second language educator.* Ann Arbor, MI: University of Michigan Press.

van Mulken, M. & van der Meer, W. (2005). Are you being served?: A genre analysis of American and Dutch company replies to customer inquiries. *English for Specific Purposes, 24*, 93–109.

Van Waes, L., Leijten, M., & Quinlan, T. (2010). Reading during sentence composing and error correction: A multilevel analysis of the influences of task complexity. *Reading and Writing, 23*, 803–834.

van Weijen, D., van den Bergh, H., Rijlaarsdam, G., & Sanders, T. (2009). L1 use during L2 writing: An empirical study of a complex phenomenon. *Journal of Second Language Writing, 18*, 235–250.

Verspoor, M., Schmid, M. S., & Xu, X. (2012). A dynamic usage based perspective on L2 writing. *Journal of Second Language Writing, 21*, 239–263.

Vyatkina, N. (2012). The development of second language writing complexity in groups and individuals: A longitudinal learner corpus study. *The Modern Language Journal, 96*, 576–598.

Vygotsky, L. (1978). *Mind in society: The development of higher psychological processes.* Cambridge: Cambridge University Press.

Wang, W. & Wen, Q. (2002). L1 use in the L2 composing process: An exploratory study of 16 Chinese EFL writers. *Journal of Second Language Writing, 11*, 225–246.

Waring, H. Z. (2005). Peer tutoring in a graduate writing centre: Identity, expertise, and advice resisting. *Applied Linguistics, 26*, 141–168.

Watanabe, Y. & Swain, M. (2007). Effects of proficiency differences and patterns of pair interaction on second language learning: Collaborative dialogue between adult ESL learners. *Language Teaching Research, 11*, 121–142.

Watson-Gegeo, K. A. (1988). Ethnography in ESL: Defining the essentials. *TESOL Quarterly, 22*, 575–592.

Weigle, S. C. & Nelson, G. L. (2004). Novice tutors and their ESL tutees: Three case studies of tutor roles and perceptions of tutorial success. *Journal of Second Language Writing, 13*, 203–225.

Weissberg, R. (2006). *Connecting speaking and writing*. Ann Arbor, MI: University of Michigan Press.

Wigglesworth, G. & Storch, N. (2009). Pair versus individual writing: Effects on fluency, complexity and accuracy. *Language Testing, 26*, 445–466.

Wigglesworth, G. & Storch, N. (2012). What role for collaboration in writing and writing feedback. *Journal of Second Language Writing, 21*, 364–374.

Willey, I. & Tanimoto, K. (2015). "We're drifting into strange territory here": What think-aloud protocols reveal about convenience editing. *Journal of Second Language Writing, 27*, 63–83.

Williams, J. (2004). Tutoring and revision: Second language writers in the writing center. *Journal of Second Language Writing, 13*, 173–201.

Winke, P. (2013). An investigation into second language aptitude for advanced Chinese language learning. *The Modern Language Journal, 97*, 109–130.

Winke, P. (2014). Testing hypotheses about language learning using structural equation modeling. *Annual Review of Applied Linguistics, 34*, 102–122.

Winke, P. & Lim, H. (2015). ESL essay raters' cognitive processes in applying the Jacobs et al. rubric: An eye-movement study. *Assessing Writing, 25*, 37–53.

Wolfe-Quintero, K., Inagaki, S., & Kim, H. Y. (1998). *Second language development in writing: Measures of fluency, accuracy, and complexity*. Honolulu, HI: University of Hawaii Press.

Wong, A. T. Y. (2000). *A study of cognition in context: The composing strategies of advanced writers in an academic context*. Unpublished doctoral thesis, The University of Hong Kong, Hong Kong.

Wood, D., Bruner, J. S., & Ross, G. (1976). The role of tutoring in problem solving. *Journal of Child Psychology and Psychiatry, 17*, 89–100.

Wray, A. (2002). *Formulaic language and the lexicon*. Cambridge: Cambridge University Press.

Xu, C. (2009). Overgeneralization from a narrow focus: A response to Ellis et al. (2008) and Bitchener (2008). *Journal of Second Language Writing, 18*, 270–275.

Yang, C., Hu, G., & Zhang, L. J. (2014). Reactivity of concurrent verbal reporting in second language writing. *Journal of Second Language Writing, 24*, 51–70.

Yang, H. C. & Plakans, L. (2012). Second language writers' strategy use and performance on an integrated reading-listening-writing task. *TESOL Quarterly, 46*, 80–103.

Yang, L. & Shi, L. (2003). Exploring six MBA students' summary writing by introspection. *Journal of English for Academic Purposes, 2*, 165–192.

Yang, R. & Allison, D. (2003). Research articles in applied linguistics: Moving from results to conclusions. *English for Specific Purposes, 22*, 365–385.

Yanguas, I. & Lado, B. (2012). Is thinking aloud reactive when writing in the heritage language? *Foreign Language Annals, 45*, 380–399.

Yasuda, S. (2011). Genre-based tasks in foreign language writing: Developing writers' genre awareness, linguistic knowledge, and writing competence. *Journal of Second Language Writing, 20*, 111–133.

Yayli, D. (2011). From genre awareness to cross-genre awareness: A study in an EFL context. *Journal of English for Academic Purposes, 10*, 121–129.

Yeung, L. (2007). In search of commonalities: Some linguistic and rhetorical features of business reports as a genre. *English for Specific Purposes, 26*, 156–179.

Yi, Y. (2010). Adolescent multilingual writers' transitions across in- and out-of-school writing contexts. *Journal of Second Language Writing, 19*, 17–32.

Yi, Y. (2013). Adolescent multilingual writer's negotiation of multiple identities and access to academic writing: A case study of a Jogi Yuhak student in a US high school. *The Canadian Modern Language Review, 69*, 207–231.

Yin, R. K. (2006). Mixed methods research: Are the methods genuinely integrated or merely parallel? *Research in the Schools, 3*, 41–47.

Yin, R. K. (2014). *Case study research: Design and methods* (5th ed.). Thousand Oaks: Sage.

Yin, Z. (2015). The use of cohesive devices in news language: Overuse, underuse or misuse? *RELC Journal, 46*, 309–326.

Yoon, H. & Polio, C. (2016). Linguistic development in two genres. *TESOL Quarterly.*

Young, R. F. & Miller, E. R. (2004). Learning as changing participation: Discourse roles in ESL writing conferences. *The Modern Language Journal, 88*, 519–535.

Yu, G. (2010). Lexical diversity in writing and speaking task performances. *Applied Linguistics, 31*, 236–259.

Zhang, C. (2013). Effect of instruction on ESL students' synthesis writing. *Journal of Second Language Writing, 22*, 51–67.

Zhang, G. (2015). It is suggested that. . . or it is better to. . .? Forms and meanings of subject it-extraposition in academic and popular writing. *Journal of English for Academic Purposes, 20*, 1–13.

Zhao, H. (2010). Investigating learners' use and understanding of peer and teacher feedback on writing: A comparative study in a Chinese English writing classroom. *Assessing Writing, 15*, 3–17.

Zhou, A. A. (2009). What adult ESL learners say about improving grammar and vocabulary in their writing for academic purposes. *Language Awareness, 18*, 31–46.

Zhou, A., Busch, M., & Cumming, A. (2014). Do adult ESL learners' and their teachers' goals for improving grammar in writing correspond? *Language Awareness, 23*, 234–254.

Zhu, W. & Mitchell, D. A. (2012). Participation in peer response as activity: An examination of peer response stances from an activity theory perspective. *TESOL Quarterly, 46*, 362–386.

Zuengler, J., Ford, C., & Fassnacht, C. (1998). *Analyst eyes and camera eyes: Theoretical and technological considerations in "seeing" the details of classroom interaction.* CELA Technical Report. Albany, NY: SUNY Center for English Learning and Achievement.

INDEX

Richards, L. 201, 214–20
Rijlaarsdam, G. 167, 171, 172
Rimmer, W. 121
Rinnert, C. 79, 84
Roberts, B. 110
Roberts, C. 189, 238
Roberts, J. K. 45
Robinson, P. 105, 118, 119
Roca de Larios, J. 149, 150, 156, 160, 166, 168, 170
Ros, C. 256
Rose, D. 132, 231
Ross, G. 231
Ross-Feldman, L. 26
Roulston, K. 190, 193, 195
routines 109
rubrics 10, 17, 24, 25, 30, 36, 113, 116, 117, 153, 256; analytic 7, 101, 119; holistic 101, 119
Ruiz-Funes, M. 107
Russell, J. 264, 265
Ryshina-Pankova, M. 140

Sachs, R. 26, 156, 159, 162
Saldaña, J. 208, 209, 213, 218
Salinas, C. S. 50, 56, 57, 60, 63
sample interview-based study 176
sampling 92, 103, 131, 141, 145, 146, 203, 204, 209, 212, 266, 269; case study research 47; ethnography 47; mixed methods research 73, 81, 88, 89; parallel 89; purposive (purposeful) 65; self-selection 89; stratified random 29
Samraj, B. 124, 126, 129, 135, 138, 139, 141
Sancho Guinda, C. 231
Sanders, T. 167, 171, 172
Santangelo, T. 266
Santos, T. 267
Sasaki, M. 78, 79, 84, 89, 149, 150
saturation (grounded theory) 212
Schallert, D. L. 49, 56, 209, 212
Schegloff, E. A. 233, 234, 241
Schellens, P. J. 175
Schiffrin, D. 232
Schleppegrell, M. J. 250
Schmid, M. S. 103, 105, 106
Schmidtke, J. 90
Schmitt, N. 3, 106, 109, 139, 182, 184, 189
Schneider, G. 130, 135
Schoonen, R. 37, 41, 42, 43, 44, 45
Schwegler, R. A. 255
Seedhouse, P. 249
Segalowitz, N. 108

segmentation 166, 167
Seloni, L. 49, 54, 58, 63, 182
semiotic field 236
sequential mixed method design 75, 76, 77, 78, 89
Séror, J. 220
Serovich, J. M. 237
Seton, B. 31
Shaw, P. 177, 180, 181, 182, 187, 192
Shea, M. 107, 112, 113, 120
Shi, L. 3, 149, 150, 155, 166, 170, 180, 182, 185, 188, 196
Shim, E. 136
Shintani, N. 21, 103, 104, 256
Short, D. J. 18, 19, 20, 22, 23
Shoukri, M. M. 112
Sidnell, J. 249
significance: statistical 26, 30
Silva, T. 3
Silver, C. 224
Silverman, D. 186
Simon, H. A. 155, 158, 161, 168, 169, 171
Simon-Maeda, A. 61, 185
Simpson-Vlach, R. 124, 125, 137
simultaneous (concurrent) mixed method design 75
Skehan, P. 105, 117, 119
Smagorinsky, P. 165, 214, 215
Soler-Monreal, C. 127, 129, 139, 140
Spack, R. 47
Spada, N. 265
speech recognition 241, 257
Spilioti, T. 273
Spino, L. A. 22, 39, 90, 162, 163, 165
Spradley, J. P. 192
Stake, R. E. 55
Starfield, S. 61, 269
step 123, 130, 131, 132, 137, 138, 139, 141, 142, 143, 144, 145, 146
Sterling, S. 90
stimulated recall (retrospective verbal protocols) 55, 56, 78, 79, 80, 84, 148, 149, 151, 152, 154, 155, 156, 157, 158, 159, 160, 163–71, 174, 178, 182, 201, 203, 206, 218, 256; augmented 156, 157, 163, 164
Stine, M. 85
Stivers, T. 249
Stoel, R. D. 37, 41, 42
Storch, N. 17, 19, 20, 23, 65, 102, 104, 106, 108, 109, 116, 179, 181, 227, 230, 243, 263
Strauss, A. 210, 211, 221, 222
Street, B. V. 47, 205, 207